FEMALE VICTIMS OF CRIME

Reality Reconsidered

Venessa Garcia

Kean University

Janice E. Clifford

Auburn University

Roslyn Muraskin

Long Island University
Series Editor

Prentice Hall
Upper Saddle River, New Jersey
Columbus, Ohio

Library of Congress Cataloging-in-Publication Data

Female victims of crime: reality reconsidered/Venessa Garcia, Janice E. Clifford,
    Roslyn Muraskin [editors].—1st ed.
        p. cm.
Includes bibliographical references and index.
ISBN-13: 978-0-13-233931-5 (alk. paper)
ISBN-10: 0-13-233931-5 (alk. paper)
    1. Sex discrimination in criminal justice administration—United States.   2. Women—Crimes
against—United States.   3. Victims of crimes—United States.   I. Garcia, Venessa.   II. Clifford,
Janice E.   III. Muraskin, Roslyn.
HV9950.F46 2010
362.88082'0973—dc22

2008039110

Vice President and Executive Publisher: Vernon Anthony
Senior Acquisitions Editor: Tim Peyton
Editorial Assistant: Alicia Kelly
Media Project Manager: Karen Bretz
Director of Marketing: David Gesell
Marketing Manager: Adam Kloza
Marketing Coordinator: Alicia Dysert
Production Manager: Wanda Rockwell
Creative Director: Jayne Conte
Cover Design: Bruce Kenselaar
Cover Illustration/Photo: Getty Images, Inc.
Full-Service Project Management/Composition: Integra Software Services Inc.
Printer/Binder: Bind-Rite/Command Web

Credits and acknowledgments borrowed from other sources and reproduced, with permission, in this
textbook appear on appropriate page within text.

Pearson Education Ltd., London.
Pearson Education Singapore, Pte. Ltd
Pearson Education, Canada, Ltd
Pearson Education–Japan
Pearson Education Australia PTY, Limited

Pearson Education North Asia, Ltd., Hong Kong
Pearson Educación de Mexico, S.A. de C.V.
Pearson Education Malaysia, Pte. Ltd
Pearson Education, Upper Saddle River,
    New Jersey

Prentice Hall
is an imprint of

www.pearsonhighered.com

10 9 8 7 6 5 4 3 2 1
ISBN-13: 978-0-13-233931-5
ISBN-10:   0-13-233931-5

DEDICATION

I dedicate this book to my best friend and husband, Michael; my daughter, Samantha; my son, John; and my mother, Norma. You all have inspired my life and made me the person I am today.

VENESSA GARCIA, PH.D.

I dedicate this book to my family and friends, who all have assisted me in so many ways to achieve both personal and professional goals. Thank you for all of your enduring love, encouragement, and support.

JANICE E. CLIFFORD, PH.D.

The authors, together, would also like to dedicate this book to several other individuals. First, they would like to dedicate this book to Dr. Michael Farrell, who we both studied under in graduate school. His dedication to current and former students, and to the pursuit of knowledge in the field of Sociology, through example, has helped shape our careers.

Second, they would like to dedicate this book to the women, men, and children who have been victimized and to their families who, likewise, have been impacted by the effects of crime. We hope that this book helps to enlighten those who may be in similar positions and to ease the suffering of crime victims.

CONTENTS

❧

FOREWORD

ꝏ

Female Victims of Crime: Reality Reconsidered

ROSLYN MURASKIN, EDITOR WOMEN'S SERIES
Long Island University

Women are victimized by the very laws that were passed to protect them. Women who are victims of rape, domestic violence, and sexual harassment do not always come out and report this act. Why? Because women appear to be treated differently as victims of these crimes—after all "she asked for it," no woman would be attacked if she did not want to be. This of course is myth but myth and reality need to be reconsidered.

The history of women in the criminal justice system demonstrates the tribulations that they have had to face since the beginnings of this country. Over these many years, it has been women who have had to make the difference, to sue for their rights in prison, and to have legislation passed so that they would be treated similar to men who are victimized. Traditional textbooks have always ignored the plight of women in the criminal justice system. This work *Female Victims of Crime: Reality Reconsidered* (as part of the Women's Series) demonstrates why overlooking women can no longer be the case. Public denigration is not acceptable to women and their relationship to the field of criminal justice. This work looks at areas of women as victims of crime, the impact of gender, race, and discrimination, specific crimes of rape and domestic violence, workplace discrimination, the role of corrections, and the future of criminal justice and the victimization of women. We need to understand that women and equality are a major part of our constitutional jurisprudence.

Violence and victimization are a major part of our criminal justice system, and for this reason alone, women cannot be segregated out of the literature, and assumed to be less than human. Violence and victimization exist in many forms within society, and there needs to be more attention paid to women as victims. Throughout history, there has been evidence of a double standard, one for men and another for women. Such disparate treatment cannot continue to exist.

Victimization of women is a common experience. Yet, many rapes are never reported. Those that are, are rarely prosecuted, and many prosecutions do not result in convictions. Victims do not report their rapes because of fear of the criminal justice system and their failure to be treated fairly as victims. Women are put on trial, and treated as defendants rather than complainants. A woman as a victim finds the attack on her self as shattering, degrading, and lowering her self-esteem. As stated in the finding of *R. v. Osolin (19930 4 S.C.R. 595, 669)*,

> it cannot be forgotten that a sexual assault is very different from other assaults. It is true that it, like all the other forms of assault, is a simple act of

violence. . . . Sexual assault is in the vast majority of cases gender based. It is an assault upon human dignity and constitutes a denial of any concept of equality for women. The reality of the situation can be seen from the statistics which demonstrate that 99 percent of the offenders in sexual assault cases are men and 90 percent of the victims are women.

Is it true that women and girls are taught from their early years to be afraid of men? A right to human dignity should prohibit bias in the criminal justice system, but does there exist for women the factor of human dignity? What is equality? Treating likes alike, unlikes unalike? Or is there a set standard for everyone? If there is a compelling state interest to treat everyone alike, then there should be no discussion on victimization of women and victimization of men. All should be treated the same. According to Catherine MacKinnon (2001),

> the law of sex discrimination, . . . has applied the sameness/difference approach to those sites of social life where sex as an inequality has been identified. Attempts to explain and change the inequality between women and men, to intervene in its dynamics or restrain its abuses, are usually premised upon a theory of the driving force or prime location or original ground of the problem. Such a theory is termed here a 'linchpin theory'—meaning, the problem turns on this pivot: If you change this, you change the whole thing. (p. 144)

Under the doctrine of constitutional law, is there sex equality or are there different rules for different folk?

According to the chapter by Brewster and Holley, "victims have become increasingly important in the study of crime . . . and more recently in the field of victimology. Women's victimization is of growing importance in the field of victimology . . . " In history, women have blamed themselves for being victims of rape, but today there is the recognition that women should have a better sense of self-worth. So is the case with domestic violence. Laws have changed demanding the arrest of the offenders of domestic violence, with the hope that the "rule of thumb" no longer exists. When women are noted as being victims of crimes such as homicide, it is more often than not that the offender is a man. As pointed out in this work by Regoeczi and Miethe, " . . . the high prevalence of female victimization by intimate partners is thought by many researchers to derive from cultural legacies in which violence against women is often normatively expected, tolerated, or even demanded within particular contexts."

By studying the stereotypical images of crime victims, we consider alternatives that are realistic in particular for women. Women are murder victims in this country more so than in any other country. Why is this? Della Giustina points out that "women are murdered by serial killers, friends, family members, intimate partners, co-workers, and strangers within a society that devalues women." What then is the reason for this and what is the solution? There exist many varied strategies that can be followed to predict what the future holds for victims of crime, primarily women. What is must be distinguished from what ought to be. Criminal justice officials must recognize that the rhetoric, though there is not enough, must include action to be taken to stop the disparate treatment of victims by the system. There needs to be social policy implementation that promotes true equality for all, not just for some.

One of the results of modern technology is the use of the Internet for porn, attracting young girls, harassment of these females, and what is referred to by Burgess-Proctor, Patchin, and Hinduja as cyberbullying. According to these authors, cyberbullying is defined as "willful and repeated harm inflicted through the medium of electronic text." Such cyberbullying brings about victimization in a manner not previously studied. They have studied how such use of the electronic age has impacted young girls as victims and indicate the reasons why the new age of technology has to be treated as part of the victimization that occurs in the twenty-first century.

There exists a negative perception about victims, in particular those who come from lower socioeconomic areas. The observation of the women who reside in these areas have a poor perception of law enforcement and as such do not report such acts of domestic violence as they should. The voices of victims must be heard. Without their voices, needed social policies cannot be put into place. Without such policies in place, not just the rhetoric, perhaps victims will feel more comfortable in standing up and speaking out. If women who are victims of domestic violence are afforded little protection or believe that they will be afforded little protection, discrimination against women as victims will continue to exist. Minority women, in particular, still feel ill at ease when reporting such cases of violence.

Interesting is the factor of the media's handling of cases of women who are victims of crime. The media impact our understanding of crime on an everyday level due to the headlines. The public appears to accept crime reporting by the media, but how do you separate myth from reality, headlines from truth? The public's knowledge of crime is principally derived from its depiction in the media. According to the chapter by Garcia and Schweikert "images have dichotomized women into good girls and bad girls . . . " Women of color are discriminated against even more by the media. Accordingly, "when we focus on victimization in society, as with all things less understood, people tend to fear what they do not understand." The ideas of victim blaming or victim facilitation are something that requires consideration by the criminal justice system. As an example, "supporting prior research, older female victims who knew their sexual predators [are] more likely to be blamed. This finding supports the existence of rape myths within the media of what constitutes a 'real rape.'" The news media continue to focus on negative criticism rather than on positive criticism. There is the court of opinion and there exists the public court of opinion as prejudiced by the media. The role of the media is to sell, and therefore, their concentration of what makes big headlines becomes of prime importance rather than the reporting of the simple truth. The mass media help to form attitudes where none has existed before. Therefore, its usefulness is in reporting what is occurring. But its usefulness is oftentimes outdone by what it does not do, that is, giving proper notice regarding victims of crime.

This work before you is a fascinating study of victims of crime and the reality that must be reconsidered. According to MacKinnon (2001),

[M]ore imagined than in real life, sex equality in law tends to be more formal or hypothetical than substantive and delivered. In legal application, the meaningfulness of sex equality varies dramatically, its observance ranging from obvious to anathema. Around the world and throughout history, in settings from the institutional to the intimate, sex equality remains more promise than fact. (p. 3)

Criminological thought has always been shaped by the idea that there exists a double standard, one for men and another for women. This work demonstrates the need for a better understanding of who victims of crime are and why we must come to grips with reality.

Reference

MacKinnon, C. (2001). *Sex equality*. New York, Foundation Press.

ACKNOWLEDGMENTS

We wish to acknowledge the encouragement given to us by Roslyn Muraskin, Series Editor of the Women and Crime Series of Prentice Hall, to write this book. We would also like to thank the Editorial Staff at Prentice Hall for all of their hard work and support in bringing this piece together. Thanks must also be extended to Frank Mortimer, who fine-tuned the particulars of our work. We would also like to thank all of the contributors, without whose work this book would not have been possible. Finally, we would like to thank the Division of Women and Crime (DWC) of the American Society of Criminology. Without the support, inspiration, and inroads accomplished by all of the women of the DWC much of the research included in the book, as well as much that has been cited, would not exist.

Venessa Garcia, Ph.D. and Janice E. Clifford, Ph.D.

ABOUT THE EDITORS

Janice E. Clifford, Ph.D., is an Associate Professor of Sociology and Criminology at Auburn University. Her areas of teaching and research include family studies, violent crime, juvenile deviance, victimization, and violence against women. She has published in several journals including the *Journal of Contemporary Criminal Justice*, *Journal of Quantitative Criminology*, *The Journal of Homicide Studies*, and *The American Sociologist*. She is a member of Alpha Kappa Delta International Sociology Honor Society, has served on the National Council, and is an advisor for the local chapter.

Venessa Garcia, Ph.D., is an Assistant Professor of Criminal Justice at Kean University. She received her M.A. and Ph.D. in Sociology at the State University of New York University at Buffalo. Her family court research resulted in a book, *Domestic Violence and Child Custody Disputes: A Resource Handbook for Judges and Court Managers*. Her research in policing has been published in the *Journal of Contemporary Criminal Justice*, *Journal of Criminal Justice*, *Police Practice and Research: An International Journal*, *Handbook of Police Administration*, and *Contemporary Issues in Law Enforcement and Policing*. She is also the author of over 20 published reports, encyclopedia entries, professional articles, and book reviews. She is currently editor of the *New Jersey Criminal Justice Educator* and deputy editor of *Feminist Criminology*. In 2005, she won the New Scholar of the Year from the Division of Women and Crime of American Society of Criminology. She currently services as Chair of the Division of Women and Crime.

ABOUT THE CONTRIBUTORS

Joanne Belknap, Ph.D., received a Ph.D. in Criminal Justice and Criminology from Michigan State University in 1986. She is Professor of Sociology at the University of Colorado. Dr. Belknap has numerous scholarly publications, most of which involve violence against women and girls and female offenders. Dr. Belknap recently published the third edition of her book *The Invisible Woman: Gender, Crime, and Justice.* She has secured almost a million dollars in grant money to conduct research on women, girls, and crime (as a principal or co-principal investigator). Recent and forthcoming empirical publications are about college campus fraternity rapes, the court processing of woman battering cases, delinquent girls transferred to adult court, a gender comparison of delinquent girls' and boys' trauma histories, and focus groups with delinquent girls and those who work with them in Ohio and Colorado. She has served on state advisory boards for female offenders and women in prison, on U.S. Attorney General Janet Reno's Violence Against Women Committee, and gave expert testimony to the Warren Christopher Commission investigating the Rodney King police brutality incident in Los Angeles. Dr. Belknap is the recipient of the 1997 national award "Distinguished Scholar of the Division on Women and Crime" of the American Society of Criminology and won the Student-Nominated University of Colorado Teaching Award in 2001 for her class "Violence Against Women and Girls." She is the past Chair of the Division on Women and Crime of the American Society of Criminology. Also, Dr. Belknap is the 2004 recipient of the Boulder Faculty Assembly Teaching Award, the most prestigious teaching award at the University of Colorado, and the 2004 Inconvenient Woman Award from the American Society of Criminology for speaking out on behalf of college women reporting rapes by football players.

Sharon Boyd-Jackson, Ph.D., is a licensed psychologist who is trained in the field of clinical psychology. She is past president of the New Jersey Chapter of the Association of Black Psychologists, and past co-chair of the Academic and Scientific Affairs Committee of the New Jersey Psychological Association. Dr. Boyd-Jackson has experience and expertise in conducting women's groups and working with adolescents and adults dealing with depression, anxiety, abuse, and race-related issues. Dr. Boyd-Jackson has trained and supervised graduate students and professional psychologists working toward licensure. She has written articles and presented on several topics related to stress, self-esteem, impact of racism, intimate partner violence and abuse, and depression in women. She is currently working on a book to assist young adults in understanding the complexities of relationships. Dr. Boyd-Jackson is presently an Associate Professor in the Department of Psychology at Kean University and maintains a part-time private practice.

Dennis R. Brewster, Ph.D., received his Ph.D. in 2002 from University of Oklahoma. Dr. Brewster is currently an Assistant Professor at Oklahoma State University, Stillwater, Oklahoma. His interests include all areas of criminal justice, with particular attention to inequality in the criminal justice system, and he is currently working on a book on Victimology. His work includes publications in *The Prison Journal* and *Deviant Behavior*, and he also has written several book chapters.

Amanda Burgess-Proctor, Ph.D., is a research analyst at the Center for Urban Studies at Wayne State University. She received her Ph.D. in Criminal Justice from Michigan State University in 2008. Her primary research interests include feminist criminology, criminological theory, intimate partner violence, and intersections of race, class, and gender. She has published articles in *Feminist Criminology*, *Violence Against Women*, *Violence & Victims*, and *Women & Criminal Justice*.

Jo-Ann Della Giustina, Ph.D., is an Assistant Professor of Criminal Justice at Bridgewater State College (Massachusetts), where she teaches courses in gender and crime, domestic violence, homicide, criminal law and procedure, and restorative justice. She received her Ph.D. in Criminal Justice from City University of New York (John Jay College) with a specialization in women and crime, and her J.D. from Chicago-Kent College of Law. As an attorney, Dr. Della Giustina was an Assistant Cook County (Illinois) Public Defender and a law clerk to Illinois Appellate Court Justice David Cerda. Dr. Della Giustina volunteers with the Alternative to Violence Project at Old Colony Correctional Center in Bridgewater, Massachusetts, and the Mt. Moriah Compassion Reentry Program, which is initiating a reentry program for women returning to Brockton, Massachusetts, from the Massachusetts Correctional Institution (MCI)-Framingham Prison. Dr. Della Giustina is a licensed attorney in Massachusetts, New York, and Illinois, has published several book chapters and journal articles, and is listed in Who's Who in America and Who's Who in the World.

Bonnie S. Fisher, Ph.D., received her Ph.D. in 1988 from Northwestern University. She is a Professor in the Division of Criminal Justice at the University of Cincinnati and a senior research fellow at the Criminal Justice Research Center. Her recent work includes examining repeat sexual victimization among college women, including stalking, and assessing the efficacy of the protective action–sexual victimization nexus. She edited *Campus Crime: Legal, Social and Political Perspectives* (2nd edition) and *Violence at Work: Causes, Patterns, and Prevention*. Professor Fisher has authored more than 100 articles, chapters, and reports on topics that include the college campus victimization, sexual victimization, stalking and violence of female college students, gendered fear, violence against older women, and workplace violence. She has been the Principle Investigator on four national-level grants funded by the Department of Justice to examine issues concerning the victimization of college students, the sexual and stalking victimization of college women, violence against college women, and responses by colleges and universities to a report of a sexual assault and one grant from the Small Business Administration to examine workplace violence issues. Professor Fisher, along with researchers at Research Triangle Institute and the University of North Carolina at Chapel Hill (UNC-Chapel Hill), recently completed a National Institute of Justice-funded grant to examine the extent and nature of alcohol- and drug-enabled sexual assault among college women. She is currently analyzing the Workplace Risk Supplement of the National Crime Victimization Survey with Dr. Lynn Jenkins at the National Institute for Occupational Safety and Health (NIOSH) and Professor James Lynch, and coediting the *Encyclopedia of Victimology and Crime Prevention* with Professor Steven Lab. She is also currently the Co-Principal Investigator on two federally funded grants: a National Institute of Health grant to address health disparity by determining injury from sexual assault and a Office of Violence Against Women grant to perform a needs assessment concerning services provided for victimized women with disabilities in the Cincinnati area.

Melissa S. Fry, Ph.D., is Research and Policy Associate at the Mountain Association for Community Economic Development (MACED) in Berea, Kentucky. Her work includes research, program evaluation, policy analysis, and advocacy. Melissa has a Ph.D. in Sociology from the University of Arizona with teaching and research interests in social inequality, public policy, and organizations.

Alesha Durfee, Ph.D., is an Assistant Professor in the Women and Gender Studies program at Arizona State University. She received a Ph.D. in Sociology from the University of Washington. Her research focuses on domestic violence, the social construction of victimization, child care utilization, and social policy. Her work has appeared in such journals as *Politics & Society* and the *Journal of Marriage and Family*. Outside of academia, she has worked as a domestic violence victim advocate in law enforcement and the criminal justice system.

Jennifer L. Hartman, Ph.D., is an Assistant Professor of Criminal Justice at the University of North Carolina at Charlotte with an Adjunct Professor appointment in the Women's and Gender Studies Department. Dr. Hartman earned her Ph.D. from the University of Cincinnati. She is the author of over 20 journal articles, academic book chapters, and technical reports focused on gender issues, domestic violence, and best court and community correctional practices. Her recent publications have focused on the gendered effects of drug users in a community setting.

Sameer Hinduja, Ph.D., is an Assistant Professor in the Department of Criminology and Criminal Justice at Florida Atlantic University. He received his Ph.D. in Criminal Justice from Michigan State University. He has written two books, and his interdisciplinary research on Internet crime and online safety is widely published in a number of academic journals. He can be reached via e-mail at hinduja@fau.edu.

Philip D. Holley, Ph.D., is currently a Professor of Criminal Justice and Sociology and Chair of the Department of Social Sciences at Southwestern Oklahoma State University in Weatherford, Oklahoma. He has been at Southwestern since 1974, teaching both criminal justice and sociology courses. His Ph.D. in sociology was granted in 1982 from Iowa State University. Research interests currently include general victimology, corrections, and deviance. Published work covers such diverse areas as prisons, rib joints, and sociologists serving as expert witnesses.

John P. Jarvis, Ph.D., is a Senior Behavioral Scientist in the Behavioral Science Unit at the FBI Academy. His work focuses on crime analysis, crime trend research, and the initiation and support of various research efforts by local, state, and federal law enforcement. His recent criminological work involves examining validity and reliability of national crime statistics, analyses of serial crimes, and measuring and exploring the behavior of computer criminals. He holds a Ph.D. in Sociology from the University of Virginia and has authored and co-authored numerous works that include recent publications appearing in the *Journal of Contemporary Criminal Justice*, the *Journal of Homicide Studies*, and the *Journal of Trauma, Violence and Abuse.* He also has served as an Adjunct Professor in social sciences at several universities.

Victoria L. Lippen, M.Ed., was employed by Hamilton County Pretrial Services in Cincinnati, Ohio for nine years as a Pretrial Release Officer, Caseworker, and Information System Specialist. Ms. Lippen earned her M.Ed. at the University of Cincinnati.

Patrick McManimon, Ph.D., received a B.S. degree in Sociology and Religion from Bradley University in 1973. He earned an M.A. in Criminal Justice and a Ph.D. in Criminal Justice from Rutgers University in 1994 and 2000, respectively. Dr. McManimon was employed with the Illinois Department of Corrections from 1973 to 1988 in various administrative positions and the Mercer County Department of Public Safety as Warden of the Mercer County Detention Center from 1988 to 1998. His research interests lie in jail and prison violence, inmate suicide, criminal justice responses to domestic violence, and sentencing policy. His teaching concentrations are corrections and research methods. Dr. McManimon has published in the *Journal of Criminal Justice Education* and *American Jails.* He serves as an expert witness in U.S. Federal District Courts on matters of prison and jail administration.

Terance D. Miethe, Ph.D., is a Professor of Criminal Justice at the University of Nevada, Las Vegas. His most recent research has focused on criminal victimization, the situational context of homicide, and the normative rules and rituals surrounding incidents of interpersonal violence.

Heather C. Melton, Ph.D., is an Assistant Professor in the Department of Sociology at the University of Utah. Her research interests center around violence against women and the criminal justice response to it. Specifically, she has published on stalking in the context of intimate partner abuse, gender differences in intimate partner abuse, criminal justice responses to stalking and intimate partner abuse, and sexual assault.

Angela M. Moe, Ph.D., is Associate Professor of Sociology and Criminal Justice, with affiliation with Gender and Women's Studies, at Western Michigan University. Her research interests include violence against women, gender and justice, and sociology of the body. Her work may be found in such journals as *Violence Against Women*, *Criminal Justice Studies*, *Women and Therapy*, *Women's Studies Quarterly*, *Journal of Contemporary Ethnography*, *Women and Criminal Justice*, and *Journal of Interpersonal Violence.* She has served as President of the Midwest Sociologists for Women and

Society; Executive Counselor for the American Society of Criminology, Division on Women and Crime; and founding member/deputy editor for the journal *Feminist Criminology.* She is currently earning a graduate certificate in holistic health care, with the aim of developing a line of action-based research in third wave feminist movement therapy.

Justin W. Patchin, Ph.D., is an Assistant Professor of Criminal Justice at the University of Wisconsin-Eau Claire. His research areas focus on policy and program evaluation, juvenile delinquency prevention, and school violence. For the past several years, he has been studying adolescent Internet use, including social networking and cyberbullying. He can be reached via e-mail at patchinj@uwec.edu.

Hillary Potter, Ph.D., is an Assistant Professor of Sociology at the University of Colorado at Boulder. Her research focuses on the intersections of race, gender, and class issues as they relate to crime and violence. Dr. Potter holds a B.A. and a Ph.D. in sociology from the University of Colorado at Boulder and an M.A. in criminal justice from the John Jay College of Criminal Justice. Dr. Potter is the author of *Battle Cries: Black Women and Intimate Partner Abuse* (New York University Press, 2008) and the editor of *Racing the Storm: Racial Implications and Lessons Learned from Hurricane Katrina* (Lexington Books, 2007).

Wendy C. Regoeczi, Ph.D., is an Associate Professor of Sociology at Cleveland State University. Her research focuses on violence and homicide, including domestic violence, gender, and racial differences in homicide, solvability factors in homicide cases, and methodological issues in studying lethal violence. She is coauthor (with Terance Miethe) of *Rethinking Homicide: Exploring the Structure and Process Underlying Deadly Situations,* published by Cambridge University Press.

Gina Robertiello, Ph.D., is Associate Professor and Coordinator of the Criminal Justice Major at Felician College, in Lodi, New Jersey. She obtained her B.S., M.A., and Ph.D. from Rutgers University, and her doctoral dissertation was published with Edwin Mellen Press, in 2004. She is the author of over a dozen articles and book chapters, and has several publications currently in press. She has also published a number of book reviews. In addition, Dr. Robertiello regularly attends and presents papers at national conferences. She guest lectures regularly and serves as a book reviewer for a number of publishing companies. Her areas of expertise include Domestic Violence, Perceptions of Police, Research Methods, and Victimology.

Shannon Santana, Ph.D., is an Assistant Professor in the Department of Sociology and Criminal Justice at the University of North Carolina Wilmington. Her research interests include violence against women, the effectiveness of self-protective behaviors in violent victimizations, workplace violence, and public attitudes toward crime and criminal justice. Her work has appeared in *Violence and Victims,* the *Justice System Journal,* and the *Security Journal.* In addition, she has also coauthored book chapters in several books including *Campus Crime: Legal, Social and Policy Issues, Violence at Work: Causes, Patterns, and Prevention,* and *Changing Attitudes to Punishment: Public Opinion, Crime and Justice.*

Erica J. Schweikert, B.A., graduated from Kean University with a degree in criminal justice in 2005. She worked for the State of New Jersey's Juvenile Justice Commission, where she worked one-on-one with juveniles utilizing numerous tools that she had learned in her field. Her research interests focus on victims, especially children, who have been lost in the system.

Susan Sharpe, Ph.D., is a Professor in the Department of Sociology, University of Oklahoma. She is the former chair of the Division on Women and Crime of the American Society of Criminology and currently serving on the Program Committee for the Academy of Criminal Justice Sciences and Outstanding Paper Committee for the American Society of Criminology. In 2006, Professor Sharp launched the journal *Feminist Criminology* as its founding editor. Professor Sharp is the editor of the text *The Incarcerated Woman*, Prentice-Hall, 2003, sole author of a 2005 book on effects of death penalty on families of offenders, *Hidden Victims*, and author of more than 30 articles and book chapters focusing on gender, nationality, crime, and the criminal justice system. She has received numerous awards, including the 2005 Good Teaching Award for the University of Oklahoma and both the Kenneth Crook and the Rufus G. Hall Faculty Awards from the College of Liberal Studies at the University of Oklahoma. Since 2005, she has conducted the annual Oklahoma Study of Incarcerated Women and Their Children for the Oklahoma Commission on Children and Youth, resulting in reports to the state legislature and policy changes.

INTRODUCTION

☙

The Gendered Nature of Victimization

VENESSA GARCIA
JANICE E. CLIFFORD

INTRODUCTION

Gendered justice and gendered victimization are social facts within our society. Gendered victimization describes the fact that most crimes tend to be committed against one gender more than the other. For example, murder is gendered in that most murder victimizations involve males, while intimate partner violence (IPV) and sexual assault are gendered in that most victims tend to be females. These social facts do not deny that both genders do experience these crimes. We can see, for example, that research has uncovered a category of murder as gender-motivated violence, known as *femicide* (as will be discussed by Della Giustina in Chapter 6). In addition to gendered victimization, research as uncovered the continued practice of gendered justice in American society (Belknap, 2007; Garcia, 2007; Martin & Jurik, 2007). Gendered justice can be found in the lack of hiring of women in criminal justice occupations, in ignoring female offenders, their circumstances, and their treatment within the system, and, in particular to this book, in ignoring female victims of gendered victimizations.

Women have been invisible, outside of the family, throughout history. Women's experiences and contributions within society have been ignored and in many cases denied. However, in the 1970s, feminists brought to the forefront the fact that crime and victimization are gendered. It was at this time that feminist scholars educated criminal justice and criminology/victimology about the *generalizability problem*, or what is commonly referred to as the *add-the-women-and-stir approach* (Belknap, 2007). The generalizability problem is the practice of criminal justice and criminology/victimology to develop theories and practices based on males' experiences—usually juvenile boys—and fitting women and girls into these theories and practices. Furthermore, approaching an understanding of females' victimization and criminal behaviors, scholars and practitioners alike assumed that females' problems were based on their inferior or dysfunctioning biology. Females were thought to be biologically dysfunctional or social misfits, thus allowing for their victim and criminal experiences. These conclusions, however, were based on a social construction of the good woman/bad woman dichotomy that tends to drive the treatment of female victims of crime by their families, by their communities, and by criminal justice officials.

This book focuses on gendered victimization as it is experienced by females. As such, the most pressing gendered victimization that females experience in our society are examined: IPV, sexual assault, stalking, workplace violence, and gender-motivated murder. However, before moving the focus further, let us examine the extent of gendered victimization with a look at differential risks of violence.

DIFFERENTIAL RISKS OF GENDERED VICTIMIZATION

Crime category is important to examine, especially when focusing on women and young children. Their victimizations are the product of their positions within society. So, while men and boys are relegated the public sphere making them more susceptible to street crimes, women and girls are relegated the private sphere making them more susceptible to crimes within the family. This is important to understand because the nature, extent, and frequency of females' victimizations, as well as the treatment they experience, are a result of their lower positions relative to males given their power in diverse realms of society. As Melissa S. Fry discusses in Chapter 2, women's lack of citizenship and political power denied their victimizations historically. Existing remnants of such conditions presently have implications for females as contemporary societal and legal responses to female crime victims reflect historical patterns.

Examining differential risk rates, victimologists have found that some groups of people are more likely than others to be victimized. Currently, in looking at violent crimes, we know that young males (teen and young adults) are more likely to be murdered, assaulted, and robbed; and that males, in general, most commonly are victimized through the efforts of strangers (Bureau of Justice Statistics, 2006). However, young women are much more likely to be sexually and physically assaulted by an intimate or former intimate partner (Belknap, 2007; Harlow, 1991). Similarly, individuals who are racial minorities are more likely to be victims of violent crimes. For example, Black males have a much greater chance of being murdered than White males (Langan, 1985). They are also more likely to be robbed (Koppel, 1987). Focusing on victim/offender relationships, murder victims tend to know or be related to their murderers in 41–52 percent of the cases (Karmen, 2007). Examining the profile of robbery victims, Rennison (1999) found that these victims more likely than not were males, Black or Hispanic, 16–19 years of age, never married, had an income of $25,000 to $34,999 (followed by an income of less than $7,500), and resided within an urban area located in the Western region of the United States.

Six million women are physically assaulted each year at the hands of intimate or former intimate partners (Straus, 1990). However, about half of the cases go unreported to the police (Fleury, Sullivan, Bybee, & Davidson, 1998; Greenfeld, Rand, & Craven, 1998). This is problematic for a variety of reasons, one in particular, because IPV is the greatest threat of injury to women between the ages of 15 and 44. In 1998, females represent over 85 percent of all IPV victims (Rennison & Welchans, 2000). Rennison (1999) identified the most common sexual assault victim as female, 16–19 years of age, Black, single, unemployed or having low income, and from large cities. Furthermore, victims tend to know their assailants in slightly over half of the sexual assault cases (Bachman & Paternoster, 1993).

EXPLANATIONS OF GENDERED VICTIMIZATIONS

Historically, criminologists and other scholars have sought the answer to the question "what distinguishes criminals from noncriminals?" As a younger discipline and a specialization within criminology (see Karmen, 2007, for a brief history of victimology), victimology specifically has sought to answer the question "what distinguishes victims from nonvictims?" While this information can be useful in allowing us to understand the general characteristics of those individuals targeted by motivated offenders, the quest has led victimology instead to focus on what is wrong with the victim and what the victim can change in order to decrease her or his chances of future victimization, i.e., serial victimization.

As discussed by Venessa Garcia and Erica J. Schweikert in Chapter 1, the problems here are that, first, this approach takes responsibility and accountability away from the offender, in a sense justifying the offender's behavior, and places it on the victim, which is reflected in the concept of "victim blaming." The second, and larger, consequence is that it ignores, even rejects, social structural causes of crime and victimization. When we are able to identify characteristics of victims that we can lay blame to, we in essence claim that individuals who do not possess these characteristics are less blameworthy and more innocent. We then mandate that individuals who possess these traits "educate" themselves and even change their lifestyles in order to prevent future victimization. Therefore, ignoring social structural causes of crime and victimization allows the problem to persist.

Victimologists have attempted to answer the question "why are these groups of people victimized?" from many angles. Social structural explanations focus on differential rates of crime, poverty, family breakdown, and neighborhood ecology (Cohen, Kluegal, & Land, 1981; Garofalo, 1986; Siegal, 1998; Sherman, Gartin, & Buerger, 1989). Others place more focus on offender-related factors such as routine activities and the motivation of offenders (Cohen & Felson, 1979; Felson, 1994, 1997). However, the focus to take hold of victimology research has been the victim-focused approach.

Examining differential risk factors, victimologists have attempted to understand why certain groups of people are at greater risk of crime victimization than other groups. For example, Skogan (1981) and Felson (1997) found that young single and childless men and women lived a certain lifestyle that exposed them to victimization. This focus was labeled lifestyles theory.

Even more focused on lifestyles and exposure, equivalent group theorists explain victimization as the result of victims and criminals sharing similar interests, engaging in similar activities, and being selected from similar social groups, i.e., youth, racial groups, or criminal groups. According to equivalent group theory, victims are the "adversaries, acquaintances, and friends" of offenders (Siegal, 1998), and tend to be defined as "fairgame." Furthermore, their criminal involvement inhibits turning/authorities for help (Siegal, 1998). This explanation may be acceptable for female-gendered victimization because much of the violence they experience is perpetrated by those closest to them. Within this discussion, it should then be interpreted to imply that females are most commonly victimized within the context of engaging in criminal activity themselves. Attempts to apply this theory have proven to be disastrous.

Equivalent group approaches have been most common in understanding murder. Wolfgang (1958) was one of the first to use this approach when he examined "victim precipitative murders" in Philadelphia from 1948 to 1952. Wolfgang found that precipitative victims were often men, having consumed alcohol, having a history of at least one violent offense, having been the first to use force, or having known the offender prior to the murder. Some victims have been described as engaging in a subintentional death by engaging in a self-destructive lifestyle (Allen, 1980) or as having a "death wish" in adhering to certain norms of a subculture of violence (Anderson, 1999; Wolfgang & Ferracuti, 1967). In this way, many victims have been attributed the role of instigator of the crime. For example, the murdered victim was the first to draw a knife, or the raped woman seduced her attacker.

Where the victim did not engage in a high-risk lifestyle or a precipitative manner, others have found a more subtle form of victim blaming, known as victim facilitation. Victim facilitation describes the cause of the victim's misfortune as the result of carelessness, or disregard to dangers (Karmen, 2007). Accordingly, victims are attributed some blame, as with the victims who do not lock their doors or who walk alone at night (see Belknap, 2001). However, borrowing from Wolfgang's victim precipitative homicides research, Amir (1971) attempted to answer the question of why women get raped. In his research, Amir identifies a category of rape victims who precipitate their victimizations through what he identifies as involving some aspect and/or degree of compliance.

Some victim typologies, which are "classification schemes that aid in the understanding of what a group has in common and how it differs from others" (Karmen, 2007, p. 104), have explained victimization through victim culpability. For instance, Mendelsohn (1940, as cited in Shafer, 1968) discusses victimization by centering on the relative culpability for the criminal act as attributable to the victim, which ranges on a continuum with varying degrees of blame from completely innocent to mostly guilty. Similarly, Schafer's (1968) typology explains victimization, in part, as related to the level of blame (i.e., full, partial, or none) attributed to victims for the circumstances surrounding the criminal act leading to their experience.

Amir's research has been one of the more extreme forms of victim blaming of female crime victims in victimology (Eigenberg, 2003); however, there have been several explanations for the occurrence of victim blaming in our society. As Van Wormer and Bartollas (2000) describe, it is the natural social psychology that allows us to deny the suffering of the victim. According to Van Wormer and Bartollas, there is a natural tendency to turn our heads from the pain that other people experience. This social psychological explanation focuses on the need to rationalize injustice, as well as on the reciprocity believed to be involved in victimization which then leads victims to internalize the blame that society places on them.

In another social psychological explanation, it is argued that "the closer we try to identify ourselves with victims, the more vulnerable we are to their suffering" (Van Wormer & Bartollas, 2000, p. 93). As a result, the victim is stigmatized in an effort to avoid *contamination*. Other, though not unrelated, explanations suggest that we hold various images of what certain criminals look and act like, such as rapists; and when the accused does not fit this image the blame is transferred to the victim, as was the case in the Glen Ridge rape of a young mentally disabled girl (Lefkowitz, 1997). Similarly, there are certain ideas about who can be a victim based on personal characteristics, cultural context, and the existence of stereotypes and myths (as Heather C. Melton discusses in Chapter 7 surrounding sexual victimization). Images of females are also held that when violated result in minimizing the suffering of the victim (Belknap, 2007). Images have dichotomized women into good girls and bad girls, or as Feinman (1986) states into "Madonnas" or "whores." To make things more complex, images of women of color prove that not all women are discriminated to an equal degree. Young (1986) argues that women of color are not given a "good girl" category. Schwartz and DeKeserdey (1997) add that the socialization of aggression and reverence for athletes lead to aggression against women off the field and a certain degree of acceptance of this violence. As a result of this extreme level of victim blaming, feminist advocates and researchers stepped in to correct the problem presented by the add-the-woman-and-stir approach (Belknap, 2007). This is where this book picks up.

THIS BOOK

In creating this book, four major themes prevailed. The first theme surrounds cultural ideologies of "doing gender" and how they affect female crime victims. Thus, Part I, Doing Gender, provides a theoretical, historical, and social context to understanding female victimization. The second theme is organized around gendered crime types. Part II is dedicated to addressing the most common female-gendered victimizations: gender-motivated murder, sexual assault, and IPV. The last two chapters of Part II examine two crime types that have either not yet been identified as gendered victimization or in which the jury is still out on the matter. These crimes are workplace violence and cyberbullying and on-line harassment.

The third and fourth themes of this book, addressed in Part III, are the responses to female victimization. The beginning of Part III examines the social response to female victimization. In this part, the treatment of female crime victims within the community setting of a shelter is examined. Within the last several chapters in Part III, the fourth and final theme of this book examines police, prosecution, court, and correctional responses. The chapters included within this part examine criminal justice responses through the eyes of the victims as well as through official documents. Also included is a focus on the criminalization of female victimization. This book provides an examination of female victimization that places it into cultural, historical, and social contexts. The chapters provide theoretical, quantitative, and qualitative examinations of the issues. It is hoped that the readers will gain an appreciation for the complexities of these issues. Only in this light can we hope to improve these social problems.

References

Allen, N. (1980). *Homicide: Perspectives on prevention.* New York: Human Sciences Press.

Amir, M. (1971). *Patterns in forcible rape.* Chicago, IL: University of Chicago Press.

Anderson, E. (1999). *The code of the streets.* New York: W. W. Norton.

Bachman, R., & Paternoster, R. (1993). A contemporary look at the effects of rape law reform: How far have we really come? *Journal of Criminal Law and Criminology, 84*, 554–574.

Belknap, J. (2007). *The invisible women: Gender, crime, and justice* (3rd Ed.). Belmont, CA: Wadsworth/Thomson Learning.

Bureau of Justice Statistics. (2006). *Criminal victimization in the United States: 2005 Statistical tables from the National Criminal Victimization Survey.* Washington, D.C.: U.S. Department of Justice, Office of Justice Programs, Bureau of Justice Statistics. NCJ 215244. Retrieved June 2, 2008, from http://www.ojp.usdoj.gov/bjs/pub/pdf/cvus05.pdf

Cohen, L., & Felson, M. (1979). Social change and crime rate trends: A routine activity approach. *American Sociological Review, 44*, 588–607.

Cohen, L., Kluegal, J., & Land, K. (1981). Social inequality and criminal victimization. *American Sociological Review, 46*, 505–524.

Eigenberg, H. M. (2003). Victim blaming. In L. J. Moriarty (Ed.), *Controversies in victimology*, pp. 15–24. Cincinnati, OH: Anderson.

Feinman, C. (1986). *Women in the criminal justice system.* New York: Praeger.

Felson, M. (1994). *Crime and everyday life.* Thousand Oaks, CA: Pine Forge Press.

Felson, M. (1997). Routine activities and involvement in violence as actor, witness, or target. *Violence and Victims, 12*, 209–220.

Fleury, R., Sullivan, C., Bybee, D., & Davidson, V. (1998). Why don't they just call the police? *Violence and Victims, 13*, 333–340.

Garcia, V. (2007). Gendered justice. In Barak, G. (Ed.), *Battleground criminal justice* (Vols. 1–2), pp. 311–319. Westport, CT: Greenwood Press.

Garofalo, J. (1986). Lifestyles and victimization: An update. In Fattah, E. (Ed.), *From crime policy to victim policy*, pp. 135–155. New York: St. Martin's Press.

Greenfeld, L., Rand, M., & Craven, D. (1998). *BJS report: Violence by intimates: Analysis of data on crimes by current or former spouses, boyfriends, and girlfriends.* Washington, D.C.: U.S. Department of Justice.

Harlow, C. W. (1991). *Female victims of violent crime.* Washington, D.C.: U.S. Department of Justice.

Karmen, A. (2007). *Crime victims: An introduction to victimology* (6th ed.). Belmont, CA: Wadsworth/Thomson Learning.

Koppel, H. (1987). *Lifetime likelihood of victimization: Bureau of Justice Statistics technical report.* Washington, D.C.: U.S. Department of Justice.

Langan, P. (1985). *BJS special report: The risk of violent crime.* Washington, D.C.: U.S. Department of Justice.

Lefkowitz, B. (1997). *Our guys: The Glenn Ridge rape and the secret life of the perfect suburb.* Berkeley: University of California Press.

Martin, S. E., & Jurik, N. C. (2007). *Doing justice, doing gender: Women in legal and criminal justice occupations* (2nd ed.). Thousand Oaks, California: Sage Publications.

Rennison, C. M. (1999). *Criminal victimization 1998: Changes 1997–1997 with trends 1993–1998. BJS NCVS.* Washington, D.C.: U.S. Department of Justice.

Rennison, C. M., & Welchans, S. (2000). *BJS special report: Intimate partner violence.* Washington, D.C.: U.S. Department of Justice.

Schafer, S. (1968). *The victim and his criminal.* New York: Random House.

Schwartz, M., & DeKeserdey, W. (1997). *Sexual assault on the college campus: The role of male peer support.* Thousand Oaks, CA: Sage Publications.

Sherman, L., Gartin, P., & Buerger, M. (1989). Hot spots of predatory crime: Routine activities and the criminology of place. *Criminology, 27*, 27–40.

Siegal, L. (1998). *Criminology* (6th ed.). Belmont, CA: West/Wadsworth.

Skogan, W. G. (1981). Assessing the behavioral context of victimization. *Journal of Criminal Law and Criminology, 72*, 727–742.

Straus, M. A. (1990). *Physical violence in American families.* New Brunswick, NJ: Transaction Publishers.

Van Wormer, K. S., & Bartollas, C. (2000). *Women and the criminal justice system.* Boston, MA: Allyn & Bacon.

Wolfgang, M. E. (1958). *Patterns in criminal homicide.* Philadelphia, PA: University of Pennsylvania Press.

Wolfgang, M. E., & Ferracuti, F. (1967). *The subculture of violence: Towards an integrated theory in criminology.* London: Tavistock.

Young, V. D. (1986). Gender expectations and their impact on black female offenders and victims. *Justice Quarterly, 3*, 305–328.

PART I

ॐ

DOING GENDER
THE GENDERED NATURE
OF VICTIMIZATION

What does it mean to *do gender*? *Doing gender* is the daily gendered activity to which all members of society are held accountable (Fenstermaker, West, & Zimmerman, 1991; Garcia, 2003; West & Fenstermaker, 1993). As such, males are required through gendered scripts to behave like males, while females are required to behave like females. Gender scripts tend to be located within the larger society and are frequently written by males. With regard to so-called gender-neutral activities, such as crime, victimization, and work, behavioral scripts are often written by men and for men (Martin & Jurik, 2007). Because all institutions are organized through gendered lines (Acker, 1992) and because gender scripts are found within the larger society, we can argue that to do gender is to *do culture*.

Criminal justice laws, processes, crimes, and victimizations, like every institution, have been defined and treated through the process of *doing culture*. Hence, laws and definitions of what is a crime and who is a victim use gender scripts defined by men for men. These social facts within our criminal justice system often do not allow for the recognition of certain victims. When gender scripts are combined with an understanding of victimization, gender-motivated crimes tend to be ignored or marginalized. Thus, female victims of family or intimate partner violence (IPV), sexual assault, or gender-motivated murder often are not allowed the status of victim.

Part I is organized around this first theme of *doing gender/doing culture* and how these ideologies affect female crime victims. Thus, Part I, Doing Gender, provides a theoretical, historical, and social context to understanding female victimization. In the first chapter, "Cultural Images—Media Images: 'Doing Culture' and Victim Blaming of Female Crime Victims," Venessa Garcia and Erica J. Schweikert defend the perspective that crime and victimization are socially constructed around gender scripts of doing gender and culture. They argue that cultural scripts of victimization apply only to females who do gender. However, for certain types of victimizations, such as IPV and sexual assault, most women are assumed to be violating gender roles. As a result, many females are blamed for victimizations against them.

Melissa S. Fry takes this conceptualization through a historical analysis in Chapter 2, "Becoming Victims, Becoming Citizens: A Brief History of Gender-Motivated Violence in the U.S. Law." Fry examines gender-motivated crimes, specifically intimate partner violence and sexual violence, arguing that women's lack of citizenship denied their victimizations throughout history. Consequently, this transcended to current practices in applying male definitions and explanations of this gender-motivated violence. Fry argues that women's fight to citizenship and political recognition is a continual struggle that is found in today's laws and practices.

In Chapter 3, "Women and Victimization: Constructing Outcomes," Dennis R. Brewster and Philip D. Holley bring the reader back to a theoretical explanation of the social construction of female victimization. Brewster and Holley argue that a general theory of victimization needs to be developed in order to understand gender-motivated violence against women. In their chapter, Brewster and Holley provide a framework for understanding the abstract concepts surrounding the construction of victimhood (i.e., harm, social reaction, victim status, and victim entitlements). The authors argue that these concepts must be fully understood and empirically tested.

The last chapter in Part I, "The Measurement, Definition, and Reporting of Female Victimization" by Janice E. Clifford and John P. Jarvis, examines the various measures used in identifying, defining, and reporting gendered victimization. Clifford and Jarvis argue that while the criminal justice system relies heavily on official accounts such as the Uniform Crime Report and National Crime Victimization Survey, in addition to these, other measures should be examined to comprehensively understand the nature and extent of violence against women.

References

Acker, J. (1992). Gender institutions: From sex roles to gendered institutions. *Contemporary Sociology, 21*, 565–568.

Fenstermaker, S., West, C., & Zimmerman, D. H. (1991). Gender inequality: New conceptual terrain. In R. Lesser-Blumberg (Ed.), *Gender, family and economy* (pp. 298–307). Newbury Park, CA: Sage.

Garcia, V. (2003). "Difference" in the police department: Women, Policing and "Doing Gender." *Journal of Contemporary Criminal Justice, 19*, 330–344.

Martin, S. E., & Jurik, N. C. (2007). *Doing justice, doing gender: Women in legal and criminal justice occupations* (2nd ed.). Belmont, CA: Sage Publications.

West, C., & Fenstermaker, S. (1993). Power, inequality, and the accomplishment of gender: An ethnomethodological view. In P. England (Ed.), *Theory on gender/feminism on theory* (pp. 151–174). New York: Aldine.

CHAPTER 1

CULTURAL IMAGES—
MEDIA IMAGES

"Doing Culture" and Victim Blaming
of Female Crime Victims

❧

VENESSA GARCIA AND
ERICA J. SCHWEIKERT

ABSTRACT

Images of victimization often follow cultural myths of who deserves to claim the status of victim. These images tend to be carried over into the criminal justice system influencing the way in which victims are treated, into the social sciences influencing the way in which victims are studied, and into the media influencing the way in which victims are portrayed. Research on crime in the media has examined perceptions of criminals, professionals, women, and other minority groups; however, images of victims, specifically female victims, in the media have been neglected. This chapter examines the cultural and media victim blaming of female victims of violent crime. The images of 328 victims in 126 newspaper stories were analyzed. It was found that victim blaming of female crime victims tends to reflect more camouflaged or subtle forms of victim blaming for all crimes as well as for sexual assault. This finding shows that media blame female victims more in line with victim facilitation. Males are blamed more directly for the occurrence of the victimizations in line with victim precipitation.

INTRODUCTION

In 1989, 28-year-old Trisha Meili was brutally raped while jogging in Central Park in New York City. The media quickly labeled her the "Central Park Jogger." Media images of Trisha Meili presented her as a health conscious, young, white woman who was brutally attacked by a gang of young Black and Hispanic teenagers (Facts On File World News Digest, 1990). The case quickly became symbolic of racial tensions in New York City focusing on the dangers faced by innocent, young, white women at the hands of young, racial and ethnic minority males. These young men were prosecuted, convicted, and incarcerated; however, 15 years after the attack they were exonerated based on DNA evidence and the confession of the actual perpetrator.

In 1991, William Kennedy Smith, nephew of the late President John F. Kennedy, was accused by Patricia Bowman of date rape at the Kennedy estate in Palm Beach, Florida. As the trial progressed, Patricia was portrayed as an unstable, promiscuous, single mother, crying rape in an attempt to damage the promising life of a vulnerable famous figure (CourtTV, 2004; Grant & Otto, 2003). The case became a battle between a mentally unstable and sexually promiscuous woman and a politically powerful man and his family, especially as portrayed by the media.

In June 2003, basketball star Kobe Bryant was accused of rape. Bryant's defense counsel adopted the same tactics used in the Kennedy Smith case. In a media frenzy, the accuser's name was released and images of mental instability and sexual promiscuity were released to the public. Newspaper stories captioned such victim-blaming titles as "Kobe Win: Sex Life of Accuser to be Aired" (Cullen & Conner, *Daily News*, August 17, 2004), "She Made Eyes at Me, Kobe Said" (Connor, *Daily News*, September 1, 2004b), "Bryant Case Could Have a Chilling Effect on Report of So-Called 'Acquaintance Rape' " (Lavoie, The Associated Press State & Local Wire, September 5, 2004), and "Kobe Told Cops She Was Aggressor" (Connor, *Daily News*, September 17, 2004a). Other stories described the repercussions of the system's failure: "'Nutty or Slutty' Rape Defense Too Easily Believed" (Eagan, *Boston Herald*, August 17, 2004) and "Kobe Bryant Case Has Lesson for Women" (McCarthy, *Newsday*, August 19, 2004). The media images described above reveal a certain ideology regarding those who deserve to hold the status "victim" and those who do not.

Institutionalization, as defined by Meyer, Boli, and Thomas, is the process whereby patterned activities become so ingrained in knowledge and custom that they become "normatively and cognitively held in place, and practically taken for granted as lawful" (1994, p. 10). The status of victim has been institutionalized in modern culture (Furedi, 1997, p. 95). Within the institution of *victimhood*, a victim is expected to behave in a certain way and to follow a certain cultural script of "weakness, loss, and pain" (Rock, 2002, p. 14; also see Altheide, 2002); otherwise, she lacks the right to claim the name *victim*. Likewise, the status of a good woman has been institutionalized. A good woman is expected to be passive, dependent, and powerless. The institutionalized image of the female victim resembles the institutionalized image of the good woman (Winter, 2002). Crime events that do not have this "ideal victim" do not involve what society has named the "innocent victim." It is often the case that the ideal victim is viewed as the helpless, unsuspecting, and powerless prey of a violent stranger. However, the image of the ideal victim becomes much more complex when we consider the intersectionality of gender, race, age, and income. Younger females tend to be viewed as more carefree or reckless, while people on the lower rung of the socioeconomic ladder have been blamed for their plight in our individualistic society. Likewise, women of color are generally not given a good girl grade which they can obtain. And yet the ideal type has been found to be the exception, not the rule, while deviations from these cultural expectations result in blaming women for their victimizations. This dual image of the victim requires that she be passive and helpless; yet, she must also show resistance to being victimized. This does not equate with the ideal female victim or the passivity and powerlessness of a good woman.

In addition to the inconsistent norms, we see this inconsistency in practice. For example, a rape victim who does not show signs of fighting back is not perceived to have been truly raped and may not find the criminal justice system willing to take action against her attacker (Belknap, 2007), while an intimate partner violence (IPV) victim who did fight back is often defined as engaging in mutual combat (Grady, 2002; Straus, 1990; Straus & Gelles, 1986) and may face arrest (Klein, 2004). Furthermore, many female victims of crime know their offenders, and holding to ideas of reciprocity (Van Wormer & Bartollas, 2000), society tends to view them as facilitating their own victimizations.

This chapter provides the framework for the rest of the book. This chapter focuses on the victim-blaming images of female victims of crime as they are portrayed by society in general and the media specifically. These images drive legal and social responses to female crime victims, as well as self-interpretations and self-labels. Social constructionism is applied in order to understand the images of female crime victims. First, the cultural images of womanhood and victimhood are examined. This is followed by an examination of victim blaming within culture. Finally, the chapter moves into an examination of how these images are reflected within the media. It is argued that media, while a reflection of the larger society, are in the business of *making*; particularly, media refine and reinforce our social constructs of victimization on a daily basis. The focus is on two forms of medium: print news media and television entertainment media. Images of crime, criminals, and criminal justice have been examined to some extent (Hale, 1998; Surette, 1984, 1992); however, crime victims have been largely ignored (see Chermack, 1995). Similarly, media images of crime victims focusing on gender are largely unexplored. This research examines the images of 328 crime victims in 126 newspaper stories from three large U.S. cities (Houston, New York City, and Los Angeles).

CULTURAL IMAGES AS MYTH

The social construction of reality is accomplished on a continual basis. It is the process by which, through interaction, individuals come to give meaning to the world around them (Loseke, 1999; Surette, 1998). In this sense, individuals consistently "do reality" or "do culture." In "doing reality," people inevitably interact and, based on that interaction, they give meaning to present and future interactions. In this way, people act and interact in the continual process of constructing reality (Gergen, 1985). It is essential to stress that people do not act and give meaning individually and in isolation (Grossberg, Wartella, & Whitney, 1998; Kappeler, Blumberg, & Potter, 2000). Rather, people act collectively, sharing systems of meaning, or ideologies of politics, class, race, gender, family, crime, and so on. In "doing culture", we construct our reality through personal experiences, social groups, including significant others and institutions, and the mass media (Surette, 1998). These interactions and constructs are experienced within systems of social differences through which the distribution of resources are organized (Grossberg et al., 1998). These differences surround class, race and ethnicity, gender, sexual identity, and age. The unequal distribution of societal resources is related to the fact that different social groups construct reality using slightly different systems of meaning, adding to the complexity of culture and meaning.

Media, however, tend to present a socially constructed reality more in line with the ideals of the dominant class of society. These ideals are taken to represent reality and are found within our systems of meaning. Futhermore, these ideals are developed and reinforced through family, peers, school, sports, religion, and media. In light of our limited experiences with crime and victimization, we give weight to media discourse which presents, on a continual basis, these ideas as reality. The importance given to "media making" increases when other sources of knowledge are not as readily available (Surette, 1998). However, as described earlier, the cultural images reproduced by the media do not always allow victims of crime to claim this status.

VICTIM BLAMING

The image of the ideal female victim is not an arbitrary one and often takes the form of victim blaming. The image comes from cultural ideologies that have been in existence for some time. These cultural ideologies involve gender relations based in patriarchy, racism, and classism, and power relations based in ideas of knowledge and legitimacy (see Chapter 2 for a further examination). There have been several explanations for the occurrence of victim blaming in our society. As Van Wormer and Bartollas (2000) describe it, it is the natural social psychology which allows us to deny the suffering of the victim. According to Van Wormer and Bartollas, there is a natural tendency to turn our head's from the pain that other people experience. This social psychological explanation focuses on the need to rationalize injustice as well as on the reciprocity believed to be involved in victimization which then leads victims to internalize the blame that society places on them. In another social psychological explanation, it is argued that "the closer we try to identify ourselves with victims, the more vulnerable we are to their suffering" (Van Wormer & Bartollas, 2000, p. 93). As a result, the victim is stigmatized in an effort to avoid contamination. Other, though not unrelated, explanations suggest that we hold various images of what certain criminals look and act like, such as rapists; and when the accused does not fit this image, the blame is transferred to the victim, as was the case in the Glen Ridge rape of a young mentally handicapped teenager (Lefkowitz, 1997).

Images of females are also held that when violated result in minimizing the suffering of the victim (Belknap, 2007). Images have dichotomized women into good girls and bad girls, or as Feinman (1986) states into "Madonnas" or "whores." To make things more complex, images of women of color prove that not all women are discriminated to an equal degree. Young (1986) argues that women of color are not given a "good girl" category. Schwartz and DeKeseredy (1997) add that the socialization of athletes to be aggressive and revered leads to aggression against women and to a certain degree of acceptance of this violence.

These social psychological explanations for blaming the victim are premised within society's belief in a just world. This idea of the world as just is not a separate ideology; instead, it is the foundation that allows for these explanations. We like to believe that we can know the causes of human behavior and social structure. We believe that this knowledge allows us to predict and control our future. In a just world we can know these things. In a just world, people "get what they deserve." When we focus on victimization in society, as with all things less understood, people tend to fear what they do not understand. It does not sit well with us to think, and even worse to know, that we do not have control and that we are vulnerable. In order to bring sense and order into our lives, to weed out the uncertainty, we reason that we can control our lives and thus control any possible victimization (Karmen, 2001). To explain victimization in a just world, as the ideology goes, we look to the victim who does not have control over her life. The victim is given the shared responsibility for her victimization through the commission or omission of some activity and has somehow, to some degree, instigated the criminal activity.

Holding to a just world ideology, society maintains an individualized focus of the world and ignores social structural explanations of crime. In this way, we have engaged in victim blaming (Ryan, 1976). When we engage in victim blaming, we define victims as different from other people, or wrong. We attribute this difference as the source of their victimization and demand that victims change their ways. The problem identified with the victim-blaming perspective is that these differences are not always in the control of individuals. For example, women who are attacked at night in dangerous neighborhoods are ridiculed for not moving to safer neighborhoods, giving no focus to the social structural barriers that do not allow many women to move out of poverty. This just world allows us to envision the victim in many ways, for example, as careless, mentally ill, deviant, and even criminal, without direct experience to support our claims. It also ignores the multiple marginality that young, poor, women of color experience in society.

MYTHOLOGY IN SOCIAL ATTITUDES

Victim-blaming images found within social attitudes apply more to female victims of domestic and sexual violence than to any other victim. Victims are said to have provoked or precipitated the rape by their promiscuous behavior (Belknap, 2007; Spencer, 1987). Gelles (1979) found that IPV and rape victims are often thought to have "asked for it" or to have deserved and even enjoyed their victimization, while in his research, Amir (1971) argued that some women precipitate their rapes.

Where the victim did not engage in a high-risk lifestyle or in a precipitative manner, others have found a more subtle form of victim blaming, i.e., victim facilitation. Accordingly, victims are attributed some blame, as with victims who do not lock their doors or who walk alone at night (Burt & Albin, 1981). When examining attitudes toward date rape, researchers have identified a cultural dating script that assumes that she owes him sex (Belknap, 2007; Sutherland, 1995) and that alcohol consumption made her careless (Scronce & Corcoran, 1995). Other victim-blaming images include her style of dress and reputation, more so than her relationship with the offender (Whatley, 1996). However, the relationship with the offender has been found to be a factor in blaming females for the rape (LeDoux & Hazelwood, 1985; Muehlenhard, Powch, Phelps, & Guisti, 1992; Sudderth, 1998). Overall, research has found that the general public holds to the same rape myths as do the police (Field, 1978) and which are in line with legal definitions (Gordon & Riger, 1989).

MYTHOLOGY IN CRIMINAL JUSTICE PRACTICE

Criminal justice practitioners often reinforce the institutionalized notion of the ideal victim when handling cases involving female crime victims. It is often found that females who step out of their socially prescribed gender roles are blamed, at least in part, for their victimizations (Belknap, 2007). Accusations of shared responsibility females experience by the criminal justice system and society at large have been identified as a second victimization. As the gatekeepers of the criminal justice system, police may often be the only agents involved in the process of victim blaming and are a major influence in the angle taken in media stories (Garcia, 2005; Surette, 1998).

Rape is the crime that more often results in victim blaming. Police are more likely to unfound rape cases (determining that the victim made a false charge) when the character or conduct of the victim is questionable or when there is a perceived lack of victim cooperation (LaFree, Reskin, & Visher, 1985). LaFree et al. (1985) also found that police perceive questionable conduct to include hitchhiking, sex outside of marriage, frequenting bars without a male, and going to the home of the accused. Other studies have found that police are less likely to believe a victim's claim if she had previous consensual sexual relations with the accused (LeDoux & Hazelwood, 1985) and if there was a prior victim–offender relationship, especially when considering class, race/ethnicity, and victim blameworthiness (Muehlenhard et al., 1992). The reliance on rape myths has also been found in the courts (LaFree, 1989). Judges and prosecutors have been found to hold the same attitudes toward rape as do the police (LaFree, 1989). Estrich (1987) found that only 35 percent of rape arrests end in convictions. Furthermore, in rape cases where female victims are divorced, are racial/ethnic minorities, or travel alone at night, there is a greater likelihood that consent is believed to have been given (Burt & Albin, 1981).

Criminal justice officials often blame female victims of IPV for instigating these crimes against them and are often reluctant to make an arrest. The traditional response has been that the family is a private institution that ought not to be violated by the government (Kantor & Straus, 1990). In following patriarchal ideologies, police officers often hold to notions that the man should be in control in the relationship (Goolkasian, 1986) or that the woman nagged him beyond control (Belknap, 2007). Today, as a result of successful lawsuits, police are now more willing to make arrests; however, arrests still only make up 15–30 percent of all dispatched calls (Bourg & Stock, 1994; Ferraro, 1989; Lawrenz, Lembo, & Schade, 1988).

Prosecutors' decisions to bring a case to trial are found to be determined by the credibility or worthiness of the victim (Baumer, Messner, & Felson, 2000; Hagan, 1983; Myers and Hagan, 1979; Stanko, 1981–1982). The victim's age, race, income, and conduct during the crime are often considered by prosecutors, judges, and juries. When abusers in IPV cases were tried in court, only 10 percent of the cases ended in a felony conviction (Blodgette, 1987). At the same time, victims have found themselves to be ignored by the judge and report being treated as unworthy of court resources (Hart, 1993). In sum, criminal justice officials hold victim-blaming images toward females differently depending on age, race, and income.

MEDIA IMAGES AS CULTURAL IMAGES

The main problem identified here is that the images presented by the media are a reflection of cultural images and are based on stereotypes rooted in prejudice. According to Grossberg, Wartella, and Whitney, the media's primary activities involve *making*: "making money, making everyday life, making meaning, making identities, making reality, making behavior, making history" (1998, p. 7). In *making*, media products become cultural forms. According to the cultural model of communication, media are a form of communication that socially construct a reality that aids in individual interpretations of meaning in everyday life. Our purpose is not to explain these media effects on human perceptions, as would analysts using the transmission model. Instead, the media are viewed as an institution communicating language and images currently existing within our social systems. In other words, media reproduce taken-for-granted images within society. Thus, one can see the similarities between media discourse and personal discourse. Furthermore, personal discourse is put into practice on a continual basis in all of our social institutions, including academia and government (Garcia & Linskey, 2003).

MEDIA IMAGES AS MYTH

It has long been known that news media are a major source of information about crime (Garcia & Linskey, 2003; Graber, 1980; Kennedy & Sacco, 2001; Skogan & Maxfield, 1981). Crime news is big business. Eleven percent of all news items are crime related and crime is the fourth largest news category (Kennedy & Sacco, 2001). Furthermore, crime news tends to focus on reports of individual crimes of violence, especially, homicide. While one can pick up the newspaper on any given day and read about crime, newspapers rarely relate crime stories to crime rates and trends in the larger society (Garcia, 2005; Garcia & Linskey, 2003).

Sometimes criminals are presented as victims or, at least, as not so criminal, but the media tend to ignore the victim. Chermack (1995) found that news media identified the victim's race in only 15 percent of the cases. Much of the background information about the victim is lacking, especially with the adaptation of forensic journalism which aims to present as many facts about a crime supported by police sources as possible. Even with the lack of background presented on the victim, Chermack found that the profile of the victim has been presented as male, white, young (17–25 years of age) and married, hardly representative of the highest risk group.

According to Soothill and Walby (1991), while we know little about the victim through media discourse, what is presented reproduces dominant values in society. Such images tend to mandate that the victim share responsibility in the victimization. Victim blaming in media discourse can take a subtle image as it tends to in print news media, or it can take an extreme image as is commonly the case in television "infotainment" and crime drama series (Garcia, 2005; Garcia & Linskey, 2003). In what follows, the prominence of media victim blaming and the question of whether victim blaming is gendered are explored. Also explored is the intersectionality of victim blaming with race, age, victim/offender relationship, and crime type.

EXAMINING MEDIA IMAGES: GENDER COMPARISONS OF CRIME VICTIMS

The data were collected from 126 newspaper stories from three large cities (Houston, Los Angeles, and New York City). The three cities were selected randomly from a list of six cities with a Uniform Crime Report total crime index of more than 100,000 incidents for 2001. Newspapers were selected from those available on LEXIS-NEXIS® and with the largest distribution: *The New York Times*, *Los Angeles Times*, and *Houston Chronicle*.

Stories were selected by searching for "crime" and "victim" or "illegal" within the full text of the story and which were printed between April 1, 2003 and April 30, 2003. Only stories that covered violent crimes, including robbery, were selected. National briefs were omitted due to the lack of detail, especially with regard to victims. International and war stories were also omitted due to the complexity of cultural images in the aftermath of 9/11, a focus this research did not address.

While commonly the unit of analysis in media studies would be the newspaper story or the television episode, here the victim is placed as the unit of analysis. For most of the newspaper articles (84%), there was more than one victim. Because the image of the victim is being examined, it did not stand to reason that the victims should be aggregated to represent an index. In many cases, one may find a robbery taking place in a couple's home, and while the man is murdered the woman is raped. There were 328 victims found in the 126 newspaper stories. The crime stories included 152 victims (46%) from *Los Angeles Times*, 97 (30%) victims from *The New York Times*, and 79 victims (24%) from *Houston Chronicle*. Media coverage of the nature of the murder and sexual victimization, the ages, and the genders of the victims were examined to determine the extent and context of victim blaming.

MEASURES OF VICTIM BLAMING

Victim blaming was the focus of this analysis; specifically, are females of gendered victimizations likely to be blamed for their victimizations? In this analysis, common social images of victim blaming were coded. Research has revealed that the complexity of attitudes and images cannot be captured in a single measure (Garcia & Cao, 2005). Therefore, 13 items that are common patterns of victim blaming (Belknap, 2007; Eigenberg, 2003) were coded into binary variables: (1) there was doubt that the offender is guilty; (2) the victim was reported to be a criminal; (3) if not a criminal, the victim was reported to be deviant usually through criminal associations, such as an addict or associating with gang members, or portrayed in any negative light, such as fighting with the murderer before being stabbed or wearing expensive clothes and carrying hundreds of dollars while only being a teenager; (4) victim was portrayed in a negative light, such as not being a very nice or good person or not well liked; (5) victim was portrayed as mentally unstable, usually involving discussion of institutionalization or accusations of mental conditions by acquaintances; (6) victim was portrayed as helpless; (7) victim was portrayed as promiscuous, such as having multiple partners or dating frequently; (8) victim was portrayed as careless in his or her actions, such as walking alone at night or going home with a stranger in order to obtain drugs; (9) victim was portrayed as being dishonest in the eyes of the police; (10) victim was portrayed as not an innocent victim by the police, such as police reporting about an ongoing conflict between the victim and offender or a fight that occurred just before the victimization; (11) victim was portrayed as not innocent by witnesses; (12) victim was portrayed as not deserving justice or the status of victim (this was usually in relation to other deviant factors noted above); and (13) victim was portrayed as instigating the victimization, such as the victim agreed to murder for hire and ended up a murder victim. While media portrayal with regard to these 13 items may not have intended to blame the victim, following cultural practices of blaming the victims, these are accurate measures.

MEDIA PATTERNS OF CRIME VICTIMS CHARACTERISTICS

In order to get an understanding of whom the media tended to portray as the most common crime victim, data were collected on gender (female = 1), age (child, teen, young adult (20–29 years), adult (30–59 years), older adult (60+ years), and victim/offender relationship. With regard to victim/offender relationship, this study examined (1) if the victim had a prior relationship with the offender (yes = 1) and (2) if the victim had family ties to the offender (yes = 1). Also coded was whether or not the crime was interracial (yes = 1). Race data were collected for White (1), Black (1), Hispanic (1), and Other. However, these data were not common elements in newspaper stories, perhaps media's response to social pressures to eliminate racism within stories. Data were also coded for crime type. This analysis focused primarily on sexual victimization represented in a binary variable (sexual victimization = 1), as this is a gendered victimization. The following analysis describes the data and examines whether victims with various characteristics were blamed for their victimizations.

The sample consisted of 137 (48%) female and 150 (52%) male victims (see Table 1.1). In 13 percent of the crimes, the victim's gender was not specified. Race was identified for only 64 (20%) victims. Hispanics represented the largest proportion of the sample (58%), followed by an even coverage of Blacks and White (17% each), and Other (11%). The stories did, however, reveal that the crimes were interracial in 38 percent of the cases. Age was much more readily identifiable than was race within the media, via the years given or the age category referred to in the story. However, there were still 26 cases (8%) missing

TABLE 1.1   Frequencies of Victim Characteristics

Variables		N	%
Sex	Male	150	52
	Female	137	48
Race	Black	9	17
	Hispanic	37	58
	White	11	17
	Other	6	11
Age	Child	39	13
	Teen	62	21
	Young Adult	71	24
	Adult	102	34
	Older Adult	28	9
Prior Relationship	Yes	160	60
Family Ties	Yes	20	8
Interracial Crime	Yes	26	38
Violent Crime	Yes	326	99
Property Crime	Yes	118	36
Sexual Assault	No	233	71
	Yes	95	29
Murder	No	157	48
	Yes	171	52

age identification. Children (up to age 12) represented 13 percent of the sample, teens represented 21 percent, young adults (20–29 years of age) 24 percent, adults (up to age 59) 34 percent, and older adults (over age 60) 9 percent. There was a prior relationship, acquaintance or intimate, in 60 percent of the sample, while the victim and the offender had familial ties in 8 percent of the cases.

As has been found in cultural definitions, as well as within victimology and criminal justice practice, this study attempted to determine if crime type, specifically sexual assault and murder, significantly influenced media victim blaming. Table 1.1 reveals that 29 percent of the victims covered in the media were sexually assaulted, while 52 percent were murdered. In other analyses not revealed in the table, the four most frequently reported crime as the primary offense were murder (52%), child molestation (15%), sexual assault (12%), and assault (6%), respectively. For both newspapers and television, violent crimes occurred in almost all of the cases (99%); while property crimes were reported in 36 percent of these cases. Obviously, these data do not reflect the actual occurrence of the crime types.

VICTIM IMAGES WITHIN NEWSPAPERS

As has been discussed earlier, sexual assault is a gendered crime in which females make up the majority of the victims. Furthermore, sexual assault and IPV crimes against women are those in which victim blaming is most likely to occur (Belknap, 2007; Garcia, 2005; Karmen, 2001). For these reasons, the focus here was on gender comparisons of media images of sexual assault victims. As seen in Table 1.2, both women and men are likely to know the offenders within newspaper stories in approximately 60 percent of the cases and women are statistically more likely to be related to the offenders (13%). These characteristics are important to examine as research shows that victims, especially female victims, who know their offenders are more likely to be blamed. This will be examined further in this chapter.

In order to understand whether females are more likely to be blamed for their victimizations, the 13 measures of blaming were examined. Table 1.2 presents gendered blaming data for all crimes in aggregate as well as for sexual assaults (gendered victimization). Though not statistically significant, the data reveal that the media are more likely to present doubt regarding the guilt of the accused when males are the victims of crimes in general, as well as of sexual assaults in particular. Examining the aggregate of crimes, males are more likely to be viewed as deviant (15%), portrayed in a negative light (22%), portrayed as dishonest by police (13%) as well as portrayed as not innocent by police and witnesses (20% and 7%, respectively), and portrayed as instigators of their victimizations (21%). The images of male victims as instigators and as not innocent victims as viewed by witnesses were found to be statistically significant. These findings provide blatant examples of victim blaming, pointing to media's role in promoting a victim precipitation ideology.

Examining the data for the aggregate of crimes for females victims, females were more likely to be portrayed as criminal (17%), mentally unstable (3%), helpless (78%), promiscuous (7%), careless (20%), and not deserving of the victim status (7%). Media images of female victims as helpless were statistically significant. Furthermore, the percentage was fairly high leading us to speculate that because the victims were helpless they were not in control and, therefore, could not be blamed. However, the

TABLE 1.2   Victim Images by Sex

	All Crimes			Sexual Assaults Only[a]		
	Male (%)	Female (%)	Total	Male (%)	Female (%)	Total
Know Offender	60	62	231	**95**	**41***	62
Related to Offender	**5**	**13***	229		7	62
Doubt of Criminal Guilt	21	16	236	40		59
Victim Criminal	11	17	287	0	11	64
Victim Deviant	15	13	287	5	14	64
Negative Light	22	21	287	0	16	64
Mentally Unstable	1	3	287	0	5	64
Helpless	**61**	**78***	287	95	93	64
Promiscuous	**0.7**	**7***	287	0	11	20
Careless	**9**	**20***	287	0	11	64
Not Honest, CJ	13	0	287	0	7	64
Not Innocent, CJ	20	12	287	0	9	64
Not Innocent, Witness	**7**	**2***	287	2	5	64
Not Deserving	3	7	287	0	7	64
Instigated Crime	**21**	**10***	287	5	7	64

*Implies the relationship is significant for the medium: $p < .05$

[a]No child under teen years was included in this analysis because young children are less likely to be blamed for sexual victimizations.

images of promiscuity and carelessness were also statistically significant. These tend to represent more camouflaged forms of victim blaming showing the media's role in promoting a victim facilitation ideology.

Next the images of sexual assault victims only were examined. This analysis did not include children (those younger than their teens) because children are less likely to be blamed for sexual assaults against them. Table 1.2 reveals that many of the relationships between victim blaming and sex do not change direction; however, it was found that when eliminating children from the analysis, none of the relationships remain significant. Images of victims as criminal do change but the media portray female sexual assault victims as more deviant than male victims, in a more negative light, as less helpless than male victims, as more dishonest in the eyes of the police, as less innocent in the eyes of the police and witnesses, and as more likely to instigate the victimization. Again, these data are not statistically significant; however, they tell us that further and more in-depth analysis is needed in order to understand the change in these relationships and to understand whether females are more likely to be portrayed as precipitating sexual assaults against them.

Table 1.2 reveals that in either analysis of the aggregate crimes or sexual assault alone, the victim–offender relationship is statistically significant (victim knowing the offender in sexual assault cases and victim related to offender in the data of aggregate crimes). As a result, the data were sorted according to this relationship and victim-blaming measures for aggregate crimes and sexual assault only were examined

TABLE 1.3   Victim Images for Victim/Offender Relationship by Sex

	All Crimes			Sexual Assaults Only[a]		
	Male (%)	Female (%)		Male (%)	Female (%)	
Doubt of Criminal Guilt	37	23	133	32	33	80
Victim Criminal	25	32	140	32	44	86
Victim Deviant	16	14	140	23	21	86
Negative Light	32	30	140	40	36	86
Mentally Unstable	1	6	140	0	5	86
Helpless	58	73	140	**49**	**72***	86
Promiscuous	**1**	**11***	69	2	10	86
Careless*	**10**	**27***	140	**15**	**33***	86
Not Honest, CJ	19	20	140	27	36	86
Not Innocent, CJ	28	21	140	36	39	86
Not Innocent, witness	10	3	140	15	5	86
Not Deserving	6	11	69	9	21	86
Instigated Crime	**30**	**13***	140	40	23	86

*Implies the relationship is significant for the medium: $p < .05$
[a]No child under teen years was included in this analysis because young children are less likely to be blamed for sexual victimizations.

(see Table 1.3). When examining only those cases in which the victim and offender have some form of relationship ($n = 140$), none of the directions of the relationships between sex and the victim-blaming measures change, except for the portrayal of females as dishonest by the police (this relationship is not statistically significant). The image of helplessness is no longer significant, though females are still more likely to be portrayed as helpless. Female images as promiscuous and careless remain significant as do images of males as instigators of their victimizations.

Moving to an examination of gendered victimization, sexual assault cases, excluding children, were analyzed. It was found that all relationships remained the same except for images of victims as deviant, negative images, images of victims as not innocent as portrayed by witnesses, and images of victims as the instigators. In these cases, males were more likely to be viewed negatively. Hence, while not significant, all of these point to the notion that male victims of sexual assault are more likely to be viewed as precipitating these crimes. Perhaps these findings reinforce the existence of the cultural denial of males as sexual assault victims. Prior to examining victim–offender relationships, females were more negatively portrayed by these factors. However, while an examination of all cases of sexual victimization revealed no significant relationships, when examining only cases where a victim–offender relationship exists, significant relationships between sex and helplessness and sex and carelessness were found. Additionally, female victims who knew their offenders were more likely to be portrayed as helpless as well as careless. In other words, while female sexual assault victims are portrayed as playing the helpless female role (72%), a third of them are also blamed for facilitating their victimizations by being careless.

CONCLUSION

The debate in society often focuses on whether or not media create violence in their audiences. In our view, and following much of the literature, media have power to influence time (as when people set aside time to view or read the news and view televised crime drama), space (as when one rearranges her furniture around the placement of a television set), and meaning (as when news stories reinforce the idea of blaming female victims in crimes of sexual assault) (Altheide, 2002; Grossberg et al., 1998; Surette, 1998). Placing the power of the media into context, we recognize that the media practice this power in a historically patriarchal, racist, and classist society and hold to ideas of family, womanhood, and goodness within these contexts. That is, the meanings reinforced by the media that sit so comfortably in our minds are based on the notion of white, wealthy, male domination. Hence, when considering images of crime and justice, social groups viewed to be the most dangerous to the interests of the ruling class include the economic, racial, and ethnic minorities. Focusing on women, threatening groups that serve as the *other* (not the norm) are those women who do not fall into the classification of white, middle/upper class, heterosexual, married, and with children.

This chapter began by arguing that the institutionalization of victimhood can be equated with the institutionalization of womanhood. Individuals who do not fit into these images do not deserve to claim these statuses and do not deserve help and sympathy; in fact, they deserve to be blamed. The focus then moved to a discussion of victim blaming in society at large, criminal justice practice, and mass media. As media are the major source of crime and victimization information, this study attempted to determine the extent and nature of media victim blaming among crime victims in general and victims of sexual assault in particular. That media help to reproduce cultural images and, at times, to define them, several important findings are in order.

First, it was found that media victim blaming was not as frequent as is commonly believed. This is significant in that media, as the primary source of crime and victim information, can have a substantial effect on personal discourse. However, that victim blaming does occur in many of the cases is enough to raise eyebrows and warrants further analysis. This is also a significant finding because people tend to use newspapers as a form of information gathering, though more research needs to be conducted to substantiate this assumption.

Second, it was found that on the surface females do not appear to be significantly blamed for their victimizations. However, in a more in-depth analysis of sexual assault victims, it was found that the different genders experienced victim blaming under different circumstances. In the bivariate analysis, victim blaming was significantly less likely to result when a sexual assault took place unless controlling for the victim–offender relationship. In this case, in gendered victimizations females were significantly more likely to be blamed as careless.

Third, supporting prior research, older female victims who knew their sexual predators were more likely to be blamed. This finding supports the existence of rape myths within the media of what constitutes a "real rape." In essence, females were more likely to be blamed in acquaintance rapes (date rape or marital rape) than were females who experienced stranger rapes. However, a larger sample is needed in order to examine these relationships for sexual assault cases only and controlling for race. It also appears that the intersectionality of gender and age makes age a significant predictor of victim blaming. Perhaps this finding suggests more complexity to the analysis of victim blaming.

The media impact our lives to the extent that they transition and declare thoughts of what is right and what is wrong. They are our primary communicators of what is going on in our society, and they offer solutions on what we should do as individuals and as a society to maintain the status quo. The problem with the media's ability to influence our "knowledge" is that it leaves little room for revealing who are the real victims in today's society. Media's ability to place judgment into our minds stigmatizes the people who are in desperate need of empathy. In the media's task of "doing culture," social systems of meaning are reinforced without the need for the media to be direct. This does not allow for empathy. The social construction of the ideal victim is reinforced through media images of "good" female victims deserving the name victim, while victim blaming is reserved for careless female victims. The mass media "do culture" in presenting victim-blaming images of females of sexual assault who do not socialize with the proper individuals and who step out of their culturally prescribed gender roles by their deviance. In presenting victim-blaming images of male victims, the media reconstruct an image of males as aggressive, if not violent, and as "fair game." In this way, media discourse resembles personal discourse; it reproduces personal discourse and, for many not directly exposed to victimization, creates it.

Discussion Questions

1. What does it mean to "do culture?" Explain the process according to social construction theory.
2. Define victim blaming. What are some explanations given for the occurrence of victim blaming?
3. What role do media play in the social construction of female crime victims?
4. Compare and contrast the media images of female and male crime victims in general and for sexual assault in particular. What are some major findings of the research?
5. Identify the major problems with media's presentation of crime victims. How do these images affect the larger culture in general and criminal justice in particular?

References

Altheide, D. L. (2002). *Creating fear: News and the construction of crisis.* New York: Aldine De Gruyter.

Amir, M. (1971). *Patterns in forcible rape.* Chicago, IL: University of Chicago Press.

Baumer, B., Messner, S., & Felson, R. (2000). The role of victim characteristics in the disposition of murder cases. *Justice Quarterly, 17,* 281–308.

Belknap, J. (2007). *The invisible women: Gender, crime, and justice* (3rd ed.). Belmont, CA: Wadsworth/Thomson Learning.

Blodgette, N. (1987). Violence in the home. *American Bar Association Journal, 1,* 66–69.

Bourg, S., & Stock, H. V. (1994). A review of domestic violence arrest statistics in a police department using pro-arrest policy. *Journal of Family Violence, 9,* 177–189.

Burt, M. R., & Albin, R. S. (1981). Rape myths, rape definitions, and probability of conviction. *Journal of Applied Social Psychology, 11,* 212–230.

Chermack, S. (1995). *Victims in the news.* Boulder, CO: Westview Press.

Connor, T. (2004a, September 17). Kobe told cops she was aggressor. *Daily News*, News Section, p. 36.

Connor, T. (2004b, September 1). She made eyes at me, Kobe said. *Daily News*, News Section, p. 12.

CourtTV. (2004). Bryant attorneys hint at strategy of focusing on accuser. *CourTV.com.* Retrieved on September 24, 2004, from http://courttv.com/trials/bryant/090803_strategy_ap.html.

Cullen, D., & Connor, T. (2004, August 17). Kobe win: Sex life of accuser to be aired. *Daily News*, News Section, p. 3.

Eagan, M. (2004, August 17). "Nutty or slutty" rape defense too easily believed. *Boston Herald*, News Section, p. 6.

Eigenberg, H. M. (2003). Victim blaming. In L. J. Moriarty (Ed.), *Controversies in victimology* (pp. 15–24). Cincinnati, OH: Anderson.

Estrich, S. (1987). *Real rape.* Cambridge, MA: Harvard University Press.

Facts on File World News Digest. (1990, August 31). Crime: Convictions in New York City jogger attack. *FACTS.com.* Retrieved on November 4, 2004, from http://www.2facts.com.

Feinman, C. (1986). *Women in the criminal justice system* (2nd ed.). New York: Praeger.

Ferraro, K. (1989) Policing woman battering. *Social Problems, 36*, 61–74.

Field, H. S. (1978). Attitudes toward rape: A comparative analysis of police, rapists, crisis counselors, and citizens. *Journal of Personality, 36*, 156–179.

Furedi, F. (1997, September 10). Princess Diana and the new cult of victimhood. *Wall Street Journal: Eastern Edition.* p. A22.

Garcia, V. (2005). *Reality reconsidered: Media images of female crime victims.* Presented at the Annual Meeting of the American Society of Criminology in Toronto, Canada, November 16–19.

Garcia, V., & Cao, L. (2005). Race and satisfaction with the police in a small city. *Journal of Criminal Justice, 33*, 191–199.

Garcia, V., & Linskey, J. (2003). *Images and consequences of crime victims in the media.* Presented at the Annual Meeting of the American Society of Criminology in Boulder, Colorado, November 19–22.

Gelles, R. (1979). *Family violence.* Beverly Hills, CA: Sage.

Gergen, K. (1985). Social constructionist inquiry: Context and implication. In K. Gergen & K. Davis (Eds.), *The social construction of the person* (pp. 3–18). New York: Springer-Verlag.

Goolkasian, G. (1986). *Confronting domestic violence: A guide for criminal justice agencies.* Washington, D.C.: U.S. Department of Justice, National Institute of Justice.

Gordon, M. T., & Riger, S. (1989). *The female fear.* New York: Free Press.

Graber, D. (1980). *Crime news and the public.* New York: Praeger.

Grady, A. (2002). Female-on-male domestic violence: Uncommon or ignored? In C. Hoyle & R. Young (Eds.), *New visions of crime victims* (pp. 71–96). Portland, OR: Hart Publishing.

Grant, P. H., & Otto, P. I. (2003). The mass media and victims of rape. In L. J. Moriarty (Ed.), *Controversies in victimology* (pp. 43–56). Cincinnati, OH: Anderson Publishing Co.

Grossberg, L., Wartella, E., & Whitney, D. C. (1998). *MediaMaking: Mass media in a popular culture.* Thousand Oaks, CA: Sage Publications.

Hagan, J. (1983). *Victims before the law: The organizational domination of criminal law.* Toronto: Butterworth's.

Hale, D. (1998). Keeping women in their place: An analysis of policewomen in videos, 1972–1996. In F. Bailey & D. Hale (Eds.), *Popular culture, crime and justice* (pp. 159–179). Belmont, CA: Wadsworth.

Hart, B. (1993). Battered women and the criminal justice system. *American Behavioral Scientist, 36*, 624–638.

Kantor, G. K., & Strauss, M. A. (1990). Response of victims and the police to assaults on wives. In M. A. Strauss & R. J. Gelles (Eds.), *Physical violence in American families: Risk factors and adaptation to violence in 8,145 Families* (pp. 473–487). New Brunswick, NJ: Transaction Press.

Kappeler, V. E., Blumberg, M., & Potter, G. W. (2000). *The mythology of crime and criminal justice.* Prospect Heights, IL: Waveland Press, Inc.

Karmen, A. (2001). *Crime victims: An introduction to victimology* (5th ed.). Belmont, CA: Wadsworth.

Kennedy, L. W., & Sacco, V. F. (2001). *Crime victims in context.* Los Angeles, CA: Roxbury.

Klein, A. R. (2004). *The criminal justice response to domestic violence.* Belmont, CA: Wadsworth/Thomson Learning.

LaFree, G. D. (1989). *Rape and criminal justice: The social construction of sexual assault.* Belmont, CA: Wadsworth.

LaFree, G. D., Reskin, B. F., & Visher, C. A. (1985). Jurors' responses to victims' behavior and legal issues in sexual assault trials. *Social Problems, 32,* 389–407.

Lavoie, D. (2004, September 5). Bryant case could have chilling effect on report of so-called "acquaintance rape." *The Associated Press, State & Local Wire,* Domestic News.

Lawrenz, F., Lembo, J. F., & Schade, T. (1988). Time series analysis of the effect of a domestic violence directive on the number of arrests per day. *Journal of Criminal Justice, 16,* 493–498.

LeDoux, J. C., & Hazelwood, R. R. (1985). Police attitudes and beliefs toward rape. *Journal of Police Science and Administration, 13,* 211–220.

Lefkowitz, B. (1997). *Our guys.* Berkeley, CA: University of California Press.

Loseke, D. R. (1999). *Thinking about social problems: An introduction to constructionist perspectives.* New York: Aldine de Gruyter.

McCarthy, S. (2004, August 19). Kobe Bryant case has lesson for women. *Newsday,* Opinion Section, p. A48.

Meyer, J. W., Boli, J., & Thomas, G. M. (1994). Ontology and rationalization in western cultural account. In W. R. Scott & J. W. Meyer (Eds.), *Institutional environments and organizations: Structural complexity and individualism* (pp. 9–27). Thousand Oaks, CA: Sage Publications, Inc.

Muehlenhard, C., Powch, I., Phelps, J., & Guisti, L. (1992). Definitions of rape: Scientific and political implications. *Journal of Social Issues, 48,* 23–44.

Myers, M., & Hagan, J. (1979). Private and public trouble: Prosecutors and the allocation of court resources. *Social Problems, 26,* 439–451.

Rock, P. (2002). On becoming a victim. In C. Hoyle & R. Young (Eds.), *New visions of crime victims* (pp. 1–22). Portland, OR: Hart Publishing.

Ryan, W. (1976). *Blaming the victim.* New York: Vintage Books.

Schwartz, M. D., & DeKeseredy, W. S. (1997). *Sexual assault on the college campus: The role of male peer support.* Thousand Oaks, CA: Sage.

Scronce, C. A., & Corcoran, K. J. (1995). The influence of the victim's consumption of alcohol on perceptions of stranger and acquaintance rape. *Violence Against Women, 1,* 214–253.

Skogan, W. G., & Maxfield, M. (1981). *Coping with crime.* Thousand Oaks, CA: Wadsworth.

Soothill, K., & Walby, S. (1991). *Sex crime in the news.* London: Routledge.

Spencer, C. C. (1987). Sexual assault: The second victimization. In L. L. Crites & W. L. Hepperle (Eds.), *Women, courts, and equality* (pp. 54–73). Newbury Park, CA: Sage.

Stanko, E. (1981–1982). The impact of victim assessment on prosecutor's screening decisions: The case of the New York county district attorney's office. *Law and Society Review, 16,* 225–239.

Straus, M. A. (1990). *Physical violence in American families.* New Brunswick, NJ: Transaction Publishers.

Straus, M. A., & Gelles, R. J. (1986). Societal change and change in family violence from 1975 to 1985 as revealed by two surveys. *Journal of Marriage and the Family, 48,* 465–479.

Sudderth, L. (1998). It'll come right back at me: The interactional context of discussing rape with others. *Violence Against Women, 4,* 559–571.

Surette, R. (1984). *Justice and the media.* Springfield, IL: Charles C. Thomas.

Surette, R. (1992). *Media, crime and criminal justice: Images and realities.* Pacific Grove, CA: Brooks/Cole.

Surette, R. (1998). *Media, crime and criminal justice: Images and realities.* Belmont, CA: Wadsworth.

Sutherland, M. D. (1995). Assaultive sex: The victim's perspective. In A. V. Merlo & J. M. Pollack (Eds.), *Women, law, and social control* (pp. 179–201). Boston, MA: Allyn & Bacon.

Van Wormer, K. S., & Bartollas, C. (2000). *Women and the criminal justice system.* Boston, MA: Allyn & Bacon.

Whatley, M. A. (1996). Victim characteristics influencing attributions of responsibility to rape victims: A meta-analysis. *Aggression and Violent Behavior, 1*, 81–96.

Winter, J. (2002). The trial of Rose West: Contesting notions of victimhood. In C. Hoyle & R. Young (Eds.), *New visions of crime victim* (pp. 173–196). Portland, OR: Hart Publishing.

Young, V. D. (1986). Gender expectations and their impact on black female offenders and victims. *Justice Quarterly, 3*, 305–327.

CHAPTER 2
BECOMING VICTIMS, BECOMING CITIZENS

A Brief History of Gender-Motivated Violence in U.S. Law

Melissa S. Fry

ABSTRACT

The history of American women's ability to claim legal protection from victimization is, in many respects, the history of women's struggle to gain access to full citizenship and all of the rights, privileges, and protections granted by the Constitution and federal and state laws. In order for a woman to be violated, she must be a person before the law, not a possession. Moreover, she must be an independent citizen, not protected chattel represented in the republic by her father, brother, or spouse. This chapter provides a brief history of the legal rights of women in the United States. Upon gaining the vote in 1920, women claimed their rightful place as actors in the American democratic system. Today, women continue to use their democratic power to bring legal recognition to gendered victimization experiences that limit women's citizenship rights and freedoms. This chapter traces the history of legal definitions of rape, legislative histories of intimate partner violence and marital rape, rape shield laws, and the Violence Against Women Act. The history of the legal recognition of women as victims is the history of women becoming whole, independent American citizens with all of the liberties and protections that entails.

INTRODUCTION

The history of women in the United States is a history marked by triumph and significant struggle. From the beginning, american women challenged our exclusion from the Constitution and continue to seek full citizenship rights through both equal protection and acknowledgment of our distinct gendered experiences. Examining the treatment of female victims of physical and sexual abuse in American jurisprudence allows us to trace the process by which women gained and continue to garner recognition of gendered victimization and, in so doing, chart a course to full independent citizenship.

Recognition of gender-motivated violence challenges a long list of cultural, political, and economic assumptions built into the U.S. Constitution and federal, state, and local legal structures. Much of the discourse surrounding the legal recognition of gender-motivated violence focuses on the need to recognize women's distinct experiences in a gendered social hierarchy. However, more recent contributions to the discussion ask that we recognize men's experiences of gender-motivated violence as well. Academic debate has broadened to challenge constructions of gender and sexuality in a way that will recognize victimization of men and boys by men, abuse in homosexual relationships, and abuse instigated by women against men. For the purpose of this discussion, however, the focus will involve conceptualizations of women as victims in rape laws (including marital exemptions), the Violence Against Women Act (VAWA), and rape shield regulations.

This chapter begins with a historical discussion of the civil rights of women from English common law to modern American jurisprudence, noting the role and impact of gendered and gender-neutral language in structuring the rights of women. Against the backdrop of a more general discussion of American women's struggles for citizenship, the focus moves to a more specific discussion of gender-motivated violence in American law and its impacts on women's rights to full citizenship, drawing clear connections between the history of women's citizenship and the struggle to adequately address gender-motivated victimization. The discussion of gender-motivated violence addresses definitions of rape and sexual assault, gender-motivated violence and the law, intimate partner violence (IPV) and marital rape, rape shield regulations, and the accomplishments and failures of the VAWA. The final section of the chapter brings the discussion full circle with a discussion of women as citizens in the twenty-first century and concluding remarks on the legislative history of women as victims and its impact on women's citizenship status in the United States.

WOMEN AND CITIZENSHIP: FROM ENGLISH COMMON LAW TO MODERN AMERICAN JURISPRUDENCE

Americans too often suffer under the false impression that the U.S. Constitution conferred equal rights on all U.S. citizens. The original document did no such thing and at no point has it explicitly included women under its protections, save granting the suffrage in the Nineteenth Amendment, ratified in 1920. The common assumption of legal neutrality fails to recognize the historical reality of U.S. law's masculinity.

> All are citizens who are free, and who are born or naturalized members of civil society. But *only those have the right of suffrage, or voting, upon whom the compact of civil society has conferred the political power.* In fact, *not more than one fifth part of the citizens, male and female, hold the right of suffrage.* (Mansfield, 1845, p. 128, *emphasis added*)

Mansfield's early treatise *Legal Rights of Women* was progressive in its concern for women's citizenship rights, but he remained a product of his time. Mansfield was confident that in supporting their citizenship, he by no means supported women's suffrage.

Like many, he recognized no contradiction in trumpeting the importance of the rights of women, while simultaneously defining those rights in terms written and enforced only by men.

Women's citizenship status, as well as perceptions of the possibility for gender-motivated victimization, in American jurisprudence is rooted in the English common laws on which early colonists modeled their governing structures (see Box 2.1). The framers and later legislators embedded women's subordination to men not only in their exclusion from access to full independent citizenship, but in the language of the laws pertaining to male citizens.

A woman's status in early colonial America was determined first by her relationship to her father and later by her relationship to her husband. The marriage ceremony itself symbolized a transfer of ownership and of responsibility.

> The legal term for the status of married women was 'coverture,' which meant that wives were 'covered' by their husbands in all areas of life, especially the control of property . . . In turn, wives could rely on courts to force husbands to provide them with the necessities of food, clothing, and shelter. (Irons, 1999, p. 11)

Coverture limited women's access to full independent citizenship, but it also protected a woman's claim to her husband's property. As a part of his property, her rights were protected insofar as any damage to a married woman was considered a violation of her husband's property rights. The rape of a young unmarried woman was a violation of her father's property rights, as the rape devalued her status in the marriage market.

Under this early formulation, laws intended to protect the rights of citizens included the protection of men's access to their own property. Women were not a part of the legislative process and without independent citizenship rights; the law represented women's interests solely in terms of the men to whom they belonged. "Thus, men wrote rape laws that protected men and the property of men" (Rowland, 2004, p. 665). The rape of a woman was the violation of her father's or her husband's property rights, and "rape" within marriage was a legal impossibility: A man had the right to access his property as he chose.

Fifty-five men produced the U.S. Constitution. "Although subject to the Constitution's terms, women were 'unacknowledged in its text, uninvited in its formulation, [and] unsolicited for its ratification' (Rhode, 1989, p. 20) . . . the Framers of the Constitution envisioned no role for American women" (O'Connor, 2003, p. 155). While drafting the young nation's charter, future President John Adams received letters from his wife, imploring him

---

BOX 2.1

AMERICAN JURISPRUDENCE IS ROOTED IN ENGLISH COMMON LAWS

"The exclusion of women from government, church, and the courts did not set the colonies apart from England, or from any other country at that time. Their legal status as 'wards' of husbands stemmed from centuries of English common law and biblical precepts that reflected male domination of every institution in society" (Irons, 1999, p. 11).

to "remember the ladies" (O'Connor, 2003, p. 155). Adams ignored her requests and she replied, "I cannot say that I think you very generous to the Ladies, for whilst you are proclaiming peace and good will to Men, Emancipating all Nations, you insist upon retaining an absolute power over Wives" (O'Connor, 2003, p. 155).

Abigail Adams, among others, pointed to the hypocrisy of the framers' position: The framers held women in high esteem in the domestic sphere, which was also seen as the nursery of citizenship, and saw women as morally and spiritually superior to men, and yet, they refused to include women as citizens (O'Connor, 2003). "By law, wives could not hold, purchase, control, bequeath, or convey property, retain their own wages, make contracts, or *bring legal actions*" (O'Connor, 2003, p. 156, *emphasis added*). The stipulation against bringing legal action precluded any legal redress for gender-motivated violence.

Women were also barred from professional careers in law and government. In 1869 Myra Bradwell filed an application to the state bar of Illinois, and in 1874 Belva Lockwood applied to law school. Both were rejected with statements about their sex and the proper roles for women. Women's exclusion from the vote, the legislative process, and even the practice of law solidified their position as noncitizens, granted citizenship privileges only through marriage and the actions of their spouses on their behalf. In marriage, women were to be subject to their husbands, as was approved by the Mississippi Supreme Court in 1824 (see Box 2.2).

Like children or chattel of the time, women were subject to whatever means men might use to control them. Conferring ownership and the rights to physically discipline women into "appropriate" behavior precluded any concept of women as victims. These laws did not simply ignore gender-based violence, they actually legitimated and legalized gender-based violence. "Not until the late nineteenth century did some states begin to criminalize wife beating" (O'Connor, 2003, p. 158).

The period of Reconstruction following the Civil War witnessed significant changes in access to citizenship, providing small openings for the advancement of women's rights. The Civil Rights Movement of former slaves and the Women's Rights Movement both had a vested interest in expanding definitions of citizenship and often worked together to fight for such expansion during Reconstruction and beyond. The Thirteenth Amendment, adopted in 1865 as the Civil War ended, abolished slavery and involuntary servitude and gave Congress the right to enforce the Amendment's provisions (Ritter, 2006, p. 15). The Fourteenth Amendment, ratified in 1868, declared, "persons born or naturalized in the United States, and subject to the jurisdiction thereof, are citizens of the United States and of the States wherein they reside" (*U.S. Constitution*,

---

> ## BOX 2.2

BRADLEY V. STATE OF MISSISSIPPI (1824)

Let the husband be permitted to exercise the right of moderate chastisement, in cases of great emergency, and use salutary restraints in every case of misbehavior, without being subject to vexatious prosecutions, resulting in the mutual discredit and shame of all parties concerned (*Bradley v. State of Miss* I Miss. 156 (1824) as cited in O'Connor, 2003, pp. 157–158).

as cited in Ritter, 2006, p. 15). The Amendment forbids states from denying citizenship rights, protects citizens' rights to life, liberty, and property, requires due process in any State interruption thereof, and grants all citizens *equal protection* under the law.

The second section of the Fourteenth Amendment "calls for a reduction in national political representation for states that deny voting rights to any *males* over the age of twenty-one" (Ritter, 2006, p. 16, *emphasis added*). The inclusion of the word *male* clarified that the intended beneficiaries of the Amendment were Black males, not women. No penalty resulted from excluding women from the political realm. Incensed by this exclusive language, some women's rights groups opposed the Amendment. Susan B. Anthony and Elizabeth Cady Stanton, active abolitionists, called on Black women to see that their interests were distinct from their Black male counterparts and that Black male suffrage would not protect the interests of Black women. Conversely, other women's rights activists, led by Lucy Stone, Henry Blackwell, and Frederick Douglass, argued, " 'this hour belongs to the negro,' fearing that debate about woman suffrage at the federal level would introduce additional controversy and endanger the passage of the Fourteenth and Fifteenth Amendments" (Evans, 1989, p. 122). Lucy Stone favored rewording to include sex, "but still supported it, reasoning that it was better for some rather than none of the disenfranchised to get the vote" (Giele, 1995, p. 59). For many women, the expansion of suffrage to include their husbands represented a political gain, even if it was not a win. White women, and particularly middle-class White women, enjoyed some level of political power through their husbands, but Black women and poor women more generally, because their spouses were also excluded from the economic and political privileges of American citizenship, had few if any of their political and economic interests represented in political institutions.

Following its passage, Susan B. Anthony and Elizabeth Cady Stanton responded by leading a charge to interpret the Fourteenth Amendment as a mandate for civic inclusion and rights (Ritter, 2006). They argued that the reconstruction amendments clearly granted them citizenship rights, but that those rights were without meaning if women were not also granted *political* rights. Anthony and Stanton recognized that male politicians would not be accountable to women and the representation of women's interests in the law until women had the power to elect them. Political rights were constitutive citizenship rights. Despite the controversy and failure to achieve full citizenship rights, the equal protection clause of the Fourteenth Amendment to the Constitution laid the groundwork for women's subsequent political successes and provided opportunities to force debate over the meaning of *citizenship* and *protection*.

A second wave of activity in favor of citizenship rights for women grew out of the social progressive movements surrounding industrialization and focused primarily on the need to get women into the political sphere through the right to vote. The obvious logic was that with the right to vote, women could at least play a role in determining who spoke on our behalf: an essential first step to having our interests represented in the law. Women were primary players in the progressive social reform movement that marked the turn of the twentieth century. Rooted in concern for the miserable conditions of America's rapidly industrializing cities, the progressive era gave rise to the Suffrage Movement and the eventual passage and ratification of the Nineteenth Amendment conferring women's right to vote in 1920 (O'Connor, 2003; Evans, 1989; Giele, 1995; Ritter, 2006). Gaining the suffrage was a huge step in women's path to full recognition of gendered experiences and a key victory in the fight for full citizenship.

Women were still not able to enjoy the right to a jury of their peers as women were excluded from the judicial process.

Equal rights in the workplace did not follow until the passage of the Civil Rights Act of 1964. Once again, the 1960s were a time when African Americans and women were struggling together for recognition as citizens. Again, the Black Civil Rights Movement took priority as gender was not originally included in the Act. In fact, gender was only added at the last minute in an effort to defeat the Civil Rights Act (O Connor, 2003).

In many respects, social change defined the 1960s and 1970s. Thirty-eight percent of women were working outside the home (O'Connor, 2003), and the women's movement pushed for the passage of the Equal Rights Amendment (ERA) to ensure that women would be protected from discrimination in all spheres (Ritter, 2006; Evans, 1989). Several states ratified the Amendment in the early 1970s. The Supreme Court responded to this shift with a broadening of their application of the Fourteenth Amendment to include protections for women. On several occasions, the Court responded to both racial and gender discrimination as violations of Fourteenth Amendment citizenship rights and protections.

In *Personnel Administrator of Massachusetts et al. v. Feeney* (1979), the Court found that a state policy of preference for U.S. veterans was inherently biased in favor of men because women were not allowed equal access to military service and were thus systematically discriminated against in civil service jobs. The 1977 *Califano v. Goldfarb* decision found similar fault with Federal Old Age policies that limited the Social Security benefits awarded to widowers in the event of a formerly working spouses, death. Widows were granted full benefit of a husband's Social Security benefit, while men were only awarded the benefit if at least half of their income was generated by the working wife. The Supreme Court found that this policy "constituted unconstitutional discrimination against female wage earners" (*Califano v. Goldfarb*). These cases are two among many in the 1970s and 1980s where the court used the equal protection clause of the Fourteenth Amendment to declare unconstitutional a variety of state and federal policies that needlessly differentiated on the basis of gender.

In addition to expanded interpretations of "equal protection," constitutional rights to privacy, as laid out in the Fourteenth Amendment as well as in due process clauses of the Fifth Amendment, were essential to the Court's decision to legalize abortion in *Roe v. Wade*. The Court's rulings in all of these cases led many to argue that the existing Amendments provided sufficient protections for women. As a result, the ERA lost momentum and failed in 1982. Though women found significant relief from workplace discrimination and harassment under these expanded interpretations of the Fourteenth Amendment, problems of gender discrimination in the workplace persisted. The American legal system and American culture both came a long way in a relatively short period of time, but laws written by and for men still contained hidden biases.

The theory of original intent, common law through precedent, and the "reasonable *man*" standard of the courts, all intended to be read as gender neutral, function to constrain women's access to full citizenship. "Original intent," also called "originalism," suggests that laws be interpreted according to the intent of the authors. Our nineteenth-century sisters noted the obvious problem that the "original intent" of the Fourteenth Amendment was to exclude women. Subscribing to Lockean republican liberal theory of their time, nineteenth-century women's rights advocates believed in women's natural inalienable human rights and believed that the framers' intent was for the founding documents to be read with this in mind, taking into account changes in considerations of different groups that would undoubtedly occur over time (Evans, 1989; Finley, 2004; Ritter, 2006). Political debate continues to revolve around arguments of original intent and the "spirit of the law," with original intent often read as a mandate for the maintenance of traditions, regardless of the inequalities they may produce.

> "Common law through precedent" has the similar problem of suggesting that even if the people involved in legal decisions in a prior case either relied on "original intent" interpretations or made decisions that reified gender inequality, these cases were legitimate sources of common law motivated on the precedent they set. Courts can avoid the binding authority of precedent "by distinguishing the cases on their facts or issues" or by "finding that the rule put forth in the previous case is *no longer valid* and by overruling it." (Jacobstein, Myron, Mersky, & Dunn, 1998, p. 6, *emphasis added*)

However, the power to determine that a rule is no longer valid lay in the hands of judges, a largely male group until fairly recently. The influence of common law through precedent is often rather conservative, maintaining traditional standards and institutions that fail to acknowledge women's equal citizenship.

Similarly, the "reasonable man standard" is applied ubiquitously to keep in mind the perceptions of those involved in a legal action. Juries generally operate under the premise that what is at issue is how a "reasonable man" would interpret a contract, an overture by a boss, an agreement with an employer, a neighbor, or a spouse, etc. The gendered language of the standard has been challenged and thus replaced in many cases with a "reasonable person" standard. As with other legal debates addressed in this chapter, the very "neutrality" of the replacement language has been questioned as well, and some courts have employed "reasonable woman" standards where appropriate. In a sexual harassment case facing the court in Alaska, the court opted for a "reasonable victim" standard (Alexander, 2000). This option recognizes that the perception of the individual claiming harassment is clearly shaped by the context of the perceived harassment, regardless of gender. Others suggest that in a society structured by a gendered hierarchy, and in a culture filled with sexualized images of women, the gender-neutral "reasonable victim" language misses the key role that cultural ideologies surrounding gender play for both perpetrators and victims of gender-motivated violence.

Women's rights activists and victims of gender-motivated violence consistently run up against the wall of bias that fails to fully appreciate the cause and context of violence against women. Gender-neutral laws consistently fall short of dealing with the complex web of culture, economics, politics, and violence that supports patterns of female victimization. The struggle for citizenship has thus required that women demand the passage of laws that specifically deal with gendered experiences of crime and violence. In order for the law to protect American women, it must deal with those crimes that are specific to women's location in the gender status order. IPV and marital rape laws, rape shield regulations, and the VAWA restructure women's place before the law by granting them "victim" status in their experiences of gender-motivated violence.

Today, women enjoy the full protections afforded by the Fourteenth Amendment and this has allowed for significant progress. The broad interpretation of the gender-neutral Fourteenth Amendment still leaves women subject to the limitations of language. The gender-neutral language of the Amendment in effect today fails to recognize that equal application of existing law may not fully protect women as victims of gender-motivated crimes. Neither criminal nor civil law in the United States is gender neutral, and therefore, equal application of U.S. law does not yield equality in outcomes. We continue to struggle with debates over "original intent," bias via common law through precedent, and the struggle to replace the gendered "reasonable man" standard with a gender-neutral standard while at the same time arguing for legal redress for gender-motivated violence.

GENDER-MOTIVATED VIOLENCE AND CITIZENSHIP IN LATE TWENTIETH AND EARLY TWENTY-FIRST CENTURY AMERICA

Despite rapid progress in women's citizenship rights from 1920 to 1964, the legacy of coverture remained apparent in the treatment of gender-motivated violence in the criminal justice and legal systems. The process of dismantling legalized gender-motivated violence in both criminal law and procedure is an important part of women's struggle for citizenship rights. Procedures and laws that support women's continued subordination and provide justifications for male violence against women prevent women from enjoying the full rights and protections of U.S. citizenship.

Early rape law protected against the devaluation of men's property through the violation of their wives' and daughters' sexual dignity and purity. Without the rights of independent citizenship, a woman was not subject to legal violation. As the property of men, women were subject to the actions of those men who "owned" them, and the law granted men full rights to control access to their daughters and to access their wives as they saw fit. Marital rape was a legal impossibility. With the passage of time and changing social dynamics, the crime of rape was separated from antiquated notions of ownership, but the legacy of these norms persisted and resulted in a largely ineffective system for protecting women and punishing offenders.

During the 1950s, the "American Law Institute, a prestigious body of judges, lawyers, and legal scholars, began an ambitious project to examine the whole of American criminal law" (Schulhofer, 1998a, p. 20). Members of the American Law Institute, concerned with low conviction rates in cases of rape, noted "three defects in the law: the resistance requirement, the undue preoccupation with victim consent, and the inclusion of too many diverse kinds of misbehavior within a single felony that carried extremely severe punishments" (Schulhofer, 1998a, p. 20). The reformers' concerns were accurate, but limited in scope. They used their findings to compose a "Model Penal Code," but their proposals rested on the same faulty assumptions about forced sexual encounters as those found in existing law at the time. They preserved the marital rape exemption and maintained rules requiring prompt filing of the complaint, corroboration of the victim's testimony, and special *cautionary* instructions for the jury (Schulhofer, 1998a, p. 20, *emphasis added*). The focus of rape prosecution was to ensure that the law could not be used by women to falsely accuse and punish men. Moreover, the assumption that women were rarely "forced" to have sex with men remained embedded in the law.

The 1970s was a decade of collaboration among women's groups in their activism around the issue of rape. In cities across the country, women's groups joined forces to bring greater attention to the problem of rape and our legal system's way of dealing with it. "[B]y 1980 all of the states and the District of Columbia had either revised, or were considering revisions to, the rape statutes in their states, and more than 400 rape crisis centers had been established" (Rowland, 2004, p. 667–668). Women were effectively organized, and rape, domestic violence, and sexual assault were on the public agenda.

The progress of the 1960s and 1970s relied on the confluence of a few major developments: First development was the success of the second wave of the women's movement that saw women moving into the labor force in large numbers and challenging systems designed to exclude them; second, and maybe even equally important, was a new focus on crime and criminals (Bevacqua, 2000). Social unrest during the Vietnam War led to public cries for social control and order, making it an opportune time to bring increased attention to rape and sexual assault as criminal offenses. "In 1968, Congress passed, and Johnson signed, the Omnibus Crime Control and Safe Streets Act (P.L. 90–351), creating the Law Enforcement Assistance Administration (LEAA) within the Department of Justice" (Bevacqua, 2000, p. 117). The establishment of the LEAA marks the successful move of crime to the institutional agenda at the federal level. The move from the more nebulous, ideological, systemic agenda to the more specific, concrete institutional or policy agenda is central to moving a concern from the realm of debate and discussion into the field of policy and implementation. In the case of sexual violence, the late 1970s was a moment of "political opportunity" (McAdam, 1982).

The Justice Department established the National Crime Victimization Survey, first administered by the LEAA under the title "National Crime Survey" and later the Bureau of Justice Statistics under the Justice System Improvement Act of 1979 (Bevacqua, 2000). The survey was designed to provide an alternative to the Uniform Crime Report (UCR) which measured only those crimes reported to the police. For taboo crimes of rape and sexual assault, the new survey instrument and sampling technique was a vital tool in bringing public attention to the problem. Activists in the anti-rape movement found that legislative proposals that were tough on perpetrators and gentle on victims received a welcome reception in the "tough on crime" climate of the 1970s.

Corroboration requirements had long held that without someone other than the victim available to confirm her story, a rape victim could not win a case in court. In 1974, Governor Malcolm Wilson, of New York, signed the corroboration repeal bill that would nullify the corroboration requirement that had previously blocked untold numbers of rape cases from ever making it to court, much less reaching conviction. The state legislature passed the bill unanimously.

While Americans were getting behind "get tough on crime" policies, feminist theory was increasingly examining the roles of race and class in shaping structures of power and the oppression of women of color and poor women.

As the third wave of feminist activism emerged, leaders drew attention to the flawed notion that rape and sexual assault were simply manifestations of male dominance. Feminist activists of the 1980s pointed to the roles of race, class, and imperialism in structuring both the experiences of sexual violence among White women and women of color, and our society's responses to these crimes. The impossibility of raping one's own property precluded any legal attention to the sexual abuse of female slaves. The ideologies that supported the injustice outlived the institution of slavery by many years and manifest in the construction of the Black woman as an insatiable whore who could not be violated (Collins, 1990). A racist criminal justice system disproportionately affected non-White communities through rape prosecution as it imprisoned far more men of color than White men for sexual assault. The criminal justice system meted out an additional blow to communities of color as it was far more likely to imprison a perpetrator whose victim was White than one whose victim was non-White, thus providing less protection to victimized Black women than to victimized White women. Moreover, Black men were far more likely than White men to pay the price for the crackdown on rape as they were more often prosecuted and convicted for rape than White men (Bevacqua, 2000).

DEFINING RAPE AND SEXUAL ASSAULT

Definitions of rape and sexual assault occupy a central location in feminist legal theory. The treatment of women in court and by the criminal justice system is closely tied to the language of the law as this determines possible interpretations and enforcement. Feminist legal theorists spend a great deal of time and energy dissecting the language of the law: for in all law, language is carefully chosen to anticipate possible interpretations at the time the legislation is drafted and into the future. Language is all we have to construct the boundaries of the law and the law carries significant cultural, social, political, and economic weight (see Box 2.3).

The Department of Justice (DOJ) definition is very general in order to encompass the wide range of definitions found across the 50 states. The broad definition allows the DOJ to collect comprehensive, if not specific, national statistics on rape. The broad definition reflects advances in recognition of the psychological aspects of sexual violence as well as a move away from the notion that the violation that constitutes rape is restricted to penile penetration of a female by a male. The language is gender inclusive and covers a wider range of violent acts that may be perpetrated against a victim.

Interestingly, the Federal Bureau of Investigation (FBI), in its UCR protocol (2005), uses a different definition, "the carnal knowledge of a female forcibly and against her will." This definition dates back to the late eighteenth century, a time when included with it were marital exemptions for rape (Schulhofer, 1998a). One explanation for the use of this definition is that UCR data come from arrest reports and therefore may over-represent

---

BOX 2.3

The United States Department of Justice defines rape as follows:

Forced sexual intercourse including both psychological coercion as well as physical force. Forced sexual intercourse means vaginal, anal or oral penetration by the offender(s). This category also includes incidents where the penetration is from a foreign object such as a bottle. Includes attempted rapes, male as well as female victims and both heterosexual and homosexual rape. Attempted rape includes verbal threats of rape.

forcible rapes that are more likely to be reported than acquaintance rapes. This far narrower definition used by the FBI has important implications for UCR statistics as it rests on the use of physical force. While the less inclusive definition may yield smaller numbers, the numbers also provide data on a more specific subset of violent crime. The FBI may be using this definition because they are most likely to be involved in this subset of cases, but the definition is a bit archaic nonetheless and has been widely critiqued. The DOJ definition tells us more about the direction of American jurisprudence as it pertains to our culture's current understandings of sexual violence.

The language found in state laws is telling and, in many cases, far more limited in scope. In some instances, states have separate laws for "rape" and "forcible rape." The very fact that rape is referred to as "forcible rape" in the law indicates Americans' ambivalent attitude toward the criminalization of rape. One might argue that the term "forcible rape" is unnecessarily redundant, for "rape" by definition involves an act of psychological or physical force. The inclusion of the adjective "forcible" provides legal wiggle room for "due resistance" arguments suggesting that lack of a properly aggressive struggle constitutes consent. Some theorists argue that the "forcible" rape distinction is important in differentiating instances of physical violence from those where coercion, manipulation, or failure for a woman to communicate nonconsent constitutes force.

In *Toward a Feminist Theory of the State*, Catharine MacKinnon (1989, p. 172) takes aim at the construction of rape found in state laws,

> [t]he law, speaking generally, defines rape as intercourse with force or coercion and without consent.[1] Like sexuality under male supremacy, this definition assumes the sadomasochistic definition of sex: intercourse with force or coercion can be or become consensual . . . In a critique of male supremacy, the elements 'with force and without consent' appear redundant. Force is present because consent is absent.

"Forcible rape" and "with force or coercion and without consent" both legitimate the court's demands that victims demonstrate an "appropriate" level of resistance to intercourse. Over the years, this requirement has led to underreporting and failures to convict. Some scholars, such as Wolfgang (1958) and Amir (1971), apply the criminological theory of victim precipitation to contextualize incidents of rape given the existence of certain conditions: 1) failure of the victim to physically resist to a certain degree and/or 2) failure of the victim to say "no" very definitively. Some argue that compliance or first agreeing to have sex and then changing one's mind does not necessarily clearly convey an individual's lack of consent. In fact, in a collection of essays on feminist legal theory, Susan Griffin takes a more critical approach to defining rape as shown in Box 2.4.

Defining rape as a form of terrorism (Griffin, 1996; MacKinnon, 1989; Rowland, 2004) brings out the real cultural, social, and economic impacts of rape in our society. Strong positions on the importance of language and the ubiquitous nature of the rape culture (Herman, 1991), while important to awakening female consciousness, have not been without their critics. Katie Roiphe (1993) is one of several feminist writers who reject the victim status that the "terrorism" concept forces on women. She argues that women are disempowered by our fear and that we must take responsibility for our sexuality and for the prevention of sexual assault. This discussion continues today and has clear implications for law and legal interpretation of context (Dressler, 1998).

BOX 2.4

CRITICAL DEFINITIONS OF RAPE

Rape is an act of aggression in which the victim is denied her self-determination. It is an act of violence which, if not actually followed by beatings or murder, nevertheless always carries with it the threat of death. And finally, rape is a form of mass terrorism, for the victims of rape are chosen indiscriminately, but the propagandists for male supremacy broadcast that it is women who cause rape by being unchaste or in the wrong place at the wrong time—in essence, by behaving as though they were free (Griffin, 1996 [1971], as cited in Rowland, 2004, p. 664).

Legal and cultural discussions of rape and sexual assault tell us a great deal about the tensions between our belief systems, power dynamics, culture, and political institutions. How we respond to and define rape, both as a physical phenomenon and as a crime, have reciprocating effects on our culture and our political system. Changing ideas about power, biology, and criminal justice shape our definitions, and our definitions, in turn, shape our beliefs about power, biology, and criminal justice. Several significant shifts in the language and policy surrounding sexual violence occurred during the mid to late 1990s, but these changes were not without challenge.

In 1995, following the passage of the VAWA of 1994, the U.S. DOJ opened a Violence Against Women Office. In 1998, a United Nations tribunal, prosecuting Rwandan authorities accused of war crimes, declared rape a crime of genocide. However, praise for such change may be premature. In addition to consistent feminist backlash against claiming victim status, some challenge the very notion that the gendered status order is a social construct. As recently as 2000, evolutionary biologists Randy Thornhill and Craig T. Palmer presented *A Natural History of Rape: Biological Bases of Sexual Coercion.* The crux of their argument is as follows:

> [t]he males of most species—including humans—are usually more eager to mate than the females, and this enables females to choose among males who are competing with one another for access to them. But getting chosen is not the only way to gain sexual access to females. In rape, the male circumvents the female's choice. (Thornhill & Palmer, 2000 as cited in Rowland, 2004, p. 656)

The two researchers may not have intended to excuse rape, but the cultural debate that followed suggests that many found the biological argument to relieve men of responsibility for forcing women to have sex. The debate is nothing new and a history of the legal treatment of women as victims of rape and sexual assault suggests that the biological assumptions inherent in the evolutionary argument permeate our cultural understandings of men, women, sexuality, and rape.

In response to concerns regarding the wide range of abuses related to sex, but not constituting rape as defined by "penetration," lawmakers created the category termed "sexual assault." For the purpose of collecting statistics, the DOJ defines sexual assault as "[a] wide range of victimizations, separate from rape or attempted rape. These crimes include attacks or attempted attacks generally involving unwanted sexual contact between victim and offender. Sexual assaults may or may not involve force and include such things as grabbing or fondling. Sexual assault also includes verbal threats" (DOJ, 2005).

"Sexual assault" allows victims to press charges without bringing the full strength of a rape charge to bear on the perpetrator. Moreover, the charge of "sexual assault" recognizes that abuses of a sexual nature extend far beyond the simplicity of rape and are distinct in character and effect from standard assault and battery.

Our culture's struggle to define and to criminalize rape and sexual assault reflects the history of women's legal status as dependents. Buttressed by a gendered hierarchy, women's status as property ensured that any violation of a woman's purity was seen as a violation of the male to whom she was legally bound, not a violation of her as an independent citizen. Efforts to define rape and sexual assault in ways that fully acknowledge women's independence from men and their right to sexual autonomy are indeed struggles for full citizenship for women.

INTIMATE PARTNER VIOLENCE AND MARITAL RAPE

Female victims have faced the greatest barriers to protection in cases where they know or are intimately connected to their abuser. In cases of extreme violence and/or stranger rape, the courts are generally sympathetic to victims. However, the majority of rapes are perpetrated by acquaintances or family members. DOJ Statistics for 2005 indicate that in 31.3 percent of rape and sexual assault cases, women knew the perpetrator well and in an additional 29.1 percent, the two were casual acquaintances. Only 31.4 percent of rapes and sexual assaults in 2005 were clearly defined as perpetrated by strangers, roughly the same proportion that knew their victims well (DOJ, 2005).

Clearly, the majority of rapes are committed by individuals known to the victim, not the violent stranger incidents that occupy the popular imagination's definition of "rape." "And yet, where 'prior relationships' exist between a victim who charges rape and the defendant who is accused of it, judges, juries, legislatures, and attorneys have long proved more skeptical of the women charging rape than of the men accused. This is true even where the 'relationship' between the victim and her attacker is not 'intimate' (i.e., master and servant or employer and employee)" (Rowland, 2004, p. 661).

Resistance to recognizing and responding to sexual violence between acquaintances and intimates is rooted in our larger cultural understandings of public and private spheres as well as the roles of men and women in intimate relationships. The "cult of domesticity" that dominated American culture in the nineteenth and early twentieth centuries clearly divided society into public and private spheres to be separately managed by men and women, respectively. The ideology placed women on a pedestal as the morally and spiritually superior sex. Women derived some power over family and household in their domestic roles, but formal doctrine and law reinforced gendered hierarchies. For example, American courts established the husband's right to whip his wife as long as the tool was no thicker than his thumb. This gave way to what we know as the "rule of thumb" (Rhode, 1989). Courts decided cases of rape and domestic violence that came before them in very subjective ways, largely dependent on circumstances and the temperament of the public official presiding. Formal action was most likely to be taken in cases where the accused were poor and/or non-White (Rhode, 1989).

Laws written, administered, and enforced by men reinforced a gendered hierarchy in social relationships and punished women whose complaints challenged the system's legitimacy. Marriage effectively protected men from rape charges on the part of their wives. Some have even gone so far as to say that a license to wed is a license to rape (Finkelhor & Yllo, 1985). Our reluctance to recognize rape within the institution of marriage is a vestige of our British history. Under British common law, a man's wife was his property and he could do whatever he wanted with his wife, short of killing her (Rowland, 2004). Along with the liberal tradition that argued that we could not own people, however, came ideas of civil autonomy and rights derived from citizenship. While the VAWA of 1994 has not yet been able to solidify protection from gender-motivated violence as a civil right (discussed in a subsequent section), today a married woman is at least granted some sexual autonomy through the elimination of carte blanche marital exemptions for rape.

The law did not recognize the possibility that a man could rape his wife until the 1970s and rape exemptions remained on the books in many states until the early 1990s. In 1977, Oregon was the first state to do away with the marital exemption to rape (Rowland, 2004). On "July 5, 1993 marital rape became a crime in all 50 states, in at least one section of the sexual offense codes, usually regarding force" (Bergen & Barnhill, 2006, p. 2). Unfortunately, loopholes for marital rape remain in other sections of state code. Only 17 states have eliminated all exemptions for marital rape. Remnants of the marital exemptions come in the form of spousal immunity to prosecution for a variety of sexual offenses not labeled "forcible rape," lesser penalties for crimes committed within marriage, and additional requirements for proving the crime (Woolley, 2007). "Twenty states currently grant or imply spousal immunity from sexual offense charges if the spouse-victim is mentally incapacitated or physically helpless" (Woolley, 2007, p. 4). In addition, 12 states grant spousal immunity for nonconsensual sex offenses including sexual imposition, sexual abuse, sexual battery, sexual contact, and sexual misconduct. "Kansas allows marriage as a defense for sexual battery" (Woolley, 2007, p. 4).

In addition to direct exemptions, several states downgrade the severity of sexual crimes if they occur within a marriage, and therefore exact lesser penalties upon perpetrators. In Oklahoma, "the crime of spousal rape requires the showing of force or violence by the perpetrator" (Woolley, 2007, p. 5). Despite our increased understanding of the emotional toll of domestic violence and the ways that the marriage relationship can act as a barrier to reporting, some states have stiffer requirements for timely reporting in cases of marital rape than for other rape cases. "Four states still require prompt complaint (usually within three months) for spousal sexual offenses but not for other rape victims" (Woolley, 2007, p. 5). In South Carolina, spouse victims have only 30 days to report. Finally, "many states require that a couple be legally separated and living apart and/or divorced at the time of the assault before certain criminal prosecutions for sexual assault can proceed" (Woolley, 2007, p. 5). Woolley argues that four key assumptions continue to underlie marital rape statutes (see Box 2.5).

These assumptions permeate legal treatment of sexual abuse within marriage, but they are also implicated in cases of IPV and acquaintance rape.

Judges, juries, and the general public demonstrate an ingrained skepticism in cases where victim and perpetrator know one another, although the majority of rapes and instances of sexual violence are perpetrated by known attackers. Two assumptions

---

BOX 2.5

FOUR ASSUMPTIONS UNDERLYING
MARITAL RAPE STATUTES

1. Legal intervention into the private marital domain is inappropriate;

2. Spousal sexual offenses are not as harmful as other rapes, so they do not warrant harsh criminal sanctions;

3. The exemption promotes marital reconciliation and the resumption of normal marital relations; and

4. There is a need to prevent vindictive wives from pursuing false charges. (Woolley, 2007, p. 4)

---

underlie the jurors' and judges' skepticism regarding cases involving acquaintances or family members: The first is the assumption that the victim's allegations are false and her motivations impure, and the second is that the " 'intercourse' between the victim and the attacker may, in fact, have been consensual" (Rowland, 2004, p. 661). This skepticism is fueled by groups such as Respecting Accuracy in Domestic Abuse Reporting (RADAR), who recently posted a report on their website titled, "The Culture of False Accusation" (RADAR, 2007). Certainly, cases of false, vindictive accusation do occur, as with other crimes. Evidentiary requirements and the legal process should help us minimize the rate and effect of such accusations. The work of groups such as RADAR may be seen as essential to maintaining the integrity of our legal responses to rape and sexual violence, but they may also provide legitimacy to those advocating policies that make it difficult for victims to find justice in the U.S. legal system.

Activists, advocates, and researchers increased attention to gender-motivated violence within intimate relationships dramatically over the last 40 years. Assumptions about gender, marriage, intimacy, and the nature of sexual violence continue to complicate the experiences of victims of gender-motivated violence in court. However, all states have made significant progress and many are leading the way in eliminating bias in the language of their rape and sexual assault statutes. Changes in state-level law and in federal policy affect women's ability to access the protections of full citizenship.

PROCESS AND PROTECTION: ARREST POLICIES AND INTERSTATE COOPERATION

Shifts in policy at the national level have provided increased protection for victims of gender-motivated violence by requiring that states honor orders of protection across state lines. In addition, the federal government provides funds for states to improve their ability to communicate with one another and to change their arrest policies to better protect victims and prevent further abuse. Both arrest policies and increased interstate cooperation have been most important in cases of stalking and domestic violence.

Historically, police response to domestic violence calls actually functioned as a deterrent to reporting in cases of gender-motivated violence. "[F]ear of reprisal, perceived social stigma, and a belief that nothing may be accomplished by reporting decrease help seeking from victims" (Jordan, 2004, p. 1419). While research findings are mixed, there is some consensus that for many years, police culture came down on the side of protecting privacy in domestic violence disputes. The same assumptions underlying rape law played out in police responses to domestic violence calls. As research and activism brought police practice into full view, law makers and law enforcement agencies responded with mandatory and preferred arrest policies that decreased instances of domestic violence calls resulting in no action on the part of local law enforcement. Police response has a significant impact on outcomes in court proceedings for IPV (Jordan, 2004). According to some advocates, changes in police response have not had a uniformly positive effect as the complexities of domestic violence and women's own physical responses to abuse can muddy the waters of culpability.

Mandatory and preferred arrest policies for managing domestic violence calls have resulted in increases in dual arrests. Women who respond to violence with violence are thus punished along with their abusers without attention to context (Finn & Bettis, 2006). By treating both parties as equally guilty, both are also able to claim "justification" for their own violent actions. Moreover, police decision processes are not gender neutral in these cases. "[W]hen police who hold patriarchal values are bound by mandatory arrest laws to make arrests, officers may engage in dual arrests to ensure their involvement in the court process, to persecute victims for exercising their rights to protection, or to deter victims from invoking police response in the future" (Finn & Bettis, 2006, p. 275). Finn and Bettis find that officers rarely take the context of domestic violence into consideration in their decision-making process. Their own perceptions of the threat of future violence are the strongest determinant of their decisions, without regard for patterns of violence in a household. While increases in police responses to domestic violence are essential to improving the state's ability to protect women from violent men, the results are neither uniform across states nor consistently positive for women.

Increased protection from local authorities has also come in the form of protection orders whereby a woman who has been threatened or previously abused can seek state protection, and penalties exist for any violation of the terms of the protection order. For example, a protection order may state that a man who has threatened an ex-spouse may not come within 500 feet of her home. If the man violates this term, he can be arrested. The effectiveness of protection orders in stopping and preventing IPV has been mixed (Jordan, 2004). Supporters of civil protective orders argue that a key element in their effectiveness is that, unlike traditional restraining orders, "most states provide an enforcement provision in protective order statutes, i.e., offenders who violate protective orders may be arrested or may face contempt of court, depending on the jurisdiction" (Crowell & Burgess, 1996 as cited in Jordan, 2004, p. 1425).

Getting these laws on the books is an important step in legitimating women's claims of abuse and providing fuller protection; however, studies indicate that even when states have mandatory arrest laws for violation of protective orders, law enforcement officers do not always arrest (Jordan, 2004). Flawed as the system may be, the issuance of protective orders does seem to lower rates of repeat violence. Because victims of IPV often move to escape the threat of their abusers, the effectiveness of protection orders lies in part on their ability to maintain effectiveness across state lines.

The VAWA of 1994 recognized the importance of interstate cooperation. The VAWA of 1994 established criminal penalties for crossing state lines to commit domestic violence or to violate protection orders. These provisions provide increased security to women who move away from abusers to protect themselves and/or their children. Chapter 2, Section 2261, of VAWA addresses interstate domestic violence,

> A person who travels across a State line or enters or leaves Indian country with the intent to injure, harass, or intimidate that person's spouse or intimate partner, and who, in the course of or as a result of such travel, intentionally commits a crime of violence and thereby causes bodily injury to such spouse or intimate partner, shall be punished.

The provisions further state that if a person causes a partner or spouse to leave the state by force, coercion, duress, or fraud and commits a crime of violence, then that person is also subject to the punishments provided in the act. The "full faith and credit" provision further states that

> Any protection order issued that is consistent with the provisions laid out in the Interstate section of the VAWA "by the court of one State or Indian tribe (the issuing State or Indian tribe) shall be accorded full faith and credit by the court of another State or Indian tribe (the enforcing State or Indian tribe) and enforced as if it were the order of the enforcing State or tribe." (VAWA Chapter 2, Sec. 2265 (a))

The interstate enforcement provisions of the VAWA are essential to women's claims to equal protection as citizens. The federal policy ensures that victims of IPV maintain their rights to equal protection as U.S. citizens when they cross state lines.

Changes in the processes of law enforcement officials and the protections provided by state and local law enforcement are essential to increasing the protections offered to women as citizens. Police action at the local level is essential to female victim's experience of citizenship rights and to their subsequent experiences in court. Changes in the legal frameworks for police action that recognize the experiences of victimization fundamentally shift women's access to equal protection rights afforded by the Constitution.

FEMALE VICTIMS IN COURT: RAPE SHIELD REGULATIONS

As activists succeeded in bringing attention to problems of gender-motivated violence, rape laws afforded women the opportunity to seek response and protection from local law enforcement and press charges against their abusers, but, aside from some progress in protection orders, they did little to protect women or to ensure that the same men would not abuse again. Particularly in the early years, laws were still written, enforced, and prosecuted by men who were raised to believe they had a right to sex. The bias built into these laws added to the victims' victimization (Rhode, 1989). In the small minority of cases where an arrest was made and the case made it to trial, women faced court battles that placed their own sexual histories, motives, and characters on trial. As previously noted, law enforcement officials as well as judges and juries were generally skeptical of women's claims of victimization.

The courts reflect a culture that recognizes rape as a "woman's" issue rather than a criminal issue (Herman, 1991; Rowland, 2004). Rowland notes that " 'consent' has long seemed more plausible to judges and juries than rape . . . Thus, gray areas have made their way into the law" (2004, p. 689). In the courtroom, the burden of proof is generally on the victim. "Proof of struggle" requirements exemplify the extent to which the onus is on the woman. The American legal requirement that courts view the accused as innocent until proven guilty is turned on its head as female victims of sex crimes are treated as guilty of filing false charges until they prove their innocence by providing evidence that they did everything in their power to avoid, prevent, and stop the attack. Historically, rape victims were also held accountable for any past sexual indiscretions as well as any sexual history with the defendant. "[T]he goal in introducing evidence of the complainant's past sexual life may be to trade on deeply rooted beliefs that loose women ask for it or can't be raped" (Rowland, 2004, p. 694). Female victims found that if they chose to press charges against their attackers, their own character and history were on trial, not the actions of their attackers.

Early feminist research on violence against women made a clear case that the experiences of women in court were a deterrent to reporting rape, sexual assault, and domestic violence. Most states had some form of "rape shield" law by 1980 (Rowland, 2004). Rape shield laws protect women who file rape charges from having their own histories put on trial, but they often contain exceptions that allow the victim's sexual history to speak to the possibility of consent or perceived consent. If one is arguing that a reasonable person would have interpreted consent from the past experiences with and actions and words of the victim, then he is able to slip in information generally excluded under rape shield laws (Rowland, 2004).

An additional obstacle to successful prosecution of rape cases is the belief that physical aggression is a "normal" part of the male role in sexual interactions (Rowland, 2004). Cultural ideologies that support a tension between desire and chastity in the female psyche support the belief that "no" sometimes means "yes." This belief casts doubt on any claim of rape as both men and women often assume that a claim of rape is simply an expression of moral regret following a sexual encounter.

Catharine MacKinnon has argued that the sexualized physical aggression pervasive in pornography contributes to cultural confusion regarding sexual violence (MacKinnon, 1989, 2005). Domination and subordination are eroticized not only in pornography, but in more ubiquitous elements of popular culture such as music, videos, and mainstream advertising.

> The gendered inferiority attributed to sexual victims, and used to target them, and the gendered superiority attached to sexual prowess, along with the eroticization of subordination and dominance, are socially imbricated with established and inculcated notions and roles of masculinity and femininity respectively. (MacKinnon, 2005, p. 240)

Pornography is protected as free speech, but women are not protected from gendered violence as a matter of civil rights. MacKinnon, a known critic of pornography, sees the *Morrison* decision (that overturned the civil redress provided to female victims of gender-motivated violence in the VAWA of 1994) as a strong statement that allows states to maintain gendered hierarchies and leaves women without sufficient legal recourse. Stephen Schulhofer (1998a) also notes, "[t]he law protects our property, labor, privacy, and other fundamental interests, but sexual autonomy—the right to choose whether and when to be sexually intimate with another person—is too often ignored (55)." The juxtaposition of protections for pornography, property, and privacy in the face of the failure to protect women's rights to sexual autonomy reinforces the stereotypes and assumptions that continue to make the courtroom an unfriendly place for victims of abuse.

Rape shield provisions at the federal level, while not bullet proof, offer significant protection to women seeking justice through the courts at all levels. Rape shield laws send a message that turning the tables on victims of rape and sexual violence is no longer a legitimate rape defense. These laws do not eliminate the demonization of female accusers, nor do they bring instant legitimacy to women's claims of victimization, but they do open the possibility for women to maintain their dignity and for courts to focus on the crimes before them rather than on the sexual histories of the accusers. These provisions as well as those regarding interstate recognition of protection orders are all part of the VAWA of 1994.

THE VIOLENCE AGAINST WOMEN ACT OF 1994

The early 1990s saw a significant increase in public discussion of violent crimes committed against women. In June 1990, the Senate Committee on the Judiciary held a hearing "to examine the rise in violent crimes committed against women, and to consider the need for legislation to enhance the ability of the criminal justice system to respond to violence against women. In 1991 a VAWA was proposed, the Senate heard research and testimony on the effects of gender-motivated violence throughout the early 1990s, and the Act went through revision and reconsideration and was passed in 1994 as Title IV of Violent Crime Control and Law Enforcement Act of 1994, P.L. 103-322, "Violent Crime Control and Law Enforcement Act of 1994" intended "to control and prevent crime" (P.L. 103-322). The VAWA provides significant funds for states to improve their ability to prevent and prosecute crimes against women. The VAWA also sets a national standard for responding to gender-motivated violence in its protection requirements and rape shield regulations for courtroom proceedings (see Box 2.6).

VAWA contributed to the expansion of women's citizenship rights by providing civil redress for rape victims. Supporters cited a large body of research on the economic impacts of gender-motivated violence and argued that the effect on interstate commerce made it a civil rights issue. A bipartisan Congress concluded that gender-motivated violence limits women's interstate travel, restricts women's choice of jobs and ability to perform those jobs, reduces national productivity, and increases medical and other costs.

> The Violence Against Women Act enjoyed widespread nonpartisan support. Indeed, while pending in Congress, "the attorneys general from 38 states urged its passage, and 36 states joined a brief supporting the law before the Supreme Court. Only one, Alabama, filed a brief asking the justices to strike the law down." (Greenhouse, 2000, A16, as cited in Rowland, 2004, pp. 698–699)

Despite widespread support from legislators, VAWA faced a tough battle concerning its constitutionality as it granted the federal government power to police "private" activity.

BOX 2.6

PROVISIONS OF THE 1994 VIOLENCE
AGAINST WOMEN ACT

- Revises and expands protections for women against violent crime.
- Directs the U.S. Sentencing Commission to promulgate revised sentencing guidelines for sex crime offenders, and mandates financial restitution to victims by offenders.
- Authorizes Department of Justice grants to states and local governments for law enforcement, prosecution, and victim services in violent crimes against women.
- Authorizes Department of Transportation grants for capital improvements to prevent crimes in public transit systems and other grants to reduce crime in public parks.
- Amends the Federal Rules of Evidence pertaining to sexual assault cases.
- Amends the Public Health and Human Services Act to authorize State use of certain funds for rape prevention and education programs.
- Amends the Runaway and Homeless Youth Act to authorize grants for runaway, homeless, and street youth who have been subjected to or are at risk of being subjected to sexual abuse.
- Authorizes various programs under the Victims of Child Abuse Act of 1990.
- Amends the Family Violence Prevention and Services Act to authorize a Department

of Health and Human Services national domestic violence telephone hotline.
- Establishes criminal penalties for crossing state lines to commit domestic violence or violate protection orders.
- Authorizes appropriations for grants for battered women's shelters, community programs on domestic violence, and rural domestic violence and child abuse enforcement.
- Establishes a civil rights cause of action for civil suits against persons who commit sexual assault and other gender-motivated crimes.
- Authorizes State Justice Institute grants for education and training of federal and state judges and court personnel on topics pertaining to violent crimes against women.
- Amends the Immigration and Nationality Act to authorize certain aliens suffering spousal abuse to petition for change in immigration status.

Title IV, subtitle A, is cited as the Safe Streets for Women Act of 1994; subtitle B as the Safe Homes for Women Act of 1994; subtitle C as the Civil Rights Remedies for Gender-Motivated Violence Act; and subtitle D as the Equal Justice for Women in the Courts Act of 1994.

Just six years after its passage, the constitutionality of VAWA's civil rights provision was defeated. The Supreme Court heard oral arguments in *United States v. Morrison* and *Brzonkala v. Morrison* on January 11, 2000. Christy Brzonkala alleged that she was forcibly raped by Antonio Morrison and James Crawford in September 1994 at Virginia Tech University. Brzonkala sought action from the University disciplinary board, which found Crawford not guilty and found Morrison guilty only of verbal abuse (though he stated that Brzonkala had said "no" twice during the incident under review). Brzonkala left school and filed charges, but a state grand jury found the evidence insufficient to charge either man with any crime. Brzonkala later sued the men under VAWA for gang rape. The defendants challenged the constitutionality of the civil rights provision that grants victims "cause of action for civil suits against persons who commit sexual assault and other gender-motivated crimes" (Title IV, VAWA, 1994), and the Justice Department intervened to defend it. The 4th Circuit Federal Court of Appeals struck down the provision on the grounds that the connection to the interstate commerce clause was too thin to warrant federal jurisdiction in such a case; thus, VAWA could not be used. The case was appealed to the Supreme Court (Taylor, 2000).

The primary issues of concern in the *Brzonkala* case were the limits of Congressional authority in legislating private party actions through civil rights provisions under the auspices of the Interstate Commerce Clause. The government defended the VAWA as within the bounds of congressional authority and as vital to the freedom of women to participate fully in society. Brzonkala's attorney Julie Goldscheid similarly defended the constitutionality of the act focusing on the extent to which gender-motivated violence limits women's access to economic activity. Michael Rosman represented Antonio Morrison and argued vehemently for states' rights. He was very clear that the federal government had no business legislating private party actions not directly related to commerce. Arguments of the defense hearken back to a clear separation of public and private that has sexual activity locked behind privacy doors not open to the federal government. The issue of women's access to citizenship was at stake in the question of whether rape could be seen as a violation of "civil" rights (see Box 2.7).

United States v. Morrison left most of VAWA intact, but it dealt a central blow to women by denying that gender-motivated violence could be seen as a violation of *civil rights*, a violation of women's access to full citizenship.

In addition to the failure to successfully establish sexual autonomy as a right of citizenship, the VAWA of 1994 did not overcome the racial biases of the criminal justice system as it pertained to gender-motivated violence. The passage of VAWA in 1994 effectively "widened the net," increasing the number of perpetrators brought under the control of the criminal justice system. The number of Latino and African American men arrested and incarcerated under VAWA is significant (Hutchison, Hirschel, & Pesackis, 1994; Rennison & Welchans, 2000). In her review of research since the passage of VAWA, Angela Moore Parmley notes with concern, "The fact that many

---

BOX 2.7

VIOLENCE AGAINST WOMEN MAY AFFECT INTERSTATE COMMERCE

[C]iting three full pages of supporting documentation offered by Congress, and noting that the legislative record offered in *United States v Morrison* was "far more voluminous than the record compiled by Congress and found sufficient in two prior cases upholding Title II of the Civil Rights Act of 1964 against Commerce Clause challenges (*United States v. Morrison*, 120 S. Ct. 1740, 1476 (2000) (Souter, J., dissenting))," the four justices concluded that "violence against women may be found to affect interstate commerce and affect it substantially . . . however, the majority ruled otherwise, prompting critics to suggest that the "federalism counterrevolution" may have inched closer to those "core issues of civil rights for which the court for so long had given Congress wide scope" (Greenhouse 2000, A16 as cited in Rowland 2004, p. 704).

men of color are brought into the criminal justice system could lead to the erroneous conclusion that these men are more violent than their Caucasian counterparts. The concern here is not just with who is in the system but who is not" (2004, p. 1425). A number of problems arise from the disproportionate imprisonment of African American men, not the least of which is that White perpetrators are disproportionately free in our communities.

From legal definitions of rape and sexual assault to recognition of the realities of gender-motivated violence in intimate relationships, changes in language impact the assumptions underlying our country's response to gender-motivated violence. Fundamental shifts in law enforcement response and the processes that accompany seeking protection from and penalties for perpetrators of gender-motivated violence have increased women's access to full citizenship. Equal protection under the law, once not accessible to women at all, is now far closer to being a reality for female citizens of the United States. In becoming fully recognized victims in U.S. law, we are also becoming fully recognized citizens.

CONCLUSION: WOMEN AS CITIZENS IN THE TWENTY-FIRST CENTURY

In his 1845 treatise, *The Legal Rights of Women*, Edward Mansfield follows his chronicle of the history of women's rights among the Hebrews and the Romans and in the feudal system, with a plan for women's rights in America. As he defines the reciprocal rights and duties of citizens and government, he states very clearly the government's responsibility "[t]o protect them [citizens] against domestic crime, or violence. . . . if Jane be violently attacked, it is as much the duty of government to protect her, and to punish the criminal, as if she had been the most important man in the nation. . . . The right to protection she has, by virtue of her *citizenship*" (Mansfield, 1845, p. 127). But under the U.S. legal system, women are doubly disadvantaged.

They are still subject to common law doctrines denying them equal jural personhood, and also, under the rubric of equality, they are denied common law protections and presumptions under the fallacious assumption that identical treatment of men and women despite their differences will provide equal protection of the laws. (Forer, 1991, p. 96)

This chapter provides a history of women's struggle for full citizenship rights as it has played out in our efforts to gain recognition of our victimization by gender-motivated violence. In gaining legitimacy for our claims to "victim" status, we have also empowered women with broader access to the full rights and responsibilities of citizenship. The denial of women's citizenship rights is rooted in the very same intimate relationships with spouses and family that have been the sites for much of our victimization. The same assumptions that justified coverture created barriers to women accessing the protection from violence perpetrated by the men who represented them.

The first step was to gain access to the political sphere. From there, women were able to begin shaping the language and definitions of the laws that provide the frameworks for legitimate action and that protect our common welfare. By affecting changes in language and definition, we are able to shape the process of law enforcement and demand the protections we need and that we have the right to demand as citizens. Courtrooms across the country are fundamentally shaped by the federal regulations that protect our citizenship rights. Furthermore, the changes brought by the VAWA of 1994 and subsequent additions in 2000 are essential. Federal policy not only provides a uniform rule book, but is also essential to providing states with the resources needed to develop the support structures and services needed to serve victims of gender-motivated violence and to prevent future generations from becoming perpetrators of such violence. Cultural, political, and economic barriers to women's full and equal citizenship rights remain.

The history documented here is one of constant conflict and tension and it continues to today. As noted throughout, many advances have met only partial success. The tension between philosophical commitments to equality and to difference that have marked women's movements for citizenship rights in the United States is central to discussions of women as victims of gender-motivated violence. The successes of women's rights movements have produced a strong and vocal constituency, but women still lack the civil right to protection from the violence they experience solely because they are women. Women now outnumber men as eligible voters and comprise nearly 30 percent of attorneys in the United States and over 50 percent of law school students (O'Connor, 2003). Our legal structure will continue to be shaped by women's increasing participation and by the growing power of the female electorate.

In a global society, discussions of women as victims and as citizens must transcend the political boundaries of nation-states. This chapter focuses on the history of women as victims in U.S. law, but a growing international sex trade requires that we conceptualize issues of sexual violence and exploitation, not simply as issues of citizenship, but rather as human rights concerns. "In February 2001, the war tribunal at the Hague formally recognized 'sexual enslavement' as a crime against humanity in convicting three Bosnian Serbs of rape" (Rowland, 2004, p. 664). Establishing the right to sexual autonomy as a right of citizenship in the United States is a very important step for American women and the protection of the U.S. Constitution, but in an increasingly global society, the failure of societies to uniformly recognize this right has far-reaching implications. The struggles for legal recognition and protection documented in this chapter continue in the United States and will increasingly play out on a global stage as we work to end female sexual slavery and abuse and create a world where, instead of assuming male access to female sexuality, we assume the human right to sexual autonomy.

Discussion Questions

1. How did women's legal status define their victim status?
2. Describe the complications that slaves/African Americans and women advocates faced in fighting for equality both in the 1860s and in the 1960s.
3. How does gender-neutral language in our laws affect women's status as victims of gender-motivated crimes?
4. How has language affected implementation of rape and sexual assault laws? How has culture affected language and in turn how has language affected culture?
5. How did VAWA address problems of violence against women? What have been some of the barriers for VAWA when advocating for women's citizenship rights?

References

Alexander, K. (2000). Note: A modest proposal: The "reasonable victim" standard and Alaska employers' affirmative defense to vicarious liability for sexual harassment. *Alaska Law Review, 17*, 297–318.

Amir, M. (1971). *Patterns in forcible race.* Chicago: University of Chicago Press.

Bergen, R. K., & Barnhill, E. (2006). *Marital rape: New research and directions.* Retrieved July 17, 2007 from http://new.vawnet.org/Assoc_Files_VAWnet/AR_MaritalRapeRevised.pdf.

Bevacqua, M. (2000). *Rape on the public agenda: Feminism and the politics of sexual assault.* Boston: Northeastern University Press.

Califano v. Goldfarb, 1977 Supreme Court of the United States, 97 S. Ct. 1021.

Collins, P. H. (1990). *Black feminist thought: Knowledge, consciousness, and the politics of empowerment.* New York: Routledge.

Department of Justice (DOJ). (2005). *Criminal victimization in the United States.* Retrieved December 30, 2006 from http://www.ojp.usdoj.gov/bjs/abstract/cvus/definitions.htm.

Dressler, J. (1998). Where we have been, and where we might be going: Some cautionary reflections on rape law reform. *Cleveland State Law Review, 46*, 409.

Evans, S. M. (1989). *Born for liberty: A history of women in America.* New York: The Free Press.

Federal Bureau of Investigation (FBI). (2005). *Uniform Crime Reports.* Retrieved July 17, 2007 from http://www.fbi.gov/ucr/05cius/offenses/violent_crime/forcible_rape.html.

Finkelhor, D., & Yllo, K. (1985). *License to rape: Sexual abuse of wives.* New York: Holt, Rinehart, and Winston.

Finley, L. M. (2004). Vision and revision: Exploring the history, evolution, and future of the Fourteenth Amendment: Putting "protection" back in the equal protection clause: Lessons from nineteenth century women's rights activists' understandings of inequality. *Temple Political & Civil Rights Law Review, 13*, 429.

Finn, M. A., & Bettis, P. (2006). Punitive action or gentle persuasion: Exploring police officers' justifications for using dual arrest in domestic violence cases. *Violence Against Women, 12*, 268–287.

Forer, L. G. (1991). *Unequal protection: Women, children, and the elderly in court.* New York: W.W. Norton and Company.

Giele, J. Z. (1995). *Two paths to women's equality: Temperance, suffrage, and the origins of modern feminism.* New York: Twayne Publishers.

Griffin, S. (1996/1971). Rape: The all American crime. In D. K. Weisberg (Ed.), *Applications of feminist legal theory to women's lives: Sex, violence, work, and reproduction.* Philadelphia: Temple University Press.

Herman, J. L. (1991). *Trauma and recovery.* New York: Basic Books.

Hutchison, I., Hirschel, D., & Pesackis, C. (1994). Family violence and police utilization. *Violence and Victims, 9*, 299–313.

Irons, P. (1999). *A people's history of the Supreme Court.* New York: Viking.

Jacobstein, J., Myron, R., Mersky, M., & Dunn, D. J. (1998). *Fundamentals of legal research.* New York: Foundation Press.

Jordan, C. E. (2004). Intimate partner violence and the justice system. *Journal of Interpersonal Violence, 19*, 1412–1434.

MacKinnon, C. A. (1989). *Toward a feminist theory of the state.* Cambridge, MA: Harvard University Press.

MacKinnon, C. A. (2005). *Women's lives-men's laws.* Cambridge, MA: The Belknap Press of Harvard University Press.

Mansfield, E. D. (1845). *The legal rights, liabilities and duties of women.* Salem: John P. Jewett & Co.

McAdam, D. (1982). *Political process and the development of black insurgency 1930–1970.* Chicago: University of Chicago Press.

Moore Parmley, A. (2004). Violence against women research post VAWA: Where have we been, where are we going? *Violence Against Women, 10*, 1417–1430.

O'Connor, S. D. (2003). *The majesty of the law.* New York: Random House, Inc.

Personnel Administrator of Massachusetts v. Feeney. (1979) Supreme Court of the United States, 442 U.S. 256; 99 S. Ct. 2282.

Rennison, C. M., & Welchans, S. (2000). *Intimate partner violence.* Washington, D.C.: U.S. Department of Justice, Bureau of Justice Statistics.

Respecting Accuracy in Domestic Abuse Reporting. (2007). *A culture of false allegations: How VAWA harms families and children.* Rockville, MD: Respecting Accuracy in Domestic Abuse Reporting. Retrieved July 17, 2007 from http://www.mediaradar.org/docs/VAWA-A-Culture-of-False-Allegations. pdf.

Rhode, D. L. (1989). *Justice and gender: Sex discrimination and the law.* Cambridge, Massachusetts: Harvard University Press.

Ritter, G. (2006). *The constitution as social design: Gender and civic membership in the American constitutional order.* Stanford, CA: Stanford University Press.

Roiphe, K. (1993). *The morning after: Sex, fear, and feminism on campus.* Boston: Massachusetts: Little Brown & Co.

Rowland, D. (2004). *The troubling history of women's rights in America.* Naperville, IL: Sphinx Publishing.

Schulhofer, S. (1998a). *Unwanted sex: The culture of intimidation and the failure of law.* Cambridge: Harvard University Press.

Taylor, S. Jr. (2000). Congress, the court, and violence against women. *The National Journal, 32,* 76–77.

Thornhill, R., & Palmer, C. T. (2000). *A natural history of rape: Biological bases of sexual coercion.* Massachusetts: Massachusetts Institute of Technology Press.

United States v. Morrison. (2000). Supreme Court of the United States, 120 S. Ct. 1740, 1476.

Violent Crime Control and Law Enforcement Act of 1994, U.S. Public Law 103–322.

Violence Against Women Act: Full Faith and Credit to Protection Orders, U.S. Code, Title 18, Sec. 2265.

Wolfgang, M. E. (1958). *Patterns in criminal homicide.* Montclair, NJ: Patterson Smith, Reprinted 1975.

Woolley, M. L. (2007). Marital rape: A unique blend of domestic violence and non-marital rape issues. *Hastings Women's Law Journal, 18,* 269–293.

Endnotes

1. LaFave, W., & Scott, A. (1986). *Substantive Criminal Law.* St. Paul: West (sec 5.11; pp. 688–689); Perkins, R. M., & Boyce, R. N. (1980). *Criminal Law.* Mineola, N.Y.: Foundation Press (p. 210).
2. Provisions as listed in Congressional Universe's Congressional Information System (CIS) Legislative History of "Violent Crime Control and Law Enforcement Act of 1994." CIS-NO: 94-PL103-322, CIS-Date December 1994. Congressional Session 103-2, Item No 575, September 13, 1994.

CHAPTER 3

WOMEN AND VICTIMIZATION

Constructing Outcomes

❧

DENNIS R. BREWSTER
PHILIP D. HOLLEY

ABSTRACT

Women's victimization is of growing importance in the field of victimology. One of the earliest and more reified positions explaining women's victimization is that of victim precipitation—in other words, victim blaming. This chapter calls for a new approach to victimology—that of a "general" victimology that can explain both criminal and noncriminal victims. In that light, our work here will introduce theoretical concepts explaining the social construction of victim status, with emphasis on crimes that are linked to women. Also considered is the impact of advocacy social movements on the creation of female victim status. Victims of crime must obtain "victim status" through social processes already in place in order to establish criteria for applying the victim status. Our theoretical position explains how the victim status is obtained based on how women are viewed in society using a constructionist approach. The constructionist approach will allow a differential explanation of status depending on not only the crime but also how women view themselves and victimization.

INTRODUCTION

Victims have become increasingly important in the study of crime—within criminology—and more recently in the field of victimology. Women's victimization is of growing importance in the field of victimology, in response to not only the rising numbers of women as criminals but also the increasing focus on women as victims. Studies of different types of victimizations suffered by women indicate that no clear-cut theoretical position has emerged that can effectively explain how society views and reacts to that victimization.

Thus, one of the overriding problems for the newly developing field of victimology is the lack of theoretical development. While researchers appear to be doing an excellent job of describing and developing differential factors involved in a study of victims, as yet a clear-cut theoretical position has not been put forth. Here a social constructionist approach is proposed to help explain society's view of women's victimization.[1] While developing the theoretical framework, two important types of victimization of women—rape and domestic violence—will be used to help explain both the reaction of women and the reaction of society.

Using a constructionist approach is beneficial to the current issue for two compelling reasons. First, social constructionism allows for the interaction of the individual and society. What that means for female victims is that while needing "victim status" to be conferred by some legitimizing social institution, victims also help determine "victim status." Second, the constructionist approach uses a dynamic rather than static approach to criminal victimization. Both the definition of what constitutes a victim and society's reaction to victimization change over time based on several factors. The constructionist approach will allow for differential views of victimization of women as society begins to change its beliefs and values.

LITERATURE REVIEW

In general women have not been a priority in either the criminological literature or the victimology literature. Where women have been included, it appears that with some exceptions the approach to female crime and victimization has been one of "add women and stir" (Chesney-Lind & Shelden, 2004), meaning that for the most part, women's victimization has fallen under many of the same theoretical frameworks developed to explain men's victimization. The problem with that type of approach does not allow for differential explanations necessary in certain types of crime.

Victimology in general and women's victimization in particular have suffered from the insistence on and persistence of the concept of "victim precipitation." The focus on how victims engage in behavior that might be seen as "cause" of their victimization is troubling to say the least. Mendelsohn (1976) opened the possibility of individual "predisposition" to being victimized, although he contended that not every victim is predisposed. He used accident data to support an argument for an "accident-prone personality" (Mendelsohn, 1976, p. 15). From the prior work of Wolfgang (1958) to current writers in the field of victimology (see Doerner & Lab, 1995; Karmen, 2007; Sgarzi & McDevitt, 2003), much attention has been given to the precipitation theme.

The literature incorporates a framework within which the criminal and the victim interact. This dynamic is described by Karmen (2007) as "shared responsibility," although the critics decry what is transpiring as "victim blaming." Motivated in part to prevent crime victimization, the almost exclusive attention to the criminal gave way to a recent interest in the victim and her/his "precipitating" behavior. Accordingly, those who become victims play an active role in the victimization experience, ensuring that "innocence" cannot simplistically describe them when drawing on the empirical evidence. To varying degrees and in numerous ways, it has been argued, "victims" contribute to their own victimization through drinking, violence, and other behaviors associated with deviant and criminal lifestyles (see Karmen, 2007).

According to Doerner and Lab (1995), "[v]ictim Precipitation deals with the degree to which the victim is responsible for his or her own victimization" (p. 9). They note that while there have been criticisms of the victim precipitation approach, much of research has still investigated how victims may or may not be involved in becoming a victim.

Karmen (2007) provides a distinction among the different forms of precipitation. He makes a distinction among victim facilitation, precipitation, and provocation. Facilitation, according to Karmen (2007), occurs where "victims unknowingly, carelessly, negligently, and inadvertently make it easier for the criminal to commit a theft" (p. 100). In other words, the victim is innocent of any intent to create his or her own harm. For example, someone whose vehicle was taken by a thief after having left the keys in the ignition has facilitated the incident, but clearly the person was not interested in having the vehicle stolen.

Precipitation, according to Karmen (2007), happens when "the person who gets hurt significantly contributed to the outbreak of violence" (p. 102). Most noted types of crimes characterizing victim precipitation are violent crimes such as murder, rape, robbery, and assault (p. 101). Provocation is, according to Karmen, even worse than precipitation (p. 102). It is during provocation that "[t]he injured party instigated an attack that otherwise would not have taken place" (p. 102). Clearly, the person who starts a fight and then is seriously injured in the fight can be seen as provoking victimization.

In contrast, Sgarzi and McDevitt offer resistance to the "practice of 'victim blaming'" (2003, p. 2), particularly in cases of rape and sexual assault. Questions about her attire and her behavior raise the possibility that she might have done things ". . . to bring the crime upon herself" (p. 2). Thus, they argue that ". . . blaming victims removes the blameworthiness of the offender . . ." (p. 2). Eigenberg (2003) argues that victim blaming means no critical examination of the political, economic, and social structures in which crime victimization occurs. Clearly, victimology in the twenty-first century continues to be beset with conflicts over victim precipitation; even when there are studies of crime "risk," there are legal and social efforts intended to prevent victim blaming by police, prosecutors, and others.

From our perspective, insufficient attention has been given to the development of a theoretical perspective that is inclusive enough to explain all types of victimization, including those of females. That quest should lead us to theory that is able to explain differing types of victimization—either physical or emotional types of harm—and differing responses to that harm. Questions such as "Does society define female victims of crime differently than men?" and "At the individual and social level, do women view victimization differently than do men?" must be explained by the theory.

In order to be able to fully understand differential harm and response to women's victimization, it is believed that a social constructionist approach is best suited to explain victimization in general and women's victimization in particular. Social construction is sociologically based on and part of the symbolic interactionist perspective. Symbolic interaction theory was developed by Cooley (1926) and Mead (1918), taking a more micro-level approach to understanding human behavior. Symbolic interactionists believe humans interact with their social environment and that the two-way interaction of people and social structure is important in understanding society and how it works. Social construction, rather than focusing on "objective" reality, seeks to examine the social construction of reality (Heiner, 2006; Kraska, 2004; Lamb, 1999). It is the exploration of that process by which ". . . constructed meanings and definitions of situations . . ." are created (Kraska, 2004, p. 137).

Of importance here is how victims view their victimization and how they play an active role in determining how they react (or not) to victimization (see Burt, 1983). Also of importance is how society views the harm to the victim and how society reacts (or not) to victimization. The interplay and processes involved in this interaction will determine who is seen in society as a "victim." Indeed, Karmen argued that victimologists study how the status of "legitimate victim" is "socially defined and constructed" (2007, p. 19).

Social construction has developed out of this symbolic interactionist perspective and has been used in dealing with such far-reaching topics as crime (Potter & Kappeler, 1998), deviance (Adler & Adler, 2006), street gangs (McCorkle & Miethe, 2002), and lesbianism (Kitzinger, 1987). Spector and Kitsuse (1977) first developed the concepts in their work on social problems in general. Social problems are social constructions, according to Spector and Kitsuse, in that society designates what is considered to be a social problem. An important part of the constructionist perspectives is the role of "claims" and "claims-makers" (for a fuller explanation of claims and claims-makers, see Best (1995), Scott (1993)). Claims-makers are individuals or groups, acting as moral entrepreneurs, who present "claims" for public digestion, typifying the very nature of what should be considered a serious problem (Best, 1995). Numerous groups can undertake claims-making, but of importance here is the claims-making and claims presented by political groups, the mass media, and social advocates in order that they promote the conferring of "victim status." Claims are statements—whether true or not—about a particular instance or situation. Oftentimes, there are counter-claims made by contending groups; such claims provide challenges to the original claims-makers. As moral entrepreneurs, these claims-makers assert moral or ethical claims based on the values of the group, although statistics may be misinterpreted or problems exaggerated and in spite of opposition from counter-claims-makers (Best, 1995; Potter & Kappeler, 1998).

While crime has been the focus of social construction (Kraska, 2004), crime victimization has also been treated as a social construction. The broad category of "victim" has been created out of a multitude of experiences defined as undeserved and harmful—rape, incest, sexual assault, domestic violence, etc.—within recent social movements (Doerner & Lab, 2005; Karmen, 2007). Once victimization is successfully claimed for a particular group of people with a particular set of undeserved and harmful experiences, individuals may seek social recognition as a victim.

It is this interaction and discussion of claims at the social and individual levels that determine whether "victim status" will be conferred or not, thus the social construction. It is our contention that victims—or more specifically "victim status"—is a social construction. Achieving victim status is neither inevitable nor automatic following harm taking place within a victimizing experience. It is contended that victim status is determined by social processes in order to verify and authenticate who is considered a victim or not. Victim status must be conferred by society or some legitimate authority in order for victims to be recognized.

It is not argued that the processes made available to those having a victimizing experience and subsequently seeking victim status are always fair, timely, or seamless, or that the outcomes are just and reasonable. The 2005 hurricane, Katrina, showed us otherwise. Clearly, those with racial, gender, class, and other minority statuses are burdened by lack of access to participation in claims-making activities as well as free, fair, and equal access to the processes by which victim status is achieved. Despite, for example, our efforts to enhance victim rights, criticisms of the criminal justice system continue (Wallace, 1998).

Furthermore, from this perspective some individuals could suffer harm and not be considered victims—as in those who lose their home in a tornado, yet are uninsured and do not live in a federally or state declared disaster area. Following that, our contention is that victim status can be accepted or rejected by the individual suffering the harm. If the individual accepts the conferred status, the individual is then entitled to be restored to their original self, or as close as can be obtained.[2]

As a result of the victim rights movement, the concept "victim" has been recast into "survivor." While some are skeptical of the utility of this concept (Lamb, 1999), as a practical matter the general preference is for "survivor" (Rock, 2002) within the victim movement. Despite the potential for assignment of a devalued label to the status of "victim," achievement of a victim status provides for entitlements (e.g., medical care, compensation, etc.) (Holley & Brewster, 2006), rewards (e.g., sympathy, attention, etc.) (Rock, 2002), and access to victim rights (Spalek, 2006).

THEORETICAL MODEL

From the societal view, Figure 3.1 provides a model representing the social process that takes place in determining whether an individual is given victim status or not. The model indicates several steps or processes that must take place in order for anyone—female or male—to be given "victim status" following a victimizing experience. A fuller explanation of how this process affects female victims of crime will follow a brief explanation of each of the concepts in the model.

FIGURE 3.1   Social constructionist model of victimization

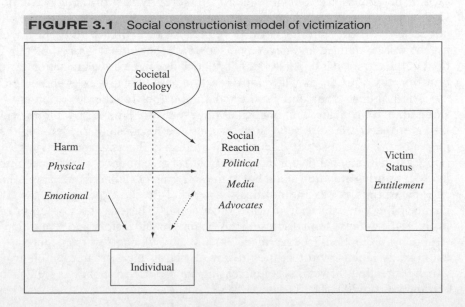

HARM

All victimization involves some type of harm. Burt (1983) refers to victims as those who are harmed, injured, or suffering. Victimization is defined as ". . . intentional or non-intentional acts of harm or injury to individuals . . . considered as unwanted, undeserved, and/or unjust . . ." (Holley & Brewster, 2006, p. 4). That harm can be either physical types of harm or emotional types of harm. Physical harm is one that involves physical injury to the person. In the case of domestic violence, that harm may be the result of hitting, slapping, or punching of the victim. It is the physical harm that is generally evidenced by police when called to the scene of a domestic dispute.

Emotional harm is much harder to see, but is also an important component of female victimization. Fear and anger are only two of the emotions that can be felt by female victims of violence. While not always producing outward appearing manifestations, emotional harm is real. For example, domestic violence victims may experience a sense of "fear of the unknown" when confronted with filing charges against the aggressor. Domestic violence literature is replete with examples of the emotional harm suffered by female victims of domestic violence (see Buzawa & Buzawa, 2003).

Harm can also include simultaneous physical and emotional harm, which is defined as the most serious of all harms. The victim must suffer from physical injury—pain and suffering—while dealing with emotional and psychological trauma at the same time. Rape victims would be examples of this type of victim. Ultimately, the crime event potentially produces financial costs associated with physical injuries as well as costs associated with missing days from work while attending court. And, to the extent that social intimates and others blame the victim for what happened, express skepticism at the victim's account, ostracize her, or apply negative labels, additional costs are accrued.

SOCIAL REACTION

Social reaction is society's response to the harm suffered by the individual within the victimizing experience. Social reaction is inherently part of the construction of the victim by society. Three main players, the political arena, the mass media, and social advocates for those suffering harm, develop how society reacts to harm. Each of these arenas will be defined and developed separately, yet do not act completely independent of the others. It is understood that politicians can be driven to action by the media or advocates, or media may develop a reaction based on advocates and politicians, etc.

The political arena may be the most important for the development of victim status, due to the ability that politicians have to create laws that would provide recognition of the victim to society, but would also be responsible for defining the entitlements of the victim status.[3] The political arena is a diverse group ranging from local politics to national political groups. The political machinery can be placed into motion in order to bring attention and relief to the suffering of victims. For example, in the case of rape victims, it was the political outlet that passed rape shield laws that have changed the view of society toward rape victims. These laws, initiated in the 1970s, prohibit the defense from discussing the victim's sexual history and reputation in court, with minor exceptions (see Karmen, 2007). While still controversial, these laws as well as those designed to protect the privacy of victims have created an environment in which protecting the victim is of increasing importance for police as well as the media (Grant & Otto, 2003).

The mass media—television, radio, Internet, and related news outlets—are important developers of social reaction to the harm of an individual. News accounts of harm or victimization can energize a society to respond to harm that is broadcast or discussed in open forums. For example, in the 2006 murder, rape, and mutilation of a college coed in New York City, the media presentations provided not only descriptive accounts of the incident, but even provided hour-long examinations of the event (i.e., The Abrams Report, MSNBC).[4]

Social advocates, functioning within social movements and particularly social movement organizations, can also play a role in providing victim status to a harmed individual. In addition, one of the most notable examples of social advocacy is Mothers Against Drunk Drivers (MADD). MADD provided information to politicians and news outlets raising the level of interest in harm created by drunk driving. Without that influence, the likelihood of laws changing protecting against drunk driving may never have been changed. Numerous social movements and advocacy groups—the anti-rape movement, Battered Women's Movement, and Take Back the Night—illustrate movements intended to address women's issues.

All of these groups can work independent of each other or may influence and interact in a way that strengthens the call for conferring victim status on an individual. For example, mass media reports of the victimization of women in domestic violence cases could be a driving force in the creation of the position of victim advocacy in the prosecutor's office. Other groups may have influence in engaging these groups as well, such as the women's movement calling attention to and demanding action in the victimization of women in both rape and domestic violence cases, as will be discussed in more detail later.

CULTURAL IDEOLOGY

Cultural ideology also plays a role in the development of victim status. Ideology is defined here as a set of beliefs and values that provide society a sense of right and wrong and a preferred way of living in the society. What values and beliefs a society has in place will guide and influence all of the actors in society—including the victim, the politicians, mass media, and social advocates. If, for example, a society sees women as property, then the politicians, mass media, and advocates will react to claims of victimization in a different manner than a society with more equalitarian views of women. That same ideological view of women will also influence women's view of their own victimization. These last two points will be discussed later in the chapter.

VICTIM STATUS

Victim status is defined as the end result of the social reaction—the definitions, discussion, authorization, verification, and authentication of the claims-making process mentioned above. Society decides whether individuals are deserving of some form of entitlement following and in direct connection to their claims of a victimizing experience and being a victim in the eyes of society. Entitlement in this sense means social recognition of the victim status as well as some type of restoration to their former self. If society deems the individuals deserving, they may be eligible for assistance through social service agencies, such as shelters or temporary housing, or help from advocacy groups and or various legal channels, such as victim compensation funds or societal protections in the form of personal protection orders designed to keep the offenders from harming them in the future.[5]

CONSTRUCTING WOMEN'S VICTIMIZATION

Using the theoretical framework set out above, the victimization of women using the crimes of rape and domestic violence is now explored. It is our contention that using this framework will allow for the differential views of female victimization over time and will also help explain how women view themselves as victims or not. In other words, using this perspective will explain how societal changes toward women have created differing responses to women's victimization over time. Also, this perspective will provide a means for us to see how women themselves might view victimization differently now in declaring a victim status or not.

RAPE

Prior to the 1970s, rape, defined here as "forced or nonconsensual sexual intercourse" (Barkan, 2006), was viewed by society much differently than it is today. Using our theoretical framework, the cultural and ideological beliefs of our society would be implicated in those different views existing over time. As a patriarchal society, women were viewed as possessions of men. Men dominated women in almost every realm of life, including sexual prowess over women. Those views of the "role" of women were passed on through the socialization process. According to Weis and Weis (1973), "The socialization processes of the male and the female act to forge the female as a victim and provide the procedure for legitimizing her in this role" (p. 7). In a patriarchal society, women are socialized to sex roles to be weak, passive, and in need of support of men. In the process of learning her role as the "proper" female, the female learns to depend on the male for protection and security. Her sexual favors become an important commodity for exchange (Weis & Weis, 1973). In other words, in each sexual encounter the woman is giving up a possession, often for the sake of love and security. When she marries, according to Weis and Weis (1973), she trades in her sexual bargaining power and becomes the property of her husband where he may sexually treat her as he wishes, even if against her will.[6]

In a patriarchal society, males are socialized to be aggressive and assertive. Males have a very strict sex role socialization that does not allow for developing an understanding of girls and their feelings and roles.[7] In this type of society, males are taught to be the sexual aggressor—taught to spread their "seed" at practically every available opportunity. Within this dual standard of sexual behavior, it is expected that males seek sexual pleasure, while females are not supposed to seek sexual pleasure. This double standard has then been implicated in rape. The equation of power with sexual domination provides the rapist a sense of power, control, and domination over the female.

Today our society views the act of rape much differently. One of the driving forces in that changing view was the women's movement. In our theoretical model, the women's movement would be an advocate group that constructs the necessary social reaction to provide women with "victim status." As claims-makers, the women's movement called for a different view of women in both society at large and the marital situation. Claims were set forth indicating the trauma that women suffer from the act of rape and the view that rape was—and is—an act of control and domination, not a sex act. That active role of claims-making and advocacy for victims of rape did bring about some change in society's reaction to rape victims in two critical ways. First, the women's movement provided the catalyst for change in the cultural ideologies of society. While certainly still not on an equal footing with men, women in American society are no longer viewed as the "property" of men. The current social reaction to victims of rape is different than in the past, with statutes being passed by all states that protect victims from a secondary victimization at the hands of the criminal justice system. For example, rape shield laws prohibit the introduction of the victim's past sexual history as evidence to be used against the victim.[8] States have also passed laws that allow the prosecution of husbands who commit the act of rape against their wives. This provides evidence supporting the theoretical position set out here (as shown in Figure 3.1).

Second, the work of the women's movement also changed the perception of the individual victim in rape cases. Under the patriarchal system, women often blamed themselves when falling victim to the act of rape. Today, the claims-making of the women's movement has provided the victim a better sense and awareness of the trauma of the act of rape, and women can now find the support necessary to stop the "self" blame.

In summary, the social reaction to the harm—both physical and emotional—caused by the act of rape created social and cultural values and practices that are much different today than existed in American society in the past. The women's movement (i.e., social advocates) created a new reaction through the claims-making process that allows women to benefit from "victim status." Social construction of a new reaction to the act of rape has created new beliefs and values in society's view of women and changed the way individual victims see themselves as victims of the act of rape. That "victim's status" has begun to provide some entitlements to victims in a manner that they are supposed to be protected from victim blaming by both the criminal justice system and society as well as providing other forms of support. While those claiming victim status must still fulfill all the requirements embedded in the processes found in the criminal justice system (i.e., reporting, giving statements, testifying if necessary, etc.), the procedures have been modified to further protect victims and their rights and to provide various entitlements within the victim status.

DOMESTIC VIOLENCE

Domestic violence, defined here as, "violence between intimates living together or who have previously cohabited" (Buzawa & Buzawa, 2003), has become a growing concern in American society. It too has connections to our patriarchal American history. Because women were viewed as being the property of men, men believed it was their "responsibility" to respond to acts that were perceived as inappropriate behavior with violence."[9] Victims were often perceived to "deserve" the violence that was committed against them.[10] Social reaction again has changed over time and the women's movement certainly often through the work of advocates,[11] but this time a political movement created change in the social reaction to victims of domestic violence.

One of the major factors in society's recent approach to domestic violence came through the Minnesota Domestic Violence studies (Sherman & Berk, 1984a, 1984b).

This was an attempt to determine the effects of arrest on domestic violence situations. The early findings of the study indicated that arrest did have a deterrent affect on offenders (Buzawa & Buzawa, 2003). Subsequent follow-up studies questioned the deterrent effect of arrest, but of importance here is that a number of large police departments (i.e., a political entity) created mandatory arrest policies (Buzawa & Buzawa, 2003). Mandatory arrest had a dual effect in that not only were offenders arrested (male or female depending on the evidence at the scene), but a growing number of dual arrests were made (both parties were arrested if evidence was seen on both individuals or if it was ambiguous as to who the offender was) (Buzawa & Buzawa, 2003).

The effects of the Minneapolis experiment also created significant changes in the views of prosecutors of domestic violence offenders. Today, prosecutors may move forward with a case with or without the testimony of the victim (Buzawa & Buzawa, 2003), thus illustrating the fact that victims may be authenticated as victims without their request or against their will. Judges have also been forced to rethink their positions on domestic violence cases due to the increased attention to the act. Issuance of "protection orders" has become an issue that judges have been forced to deal with (Buzawa & Buzawa, 2003). The Violence Against Women Act of 1994 calls for protection orders to fall under "full faith and credit" protections between states, meaning that a protection order issued in one state must be recognized in all other states. One of the provisions of the act requires that when a protection order is issued, the offender must surrender to law enforcement all firearms. Judges have been reluctant to take the firearms of locals, especially if they are located in areas of the country that hunt game as sport.[12]

The changes brought about by the Minneapolis experiment have had some impact on the acquisition of "victim status," especially for women. It has brought the plight of women in violent home situations to the forefront, but has not totally changed the patriarchal thinking of all of the actors in the criminal justice system. In this case, both advocates and political mechanisms have not had the fuller impact as was noted in the case of rape. In the theoretical model presented here, the implication of women being perceived as "less" than totally innocent may be affecting the outcome.

In summary, our theoretical model can explain differential reaction to crimes committed against women over time as well as explain the differential perception of women toward themselves when a victim of domestic violence. In this case, the cultural beliefs and values that guide society have not responded as openly to victims of domestic violence that were seen with victims of rape. The reasons for that differential response can be found in either the difference in the level of perceived harm or the differential cultural beliefs and values toward the victim's background, i.e., the race, age, marital status, and sexual orientation of the victim, as well as the victim's behavior.

CONCLUSION

The examples above provide, at a minimum, anecdotal and preliminary evidence that supports our theoretical position that "victim status" for women in cases of rape and domestic violence is a social construction. The model provides for different types of responses to harm—be it physical or emotional harm. The examples also indicate differing levels of reaction to physical harm. In this case, the reaction to physical harm for the crime of rape is more significant than the response to harm created by the crime of domestic violence.[13]

The social reaction to harm is shaped and formed by two sets of variables. First, political entities, mass media outlets, and advocates for victims play a role in whether a society will provide the desired "victim status." Each of these social entities may well work in all cases and may sometimes compliment each other in raising awareness of the harm created by these crimes. Second, the beliefs and values (cultural ideologies) of a society also affect the social reaction to harm. Both examples noted above point to the lingering effects of a patriarchal society in the historical views of women as victims. Through the work of political groups, mass media, and advocates, the level of social reaction can rise to the extent that those cultural ideologies are changed over time. Cultural lag accounts for the time between the passage of laws and the acceptance of and change in the ideological beliefs. In other words, there can be substantial time before change is truly reified into the socialization process of men and women.

Finally, if granted, victim status varies by how they are viewed with respect to where the victim falls along the continuum of totally innocent to victim precipitated. If the victim is seen as totally innocent, society will be more amenable to grant entitlements than if the victim is seen as somehow instigating the incident. Victim entitlement can vary by the type and severity of the crime. For example, state statutes have been created to keep the past sexual activity of the victim out of rape cases providing for more rights to rape victims (remembering the loopholes in the laws), yet the entitlements for victims of domestic violence appear to be much less. One of the major reasons for differing entitlements is that domestic violence is most likely defined as a misdemeanor, rather than as a felony, as is the case for most rape cases.

The true test of any theory is the empirical testing. The social construction of victim status provides abstract concepts (harm, social reaction, victim status, and victim entitlements) that can be empirically tested. For example, it is possible to measure differing levels of physical harm and while more difficult, it is also possible to measure emotional harm. The degree and extent of desire to achieve victim status by those confronted with a victimizing experience in their lives can be measured. Social reaction can be empirically measured through several methods, such as the amount of legislation enacted (as in the rape shield laws and marital rape laws) or the number of newspaper articles reporting incidents of reaction to the plight of others.

Whether individuals receive victim status is empirical in the sense that victims have received recognition in formal means through actions of social institutions.[14] Victim status also varies on the continuum of totally innocent to victim participation in the incident causing the harm. Finally, victim entitlements can be extensive and more protective, or lesser protective depending on the type of victim status conferred, as mentioned above. Future research should address whether gaining victim status has any unanticipated (either positive or negative) impacts on the victim. Questions such as "Does providing victim status to domestic violence victims cause them to be re-victimized later?" must be explored empirically in order to determine the full impact of the victimization process.

As with any new paradigm, the challenge for researchers now is empirically testing the relationships found in our theoretical model beyond anecdotal and preliminary data. Rigorous measurement of the concepts and testing of the relationships is necessary to fully establish the social construction of victims through this model. As with any theoretical position, new concepts and differing types of measurements may be found during the empirical testing phase.

Both academics and practitioners can benefit from empirically testing and further development of this theoretical position. Academics will benefit from the "sense of knowing" (Reynolds, 2007) how the process of determining how society verifies and authenticates which individuals receive entitlements and which do not. For practitioners, the benefits will be in knowing how to further the entitlements to victims through the level of social reaction. As the example above indicates, some advocates (i.e., the women's movement) have the power and ability to create a strong enough social reaction to bring about change in cultural beliefs and values. In order to better deliver the entitlements, practitioners must develop a strong advocacy position in conjunction with political entities and mass media to fully develop the social construction of victims.

Discussion Questions

1. Describe the victim-blaming ideology that dominates victimology.
2. Explain the social constructionist theory and describe how it may explain victimization.
3. Describe Brewster and Holley's social construction model of victimization.
4. How does the social construction model of victimization explain the change in victim status of rape victims?
5. How does the social construction model of victimization explain the change in victim status of domestic violence victims? How are rape victims different from domestic violence victims?

References

Adler, P. A., & Adler, P. (Eds). (2006). *Constructions of deviance* (5th ed.). Belmont, CA: Thomson/Wadsworth.

Barkan, S. E. (2006). *Criminology: A sociological understanding.* Upper Saddle River, NJ: Pearson-Prentice Hall.

Best, J. (Ed.). (1995). *Images of issues: Typifying contemporary social problems.* New York: Aldine de Gruyter.

Burt, M. (1983). A conceptual framework for victimological research. *Victimology, 8*, 261–268.

Buzawa, E. S., & Buzawa, C. G. (2003). *Domestic violence: The criminal justice response.* Thousand Oaks, CA: Sage Publications.

Chesney-Lind, M., & Shelden, R. G. (2004). *Girls, delinquency, and juvenile justice* (3rd ed.). Belmont, CA: Wadsworth Publishing.

Cohen, S. (2002). *Folk devils and moral panics* (3rd ed.). New York: Routledge Publishing.

Cooley, C. H. (1926). The roots of social knowledge. *American Journal of Sociology, 32*, 59–79.

Doerner, W. G., & Lab, S. P. (1995). *Victimology.* Cincinnati, OH: Anderson Publishing Company.

Eigenberg, H. M. (2003). Victim blaming. In L. J. Moriarty (Ed.), *Controversies in victimology* (pp. 15–24). Cincinnati, OH: Anderson.

Grant, P. H., & Otto, P. I. (2003). The mass media and victims of rape. In L. J. Moriarty (Ed.), *Controversies in victimology* (pp. 43–56). Cincinnati, OH: Anderson Publishing Co.

Heiner, R. (2006). *Social problems* (2nd ed.). New York: Oxford.

Holley, P. D., & Brewster, D. (2006). *The search for victim status: Positive and negative factors.* Paper presented at the Annual Meetings of the American Society of Criminology, Los Angeles, CA.

Karmen, A. (2007). *Crime victims: An introduction to victimology* (6th ed.). Belmont, CA: Wadsworth Publishing.

Kitzinger, C. (1987). *The social construction of lesbianism.* Beverly Hills, CA: Sage.

Kraska, P. B. (2004). *Theorizing criminal justice.* Long Grove, IL: Waveland Press.

Lamb, S. (Ed.). (1999). *New versions of victims.* New York: New York University Press.

McCorkle, R. C., & Miethe, T. D. (2002). *Panic: The social construction of the street gang problem.* Upper Saddle River, NJ: Prentice-Hall.

Mead, G. H. (1918). The psychology of punitive justice. *American Journal of Sociology, 23,* 577–602.

Mendelsohn, B. (1976). Victimology and contemporary society's trends. *Victimology, 1,* 8–28.

Potter, G. W., & Kappeler, V. E. (1998). *Constructing crime.* Prospect Heights, IL: Waveland Press.

Reynolds, P. D. (2007). *A primer in theory construction.* Boston, MA: Allyn and Bacon Publishing.

Rock, P. (2002). On becoming a victim. In C. Hoyle & R. Young (Eds.), *New visions of crime victims* (pp. 1–22). Portland, OR: Hart Publishing.

Scott, W. J. (1993). *The politics of readjustment: Vietnam veterans since the war.* New York: Aldine De Gruyter Publishing.

Sgarzi, J. M., & McDevitt, J. (Eds). (2003). *Victimology: A study of crime victims.* Upper Saddle River, NJ: Prentice Hall Publishing.

Sherman, L. W., & Berk, R. A. (1984a). *The Minneapolis domestic violence experiment.* Police Foundation Reports, 1.

Sherman, L. W., & Berk, R. A. (1984b). The specific deterrent effects of arrest for domestic assault. *American Sociological Review, 49,* 261–272.

Spalek, B. (2006). *Crime victims.* New York: Palgrave MacMillan.

Spector, M., & Kitsuse, J. L. (1977). *Constructing social problems.* New York: de Gruyter.

Wallace, H. (1998). *Victimology.* Boston, MA: Allyn and Bacon.

Weis, K., & Weis, S. (1973). Victimology and the justification of rape. In I. Drapkin & E. Viano (Eds.), *Victimology: A new focus* (pp. 3–27). Lexington, MA: Lexington Books.

Wolfgang, M. E. (1958). *Patterns in criminal homicide.* Philadelphia, PA: University of Pennsylvania Press.

Endnotes

1. Actually, we are calling for a theory of "General Victimology," which would include all victims whether that victimization occurs from criminal or noncriminal activity. This chapter includes a condensed version from that larger theoretical position—that of explaining women's victimization.

2. We do not argue that every victim is entitled to the same type of restoration. For example, some victims may receive compensation from compensation funds, while others may receive property that was taken from them. We also recognize that for women, entitlement may never be able to provide a return to the former self. Victims of rape or domestic violence, for example, are more than likely changed forever in terms of psychological and physical damage that is impossible to return to a pre-victimization status.

3. We are not suggesting that the political setting is necessarily first in recognizing that harm has befallen an individual—it may well be that the mass media or social advocates are the first to notice the harm, only that in order for official recognition to be fully implemented, there must be some legitimate authority (political) recognition.

4. It is not our contention here to vouch for the accuracy of the media presentations presented to the public. Research on the accuracy of media depictions has been discussed elsewhere beginning with Cohen (2002) and continue to the present.

5. Entitlements may take many forms. In our call for a general victimology, those entitlements might take the form of low-interest loans to rebuild a home after a hurricane or tornado, or the form of cash payments for

disaster relief following a drought or flood for farmers.

6. Prior to the 1970s, many states did not prosecute men accused of raping their wives.

7. It would be much better, in a patriarchal society, for a girl to be viewed as a "tomboy," than for a male to be seen as a "sissy."

8. The authors do acknowledge that rape shield laws do have loopholes that have allowed women's sexual history into evidence in certain situations.

9. Alabama had a state statute on the record until recently that said men were allowed to beat their wives as long as the stick was not larger than their thumb. Similar laws can be found in a number of states.

10. In a personal interview with a judge in Alabama, one of the researchers was told, "If I had to put up with her, I might have to knock her down too."

11. We do not deny that the original claims-making of the women's movement created advocacy for women in the instance of domestic violence. We are interested here in knowing how the political organization (in this case the criminal justice system) played a role in changing cultural ideologies.

12. It should be noted that the reluctance to make the offender comply with the firearms portion of the statute places a judge in a position of liability if the offender would use a firearm against a victim in the future. Also, if judges fail to fully comply with the provisions in the federal statute, states could lose all federal monies.

13. We fully understand that physical violence is involved in domestic violence, but are referencing the legal distinction in the two crimes.

14. Again, in our larger work, recognition of victim status can be conferred by government agencies such as the Federal Emergency Management Agency.

CHAPTER 4

THE MEASUREMENT, DEFINITION, AND REPORTING OF FEMALE VICTIMIZATION

∾

JANICE E. CLIFFORD AND
JOHN P. JARVIS

ABSTRACT

This chapter discusses various existing measures that identify, define, and report on differing aspects of crime and victimization in the United States. In particular, it focuses on the measures that convey information about the nature and extent of violence against women in various contexts. These include source data provided by law enforcement contained in official reports and the self-reported experiences of individuals through victim accounts. While each of these approaches assists in informing about criminal activity and victimization, it is suggested that multiple measures be examined simultaneously to engage in a more comprehensive understanding.

INTRODUCTION

Addressing violence in American society has yielded the use of a multi-disciplinary approach. As such, violence perpetrated against women, in particular, has become a central focus of prevention and intervention strategies by professionals in the fields of public health, social work and law enforcement. Likewise, strategies aimed at eradicating such incidents have been implemented at the both the community and legislative levels. However, all of these efforts have been met with limited success given the difficulty of identifying the extent to which criminal incidents involving female victims occur. This is due in part to the variation in definitions of behaviors and the circumstances that comprise incidents of violence against women.

Crime, it could be argued, is one of the most serious social problems in America. There is continued concern about crime and risks of victimization even though various indicators yield that in 2005 both violent and property crime rates, comparatively, were at the lowest levels since 1994 (Bureau of Justice Statistics, 2006). Similarly, the Federal Bureau of Investigation (FBI) (2006) reported that over a 10-year period 1996–2005 violent crime decreased by 17.6 percent and property crime decreased by 13.9 percent. However, even given what appears to be a positive trend, such concern is not new. Instead, it is reflective of the continuing focus American society has on health and safety issues. In particular, crime has been a focus of inquiry by various entities in society to include the criminal justice system, medical community, and social service agencies as they relate to offending and injuries that may result from victimization. Thus, there are various sources that can be examined to inform us about the differing aspects of crime that pertain to the offender, victim, the offense, and other circumstances of these incidents.

DEFINITIONAL ISSUES

In order to more comprehensively identify the nature and extent of violence against women, two definitional issues at the outset must be addressed. The first question is that of "what constitutes violence against women?" In response, consider the various agencies or institutions that victims of these crimes may turn to for assistance. Each defines these incidents differently based upon the nature of the cases that come to their attention. For example, while the police are certainly one avenue for information, medical institutions and social service organizations often see differing kinds of cases than the criminal justice system and the resulting numbers reported by these entities differ. Complicating this issue is societal change that may impact the character of the cases as well as their frequency. That is, given the complex nature of interactions between individuals which exist in contemporary society, categorizing these modern relationships often elude clear definitional categories. As such, the relationship categories used in crime and survey data most often are family, acquaintance, stranger, and unknown (see FBI, 1992, 2004). Individuals initially seeming to be strangers, in certain situations, may in fact be acquaintances rather than truly complete strangers. That is they may not be absolute strangers, but they may be relative strangers (e.g., the retail store clerk, the public transportation passengers or the box office attendant).

Second, is the issue of "how to measure and identify violence?" The identification and reporting of violent behavior is an obstacle to adequate measurement as many agencies vary in their operational classification of behavior of criminal acts. For example, law enforcement, medical professionals, and social service personnel may each define such behavior differently. While some injurious behavior is clearly beyond interpretative differences, in some cases similar actions may not result in the same designations of violence. Typically, this is a result of either the nature and circumstances of the case or the ability of the particular agency personnel to be able to definitively ascertain that such behavior has taken place. For example, psychological and emotional injuries may be considered a form of violence by some but may not be by others. As such, some behaviors may not be reported to legal authorities or others who may be able to assist in the case. It is important to note that these identification and reporting challenges are not restricted to incidents of violence against women. Whenever measurement and identification of socially defined behaviors are sought, such definitional and reporting ambiguities often emerge.

MEASURES OF CRIME AND VICTIMIZATION

In the past, definitional and methodological issues have been perhaps of less concern than simply being able to obtain reliable estimates of victimizations. Such information has historically been gleaned from victim accounts, national or local reporting of prolific criminal cases, or from other anecdotal information. In fact, such sources of information continue to influence the public perceptions of what constitutes violence against women. However, more recent efforts to obtain systematic and objective information on female victimization is available. Since the early 1990s, pursuant to an Act of Congress (the Violence Against Women Act), several sources of data have emerged. These include, but are not limited to, the Uniform Crime Reports (UCR), the National Crime Victimization Survey (NCVS), and other large and small scale surveys. With this expanded information, efforts to control and understand domestic violence have also extended to violence against women in general-not just those instances involving domestic relationships.

While there are new and improved sources for garnering information pertaining to violence against women, contentions remain as to apparent contradictions and inconsistencies that these data sources seem to reveal (Bachman, 2000). However, many of these reporting disparities are likely more of a technical than substantive nature depending upon how the data are used and for what purposes (Schwartz, 2000). As such, varying definitional debates, at least partially, explain variances in the data that often inform policy and practice discusssions regarding the incidence and prevalence of violence against women (for a similar debate pertaining to crime reporting in general, see FBI 2004, pp. 502-504).

OFFICIAL REPORTS

Uniform Crime Report

Historically, what most research has typically focused with respect to crime was either the offender or to a lesser degree the criminal act. To this end, it was not until the late 1920s with the development of the UCR, through the initiative by the International Association of Police Chiefs, that steps were taken to systematically compile information about criminal activity occurring in the United States. Beginning in 1930, the FBI took the responsibility for collecting, analyzing, and disseminating information on criminal incidents nationwide.

Currently, these data reflect the reporting of approximately 18,000 law enforcement agencies (city, university and college, county, state, tribal, and federal law enforcement agencies) across the country. Structurally, the UCR has been divided into two parts. The first part contains Part I offenses, or index offenses, which are considered to be the most serious crimes among violent and property offenses. The violent crimes include the offenses of murder and nonnegligent manslaughter, forcible rape, robbery, and aggravated assault. Data from the 2005 UCR show 1,390,695 of these violent crimes were reported to law enforcement during that year. Similarly, 10,166,159 property crimes (including burglary, larceny-theft, motor vehicle theft) were reported to law enforcement in 2005 as well (FBI, 2006). The second part of the UCR contains information on nonindex offenses (known as Part II offenses), which contain comparatively less serious violent and property crimes, public order offenses, and status offenses.

While this source provides information on some offender traits (i.e., age, sex, race) and some circumstances (i.e., weapon use, location of incident) for selected offenses, no information, however, is available about the victim, with the exception of homicide. More detailed reporting on the dynamics of lethally violent events are contained in the Supplementary Homicide Report (SHR) section of the UCR. These data not only report victim and offender demographics but also describe the circumstance, victim–offender relationship, and weapon use for each homicide incident.

For example in 2005, there were 14,860 homicides. Of the known victim–offender relationships, homicides committed were 11.9 percent by a family member of the victim, 30.4 percent by someone known to the victim, and 13.9 percent by a stranger. Less than one-quarter (21.2%) of homicide victims were female, of which over three-fourths (86.7%) were over age 18. In particular, females between the ages of 18 and 24 had the highest homicide rates per 100,000 in the same age-based population (Fox & Zawitz, 2008). Homicide of females is most commonly perpetrated by males (90.8%), as a small proportion of the women were killed by another female (9.2%). The majority of female victims were White comprising 61.1 percent, 33.2 percent were Black, and 5.7 percent were members of other races. Thus, Black women were overrepresented as homicide victims given they constituted 13 percent of the female population in that year (U.S. Census Bureau, 2008).

While female victims of homicide are proportionately less common than male victims, regardless of the sex of the perpetrator, it is worthy to note that in incidents where a person is killed by an intimate partner, defined as spouse, ex-spouse, boyfriend, or girlfriend, data from 2005 indicate that over three-quarters (78.2%) were female victims (Fox & Zawitz, 2008). This very much could be related to that fact that females were most commonly killed in a situation involving some type of an argument (32.4%) compared with other type of situations involving drugs, brawl, romantic triangle, gang activity, or commission of any felony (FBI, 2006).

While the SHR can more readily inform us about incidents resulting in death, it unfortunately provides little, if any, details relating to other types of assaultive behaviors which do not have nonlethal outcomes such as rape and assault (Kilpatrick, 2004).

National Incident-Based Reporting System

In an effort to respond to the need for a more detailed examination of criminal incidents, a revision of the UCR Program was sought in the mid-1980s. The motivation was to establish a law enforcement data collection system that afforded more detailed examination of crime and law enforcement responses to criminal incidents. A by-product of this effort also would create a more comprehensive law enforcement reporting mechanism for examining violence against women.

The National Incident-Based Reporting System (NIBRS), originally devised as a revision to the UCR system, is a complete redesign of the original summary reporting that was characteristic of UCR data. This revised system, ultimately to be employed by all police departments in the nation, includes data on up to 53 different aspects of a criminal incident that comes to the attention of law enforcement (e.g., relationship between victim to offender, involvement of weapons, victim injury, etc.) and accounts for up to 46 different offenses that may take place in a criminal incident (see NIBRS Handbook FBI, 1992). Of particular merit is that this data is incident-based. That is, all offenses and associated data for both the offenses and the other incident characteristics are reported in NIBRS. As such, all crimes against persons (including, but not limited to, homicide, rape, aggravated assault, and robbery) that are reported in NIBRS contain additional information relating to the nature and circumstances surrounding that criminal incident. For example, the location, the number of individuals involved in the incident, the extent of injuries sustained, and the presence of substance abuse are available data elements in NIBRS. Unfortunately, while this additional detailed information is not only important but essential, there are computational complications associated with using this data source (see Akiyama and Nolan, 1992). However, many of these can and have been overcome with the use of more advanced computing technologies that are now available. As such, several efforts to utilize this data to support studies of domestic violence have emerged. For example, Thompson, Saltzman, and Bibel (1999) examined data from Massachusetts to determine that as many as 10 percent of women victims have experienced more than one offense in the incident. They also found that intimate partners were more likely to commit simple assault, intimidation, and aggravated assault than non-partners (Thompson et al., 1999).

Additionally, the FBI issued a special report on family violence (FBI, 1999) using 1998 NIBRS data which showed 1.6 million criminal incidents reported. Of these, victims of violent offenses were 112,042 instances (FBI, 1999). As such, according to this study, about 27 percent of all violence was determined to be family related and 58 percent involved female victims. Up to 43 percent of victims of violence have been found to be family related in more recent analyses of FBI data (FBI, 2004).

Studies like those noted above provide further insights into the changing dynamics of violence against women. Curbing what seems like a constant occurence of incidents of this nature depend upon the development of policies and practices that are responsive to the patterns that these studies reveal. For example, neighborhood level efforts to educate the community about potential risks and prevent further victimizations of women may be informed by analyses of the time, location, and daily occurrences of criminal incidents that involve various types of violence against women.

The promise of incident-based analyses, such as NIBRS is substantial. However, NIBRS data, like many data sources relevant to understanding crime and violence, does not adequately capture all the information that is necessary for responding to the challenges of violence against women. For example, NIBRS data currently provides no mechanism for analyzing repeat offenders or repeat victimizations which are thought to be common occurrences in abusive intimate partner relationships. Additionally, the data elements currently available in the NIBRS data do not support identification of some important aspects of both violence and violence against women. For instance, workplace designations are not available, location codes are often too general, injury codes lack specificity, and substance abuse data is somewhat limited. Consequently, victimizations involving these circumstances are difficult to examine and may be obscured or unavailable in NIBRS.

Finally, as with other data collection efforts, if victimizations are not reported to the police then these events will not be accounted for in a data set that reflects those events that come to the attention of the police. As such, variations from law enforcement data may be observed when comparing comparable data from other sources (medical, health, social services, etc). Such variation may also be made more complex when considering that NIBRS is not completely national in its scope. That is, NIBRS data currently reflects reports from just 25 states covering 20 percent of the U. S. population (FBI, 2004). Much of this data is reported form small-to medium-sized rural jurisdictions. Therefore, the NIBRS-based picture of violence against women may be more likely a reflection of the reporting jurisdictions than of a picture of overall violence against women since many urban jurisdictions are not yet reporting their victimizations in NIBRS format to the FBI.

While this contention is not negligible, recent increases in law enforcement participation in NIBRS and the current emphasis on enhancement of crime-reporting content and frequency in support of initiatives to combat terrorism hold promise for the future. In fact, not just NIBRS reporting, but other crime and disorder data collection efforts may also benefit from the current emphasis in law enforcement to develop intelligence-based capabilities. As such, information systems that may develop to deter crime and terrorism may prove beneficial to examinations of the dynamics of violence against women as well as other domestic crime problems.

If these developments provide an opportunity for more analysis and better efforts to formulate effective strategies for confronting not only violence against women but also a number of other crime problems, then all will benefit regardless of the impetus. Nonetheless, the difficulties of obtaining systematic quality data reflecting the incidence of violence against women are not limited to the issues noted above either. In fact, any expectation that a single large-scale national reporting system would provide all the advocates and authorities may need or desire is quite unrealistic. This said, it can be contend that NIBRS, more than all other law enforcement data, has shown significant progress toward a more comprehensive and detailed source for data pertaining to violence against women.

VICTIM ACCOUNTS

As official reports are informative, it is important to reflect on the fact that these accounts only represent the crimes known to law enforcement, thus leading to the existence of "dark figures" that which are not reported to any authority (i.e., police, medical or social services personnel). Therefore, it is necessary to examine other sources of data to more fully comprehend the nature and extent of crime and female victimization in the United States. One source that can potentially inform us about the unknown, or unreported, incidents is the NCVS, which is compiled through joint efforts of the Bureau of Justice Statistics (BJS) and the U.S. Census Bureau.

National Crime Victimization Survey

Since its inception in 1973, data have been collected nationwide annually, and the NCVS currently includes approximately 77,000 households comprised of nearly 134,000 persons. The NCVS examines the frequency of victimization, victim and offender characteristics, victim–offender relationship, offense characteristics (time, location, weapon use), consequences (injury, financial loss, time lost from work), and reporting of criminal victimization in the United States. Based on interview reports with persons aged 12 and older who have been victims of crime, estimates are made as to the likelihood of victimization for segments of the population for completed and attempted violent crimes (rape, robbery, sexual assault, and assault), personal thefts (purse snatching, pick pocketing), and property crimes (theft, motor vehicle thefts, and household burglary).

For 2005, the most recent year for which comprehensive data are available, the NCVS reported that there were 5,173,720 violent crime and 18,039,930 property crime victimizations. Compared with UCR figures for the same year, the extent of criminal behavior was far greater than what is reflected in law enforcement reports.

This may be attributed to the fact that victims reported less than half (47.4%) of violent crimes and even fewer property crimes (39.6%) and personal thefts (35.2%) to the police (Bureau of Justice Statistics, 2006). However, reporting of crimes has actually increased between 1993 and 2005 (Catalano, 2006).

Correspondingly, there were differences in reporting by gender. Female victims were more likely to report violent crime incidents to the police than were males. Interestingly, females were more likely to report victimizations to the police when the perpetrator of the violence were strangers, even though they were victimized in higher proportions for all violent offenses by someone that they knew. Of the known perpetrators, acquaintances constituted the largest proportion of offenders against females for all violent crime, compared with intimates (spouses and ex-spouses) and other relatives. Comparatively, males were victims of violent crime in higher proportions by strangers, but more likely to report if the perpetrator was a nonstranger.

Likewise, difference in reporting of violent crime to the police occurs by age with the youngest cohort of those between 12 and 19 years of age reporting the smallest percentage of crime against them (34.5%) and person aged 65 and older reporting the largest proportion (68.2%). However, 12–19 year-olds reported a greater number of incidents of rape/sexual assault to the police than any other age group (Bureau of Justice Statistics, 2006).

The reluctance of individuals to report the incident to the police has been associated with feelings that the victimization is a private or personal matter, the offender was unsuccessful in completion of the crime, or that they reported the incident to an official other than law enforcement personnel. Most commonly, individuals reported their victimization to the police in proactive efforts to either stop or prevent the incident or to prevent further crimes by the offender against themselves (Bureau of Justice Statistics, 2006). The degree to which crime occurs in the United States can be uncovered somewhat more extensively by examining victim accounts. However, it is noted that these statistics similar to other official reports are again only reflective of what victims are willing to disclose within the context of interactions with police or NCVS data collection efforts. While some incidents of violence against women may and do come to the attention of other authorities or community assistance centers, the official reports of the NCVS and UCR (and most police data relating to criminal behavior) do not give any specific indication of the noncriminal behaviors that may occur (i.e., forms of verbal or psychological abuse).

NATIONAL VIOLENCE AGAINST WOMEN SURVEY

Other efforts such as the National Violence Against Women Survey (NVAWS), likewise, inform us about the experiences of men and women in various types of victimization. This nationwide data collection was conducted in 1995–96 by the Center for Policy Research in order to measure the extent of violence against women. Jointly sponsored by National Institute of Justice (NIJ) and the Centers for Disease Control and Prevention (CDC), 8,000 women and 8,000 men aged 18 and older were interviewed by phone about their rape, stalking, and intimate partner violence victimization experiences. Based on the reported number of incidents by participants in the study, in conjunction with population statistics for the same time period, estimates were calculated as to the extent victimization occurred nationwide for both annual and lifetime prevalence for men and women aged 18 and older. However, these findings may underestimate the actual number of victimizations as juveniles, homeless persons, and those persons living in institutional settings and persons without a telephone are excluded.

Although rape and intimate partner violence are "supposedly" gender-neutral crimes, the majority of victims were found to be women. Accordingly, 17.6 percent of women and 3 percent of men had ever been a victim of rape (Tjaden & Thoennes, 2006), while 51.9 percent of women and 66.4 percent of men have ever experienced a physical assault (Tjaden & Thoennes, 1998).

Offending patterns indicate that the majority of perpetrators of both rape and intimate partner violence were male. This in particular was true in instances of male rape, where males also were most commonly the perpetrators. In crimes such as rape, females typically knew their offenders and were victimized in highest proportions by a current or former intimate partner (spouse, cohabiting partner, dates, boyfriend, girlfriend); males were much more likely to be victimized by either an acquaintance or a stranger. However, women compared with men are much more likely to be a victim of rape at the hands of all type of offenders (intimate, acquaintance, relative other than spouse, stranger).

Similar to recent NCVS information (Bureau of Justice Statistics, 2006), the NVAWS data also reflect women underreporting crimes to the police, as one in five females informed authorities about their being raped in adulthood (Tjaden & Thoennes, 2006). Additionally, women were more likely to report the incident if the perpetrator was a nonintimate. Failure to report the incident primarily was based on fear of retaliation by the perpetrator, feeling of embarrassment, feeling that rape was a minor incident or one should not view the episode as a police matter (Tjaden & Thoennes, 1998, 2000, 2006).

Some findings from the NVAWS report are also congruent with previous research with respect to onset of sexual victimization. For instance, the National Women's Study (NWS) conducted in 1990 (National Victim Center & Crime Victims Research Center, 1992) reported that 61 percent of women were raped before their 18th birthday; data from the NVAWS substantiate that rape tends to occur at an early age, but disproportionately by gender as over half (54%) of women and almost three-quarters (71%) of males experienced rape before turning eighteen.

CONCLUSION

While law enforcement data portray some aspects of violence against women, self-report studies sometimes show complementary information but more often give us insight into why such incidents are not brought to the attention of police. Locality-based studies, on the other hand, provide for insights into the local context in which women become victims of violence. These different sources of information provide a wealth of information regarding the measurement, definition, and reporting of incidents of violence against women. Such national efforts to determine the nature and scope of violence against women are not the only sources of data. In fact, some even argue that the definitional, methodological, and aggregation issues in national level data perhaps obscure the contextual aspects and local environment in which violence against women occurs. It should be noted that this same perspective is also held about crime data generally. In short, all crime is local.

To this end, locality-based studies of violence against women have also emerged. One such study is the Chicago Women's Health Risk Study (CWHRS). One particular strength of this approach is the ability to customize the data collection to explore aspects of violence against women that are not included in the national data collection. In the CWHRS, for example, interviews of individuals that may have knowledge of the daily lives of the disputants in these victimizations are conducted. That is, friends, neighbors, or others in the social circle of the victim are polled for data. The resulting information provides a context to better interpret and understand the varying perspectives that the data may reflect. As such, localized studies also hold some promise in contrast to the large-scale national data collection efforts embodied by the UCR and the NCVS. Nonetheless, no single source of data is likely to answer all of the questions that arise when it comes to the victimization of women. Perhaps the most fruitful course for improving our knowledge of violence against women is not to debate which data source is better or which one provides the most insight. Efforts may be better focused on pursuing a more productive course for extending our knowledge and understanding of the causes and correlates of violence against women. That is, to employ multi-agency, multi-method, and multi-trait means for gathering data and information to inform strategies for preventing violence against women (Gelles, 2000, p. 802).

Discussion Questions

1. What is the utility of examining multiple measures to inform us about crime and victimization?
2. What conclusions can be drawn from comparing the data from various sources about the nature and extent of violence perpetrated against women?
3. What factors should be considered in future efforts to measure violence against women?
4. What are some of the limitations of law enforcement data in measuring, defining, and reporting violence against women?
5. What are some of the advantages and disadvantages of self-report data sources pertaining to violence against women?

References

Akiyama, Y., & Nolan, J. (1999). Methods for understanding and analyzing NIBRS data. *Journal of Quantitative Criminology, 15*(2), 225–238.

Bachman, R. (2000). A comparison of annual incidence rates and contextual characteristics of intimate-perpetrated violence against women from the National Crime Victimization Survey (NCVS) and the National Violence Against Women Survey (NVAWS). *Violence Against Women, 6*(8), 839–867.

Bureau of Justice Statistics. (2006). *Criminal victimization in the United States: 2005 Statistical tables from the National Criminal Victimization Survey.* Washington, D.C.: U.S. Department of Justice, Office of Justice

Programs, Bureau of Justice Statistics. NCJ 215244. Retrieved May 15, 2008, from http://www.ojp.usdoj.gov/bjs/pub/pdf/cvus05.pdf

Catalano, S. (2006). Criminal victimization, 2005. *Bureau of Justice Statistics Bulletin.* Washington, D.C.: U.S. Department of Justice, Office of Justice Programs, Bureau of Justice Statistics. Retrieved May 26, 2008, from http://www.ojp.usdoj.gov/bjs/pub/pdf/cv05.pdf

Federal Bureau of Investigation (FBI). (1992). *Uniform crime reporting handbook: NIBRS edition.* Washington, D.C.: Department of Justice, Federal Bureau of Investigation.

Federal Bureau of Investigation (FBI). (1999). *Crime in the United States, 1998.* Washington, D.C: Department of Justice, U.S. Government Printing Office.

Federal Bureau of Investigation (FBI). (2004). *Crime in the United States, 2003.* Washington, D.C.: Department of Justice, U.S. Government Printing Office.

Federal Bureau of Investigation (FBI). (2006). *Crime in the United States, 2005.* Retrieved May 16, 2008 from http://www.fbi.gov/ucr/05cius/

Fox, A., & Zawitz, M. (2008). *Homicide trends in the United States.* U.S. Department of Justice, Bureau of Justice Statistics. Retrieved May 23, 2008, from http://www.ojp.usdoj.gov/bjs/homicide/homtrnd.htm#contents

Gelles, R. J. (2000). Estimating the incidence and prevalence of violence against women: National data systems and sources. *Violence Against Women, 6*(7), 784–804.

Kilpatrick, D. G. (2004). What is violence against women? Defining and measuring the problem. *Journal of Interpersonal Violence, 19*(11), 1209–1234.

National Victim Center & Crime Victims Research Center (1992). *Rape in America: A report to the nation.* Arlington, VA: National Victim Center and Charleston, SC: Crime Victims Research Center. Retrieved May 20, 2008, from http://academicdepartments.musc.edu/ncvc/resources_prof/rape_in_america.pdf

Schwartz, M. D. (2000). Methodological issues in the use of survey data for measuring and characterizing violence against women. *Violence Against Women, 6*(8), 815–835.

Thompson, M. P., Saltzman, L. E., & Bibel, D. (1999). Applying NIBRS data to the study of intimate partner violence: Massachusetts as a case study. *Journal of Quantitative Criminology 15*(2), 163–180.

Tjaden, P., & Thoennes, N. (1998). *Prevalence, incidence and consequences of violence against women: Findings from the National Violence Against Women Survey.* Washington, D.C.: U.S. Department of Justice, Office of Justice Programs, National Institute of Justice. Retrieved May 14, 2008, from http://www.ncjrs.gov/pdffiles/172837.pdf

Tjaden, P., & Thoennes, N. (2000). *Full report of the prevalence, incidence, and consequences of violence against women: Findings from the National Violence Against Women Survey.* Washington, D.C.: U.S. Department of Justice.

Tjaden, P., & Thoennes, N. (2006). *Extent, nature, and consequences of rape victimization: Findings from the National Violence Against Women Survey.* Washington, D.C.: U.S. Dept of Justice, Office of Justice Programs, National Institute of Justice. Retrieved May 14, 2008, from http://www.ncjrs.gov/pdffiles1/nij/210346.pdf

U.S. Census Bureau. (2008). *Annual estimates of the population by sex, race, and Hispanic Origin for the United States: April 1, 2000 to July 1, 2007.* National Population Estimates. NC-EST2007-03. Retrieved May 26, 2008, from http://www.census.gov/popest/national/asrh/NC-EST2007-srh.html

☕

GENDERED CRIMES: THE CONTEXT OF FEMALE VICTIMIZATION

How is a *victim* defined? What does it mean to be a *victim*? Contextualizing victimization is important as the term *victim* is used in an array of contexts, with differing connotations. This includes natural disasters, war, accidents, health conditions, and crime. In a general sense, the Merriam-Webster Dictionary (2008) defines *victim* in several ways:

1. [A] living being sacrificed to a deity or in the performance of a religious rite,
2. one that is acted on and usually adversely affected by a force or agent [to include]: one that is (1) injured, destroyed or sacrificed, (2) subject to oppression, hardship or mistreatment, (3) tricked or duped.

Other definitions of *victim* are specific to the context of the situation as in the National Crime Victimization Survey (NCVS) that defines it as "the recipient of a criminal act, usually in relation to personal crimes, but also applicable to the household" (Bureau of Justice Statistics, 2006, p. 142). The NCVS is the measure used to report on the nature and extent of violent crime, personal theft and property crime victimizations occurring annually in the United States.

Regardless of how the term *victim* is defined, one thing that victims have in common is the experience of suffering, "loss, injury or hardship" (Karmen, 2007, p. 1) by forces beyond one's control or not of personal choice. Even when narrowing the definition of *victim*, however, there are situations, such as victimization that occurs in cyberspace, that go unaccounted for in official measures such as in the NCVS or the Uniform Crime Report (see Chapter 4 for discussion of these measures). Moreover, contextualizing victimization as "an asymmetrical interpersonal relationship that is abusive, painful, destructive, parasitical, and unfair" (Karmen, 2007, p. 1), regardless of the context, may be most informative to our identification and understanding of the experiences of individuals, and in particular females as *victims*.

It is to this end that Part II examines the types of offenses and differing contexts for crimes perpetrated against females, in particular, those involving females as a large proportion of all victims. Also, within this section, there is discussion of diverse theoretical frameworks to explain the victimization of females in these varying contexts. Further, it is conveyed that acknowledgment of "victim" status is based on the contextual and situational circumstances surrounding the criminal events and the identified characteristics of those who are recipients of the criminal act. Thus, implications exist for victimization in various areas of both personal and social life, to include victim self-identification, societal recognition of victimization, and response to the victim by the criminal justice system.

Beginning this section, Wendy C. Regoeczi and Terance D. Miethe in Chapter 5, "Leading Lethal Lives? Variations in the Structure, Context, and Criminal Justice Response to Female Homicide Victimization," orient the reader to the different types and contexts of homicide involving women as victims. They inform us about homicide incidents involving females, through examination of city-level and national homicide data. In their analysis, the authors distinguish variations in victim characteristics, offender traits, and other offense circumstances as they relate to different victim–offender relationships (i.e., stranger and known offenders). Regoeczi and Miethe argue that contextual aspects of the homicide event itself influence the view of women as victims, responses by society and those of the criminal justice system to the crime.

In Chapter 6, "The Impact of Gender, Race, and Class Discrimination on Femicide Rates," Jo-Ann Della Giustina continues with an examination of female homicide by examining the significance of race and class as factors linked to victimization. Della Giustina examines at the differing economic, social, and political positions of women in various cities in relation to femicide rates for distinctive groups of women. She frames the study within intersectionality theory, which suggests that multiple forms of inequality, i.e., race, gender, and class, should be considered simultaneously, as factors contributing to violence against women, particularly for Black women. Della Giustina raises the question about the application of this theory to explaining the circumstances surrounding female homicide. As such, she argues that the killing of women of all races manifests from many sources to include discrimination and racial oppression, and in some instances serves as a backlash against progress they have made in various societal realms.

Heather C. Melton in Chapter 7, "Rape Myths: Impacts on Victims of Rape," turns our attention to sexual violence. Just as Melton identifies the different myths about rape, she presents various theoretical explanations for why they exist and the factors contributing to their acceptance in society. Melton argues that these myths are entrenched in American culture and serve to shape victim and societal views about the crime of rape, the context of victimization, and correspondingly who is identified as a victim. Further, Melton states that the existence of rape myths has many implications for victim interaction with criminal justice personnel and for case processing at various stages in the criminal justice system process.

In Chapter 8, "Domestic Violence: Overview of Theoretical Etiology, Psychological Impact and Interventions," Sharon Boyd-Jackson brings to our awareness the nature and extent of domestic violence. In doing so, Boyd-Jackson discusses the differing behaviors perpetrated against females within the context of physical abuse, sexual abuse, and stalking. In assisting the reader to understand why such victimizations occur, Boyd-Jackson applies sociological, feminist, and psychological perspectives to explain the existence of domestic violence.

Chapter 9, "Workplace Violence: Identifying Gender Differences and Similarities," by Shannon A. Santana and Bonnie S. Fisher educates the reader about a special context for victimization. They point out that differing contexts exist surrounding the experiences of males and females as victims of workplace violence. Santana and Fisher identify these circumstances with respect to types of victimization—homicide, rape and sexual assault, robbery, stalking and domestic violence, victim–offender relationship, and the associated risk of victimization by occupation. Further, the authors convey how knowledge about these incidents can be used to inform security and violence prevention efforts and future research on victimization in this context.

The last chapter in Part II, Chapter 10, by Amanda Burgess-Proctor, Justin W. Patchin, and Sameer Hinduja, again educates the reader about a special context of victimization that occurs in cyberspace. In "Cyberbullying and Online Harassment: Reconceptualizing the Victimization of Adolescent Girls," the authors present findings from their analysis of online surveys completed by adolescent girls about various aspects of their online experiences. It concludes with a discussion of the differing types of victimization behaviors the girls have encountered and the resulting array of physical and emotional consequences that impact their school and home lives.

References

Bureau of Justice Statistics. (2006). *Criminal victimization in the United States: 2005 Statistical tables from the National Criminal Victimization Survey.* Washington, D.C.: U.S. Department of Justice, Office of Justice Programs, Bureau of Justice Statistics. Retrieved May 31, 2008, from http://www.ojp.usdoj.gov/bjs/pub/pdf/cvus05.pdf.

Karmen, A. (2007). *Crime victims: An introduction to victimology* (6th ed.). Belmont, CA: Thompson/Wadsworth.

Victim. (2008). In *Merriam-Webster Dictionary.* Retrieved May 31, 2008, from http://www.merriam-webster.com/dictionary/victim.

CHAPTER 5

LEADING LETHAL LIVES? VARIATIONS IN THE STRUCTURE, CONTEXT, AND CRIMINAL JUSTICE RESPONSE TO FEMALE HOMICIDE VICTIMIZATION

◈

WENDY C. REGOECZI AND TERANCE D. MIETHE

ABSTRACT

This chapter will discuss variations in the types and contexts of homicides involving women as victims. Differences in victim, offender, and event attributes will be examined for female victims killed by parents, intimates, friends/acquaintances, and strangers using both national (Supplementary Homicide Report) and city-level (Cleveland) homicide data. Both quantitative and qualitative approaches will be used to study these variations. The chapter will also address how social responses and criminal justice and societal images of female homicide victims are strongly influenced by the context in which women are killed.

INTRODUCTION

It is well established that when women are the victims of homicide, the most likely perpetrator is a male intimate partner (Browne & Williams, 1989; Kellermann & Mercy, 1992; Wilson, Johnson, & Daly, 1995). The number of women killed by strangers is proportionally small (Kellermann & Mercy, 1992). For both types of homicide situations involving female victims, there are various structural and contextual factors associated with them.

This chapter examines differences in victim, offender, and event attributes for female victims killed by intimates, other family members, friends/acquaintances, and strangers. After reviewing general findings from previous research, comprehensive homicide data derived from files of the Cleveland Police Department are analyzed using qualitative and quantitative methods. The results of these analyses are then discussed in terms of how the differential images of female homicide victims and the criminal justice response to them are strongly influenced by the particular social context in which women are killed.

THE CONTEXT OF FEMALE HOMICIDE VICTIMIZATION

The overwhelming majority of research on female homicide victims examines women killed by intimate partners. This body of literature reports a general decline in female victims of intimate partner homicides between the 1970s and 1990s (Rosenfeld, 1997), with a particularly large drop for African American women (Browne & Williams, 1993; Rosenfeld, 1997). However, this decline appears to be limited to married partners; unmarried women killed by their boyfriends have been increasing (Browne & Williams, 1993; Rosenfeld, 1997). Furthermore, the reduction in married women killed by their husbands is significantly smaller than the decline in married men killed by their wives (Browne & Williams, 1989, 1993; Browne, Williams, & Dutton, 1999).

Female intimate homicide victims are frequently killed with guns (Rosenfeld, 1997), and are often estranged from their partners (Campbell, 1992; Dawson & Gartner, 1998a; Gartner, Dawson, & Crawford, 1999; Johnson, 1996; Wallace, 1986; Wilson & Daly, 1993). When killed by an intimate partner, women are more likely than men to be killed outside of their homes, to be killed along with other victims, and to be "overkilled" (experience excessive violence often including multiple weapons and wounds) (Cazanave & Zahn, 1992; Crawford & Gartner, 1992; Gartner, Dawson, & Crawford, 1999; Wolfgang, 1958). It is also more likely that their killer will commit suicide (Dawson & Gartner, 1998b).

In his seminal book on homicide, Wolfgang (1958, p. 252) defined a victim-precipitated homicide as follows:

> The term victim-precipitated homicide is applied to those criminal homicides in which the victim is a direct, positive precipitator in the crime. The role of the victim is characterized by his having been the first in the homicide drama to use physical violence directed against his subsequent slayer. The victim-precipitated cases are those in which the victim was the first to show and use a deadly weapon, to strike a blow in the altercation—in short, the first to commence the interplay of resort to physical violence.

While victim precipitation is a major element in most dispute-related homicide situations, the killing of women by intimate partners is typically not precipitated by the victim's physical violence (Rosenfeld, 1997). However, a history of domestic violence against the female victim leading up to her death is common in these homicide situations (Browne, 1987).

When women are killed by nonintimate partners, their homicides occur in a wide array of situational contexts. For example, the victims of sexual homicide (i.e., homicides that occur within the context of sexual assaults) are disproportionately female and the offenders in these homicides are often strangers (see Hickey, 2002; Ressler, Burgess, & Douglas, 1988). Based on national homicide data (i.e., the FBI's Uniform Crime Reporting Program's Supplemental Homicide Reports [SHR]), sexual assault and rape are the criminal circumstances in far less than 1 percent of homicides known to the police (FBI, 2004).

Another circumstance for female homicide victimization by nonintimate partners involves situations of personal or institutional robbery. In these deadly situations, the female victim is a customer or employee in a commercial business establishment or the unsuspecting target of a lethal street mugging. SHR data for 2004 indicate that robbery is the lethal circumstance in about 11 percent of homicides with a known motive. Approximately 5 percent of female homicide victims are killed within robbery situations.

The remaining situational contexts for female homicide victimization by nonintimate partners are wide and varied. For example, women who participate in deviant or criminal lifestyles (e.g., prostitution, drug abuse) are often victimized by acquaintances and strangers within this context. However, these situational contexts represent only about 3 percent of the homicides involving female victims (FBI, 2004). Lethal abuse of female children by parents or other caregivers, juvenile gang killings, sniper shootings, and situations of workplace homicides by disgruntled employers are other contexts for female victimization by nonintimate partners.

THE CURRENT RESEARCH STUDY

The current study involves both quantitative and qualitative analyses of the situational context of female homicide victimization. Detailed incident reports derived from the Homicide Unit of the Cleveland Police Department are the primary data used in the current study.[1] The Cleveland homicide data file was coded, compiled, and constructed by the first author. The particular characteristics of these city-level data are summarized below.

The Cleveland homicide data involve detailed information that was coded from each homicide file between 1998 and 2002 ($N = 414$), including many victim, offender, and event characteristics not present in publicly available homicide data sets such as the SHR. A narrative for each homicide was constructed describing the events leading up to the homicide, including any verbal exchanges between the victim and offender (if known). This data collection effort took 16 months to complete.

The data set included 13 police justifiable homicides that were eliminated for the purposes of these analyses. In addition, there were 16 cases where the actual offense occurred prior to 1998 even though the death occurred between 1998 and 2002. These cases were also dropped, resulting in a final data set of 385 victims. Of these cases, about one-quarter (25.2%) of the victims was female, which is similar to the national average.[2]

The method of qualitative comparative analysis (QCA) was used to identify the common combination of offender, victim, and situational aspects that underlie different types of female homicide victimization. An interpretive analysis was also conducted on the homicide narratives to explore common themes and patterns in the dynamics of these homicide situations. We have previously used these analytic approaches to explore the structure and process underlying homicides reported in the SHR (see Miethe & Regoeczi, 2004).

RESEARCH FINDINGS

Several types of comparative analyses were conducted to explore the nature and characteristics of female homicide victimization. These results are summarized below.

FEMALE VERSUS MALE VICTIMS OF HOMICIDES

An interesting question to start with is whether and how female victims differ from male victims of homicide. Table 5.1 compares male and female victims on a number of victim, offender, and event characteristics.

TABLE 5.1   Victim and Offender Characteristics of Cleveland Homicides, 1998–2002

	Female Victims, % (N)	*Male Victims, % (N)*
Victim Race/Ethnicity (N = 385)		
White victim	26.8 (26)	24.7 (71)
Black victim	70.1 (68)	70.5 (203)
Hispanic victim	3.1 (3)	4.2 (4.2)
Other race	0 (0)	0.7 (2)
Victim Age (N = 385)		
0–17 years old	20.6 (20)	9.0 (26)
18–24 years old	11.3 (11)	26.7 (77)
25–39 years old	33.0 (32)	36.8 (106)
40–59 years old	26.8 (26)	20.1 (58)
60 years and over	8.2 (8)	7.3 (21)
Victim Marital Status (N = 320)		
Single	57.5 (50)	73.0 (170)
Married (legal or common-law)	25.3 (22)	17.2 (40)
Separated	1.1 (1)	1.7 (4)
Previously married	16.1 (14)	8.2 (19)
Multiple Victims (N = 385)		
Yes	6.2 (6)	3.8 (11)
No	93.8 (91)	96.2 (277)
Victim/Offender Relationship (N = 385)		
Intimate partner	45.4 (44)	3.1 (9)
Other family	15.5 (15)	6.9 (20)
Friend/acquaintance	20.6 (20)	42.7 (123)
Stranger	8.2 (8)	22.9 (66)
Unknown	10.3 (10)	24.3 (70)
Victim Prior Criminal Record (N = 375)		
No prior criminal record	63.5 (61)	25.4 (71)
Prior record for violent offenses	12.5 (12)	40.5 (113)
Prior record for nonviolent offenses	24.0 (23)	34.1 (95)

(continued)

TABLE 5.1   *(continued)*

	Female Victims, % (N)	*Male Victims, % (N)*
Offender Race/Ethnicity (*N* = 330)		
White offender	20.7 (18)	19.3 (47)
Black offender	73.6 (64)	77.4 (188)
Hispanic offender	5.7 (5)	2.9 (7)
Other race	0 (0)	0.4 (1)
Offender Age (*N* = 297)		
0–17 years old	9.3 (8)	9.0 (19)
18–24 years old	22.1 (19)	39.8 (84)
25–39 years old	37.2 (32)	36.0 (76)
40–59 years old	27.9 (24)	13.3 (28)
60 years and over	3.5 (3)	1.9 (4)
Offender Gender (*N* = 332)		
Female	17.0 (15)	7.8 (19)
Male	83.0 (73)	92.2 (225)
Multiple Offenders (*N* = 329)		
Yes	12.6 (11)	28.1 (68)
No	87.4 (76)	71.9 (174)
Offender Prior Criminal Record (*N* = 291)		
No prior criminal record	25.6 (22)	19.0 (39)
Prior record for violent offenses	54.7 (47)	47.3 (97)
Prior record for nonviolent offenses	19.8 (17)	33.7 (69)

Examining victim characteristics first, there are few gender differences with respect to the victim's race. However, very stark differences emerged for the victim's age; almost 21 percent of female victims were under the age of 18 compared with only 9 percent for male victims. By contrast, 27 percent of male victims were between 18 and 24 years of age, compared with 11 percent of female victims. Male victims were much more likely to be single (73%) compared with female victims (58%), while female victims were more likely to be married than males. Although fewer than 5 percent of all cases involved multiple victims, homicides involving female victims were almost twice as likely to involve additional killings.

Differences across victim/offender relationship categories are striking: Almost half of all of the female victims in the data set (45%) were killed by an intimate partner compared with only 3 percent for male victims. Male victims were far more likely than female victims to be killed by a friend/acquaintance, stranger, or someone of unknown relationship. Over 40 percent of male victims had a prior criminal record that included violent offenses, whereas fewer than 13 percent of female victims had violent prior criminal histories. In fact, the majority of female victims had no prior criminal history (63%); only one-quarter of male victims had no past criminal record.

The offender characteristics in male and female homicide victimization also reveal some variation by gender. As with the victim's race, few gender differences were found in the race of the offender. With respect to offender age, a much higher percentage of male than female victims were killed by someone 18–24 years old (40% vs. 22%, respectively), whereas women were more likely to be killed by someone 40–59 years of age than were males (28% vs. 13%, respectively). Multiple offenders were over twice as prevalent in homicides involving male victims than female victims. Male victims were also more likely than female victims to be killed by an offender with a prior record of nonviolent offenses (34% vs. 20%, respectively).

Based on characteristics of the offense or incident attributes (see Table 5.2), a much higher percentage of women than men were murdered out of jealousy (16% vs. 2%) and a greater percent of cases involving male than female victims were felony-related

TABLE 5.2 Incident Characteristics and Criminal Justice Outcomes of Cleveland Homicides, 1998–2002

	Female Victims, % (N)	Male Victims, % (N)
Circumstances Surrounding Offense (N = 385)		
Felony-related	10.3 (10)	19.8 (57)
Altercation/argument/ dispute	28.9 (28)	27.8 (80)
Revenge/retaliation	8.2 (8)	11.8 (34)
Jealousy	15.5 (15)	1.7 (5)
Self-defense/defense of others	0 (0)	6.9 (20)
Other	22.7 (22)	16.3 (47)
Unknown	14.4 (14)	15.6 (45)
Victim-Precipitated Homicide (N = 303)		
Yes	6.0 (5)	25.5 (56)
No	94.0 (78)	74.5 (164)
Honor Contest (N = 276)		
Yes	4.8 (4)	21.8 (42)
No	95.2 (79)	78.2 (151)
Third Parties Present		
Yes	25.8 (23)	67.3 (169)
No	74.2 (66)	32.7 (82)
Primary Weapon (N = 385)		
Firearm	35.1 (34)	71.9 (207)
Knife/cutting instrument	17.5 (17)	8.7 (25)
Assault	12.4 (12)	9.7 (28)
Blunt instrument	11.3 (11)	3.8 (11)
Strangulation	9.3 (9)	0.7 (2)
Other	12.4 (12)	4.5 (13)
Unknown	2.1 (2)	0.7 (2)
Location of Offense (N = 382)		
Residence	62.5 (60)	24.5 (70)
Other private indoor	1.0 (1)	3.1 (9)

(*continued*)

TABLE 5.2 *(continued)*

	Female Victims, % (N)	*Male Victims, % (N)*
Private outdoor	8.3 (8)	10.8 (31)
Public indoor	1.0 (1)	6.3 (18)
Public outdoor	16.7 (16)	39.2 (112)
Vehicle	9.4 (9)	15.4 (44)
Workplace	1.0 (1)	0.7 (2)
Homicide Occurred During Daytime (N = 307)		
Yes	40.0 (26)	24.0 (58)
No	60.0 (39)	76.0 (184)
Homicide Occurred on Weekend (N = 377)		
Yes	29.8 (28)	30.4 (86)
No	70.2 (66)	69.6 (197)
Clearance Status (N = 385)		
Uncleared	14.4 (14)	27.4 (79)
Cleared by arrest	82.5 (85)	71.5 (206)
Exceptionally cleared	3.1 (3)	1.0 (3)
Most Serious Charge (N = 293)		
No charges	9.4 (8)	6.7 (14)
Aggravated murder	58.8 (50)	51.9 (108)
Murder	23.5 (20)	25.0 (52)
Voluntary or involuntary manslaughter	2.4 (2)	11.5 (24)
Other	5.9 (5)	4.8 (10)
Case Disposition (N = 284)		
Found guilty by judge or jury	27.5 (22)	27.9 (57)
Plead guilty	56.3 (45)	48.5 (99)
Found not guilty by judge or jury	2.5 (2)	8.3 (17)
Other	13.8 (11)	15.2 (31)
Minimum Prison Sentence (N = 222)	Mean = 23.2 years (std. deviation = 24.5)	Mean = 18.1 years (std. deviation = 16.9)

(20% vs. 10%).[3] Compared with the killing of women, homicides of males were more likely to be victim-precipitated by physical violence (26% vs. 6% for females), to involve honor contests (22% vs. 5%), and to occur in the presence of others not involved in the violence (67% vs. 26% for women). Male victims were far more likely than female victims to be murdered with a firearm (72% vs. 35%) and to occur in a public outdoor location (39% vs. 17%). By contrast, female victims were more likely to be killed with a knife, with a blunt instrument, or by way of strangulation than males. Over 62 percent of women were killed in a residence compared with less than a quarter of men. Women were killed during the daytime at a much higher percentage (40%) than men (24%). There were no major gender differences in whether the homicide occurred on a weekend (70% occurred on the weekend for both genders).

There are also some gender differences in the criminal justice outcomes of these homicide cases. Homicides involving female victims were more likely to be cleared by arrest (83%) or exceptionally cleared[4] (3%) than cases involving male victims (72% cleared by arrest; 1% exceptionally cleared). Female victim homicides were somewhat more likely to result in either no charges or charges of aggravated murder,[5] while male victim homicides were more likely to result in charges of voluntary or involuntary manslaughter. Killings of females were somewhat more likely to result in a guilty plea by the offender than killings of males (56% vs. 49%, respectively) while the reverse is true for not guilty findings by judges or juries (3% vs. 8%). Cases involving female victims resulted in longer average minimum prison sentences than cases involving male victims (23 years vs. 18 years). The only two cases in the data set where the defendant was given the death penalty both involved male victims.

FEMALE VICTIMS OF INTIMATE PARTNER HOMICIDES

The Cleveland homicide data set included 44 women killed by an intimate partner (spouse, ex-spouse, common-law spouse, ex-common-law spouse, boyfriend, or ex-boyfriend).[6] Almost one half of these women were killed by a boyfriend or ex-boyfriend (48%).

To examine the joint distribution of victim, offender, and incident attributes in homicide situations, the method of QCA was used to establish the most dominant situational contexts. This QCA of situations of women killed by intimate partners included the following attributes: victim age (40 and over vs. under 40 years); offender with prior arrests for domestic violence; weapon (firearm or knife); circumstances (argument or jealousy); and residential location.[7] The four profiles most commonly found account for approximately 30 percent of the female intimate partner homicide victim cases (see Box 5.1).

The most common of these situational profiles involves a woman under age 40 who was killed by a male with prior arrests for domestic violence and with a weapon other than a firearm or knife after an argument in a residential location. The following cases depict this type of profile:

- The Suspect got off of work around 7:00 P.M. on the night in question. After leaving work he stopped for some beers, reportedly drinking four 40-ounce beers. When the Suspect arrived home around 11:45 P.M. the Victim (his wife) told him she was seeing somebody else. According to the Suspect, the marriage had been on shaky grounds for 4–5 weeks. A fight ensued between the Suspect and Victim during which he strangled her. At the time of his arrest, the Suspect reportedly stated "we was just arguing, I was drunk, she said she was cheating on me and I just snapped, then I choked her." The Victim had been choked by the Suspect several weeks earlier but did not file a police report (Cleveland case: 99-39).

- On the evening leading up to her death, numerous individuals were over at the Victim's and Suspect's house drinking. The Victim became very intoxicated during the evening, at one point falling off a bar stool that broke. The Suspect was upset at that idea that everyone would come over to this house and drink

BOX 5.1

MOST COMMON PROFILES OF FEMALE HOMICIDE VICTIMIZATIONS BY INTIMATE PARTNER

N = 4	Victim less than 40 years of age	Offender with prior arrests for domestic violence	Weapon other than firearm or knife	Argument	Residential location
N = 3	Victim 40 years and over	Offender with no prior arrests for domestic violence	Weapon other than firearm or knife	Argument	Residential location
N = 3	Victim less than 40 years of age	Offender with no prior arrests for domestic violence	Firearm	Argument	Residential location
N = 3	Victim less than 40 years of age	Offender with no prior arrests for domestic violence	Knife	Argument	Residential location

and take advantage of his wife so he told them they could no longer come to his house to drink and asked everyone to leave. The Suspect then went upstairs. The Victim went storming upstairs and the Victim and Suspect had an argument about the issue. The Suspect stated he told the Victim she could leave with everyone else and the Victim became angry and stated she would leave. Then the Victim attempted to wake up her daughter and take her with her. The Suspect reports slapping the Victim with his open hand across her face and pushing her away from the children's bedroom. During this argument, the Victim got up and ran to the bathroom where she threw up. Two witnesses report during this argument that the Victim was lying on the floor, balled up, with blood on her mouth. They asked the Suspect if they could help the Victim, and Suspect told them it was none of their business and to stay out of it. One of the witnesses pointed out that the Victim's mouth was bleeding and could she get something to wipe her mouth. The Suspect replied "no, f*** her, let her lie there." The witness then asked the Suspect to call 911, but the Suspect told them no, the Victim was just faking it. At one point the Suspect threw the Victim from the bathroom doorway onto the kitchen floor by the kitchen table. The Victim got up off the floor and went into the dining room and sat in a chair. The Suspect followed her and they began to argue and cuss at other. The Suspect punched the Victim in the stomach. The Victim and Suspect then went to their bedroom where they continued arguing. Sometime later the Suspect was seen carrying the Victim out of the bedroom in his arms, claiming Victim just "fell out." They carried the Victim outside hoping fresh air would revive her. They then carried the Victim back into the bedroom, and it appeared as if the Victim was coming around. The Victim then ran out of the bedroom and into the bathroom where she threw up blood. Early the next morning the Victim began shaking like she was having a seizure. EMS was called. The Victim died as a result of blunt impact to the head, with multiple brain injuries and scattered bruises to her head, torso, and extremities. The Victim had old fractures to the ribs that were healing (the Suspect admitted to breaking the Victim's ribs the previous summer). The Suspect's previous girlfriend had made two felonious assault reports on the Suspect. The Victim also made two felonious assault reports on the Suspect but never pressed charges (Cleveland case: 99-12).

It is clear that these women were subject to prior violence before the lethal event. While an argument directly preceded their deaths, the violent nature of the men with whom they shared their lives is the more important factor influencing the direction and (shortened) length of their lives. There are many more cases in the data set that include histories of domestic violence than cases where the offender has an official arrest record for a domestic violence offense. In fact, of the 44 cases involving women killed by an intimate partner that were examined here, 36 were known to have been subject to prior violence by the perpetrator. Their attempts to protect themselves from this chronic abuse were sadly unsuccessful, as is evident in the following cases:

- According to the Suspect, this particular day he went over to the Victim's house (his wife) to "get" his brother-in-law (the Suspect had reportedly been jailed twice due to reports by the Victim's brother to the police). The Suspect crawled through the kitchen window to get into the house. Once in the house, he went into the basement and got a rubber hammer. He brought the hammer upstairs, went into another room, and sat down with the hammer thinking about hitting his brother-in-law with it. The Victim entered the house through the side door. The Suspect got up and went into the kitchen. When the Victim saw the Suspect, she started screaming. The Suspect went over to the Victim and grabbed her mouth to tell her to shut up. The Suspect was still holding the hammer and the Victim grabbed it from him. The Suspect saw a knife on the top of the microwave, which he grabbed and started stabbing her. The Victim was stabbed over 75 times (final count was 99 wounds). The Victim had taken out a temporary protection order two days prior. The Suspect had prior arrests for domestic violence, including an arrest for domestic violence six days before he killed the Victim. On that particular day, the Victim was at home with her daughter when she decided to take a nap. A short time later the Suspect had come home intoxicated and started yelling at her because she was sleeping, calling her a bitch and whore. The Victim left the house with their daughter but the Suspect followed stating that he wasn't going to allow her to leave. The Victim began walking towards the driver's side of the truck when the Suspect grabbed a 6-foot ladder that was in the bed of the truck and threw it against a fence in their front yard, stating "I'll f*** you up so bad bitch, that you'll die." He then grabbed another ladder and threw it at the Victim. He picked up a ladder and started striking it against the Victim's truck, denting the passenger door and rear fender. The Victim's brother, who had been called out by the daughter, appeared from his house next door. The Suspect stated to his brother-in-law "you want some of me?" and threw a ladder at him nearly striking him. At this time the Victim and their daughter fled on foot to a convenience store to call the police. The Victim had sent their daughter to live at a friend's house after this last altercation because she feared for her safety. After being arrested for murdering his wife, the Suspect reportedly approached another individual with whom he was incarcerated offering to pay him to murder his brother-in-law (Cleveland case: 00-29).

- The Suspect, who is the Victim's common-law husband, strangled the Victim, put her in the trunk of her car, and drove her to another location. The Suspect was reportedly jealous over the Victim and told others he thought the Victim was seeing other men. The Suspect was also jealous about the Victim making more money than him (he was reportedly envious of the Mercedes the Victim bought). The Victim was attempting to get rid of the Suspect for the last year, and finally three weeks ago she went to her brother's house with some eviction papers to get help filling them out (the Suspect was living with the Victim in a home she owned). The Suspect had told his friend he was not going anywhere and was not leaving the house. The Victim had been sleeping on the couch the past several months. The Victim had told others that she was afraid of the Suspect, and she was previously granted a restraining order against him. On one occasion, the Suspect tied up the Victim and left her bound while he left for Cincinnati with another female. Another time the Suspect broke the Victim's neck, requiring hospitalization and surgery. In 1997 the Victim was treated for lethargy. Around this time, the Victim was complaining of being tired all the time and she found a needle in her apartment and thought the Suspect might have tried to drug her. The Suspect was also arrested in 1997 for a domestic violence incident during which the Suspect starting choking the Victim and banging her head against the wall during an argument. He succeeded in pushing her head right through the wall. In February 1999, the Victim reported another assault by the Suspect. In July 2000, the Suspect pleaded guilty to domestic violence and was sentenced to two years of Community Control sanctions. The Suspect served 30 days in county jail, and was ordered to complete 200 hours of community service, receive treatment for drugs and alcohol, and again enroll in the Batterer's Program. The Suspect was also arrested in 1995 for domestic violence incident involving his now ex-wife in which he threw her to the floor, struck her head against the wall, seized her by the throat, and bent her fingers back. The Suspect pleaded no contest to this charge, was placed on probation, and was ordered to complete family violence programs. In May 1996, he violated his probation and the Court extended his probation for one year, and ordered him to enter Batterers Intervention Programs (Cleveland case: 00-54).

This last case raises the issue of the criminal justice response to the killing of women by their intimate partners. In 6 of the 44 cases, the offender committed suicide. Of the remaining 38 cases, 63 percent of the offenders were initially charged with aggravated murder and another 34 percent were charged with murder. Over three-quarters of the offenders pleaded guilty (76%). The prosecutor declined to issue papers in two cases. Approximately 16 percent were found guilty by a judge or jury. Three of the offenders received life without parole. On the other end, 6 offenders received a minimum prison term of 10 years or less for their crime. The most common minimum prison sentence was 15 years, given to over 37 percent of the offenders who were found or pleaded guilty.

FEMALE VICTIMS OF OTHER FAMILY HOMICIDES

There were 35 cases of individuals killed by other family members in Cleveland between 1998 and 2002, 15 of which were female. The majority of these cases involved either a parent killed by a child (47%) or a child killed by a parent (40%).

The following victim, offender, and incident attributes were used to develop QCA profiles of the most common situational contexts in which females are killed by other family members: victim age (6 years and under vs. 7 years and older); offender age (25 years and under vs. over 25 years); offender gender; weapon (firearm or assault); circumstances (child abuse/endangerment); and residential location.[8] Three most common profiles, displayed in Box 5.2, account for approximately 47 percent of the female victims killed by other family members.

The most common homicide situation in this context involves a young female (6 years or younger) killed by a female 25 years or younger in a residence with no one else present where the death did not result from a gunshot, beating, child abuse, or endangerment. These cases in Cleveland involved very young children killed during house fires believed to be set by their mothers seeking to claim insurance money or to commit revenge against their husbands. The following narrative illustrates such a scenario:

- The female Victims, aged two and three years, died during a fire at their home. The Cleveland Police Arson Unit ruled this fire an arson that was started by placing flame on some combustible material. That material could be, and probably was, melted candle wax. According to the Suspect (the Victims' mother), she had left a large scented candle burning in the dining room while she went to use the

---

BOX 5.2

MOST COMMON PROFILES OF FEMALE HOMICIDE VICTIMIZATIONS BY OTHER FAMILY MEMBERS

$N = 3$	Victim 6 years or younger	Offender 25 years or younger and female	Weapon other than firearm or assault	Not child abuse or endangerment	Residential location and no others present
$N = 2$	Victim 6 years or younger	Offender over 25 years and male	Assault	Child abuse or endangerment	Residential location and no others present
$N = 2$	Victim 6 years or younger	Offender over 25 years and female	Weapon other than firearm or assault	Child abuse or endangerment	Residential location and no others present

bathroom. Candles were also left unattended in the living room and on top of the dining room table. No accelerant was used. The fire originated in the dining room, which had cheap wooden paneling. That paneling caused the fire to progress very rapidly. The Arson Unit's conclusions were confirmed at trial with the testimony of an independent expert. When the Suspect first went to a neighbor's house to ask for help, she did not tell the neighbor that her kids were still in the house until after the neighbor's sister asked about the children. She then made no effort to follow the neighbor who tried to get into the burning house. The Suspect was heard to have said that she started the first fire and when she went to do the next one the first one got out of hand. It happened so quickly that she ran out of the house. It wasn't her intention to hurt her kids; "it was an insurance thing." Six weeks prior to the fire, the defendant purchased an insurance policy on the contents of the house valued at $40,000, an amount viewed as unreasonable. The Suspect had each of her children insured for $5,000 with herself as the beneficiary. Ten days after the death of her children, the Suspect attempted to perpetrate insurance fraud (Cleveland case: 00-08, 00-09).

There is no apparent evidence in the cases falling into this dominant profile of these female children experiencing ongoing abuse or neglect at the hands of a parent. And while the actions of the parents in all three cases are clearly reckless, it is not clear that they meant to kill their daughters in the process of committing an arson offense. By contrast, in the other two dominant profiles, there were older (i.e., over 25 years) male and female offenders endangering young girls (i.e., 6 years and under) in the privacy of a home environment. An examination of the actual case narratives underscores the importance of the qualitative aspect of this study, as these profiles do not always depict a situation of child abuse taken too far. Consider the following narrative:

- The Victim is a three-year-old girl who was being babysat by her aunt along with five other children. The aunt has five children, including a seven-year-old son. The Victim and this seven-year-old cousin went upstairs to play in his mother's bedroom. While jumping on the bed, a handgun fell out of the hiding place between the mattress and box spring. The seven-year-old cousin picked up the gun and started playing with it. He then pointed it at the Victim and pulled the trigger, firing one time. The bullet struck the Victim in the forehead above the left eye. The Victim sustained a single gunshot wound to the left side of the head. The Victim was about 18 inches away from her cousin when he fired the shot. No charges were filed against the boy although at the time of this incident he was under suspension from school for throwing rocks. When he was six years old, he was arrested for having an illegal weapon on school property. He had brought a knife to school, displayed the knife to several students, and made statements about robbing and cutting someone. When asked what would happen if he killed someone, he responded "so?" His father, to whom the gun in this homicide belonged, was charged with involuntary manslaughter (Cleveland case: 01-19).

Although the young boy in this homicide was not deemed culpable by the authorities given his tender age, it is clear that his violent history has put him on a destructive path, which resulted in the death of a little girl when his life overlapped with that of his younger female cousin.

The contexts in which female parents are killed by their children in Cleveland are extremely varied and do not seem to reveal any common themes. The offenders are typically female (71%), and the killings were committed with a variety of weapons (knives, blunt instruments, assaults, fire), and mostly fall into the "other circumstances" category (demonstrating the difficulty in trying to "fit" them into common contexts of lethal violence). The following narratives serve as useful illustrations of the unique nature of the deaths of women at the hands of their children in Cleveland:

- The Suspect (who is the son of the Victim) had a CD player that was not operating correctly. A few weeks before this homicide, he gave his player to his sister who had originally purchased it for him. The sister was to return the CD player to have it fixed or replaced. A few days prior to this homicide, the sister's boyfriend brought a replacement CD player to the Suspect. The Suspect did not like the replacement because it was not the same kind that he had so he threw it back (apparently it was the same as the original player, only a different color). The Suspect states he was angry about not getting his CD player back or a new one just like it. His sister stated that the day before the homicide, the Victim called her at work saying she was afraid and told her that if she didn't get the Suspect his stereo he was going to kill her (the Victim). The sister further reports that early on the morning of the day in question the Suspect repeatedly called her stating that he wanted his CD player. His sister told him there was nothing she could do about the player and that he should have kept the replacement. The Suspect replied that he was going to the prosecutor. The Suspect hung up the phone with his sister and was very angry. The Suspect became increasingly angry, got some bundles of newspapers that were in the living room by the couch (a stack approximately 3 feet high), and started them on fire using matches. The Suspect set the fire in the living room near the stairs leading up. After starting the fire, he ran out the back door. The Suspect later stated that he knew his mother was upstairs when he started the fire. According to family members, the Suspect is "mentally slow" and prone to becoming angry when he does not get his way. The Suspect's father (the Victim's husband) was in jail at the time of this homicide for domestic violence against his wife and was reportedly more concerned about the life and home insurance than the death of his wife (Cleveland case: 00-58).
- The Suspect had been released nine months ago from a New York state penal institution after serving eight years and he had returned to Cleveland to live with his mother (the Victim). The Victim was divorced and suffered from a number of health problems, including back problems, bronchitis, asthma, and diabetes, and would sometimes use an oxygen mask. The Victim was last seen on December 17 and a neighbor reports seeing the Suspect carrying stuff from the house (TV, VCR) since that time. The Suspect approached a friend about purchasing a radio belonging to the Victim several days later. The Suspect also tried to sell the Victim's computer to a neighbor, as well as her Christmas decorations. The Victim's body was discovered December 20 in the basement of her home when concerned family members who could not get a hold of her were let into the home by the landlord to find it ransacked. The Suspect had stabbed his mother in the neck and had reportedly been selling stuff from the house ever since. The Victim had apparently had a neighbor hold a bunch of her belongings

(computer, radio, etc.) while she was out of town recently because she feared the Suspect would take her things. The Victim also told a neighbor she was afraid of the Suspect because she thought he was on drugs. The Suspect is an admitted crack user, stating he has a heavy crack addiction and averaging two to three hits a day. The Suspect has an extensive criminal history, dating back to 1978 when he was adjudicated a delinquent for robbery at age 15 (Cleveland case: 02-86).

The threats of lethal violence facing these women are intricately intertwined with their own roles as mothers of dangerous children. They appear to have been aware of the danger but unwilling to turn their backs on their children to increase their own safety and security.

In terms of criminal justice outcomes for female victims of other family homicides, in 14 of the 15 cases charges were filed, the majority of which were aggravated murder (71%). In five of the cases the offender pleaded guilty, and in another five they were found guilty by a judge or jury. The average minimum sentence in cases of females killed by other family members was 21 years. This is slightly higher than the average of 19.6 years given to offenders killing female intimate partners.[9]

FEMALES KILLED BY FRIENDS AND ACQUAINTANCES

There were 143 cases of individuals killed by friends and acquaintances in Cleveland between 1998 and 2002, 20 of which were female (14%). It is clear that homicides between nonfamily members who know one another are the domain of males, because 92 percent of the offenders and 86 percent of the victims of friend/acquaintance homicides were male.

The QCA of the situations of females killed by friends/acquaintances included the following victim, offender, and incident attributes: victim age (24 years and under vs. 25 years and over); victim race (non-White vs. White); offender age (24 years and under vs. over 25 years); offender race (non-White vs. White); weapon (firearm); circumstances (argument); third parties present; and residential location. Three most common profiles account for 35 percent of the females killed by friends or acquaintances (see Box 5.3).

The most common of these involves a non-White female victim under 25 years old killed by a non-White male offender under the age of 25 with a firearm in a nonresidential location in the presence of others as a result of circumstances other than an argument. In all three situations, the death of the female appears to be the result of being in the wrong place at the wrong time, as is illustrated in the following two narratives:

- The Suspect reports that on the morning of this incident he was looking for some socks. Both of his parents were gone from the house, and the Suspect was there with his cousin who had been staying with him for about a week. The cousin told the Suspect there were some socks in a drawer in his father's room. The Suspect pulled out the top drawer of the dresser in the bedroom and saw a gun. The gun was already loaded. The Suspect took the gun into the living room and showed it to his cousin. The cousin gave it back to him and told the Suspect to put it away. Instead the Suspect took the gun and started waving it around and took the clip out. He then put the clip back into the gun and

> **BOX 5.3**

MOST COMMON PROFILES OF FEMALE HOMICIDE VICTIMIZATIONS BY FRIENDS/ACQUAINTANCES

$N = 3$	Victim under 25 years and non-White	Offender under 25 years, non-White, and male	Firearm	Not precipitated by an argument	Nonresidential location and third parties present
$N = 2$	Victim under 25 years and non-White	Offender under 25 years, non-White, and male	Weapon other than a firearm	Not precipitated by an argument	Residential location and no others present
$N = 2$	Victim under 25 years and non-White	Offender under 25 years, non-White, and female	Weapon other than a firearm	Argument	Nonresidential location and third parties present

started pointing the gun around and clicking the gun, pulling the slide back and chambering a round. The Suspect then continued to point the gun around the house. The cousin then took the gun from the Suspect and put it away. While the cousin took a nap, the Suspect retrieved the gun, went into the backyard and started showing it off. On the other side of the fence were four or five girls the Suspect knew, including the Victim. During this time the Suspect kept clicking the gun. The girls started saying the gun was not real. The Suspect then took the clip from out of the gun, took a bullet out of his pocket, and put it in the clip. He showed it to everybody, and then stuck the clip back in the gun. The Suspect asked if they wanted him to shoot the tree and nobody said anything. As the Victim turned away to pick up a tissue, the Suspect fired the gun and hit the Victim in the back. The Victim ran a short distance and collapsed. The Suspect was seen with the gun on at least three separate occasions in the days before the shooting, pointing the gun at various people (including putting it in people's faces and on foreheads) and cars. The Suspect's father had been told by more than one parent in the neighborhood that the Suspect was in possession of the gun (Cleveland case: 99-44).

- The two Suspects were being driven around by two other males. Suspect 1 instructed one of these males to give him a ride to the drive-through on East 117th and Superior so they could get some more alcohol to drink. Upon arriving, they parked on the street next to the drive-through. Suspect 2 got out of the vehicle and walked to the front of the drive-through, and then returned immediately to the vehicle, informing Suspect 1 that a particular individual was at the drive-through. Suspect 1 got out of the vehicle and walked with Suspect 2 to the front of the store. The Victim's boyfriend (who was also killed in this incident) came out of the store and went to get into the passenger side of a car out front. Suspect 1 walked over to the Victim's boyfriend and fired two shots at him. He fell to the ground. Suspect 1 then stood over the Victim's boyfriend and shot him in the chest. The Victim began screaming. Suspect 1 then handed the gun to Suspect 2 and told him he had "better do her" (the Victim) or be killed by Suspect 1. Suspect 1 then took off running. Suspect 2 reports that he closed his eyes, pointed the gun at the Victim, and pulled the trigger twice. The Victim sustained two gunshot wounds, one to the right chest and one to the right back. A suggested motive for the shooting was that Suspect 1 had a girlfriend whom he had dated on and off for the past three and a half years. This girlfriend had also slept with the Victim's boyfriend, and he impregnated her twice, both times resulting in abortions (Cleveland case: 01-34).

The female victims in these cases had no known violent histories themselves and were more victims of circumstance than anything. The easy access to firearms in the inner-city neighborhoods where they lived out their lives was certainly a contributing factor to their deaths. Simply going about their routine activities in an environment where guns can be obtained by virtually anyone with little concern and can be used to carry out revenge made life lethal for these young females.

By contrast, the two young females killed by other young, non-White females over arguments in the presence of others (profile 3) present a very different kind of situational context for lethal violence:

- The Suspect's younger brother was shooting dice in the hallway outside of the Suspect's apartment with several other people, including the Victim. The Victim came out the loser in this craps game, with the Suspect's brother winning all of the Victim's money (reported to be about $200). The Victim became angry, saying "hell no" to the Suspect's brother as he reached for her money. The Victim punched him in the face and tried to get her money back. A fight ensued. A loud commotion was heard in the hallway, and the Suspect's brother called out to the Suspect who came out of the apartment to check on things. The Suspect, with the help of several other females, retrieved the money the Victim had put in her pocket. The Victim then left the hallway where the game took place and walked out front of the apartment, while the Suspect went back into her apartment. As the Suspect walked into her living room, the living room front window was broken by a rock which was found lying on the floor (statements reveal that the Victim picked up a rock from the courtyard and threw it through the window). At this point, the Suspect grabbed a knife from her kitchen and ran back outside the apartment again. By this time, the Victim, who had been reaching for another large rock to throw, was involved in a physical altercation with the Suspect's brother, who threw his bicycle at her after witnessing the Victim break the window. The Suspect, along with some of her friends, became involved in the confrontation with the Victim. A physical fight developed, during which the Victim was stabbed by the Suspect. The Victim then attempted to run away but fell in the courtyard (Cleveland case: 99-30).

- The Suspect and Victim had known each other for about six years and were good friends. According to the Suspect, their relationship had deteriorated about a month and a half earlier over the Victim wanting the Suspect to join her in private dance parties. The last time the Suspect and Victim were together was approximately three months earlier, at which time the Victim left some of her property at the Suspect's home. The Suspect reports that she then began to receive calls from the Victim who threatened to "kick her ass." On the day in question, the Victim called the Suspect and told her she was coming over and that the Suspect better have her stuff ready when she got there. The Suspect told the Victim that because the Victim had stolen her pager and broken it, she was not getting anything back. The Victim arrived at the apartment, knocked at the door, and was let in by the Suspect. An argument ensued, which escalated into a physical altercation, during which the Suspect and Victim were pulling each other's hair and throwing punches. The Suspect's sister told the Suspect and Victim to stop fighting and take it outside. The Suspect then grabbed the Victim's duffel bag and threw it out the window. The Suspect took a kitchen steak knife off the coffee table in the living room and followed the Victim downstairs. Once outside, they began to fight again and the Suspect pulled out the knife from her rear pocket and was waving it around while they continued fighting. The fight moved out to the middle of the street. They continued fighting and then fell to the ground. The Suspect sat on top of the Victim, holding the knife to her throat, and told the Victim "keep on f***ing with me and I am going to hurt you." The Suspect then got up, kicked the Victim in the mouth, took the Victim's wallet and cell phone, and walked up to the apartment, placing the knife on the arm of the sofa. The Victim got up, walked a few steps, and then fell on her face on the sidewalk. When asked what happened, the Suspect stated, "she (the Victim) thought she was going to come over and kick my butt. Ain't nobody coming over to my house and kicking my butt." The Suspect reportedly wasn't upset over the fight, and according to witnesses she seemed "hyped" and "pumped up" immediately afterwards. The Suspect also had two additional knives in her purse (Cleveland case: 02-49).

All of the young women in these cases are caught up in a culture where violence is used as a means of settling disputes, where weapons are readily available to escalate the confrontation to another level of violence, where a willingness to resort to violence becomes necessary for saving your reputation, and not letting others take advantage of you is an important value. Both victims were at least active participants in the violence that ultimately led to their deaths, and in the first case the victim was clearly the first to use violence. Thus, while females killed by intimate partners are not likely to be victim precipitated, there is evidence of this kind of provocation Wolfgang (1958) had in mind in some of the killings of women by female friends and acquaintances.

What was the court's perspective on these kinds of cases? Of the 20 cases, 17 resulted in arrest (2 remained uncleared while 1 offender committed suicide). Nine of the 17 (53%) were charged with aggravated murder and another 4 (24%) were charged with murder. Seven offenders pleaded guilty, and eight were found guilty by a judge or jury. Two offenders received sentences of life without parole, with the remaining sentences ranging from 3 to 37 years minimum. The average minimum sentence for female victims of friends and acquaintances was 19 years,[10] lower than the average for either female victims of intimate partners or other family members.

FEMALES KILLED BY STRANGERS

There were 74 stranger killings in Cleveland between 1998 and 2002, only 8 of which had female victims (11%). Similar to acquaintance homicides, stranger killing is the domain of males; 99 percent of the offenders and 89 percent of the victims of stranger homicides were male.

The QCA of the situations of females killed by strangers included the following victim, offender, and incident attributes: victim race (non-White vs. White); offender age (under 40 years vs. 40 years and over); offender race (non-White vs. White); offender gender; weapon (firearm); circumstances (felony and argument); and outdoor location.

The two most common profiles, displayed below, account for 63 percent of the females killed by strangers (in fact all eight cases fell within only five distinct profiles). The most dominant of these involves a non-White female killed by a non-White male less than 40 years of age with a firearm outdoors in a situation precipitated by something other than a felony or argument (see Box 5.4).

An examination of the corresponding narratives to these cases reveals quite varied processual elements underlying these three homicides. One case involves a young female victim and her friend becoming involved with some drug dealers when purchasing some wet (marijuana cigarettes dipped in formaldehyde). The female was shot when they complained the cigarette was not dipped enough and they wanted it dipped again. The second female victim was an innocent bystander who was shot by a group of young Black males in a car during a drive-by retaliation shooting. The third victim was shot in her car by a known user of wet on New Year's Eve when she left a pub to purchase nylons at a gas station. While the first victim's dangerous lifestyle of purchasing drugs from street dealers is a contributing factor in her death, the other two victims appear to have been leading lethal lives only to the extent that they were exposed to dangerous neighborhoods and motivated offenders. The killing of the female in the drive-by shooting, for example, occurred in the ward with the fourth highest (of 21) number of homicides during that five-year period.

BOX 5.4

MOST COMMON PROFILES OF FEMALE HOMICIDE VICTIMIZATIONS BY STRANGERS

$N = 3$	Non-White victim	Offender under 40 years, non-White, male	Firearm	Not felony- or argument-related	Outdoor location
$N = 2$	White victim	Offender under 40 years, non-White, male	Weapon other than a firearm	Felony	Nonoutdoor location

All eight of these stranger homicides of women were cleared by arrest, and all but one resulted in charges of aggravated murder. Half of the cases resulted in guilty pleas and three in guilty findings by a judge or jury. The minimum prison sentences ranged from 3 to 50 years, with an average minimum sentence of 18 years, the lowest of the four relationship categories examined here.

DISCUSSION AND CONCLUSIONS

The lethal victimization of women in Cleveland in the late 1990s and early twenty-first century mirrors a number of national patterns, particularly the disproportionate killing of women within the context of intimate partner homicides. Similar to prior research, many of these women had histories of domestic violence victimization by the partner that ultimately killed them.

Various types of cultural explanations have been applied to explain the onset and distribution of domestic abuse and other forms of interpersonal violence. In particular, the high prevalence of female victimization by intimate partners is thought by many researchers to derive from cultural legacies in which violence against women is often normatively expected, tolerated, or even demanded within particular contexts. "Honor killings" of wives, sisters, or female offspring for sexual improprieties in non-Western cultures and the "rule of thumb" within Western culture that presumably permitted striking wives with a stick of a thumb's width are clear examples of these cultural traditions (see Miethe & Deibert, 2007).

Several subcultural explanations have also been offered to explain interpersonal violence. Among these theories are the "subculture of violence" (Wolfgang & Ferracuti, 1967), the "code of the street" (Anderson, 1999), and the "subculture of exasperation" (Harvey, 1986). Within these theoretical approaches, high rates of domestic assault and other forms of interpersonal violence are viewed as manifestations of cultural traditions, compulsive and hyperactive masculinity, frustration, and powerlessness experienced by the socially and economically disadvantaged. The Cleveland homicide narratives analyzed in this study are also suggestive of these cultural themes as predisposing and precipitating conditions for female homicide victimization. For the vast majority of these homicides, the perpetrator is a male, and most of these homicides are the lethal consequences of the dynamic expression of male dominance and control. The relative powerlessness of particular groups (e.g., poor, minority women) makes them especially vulnerable to prolonged histories of physical abuse that are ultimately terminated by lethal violence. When these women are homicide offenders against their male intimate partners, the narrative accounts also suggest that many of their killings represent a type of "self help" that occurs when other legitimate opportunities for dispute resolution are not available. Under these conditions, both homicide victimization and offending by women may be indicative of a cultural response to the daily frustration and powerlessness experienced in the world of the urban poor and the "truly disadvantaged" (Wilson, 1987, 1996).

In terms of the criminal justice response to female homicide victims, the average minimum sentence given to offenders killing female victims ranged from 18 years for stranger homicides to 21 years for other family homicides. The average minimum sentence for women killed by an intimate partner was nearly 20 years, but several of these offenders received very short sentences, as minimal as 6 months. It is likely more than coincidence that all but one of the offenders who received a sentence of less than 10 years killed a female intimate partner who was a heavy drinker, drug user, or both.

Previous research has used various terms to describe the potentially contributory role of victims in crime events. Some of these terms include victim precipitation, facilitation, and victim proneness (see Fattah, 1991; Karmen, 1984). Within this specific context and patriarchal societies in general, female homicide victims may be especially prone to legal and cultural attributions of blame and partial responsibility for their victimization. Responses by the public and the media to female victims who are minority, poor, lesbian, prostitutes, or drug users are particularly likely to involve victim blaming (Caputi & Russell, 1992). Yet even in cases where victims were involved in deviant lifestyle activities (e.g., drug users, alcohol abusers), our analysis of Cleveland homicides provides little empirical evidence to support these characterizations of female homicide victimization. However, it remains important to study these stereotypical images of crime victims because they often determine the nature and gravity of the cultural and criminal justice responses to female homicide victimization. Without realistic alternatives for these women, their high exposure to dangerous persons and situations are the precursors for leading lethal lives.

Discussion Questions

1. What are the different contextual and structural factors associated with homicide incidents involving female victims?
2. What are the significance of personal demographics such as age, gender, and race in homicide victimization?
3. What are the differing contexts of homicide for female juvenile and adult female victims?
4. What are the circumstances surrounding incidents where females are killed by family, intimate partners, friends and acquaintances, and strangers?
5. How were qualitative and quantitative research methods used in the study to examine the context of female homicide victimization?

References

Anderson, E. (1999). *Code of the street: Decency, violence, and the moral life of the inner city.* New York: W. W. Norton.

Browne, A. (1987). *When battered women kill.* New York: Macmillan/Free Press.

Browne, A., & Williams, K. R. (1989). Exploring the effect of resource availability and the likelihood of female-perpetrated homicides. *Law and Society Review, 23,* 75–94.

Browne, A., & Williams, K. R. (1993). Gender, intimacy, and lethal violence: Trends from 1976 through 1987. *Gender & Society, 7,* 78–98.

Browne, A., Williams, K. R., & Dutton, D. G. (1999). Homicide between intimate partners. In M. D. Smith & M. A. Zahn (Eds.), *Homicide: A sourcebook of social research* (pp. 149–164). Thousand Oaks, CA: Sage.

Campbell, J. C. (1992). If I can't have you, no one can: Power and control in homicide of female partners. In J. Radford & D. E. H. Russell (Eds.), *Femicide: The politics of woman killing* (pp. 99–113). New York: Twayne.

Caputi, J., & Russell, D. E. H. (1992). Femicide: Sexist terrorism against women. In J. Radford &

D. E. H. Russell (Eds.), *Femicide: The politics of woman killing* (pp. 13–21). New York: Twayne.

Cazanave, N. A., & Zahn, M. A. (1992). Women, murder and male domination: Police reports of domestic violence in Chicago and Philadelphia. In E. C. Viano (Ed.), *Intimate violence: Interdisciplinary perspectives* (pp. 83–97). Washington, D.C.: Hemisphere.

Crawford, M., & Gartner, R. (1992). *Woman killing: Intimate femicide in Ontario 1974–1990.* Toronto, Canada: Government of Ontario, Ministry of Social Services, Woman's Directorate.

Dawson, M., & Gartner, R. (1998a). Differences in the characteristics of intimate femicide: The role of relationship state and relationship status. *Homicide Studies, 2,* 378–399.

Dawson, M., & Gartner, R. (1998b, November). *Male proprietariness or despair? Examining the gendered nature of homicides followed by suicides.* Paper presented at the Annual Meeting of the American Society of Criminology, Washington, D.C.

Fattah, E. A. (1991). *Understanding criminal victimization: An introduction to theoretical victimology.* Scarborough, Ontario: Prentice-Hall Canada Inc.

Federal Bureau of Investigation. (2004). *Crime in the United States 2004: Uniform crime reports.* Washington, D.C.: U.S. Government Printing Office.

Gartner, R., Dawson, M., & Crawford, M. (1999). Woman killing: Intimate femicide in Ontario, 1974–1994. *Resources of Feminist Research, 26,* 151–173.

Harvey, W. B. (1986). Homicide among young Black adults: Life in the subculture of exasperation. In D. F. Hawkins (Ed.), *Homicide among Black Americans* (pp. 153–171). Lanham, MD: University Press of America.

Hickey, E. W. (2002). *Serial murderers and their victims* (3rd ed.). Belmont, CA: Wadsworth/Thomson Learning.

Johnson, H. (1996). *Dangerous domains: Violence against women in Canada.* Toronto, Ontario: Nelson Canada.

Karmen, A. (1984). *Crime victims: An introduction to victimology.* Belmont, CA: Wadsworth.

Kellermann, A. L., & Mercy, J. A. (1992). Men, women, and murder: Gender-specific differences in rates of fatal violence and victimization. *Journal of Trauma, 33,* 1–5.

Miethe, T. D., & Deibert, G. R. (2007). *Fight time: The normative rules and routines of interpersonal violence.* Long Grove, IL: Waveland Press.

Miethe, T. D., & Regoeczi, W. C. (2004). *Rethinking homicide: Exploring the structure and process underlying deadly situations.* Cambridge: Cambridge University Press.

Ressler, R. K., Burgess, A. W., & Douglas, J. E. (1988). *Sexual homicide.* Lexington, MA: Lexington Books.

Riedel, M. (1999). Sources of homicide data. In M. D. Smith & M. A. Zahn (Eds.), *Studying and preventing homicide: Issues and challenges* (pp. 31–52). Thousand Oaks, CA: Sage.

Rosenfeld, R. (1997). Changing relationships between men and women: A note on the decline in intimate partner homicide. *Homicide Studies, 1,* 72–83.

Wallace, A. (1986). A typology of homicide. In A. Wallace (Ed.), *Homicide: The social reality* (pp. 83–109). New South Wales: Bureau of Crime Statistics and Research.

Wilson, W. J. (1987). *The truly disadvantaged: The innercity, the underclass, and public policy.* Chicago, IL: University of Chicago Press.

Wilson, W. J. (1996). *When work disappears: The world of the new urban poor.* New York: Vintage Press.

Wilson, M., & Daly, M. (1993). Spousal homicide risk and estrangement. *Violence and Victims, 8,* 3–16.

Wilson, M., Johnson, H., & Daly, M. (1995). Lethal and non-lethal violence against wives. *Canadian Journal of Criminology, 37,* 331–361.

Wolfgang, M. (1958). *Patterns in criminal homicide.* Philadelphia: University of Philadelphia Press.

Wolfgang, M., & Ferracuti, F. (1967). *The subculture of violence: Toward an integrated theory in criminology.* London: Tavistock.

Endnotes

1. The first author would like to thank former Cleveland Police Chief Edward Lohn, Lieutenant Petkac, Sergeants Farinnaci and Rowley, and Detective Stevers for their assistance in accessing the files and collecting information on the cases during this time period.

2. The data set is a victim-based file with each victim constituting a case. Rather than exclude cases with multiple offenders, the categories of the first offender are used. This should not have a major impact on the results for two reasons: (1) there are relatively few cases ($N = 11$) involving female victims killed by multiple offenders in the data set; and (2) the "primary" offender in each homicide (e.g., the one who actually pulled the trigger) was listed as the first offender in each case during data collection and subsequently in the construction of the statistical data file.

3. Felony-type homicides include killings done during the commission of such acts as robbery, burglary, sexual assaults, and other felonies.

4. An exceptional clearance refers to a case that is closed without an arrest as a result of various circumstances beyond the control of police departments, such as the offender committing suicide, making a deathbed confession, dying from an accident or natural causes before they are arrested, denial of extradition to the jurisdiction where the homicide took place, or the district attorney refusing to prosecute (Riedel, 1999).

5. Aggravated murder cases include such situations as premeditated killings, felony-related homicides, or the killing of a law enforcement officer.

6. There were no female victims of homicides involving homosexuals during the five-year period examined here.

7. Because only three of the homicides were interracial and all of the offenders were male, offender gender, offender race, and victim race were not included in the analysis.

8. Because all but one homicide were intraracial, offender and victim race were not included in the analysis.

9. The life without parole sentences given to the three men who killed their intimate partners were each given a value of 50 years in this calculation.

CHAPTER 6

THE IMPACT OF GENDER, RACE, AND CLASS DISCRIMINATION ON FEMICIDE RATES

JO-ANN DELLA GIUSTINA

ABSTRACT

Thousands of women are killed each year in the ultimate form of violence against women. They are murdered by serial killers, friends, family, intimate partners, coworkers, and strangers in a society that devalues women. Femicide (murder of women) is a leading cause of death of women in the United States. This chapter evaluates the femicides of Black women and White women in 106 cities in relation to gender, race, and economic class, which are integral to the role expectations, behavioral influences, and life experiences that structure women's lives and responses to their surroundings. This approach allows for a multilayered analysis that examines the multiple oppressions women face in their lives. This study finds an increase in the number of Black women and White women being murdered in those cities where women have advanced in the social, economic, educational, and political arenas, thus indicating a backlash against women's progress. Moreover, Black women are murdered more often in those cities where there is greater racial oppression, including economic, social, and political discrimination, and White women are murdered more often in cities that are less economically privileged than other cities.

INTRODUCTION

Thousands of women are killed every year in an ultimate act of violence against women. In fact, American women face a higher risk of being murdered than women from any other industrial nation except Russia. The United States represents 32 percent of the female population in 25 advanced countries, but 70 percent of all femicides in those countries combined. A woman in the United States is eight times more likely to be murdered than a woman in England and Wales, five times more likely to be murdered than a woman in Germany, and three times more likely to be murdered than a woman in Canada. In fact, the U.S. femicide rate is five times higher than that in the other advanced countries combined (Hemenway, Shinoda-Tagawa, & Miller, 2002). The only exception is

Russia, which has a femicide rate that is three times higher than that of the United States (Chervyakov, Shkolnikov, Pridemore, & McKee, 2002; Human Rights Watch, 1997). During the 1990s, the femicide rate for U.S. women was 4.2 per 100,000 women. For European women, the femicide rates ranged from 0.5 to 2.4 per 100,000 women depending on the country (Salfati, 2001), and the Russian femicide rate was 12–15 per 100,000 women (Chervyakov et al., 2002; Human Rights Watch, 1997).

Women are murdered by serial killers, friends, family members, intimate partners,[1] coworkers, and strangers within a society that devalues women. In the United States in 1997, femicide (the homicide[2] of women) was the leading cause of death for Black women aged 15–34, the second leading cause of death for all women aged 15–24, the fourth leading cause of death for all women under 45 years of age, and the leading cause of on-the-job deaths for all women (Frye & Wilt, 2001; Moracco, Runyan, & Butts, 1998; Oliver, 2000). From 1976 to 1996, 105,175 women were killed, representing 23.7 percent of all homicide victims (Greenfeld et al., 1998). Similarly, in 2002, 23.1 percent of all homicide victims were women (1,905 White women and 1,184 Black women) (Federal Bureau of Investigation, 2004). The femicide rate (per 100,000 women) increased from 2.6 in 1965 to 4.5 in 1995 (Moracco et al., 1998; Smith & Kuchta, 1995).

The femicide rates of poor, young, minority women are higher than for others; however, the multiple predictive influences are unknown as of yet. Women of diverse races are differently situated in society and differently affected by homicide, so that the social conditions leading to the murders of Black women and White women cannot be assumed to be the same. Examining homicide rates separately by race allows for a richer, multidimensional analysis of the relationships of various predictive factors on the homicide victimization of women.

Femicide rates of Black women and White women are examined in this study in relation to the social structural factors of gender, race, and class, which are integral to the role expectations, behavioral influences, and life experiences that structure women's lives and responses to their surroundings. A woman's actions emanate from the totality of her life experiences. This approach allows for a multilayered analysis that investigates the multiple oppressions women face in their lives.

PATTERNS OF FEMICIDE

Despite these statistics, homicide researchers have largely ignored women, instead focusing on men, who are approximately three-fourths of all homicide victims. Because of their large numbers, any unique gendered patterns or characteristics of homicide are overshadowed by the statistics on male homicide victimization (Moracco et al., 1998). Nevertheless, we cannot assume that the factors associated with homicide against men affect women in the same manner. When male homicide victims are studied separately from female homicide victims, some differing patterns emerge (Zahn & McCall, 1999), including that most male victims are killed by strangers while most female victims are killed by someone they know. Moreover, men are more at risk of being killed by a friend or acquaintance whereas women are at a higher risk of being killed by an intimate partner (Johnson, 1994). We must be careful about assuming, however, that most femicide victims are killed by an intimate partner. While women are 75 percent of the victims of intimate partner homicide, many femicide victims, maybe a majority, are killed by someone who is not an intimate partner (Fox & Zawitz, 1999; Rennison, 2001, 2003; Rennison, 2003). For that reason, femicide research needs to go beyond the study of intimate partner femicide.

SOCIAL CONTEXT OF FEMICIDE

It has only been in the last decade that femicide research has begun to appear to any significant extent. Much of our knowledge is centered on individual-level characteristics and risk factors, such as the ethnicity, race, age, education, financial status, and emotional or mental state of the individual offender and victim, as well as the circumstances surrounding the incident. While it is important to recognize individual characteristics, to fully understand femicide we must view the homicide of women in larger social contexts. An individual's attitudes and behavior are a response to her or his specific situation within a community so that the community's characteristics and structures affect the individual's actions.

Macro-level social structural analysis is the process of studying the patterns of society as a whole instead of individuals or small groups of people. It focuses on social structural determinants as the explanation for crime patterns, which differs from the traditional American philosophy of individualism. Social structure is the pattern of social relationships and social institutions through which individual behavior is expressed. It holds a society together to form the collective reality and is greater than the sum of its individuals (Durkheim, 1951). In that way, the structure of society influences trends, including femicide trends. Whereas individual-level factors may explain a single femicide, social structural factors influence the femicide rates, that is, the level of femicide in society. Sampson (1985) describes this approach:

> Rather than seeking to explain individual involvement in criminal behavior, proponents of the structural perspective have attempted to isolate characteristics of macro social units that lead to high rates of criminality. The genesis of the social ecological model is that community structure has independent effects on crime that are not strictly disaggregable to [the] individual level. (p. 647)

Gender, race, and class are integral to the behavioral influences, role expectations, and life experiences that structure people's lives and responses to their surroundings. A person's actions emanate from the totality of his or her life experiences. In the United States, very different life experiences shape men and women, White people and Black people, and the rich and the poor. In that context, a person's gender, race, and class predict the chances of becoming a homicide victim.

This study investigates whether the macro-social structural factors of gender, race, and class predict the variation in the femicide rates across medium and large U.S. cities. This research is one of many efforts to develop a complex view of violence against women grounded in the feminist perspective that women's lives are shaped by the interconnection of the multiple oppressions of gender, race, and class, which are embedded in the social structure. Women are affected not only by their gender, but by all aspects of their lives, including their race and their socioeconomic class. To focus on only one area of a woman's life ignores her as a full human being. Developments in both theory (e.g., intersectionality) and method (e.g., path analysis) allow a more layered and integrated approach to studying femicide.[3]

INTERSECTIONALITY THEORY

During the nineteenth century, Black feminists described their lives as being a combination of racial and gender oppressions (St. Pierre Ruffin, 1895; Truth, 1972). That perspective re-emerged in the 1970s when feminists of color (Black, Latina, Asian, and Native American feminists) rejected the idea that women of color must decide whether they are more discriminated by racial oppression or gender inequality. They explained their oppression as multiple, interlocking oppressions. A combination of gender, race, and class, and not any one of these factors alone, shapes a woman's identity, status, and circumstance. Focusing exclusively on patriarchal domination, as traditional feminist thought does, obscures the reality of the lives of these women, who are differently situated in the economic, social, and political worlds than are White women (Mansbridge, 1999; Richie, 2000). A woman's social context is created by interconnecting systems of power (e.g., patriarchy, race subordination, capitalism) and oppression (racism, sexism, and classism) (Bograd, 1990).

Any analysis of violence against Black women in the United States must consider this country's racial history. Black feminists locate their critical analysis of the oppression of Black women in the United States in their long history of sexual abuse, racial oppression, class exploitation, and social control, which situates them differently from White women (and other women of color). For Black feminists, a feminist critique of rape, incest, and battering necessarily includes an analysis of racist oppression rooted in the slave system, lynchings of Black men, and the Jim Crow legal system (Mansbridge, 1999). The history of African American women is the history of slavery, which brought the vast majority of the ancestors of American Black women to this country to work as slaves (Collins, 1990). Slave women suffered violence at the hands of their husbands, other slave men, and slave owners. Raping a slave woman was legal whereas raping a White woman was a crime (White, 1985).

The traditional feminist analysis of wife beating focuses on marriage as the institution in which the wife is the property of her husband and the husband dominates over his wife on the basis of male ownership, property distribution, and control of subsistence goods (Dobash & Dobash, 1979). That type of marriage did not exist for slave women, who were the property of the slave owner. Because the slave husband had no property of his own to control, any power or control he had over his wife could not be based on his providing food, clothing, or shelter, which came from the slave owner. Moreover, intrafamily relationships had to conform to the work and social patterns of the slave system, including the sale and separation of husbands from their families (White, 1985).

Several theorists, such as Collins (1990) and Crenshaw (1991), applied the multiple oppressions' perspective to violence against women of color. Crenshaw (1991) created the term "intersectionality" to describe how the interconnecting aspects of women's complicated lives sometimes merge in violence. Intersectionality theory diverges from the narrow feminist emphasis on gender inequality as the primary factor responsible for intimate partner violence against women. Instead, it argues that gender inequality intersects with other structures of power and oppression, such as racial oppression and class exploitation, to trigger violence against women of color (Collins, 1990; Crenshaw, 1991; Davis, 1983; Hooks, 1989; Wing, 2003). Women live within social contexts where their attitudes and behavior are a response to community situations so that the community's characteristics and structures affect their risk of becoming a homicide victim. Although this theory was originally developed in the context of women of color, the concept of intersectionality has been applied to White women, who also experience multiple oppressions. However, White women experience privilege, not oppression, based on their skin color (Fine & Weiss, 1998).

Racialized violence, classed violence, and state violence may be integrated into the lives of many marginalized women (e.g., women of color, poor women, and immigrant women) who also experience intimate partner violence (Crenshaw, 1991). These women often experience multilayered and routinized forms of domination that converge to obstruct their ability to create alternatives to the abusive relationships. For example, poor women may experience chronic violence in their community, which may result from the strains of class inequality (Messner & Rosenfeld, 1999; Oliver, 2000). Lacking the economic means to escape an unsafe neighborhood can be considered a form of violence against women so that ending intimate partner violence may not necessarily end the violence in the lives of these women.

In addition, Crenshaw (1991) suggests that the link between patriarchy and racism may contribute to the cycle of intimate partner violence. She argues that the violence of men of color against their intimate partners may be a reaction to being denied the power and privilege White men have throughout all spheres of their lives.

This intersectionality perspective is changing the way in which researchers are approaching the study of violence against women (see e.g., Sokoloff, 2005). There is an increasing focus on disaggregating victims by race and ethnicity as well as investigating how class status affects the prevalence of the violence. Not all women are similarly situated so that treating them in the same way may obscure important distinctions that could help to explain the causes of violence against them. For that reason, this study considers whether the intersectionality theory predicts the variations in the femicide rates.

METHODOLOGY

This study examines the femicide rates in 106 medium and large cities in the United States (population of 170,000 or greater) for the years 1998 through 2001.[4] Cities are used as the units of analysis because they are the best social space in which to measure the relevant theoretical concepts with available data. Cities are coherent social units that are broad enough to ensure that most homicide victims are residents of the unit, but are more homogenous than Standard Metropolitan Statistical Areas (metropolitan areas), counties, or states, which can vary greatly from one area to another. Moreover, public policy, education, police protection, and other institutional decisions are more often made at the city level rather than at neighborhood levels.

Analysis in this study includes the murders of Black women and White women by both men and women regardless of the motive or the relationship between the victim and the offender.[5] The overall and race-specific femicide rates are gathered from the Federal Bureau of Investigation's Supplementary Homicide Reports (SHR) (Federal Bureau of Investigation, 1998, 1999, 2000, 2001) and the National Center for Health Statistics of the Centers for Disease Control (CDC) (Centers for Disease Control, 1998, 1999, 2000, 2001) data.

PATH MODELING

This research uses path analysis to explain how gender, race, and class inequalities predict variations in the femicide rates of Black women and White women. Path analysis is a multivariate regression method that predicts the expected change in the dependent variable as a result of the change in the independent variable while controlling the remaining variables. This method is particularly suited to study macro-level social structural factors because the entire landscape can be viewed as a whole instead of merely seeing the individual details separately. Figure 6.1 is the model used in this study. The curved arrows with double arrowheads show the associated, nonpredictive relationships between the independent variables.[6]

VARIABLES IN THE MODEL

Dependent Variable

This study includes 4,403 femicides of women 16 years old and over for the years 1998 through 2001 in the 106 cities studied. During that time, the total number of female victims (4,947) represented 17.95 percent of the 27,566 people murdered in those cities.

The femicide rates are calculated as follows:

Femicide rate (overall and race-specific) = $(I/P) \times 100{,}000 / 4$, where I = total number of reported incidents of murder and nonnegligent manslaughter of women victims 16 years old and over (overall and race-specific), and P = the total population of women 16 years old and over (overall and race-specific) in the city.[7]

Independent Variables

To study the relationships between the structural factors and the femicide rates, this study examines three macrostructural theoretical concepts measured by several social, economic, and political independent variables and are combined to create separate indices[8]: gender inequality, racial inequality, and class inequality[9] (see Table 6.1 for a list of all study variables).

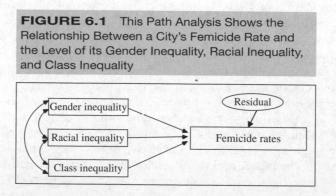

FIGURE 6.1 This Path Analysis Shows the Relationship Between a City's Femicide Rate and the Level of its Gender Inequality, Racial Inequality, and Class Inequality

TABLE 6.1	Variables Used in the Model of Predictors of Femicide
Gender Inequality Index[a]	A composite of:
	Ratio of female to male unemployment
	Ratio of female to male poverty
	Ratio of male to female median income
	Ratio of male to female college education
	Ratio of male to female in elite occupations
	SBA Women's Centers
	% of City Council members who are male
Racial Inequality Index[b]	A composite of:
	Ratio of Black to White unemployment
	Ratio of Black to White poverty
	Ratio of White to Black median income
	Ratio of White to Black college education
	Ratio of White to Black elite occupations
	% of City Council members who are White
Class Inequality Index[c]	A composite of:
	Ratio of city to U.S. median income[c]
	Ratio of city to U.S. college education[c]
	Ratio of city to U.S. above-poverty level[c]
	Ratio of city to U.S. population employed[c]

[a]To remain consistent in measuring inequality, some measures are expressed as the ratio of women relative to men while other measures are expressed as the ratio of men relative to women.

[b]To remain consistent in measuring inequality, some measures are expressed as the ratio of Whites relative to Blacks while other measures are expressed as the ratio of Blacks relative to Whites.

[c]Because these class variables measure equality, to avoid confusion when comparing the gender and race variables, which measure inequality, the class equality measures are multiplied by a constant of −1.0 to create class inequality factors.

GENDER INEQUALITY INDEX

Relative gender inequality, which reflects the relationship of women's status in society to men's status in society, includes measures of education, income, poverty, occupational attainment, employment levels, business opportunities, and political power (Baron & Straus, 1984, 1987; Dobash & Dobash, 1979; Ellis & Beattie, 1983; Martin, 1983; Stout, 1993; Yllö, 1983).

GENDER SOCIOECONOMIC INEQUALITY

This analysis uses the median income (the ratio of male to female median income) of men working full-time relative to the median income of women working full-time as well as unemployment (the ratio of female to male unemployment) measured as the percent of women 16 years old and over in the civilian labor force who are unemployed relative to the percent of men 16 years old and over in the civilian labor force who are unemployed. This eliminates women who voluntarily choose to remain outside the labor force. Educational attainment (the ratio of male to female college education) is operationalized as the percent of men 25 years and over with a college education (BA degree or higher) relative to the percent of women 25 years and over with a college education.

Although professional and managerial occupations are a minority of all occupations in the United States, they are regarded as assuring middle-class status. They offer relatively greater autonomy, power, control, and rewards than do "nonprofessional" occupations (Sokoloff, 1992) and reveals progress for women in all occupations (Schwartz, 1992). Accordingly, the ratio of male to female in elite occupations is measured by the percent of men 16 years old and over who have a professional or managerial occupation relative to the percent of women 16 years old and over who have a professional or managerial occupation.[10]

A poverty indicator is included to observe whether any increase in economic equality with men is offset by a disproportionate number of women living below the poverty level. Poverty (the ratio of female to male poverty) is measured as the percent of women living below the federal poverty level relative to the percent of men living below the federal poverty level. A measure of Small Business Administration (SBA) Women's Centers is included in this measure, measuring one area where women have made some progress in owning their own businesses (SBA Women's Centers).

GENDER POLITICAL INEQUALITY

Low representation in elected office is considered one of the factors preserving inequality in other spheres of society. Women's rights advocates cite the lack of elective political power as a source of women's inability to change their lives or the laws affecting them (National Commission on the Observance of the International Women's Year, 1978). Women's relative political power is measured as the percent of City Council members who are men.

RACIAL INEQUALITY INDEX

Racial inequality has been a focus of much homicide research. Black people are over-represented as both homicide offenders and victims (Hawkins, 1995; Messner & Rosenfeld, 1999). Furthermore, crime may be an adaptive response of Black people to institutionalized racism, which is measured by the race-based disadvantage variables (Mann, 1995). Because most homicide is intraracial (Blau & Blau, 1982; Fox & Zawitz, 2003), race-based disadvantage may affect the level of murders of Black women. In accordance with previous research, relative disadvantage is used in this study. This includes joblessness (unemployment and underemployment), median income, poverty, college education, professional and managerial occupations, and political power.

RACIAL SOCIOECONOMIC INEQUALITY

Several studies of Black violence have emphasized its connection to economic inequality (Blau & Blau, 1982; Land, McCall, & Cohen, 1990; Parker, 2001; Parker & McCall,

1997) while others have found that race has an effect on murder independent of any economic deprivation (Bailey, 1984; Logan & Messner, 1987; Parker & Johns, 2002; Peterson & Krivo, 1993). Possible socioeconomic indicators of increased violence in the Black community include unemployment, underemployment, and marginal employment as well as few opportunities to acquire the education necessary to become gainfully employed (Mann, 1995).

Blocked access to education and employment opportunities created by racial discrimination has caused chronic frustration among many Black men, who may direct their anger against society toward Black women by using violence (Bell, 1992; Mann, 1995; Oliver, 2000). In this research, joblessness (the ratio of Black to White unemployment) is operationalized as the percent of the Black population 16 years old and over who are either unemployed or not looking for employment relative to the White population 16 years old and over who are either unemployed or not looking for employment. This does not include persons who are in the military. Poverty (the ratio of Black to White poverty) is measured as the percent of the Black population living below the federal poverty level relative to the percent of the White population living below the federal poverty level.

Educational inequality (the ratio of White to Black college education) is the percent of White adults 25 years and over who have a college education (BA degree and higher) relative to the percent of Black adults 25 years old and over who have a college education (BA degree or higher) (Messner & Golden, 1992). Racial disparities in income (the ratio of White to Black income) are measured by the median income of the White population 16 years old and over working full-time relative to the median income of the Black population 16 years old and over working full-time.

Racial disadvantage in professional and managerial occupations (the ratio of White to Black elite occupations) is measured as the percent of White men and women 16 years old and over who have a professional or managerial occupation relative to the percent of Black men and women 16 years old and over who have a professional or managerial occupation.[11]

RACIAL POLITICAL INEQUALITY

Racial inequality is not limited to socioeconomic inequality. Political inequality is important because a lack of Black elected representation helps to maintain racial inequality in all spheres of society. To measure political inequality, this study includes a measure of the percent of City Council members who are White.

CLASS INEQUALITY INDEX

To measure class inequality, median income, poverty level, employed labor force, and the level of college education in the cities are used. Median income is measured as the median income of the city's population 16 years old and over working full-time relative to the median income of the U.S. population 16 years old and over working full-time (ratio of city to U.S. median income). Also used is the percent of the city's total population living at or above the federal poverty level relative to the

U.S. total population living at or above the federal poverty level (ratio of city to U.S. above-poverty level).

Because the American dream is based on attaining the good life, the failure to attain a high status can lead to anger, frustration, and violence (Bell, 1992; Mann, 1995). As a measure of employment levels, this study uses the percent of the city's total population employed in the labor force relative to the U.S. total population employed in the labor force (ratio of city to U.S. population employed). Finally, education (the ratio of city to U.S. college education) is measured as the percent of the city's population 25 years old and over with a college education (BA degree and higher) relative to the U.S. population 25 years old and over with a college education (BA degree and higher).

RESULTS

The path analysis models show that gender, race, and class predict the variances in the overall femicide rates as well as the femicide rates of both Black women and White women.[12]

Overall, a city's greater racial and class inequalities predict a higher femicide rate whereas greater gender inequality predicts a lower femicide rate (as compared with other cities).[13] These significant, moderate predictors account for 37 percent of the variance in the overall femicide rates, which means that a city's level of gender, race, and class inequality accounts for more than one-third of the variation in its overall femicide rate (see Figure 6.2).

When femicide rates are disaggregated, the gender, race, and class inequality indices account for almost one-fourth (22%) of the variance in the Black femicide rate (see Figure 6.3) and 29 percent of the variance in the White femicide rate (see Figure 6.4).

In those cities where women have a greater gender inequality, or a lower gender status, women are murdered at a lower rate than in those cities where women experience a higher status, when controlling the effects of racial and class inequality. This pattern applies to both Black women and White women although it is more significant for Black women.

This gender backlash can occur when the advancement of women is considered a threat to male dominance and violence is used to eliminate that threat (Vieraitis & Williams, 2002). Gender backlash theory asserts that increased gender equality can

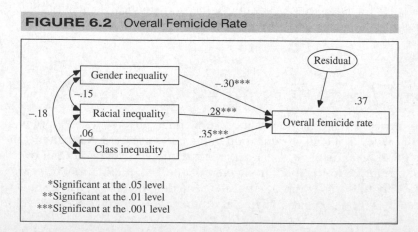

FIGURE 6.2   Overall Femicide Rate

*Significant at the .05 level
**Significant at the .01 level
***Significant at the .001 level

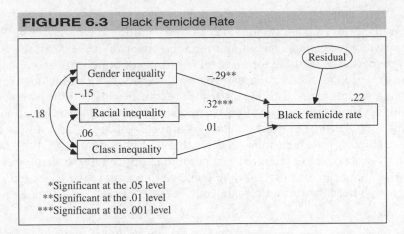

FIGURE 6.3   Black Femicide Rate

*Significant at the .05 level
**Significant at the .01 level
***Significant at the .001 level

result in increased violence due to men fearing that the improvement in women's status will threaten their own social power. Men may use violence to maintain dominance over women who want to be more independent of men (Russell, 1974; Whaley, 2001; Whaley & Messner, 2002).

Backlash can also be explained as the response to increased stress and conflict created by pro-woman policies and programs. When a man's normative goal of power and control is threatened, his frustrated attempts to achieve those goals may lead to severe, and sometimes lethal, attempts to regain control (Dugan, Nagin, & Rosenfeld, 2000; Wells & DeLeon-Granados, 2004). The gender backlash results are in accordance with previous studies that found that social structural gender equality is associated with higher femicide rates (Avakame, 1999; Bailey & Peterson, 1995; Brewer & Smith, 1995; Whaley & Messner, 2002).

In contrast to the effect of gender inequality, greater racial and class inequality are significant, moderate predictors of higher overall femicide rates. When controlling gender and class inequalities, greater racial inequality in a city (compared with other cities) predicts higher overall and Black femicide rates, but has little effect on the White femicide rate. This supports the racial inequality theory, which suggests that greater racial inequality means higher homicide rates for Black people. The findings also suggest that White women are not protected by racial privilege.

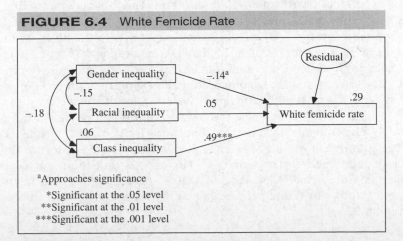

FIGURE 6.4   White Femicide Rate

[a]Approaches significance
*Significant at the .05 level
**Significant at the .01 level
***Significant at the .001 level

A city with a lower socioeconomic class status (as compared with other cities) will have higher overall and White femicide rates, but there is no effect on Black femicide rates, when controlling gender and racial inequalities. To be clear, the class inequality index measures a city's overall level of socioeconomic status compared with other cities, regardless of race, whereas the racial inequality index includes some social and economic variables.[14] This means that the femicide rate of Black women is predicted by the level of social and economic inequality of a city's Black population relative to its White population, but not by a city's overall class status relative to the class status of other cities. A possible explanation for these findings may be that the racial composition of most of these cities may be predominantly White, so that a city's class status may be more relevant to the White femicide rate than to the Black femicide rate. This suggests a need for further research on the effect of class on femicide rates.

DISCUSSION

The conclusions of this research supplement the existing literature and contribute to a more complete understanding of the complexity of femicide as a social phenomenon. This study fills a void in the homicide literature, specifically in the femicide literature, by adding to the research in several ways. Until recently, empirical homicide studies have almost exclusively focused on men, either as perpetrators or as victims. When women have been studied in relation to homicide, those studies have largely been descriptive studies or have focused on women as offenders. Even empirical research on intimate partner homicide, which disproportionately affects women, has not generally been disaggregated by the victim's gender.

This study continues a line of research that examines the structural effects of gender, racial, and class inequalities on femicide rates. It takes a multi-institutional focus by examining the relationship between the femicide rates and gender, racial, and class inequalities in a path analysis. None of the previous studies has examined these inequalities in a single model.

Moreover, this study separately analyzes the effects of gender, racial, and class inequalities on the femicide rates of various cities. Crenshaw (1991) asserts that women of color intersect differently with gender, race, and class than do White women so that their experiences with violence are different. This study supports that idea. While a city's increased gender inequality (as compared with other cities) predicts lower overall femicide rates as well as the femicide rates for both Black women and White women, a city's greater racial inequality (as compared with other cities) predicts higher overall and Black femicide rates, with little or no effect on White femicide rates, and a city's lower class status (as compared with other cities) predicts higher overall and White femicide rates, with little or no effect on Black femicide rates.

In other words, fewer Black women are murdered in cities where Black people have gained a higher racial status, but more Black women are murdered in cities where women enjoy a higher gender status. There is little effect as the city's overall socioeconomic class status changes. This means that the femicide rates of Black women are predicted by the level of a city's social and economic inequality of Black people relative to White people, but not by a city's overall class status relative to other cities.

Like Black women, more White women are murdered in cities where women enjoy a higher gender status, but a city's level of racial discrimination has little effect on the murder of White women, which means that White women do not benefit from race privilege. By contrast, as the city's overall socioeconomic class environment declines (compared with other cities), more White women are murdered.

This research reinforces the idea that women face multiple oppressions that may lead to their murder. Research focusing on gender oppression alone has obscured the reality of women's complicated lives. Greater racial oppression of Black women, including economic, social, and political discrimination, and greater class oppression of White women are predictors of higher femicide rates. A woman's social context combines interconnecting systems of power (patriarchy, racial hierarchy, and capitalism) and oppression (sexism, racism, and classism). Oppression is more than a lack of equal rights. Hierarchical power relations create and maintain a society where those people with greater power control those with lesser power. In a society where wealthy White men hold the power, women are devalued, Black people are considered dispensable, and working-class people are relegated to the lower rungs of society. U.S. society embodies a stratified system that maintains a social climate within which violence against women is a manifestation of the power relations between men and women, between White people and Black people, and between the wealthy and working people.

Gender backlash, which results in more women being murdered as women gain greater gender status, indicates that our society needs to go beyond equal rights for women. While women have gained greater access to college and better jobs, the message of current popular culture is that women cannot, and should not, have it all. Instead, women are told that they must choose between having a family and a career, and a traditional family with traditional gender roles is more acceptable. Moreover, popular films, advertising, and music videos tell men and women that women exist to be sex objects. Even violence against women is rampant in popular culture.

Our society needs to establish that violence against women is not acceptable behavior. There should be a zero-tolerance policy against all violence against women, which includes sexual harassment, acquaintance rape, and the portrayal of women as sex objects. Social hierarchies cannot condone violence against women if the level of femicides is to decline.

Yet, gender hierarchical relations are only one part of the femicide puzzle. The more racial inequality in a city, the higher the femicide rate of Black women. White women are neither helped nor hindered by changes in a city's level of racial discrimination against the Black population, which indicates that they do not experience protection based on their racial status. According to Crenshaw (1991), racism is linked to patriarchy to the extent that racism denies men of color the power and privilege enjoyed by White men. This may explain why the Black femicide rate is higher in those cities where women gain greater status than men but Black people experience higher levels of racial discrimination. Because most femicides are intraracial (Parker, 2001), most Black women are murdered by Black men, who may be threatened by the rising status of women while being held down socially, economically, and politically by racial oppression. Oliver (2000) suggests that blocked opportunities lead many Black men to direct their anger against society toward their intimate partners.

To address the high levels of Black women being murdered, a comprehensive social policy that promotes racial equality for Black women and Black men relative to

White women and White men will begin to eliminate the social, economic, and political disparities between Black people and White people, which in turn should result in lower femicide rates for Black women.

Cities with a lower overall class status (as compared with other cities), regardless of racial makeup, have higher overall and White femicide rates, but the level of Black femicides is not affected by changes in a city's class status. These findings suggest that White men, who are the majority of perpetrators against White women (Blau & Blau, 1982; LaFree, 1999; Moracco et al, 1998; Parker, 1989), may be more oppressed by class status than helped by their racial privilege. To lessen the number of White women who are murdered, a city's social and economic health must improve. More jobs, better jobs, less poverty, and more people graduating from college should lead to fewer murders of White women.

This research is only the beginning of the effort to disentangle the multi-faceted relationships among gender, race, class, and femicide. More research and discussion concerning the effect of interlocking oppressions on femicide rates will advance this area of study. Future research needs to include longitudinal studies as well as studies that disaggregate femicide by victim–offender relationships and by the motivations of the perpetrators. While this research is an important piece of the femicide puzzle, it is only the beginning of the process of understanding the predictors, causes, and risks of femicide.

Discussion Questions

1. Describe what is meant by the term *femicide*.
2. What are the social factors that contribute to the existence of femicide?
3. How can intersectionality theory be applied to explaining the differing femicide rates among women based on race and class?
4. In what context does inequality contribute to the perpetration of violence against women?
5. Identify the main findings in this study and discuss how they could be used to inform policy or legislation aimed at reducing the victimization of women?

References

Avakame, E. F. (1999). Females' labor force participation and intimate femicide: An empirical assessment of the backlash hypothesis. *Violence and Victims, 14*(3), 77–291.

Bailey, W. C. (1984). Poverty, inequality, and city homicide rates. *Criminology, 22*(4), 531–550.

Bailey, W. C., & Peterson, R. D. (1995). Gender inequality and violence against women. In J. Hagan & R. D. Peterson (Eds.), *Crime and Inequality* (pp. 174–205). California: Stanford University Press.

Baron, L., & Straus, M. A. (1984). Sexual stratification, pornography, and rape in the United States. In N. M. Malamuth & E. Donnerstein (Eds.), *Pornography and sexual aggression* (pp. 185–209). Orlando, FL: Academic Press.

Bell, D. (1992). *Faces at the bottom of the well: The permanence of racism.* New York: Basic Books.

Blau, J. R., & Blau, P. M. (1982). The cost of inequality: Metropolitan structure and violent crime. *American Sociological Review, 47*(1), 114–129.

Bograd, M. (1990). Feminist perspectives on wife abuse: An introduction. In K. Yllö & M. Bograd (Eds.), *Feminist perspectives on wife abuse* (pp. 11–26). Newbury Park, CA: Sage.

Brewer, V. E., & Smith, M. D. (1995). Gender inequality and rates of female homicide victimization across U.S. Cities. *Journal of Research in Crime and Delinquency, 32*(2), 175–190.

Centers for Disease Control. (1998). Retrieved December 1, 2004, from http://www.cdc.gov.

Centers for Disease Control. (1999). Retrieved December 1, 2004, from http://www.cdc.gov.

Centers for Disease Control. (2000). Retrieved December 1, 2004, from http://www.cdc.gov.

Centers for Disease Control. (2001). Retrieved December 1, 2004, from http://www.cdc.gov.

Chervyakov, V. V., Shkolnikov, V. M., Pridemore, W. A., & McKee, M. (2002). The changing nature of murder in Russia. *Social Science & Medicine, 55,* 1713–1724.

Collins, P. H. (1990). *Black feminist thought.* London and New York: Routledge.

Crenshaw, K. (1991). Mapping the margins: Intersectionality, identity politics, and violence against women of color. *Stanford Law Review, 43,* 1241–1299.

Davis, A. Y. (1983). *Women, race & class.* New York: Vintage Books.

Dobash, R. E., & Dobash, R. (1979). *Violence against wives.* New York: Free Press.

Dugan, L., Nagin, D., & Rosenfeld, R. (2000). Exposure reduction or backlash? The effects of domestic violence resources on intimate partner homicide. *Final report to the National Institute of Justice.* NCJRS 186194.

Durkheim, E. (1951/1897). *Suicide: A study in sociology.* New York: Free Press.

Ellis, L., & Beattie, C. (1983). The feminist explanation of rape: An empirical test. *Journal of Sex Research, 19*(1), 74–93.

Federal Bureau of Investigation. (1998). *Supplementary homicide reports.* Washington, D.C.: Federal Bureau of Investigation.

Federal Bureau of Investigation. (1999). *Supplementary homicide reports.* Washington, D.C.: Federal Bureau of Investigation.

Federal Bureau of Investigation. (2000). *Supplementary homicide reports.* Washington, D.C.: Federal Bureau of Investigation.

Federal Bureau of Investigation. (2001). *Supplementary homicide reports.* Washington, D.C.: Federal Bureau of Investigation.

Federal Bureau of Investigation. (2004). *Crime in the United States, 2002.* Retrieved June 3, 2007, from http://www.fbi.gov/ucr/cius_04/

Fine, M., & Weis, L. (1998). *The unknown city: Lives of poor and working-class young adults.* Boston, MA: Beacon Press.

Fox, J. A., & Zawitz, M. W. (1999). *Homicide trends in the United States.* Washington, D.C: U.S. Department of Justice. NCJ 173956.

Fox, J. A., & Zawitz, M. W. (2003). Homicide trends in the United States: 2000 update. *Bureau of Justice Statistics Crime Data Brief.* Washington, D.C.: U.S. Department of Justice. NCJ 197471.

Frye, V., & Wilt, S. (2001). Femicide and social disorganization. *Violence Against Women, 7*(3), 335–351.

Greenfeld, L. A., Rand, M. R., Craven, D., Klau, P. A., Perkins, C. A., Ringel, C., Warchol, G., Maton, C., & Fox, J. A. (1998). *Violence by intimates: Analysis of data on crimes by current or former spouses, boyfriends, and girlfriends.* U.S. Department of Justice, Office of Justice Programs, Bureau of Justice Statistics. Washington, D.C.: U.S. Government Printing Office. NCJ-167237.

Hawkins, D. F. (1995). What can we learn from data disaggregation: The case of homicide and African Americans. In M. D. Smith & M. A. Zahn (Eds.), *Homicide: A sourcebook of social research* (pp. 195–210). Newbury Park, CA: Sage.

Hemenway, D., Shinoda-Tagawa, T., & Miller, M. (2002). Firearm availability and female homicide victimization rates among 25 populous high income countries. *Journal of the American Medical Women's Association, 57*(2), 100–104.

Hooks, B. (1989). *Talking back: Thinking feminist thinking black.* Boston, MA: South End Press.

Human Rights Watch. (1997). Russia: Too little, too late: State response to violence against women. *Human Rights Watch, 9*(13). Retrieved on June 1, 2008, from http:/www.hrw.org/reports97/russwmn/

Johnson, H. (1994). Risk factors associated with non-lethal violence against women by marital partners. In C. Block & R. Block (Eds.), *Trends, risks, and interventions in lethal* violence: *Proceedings of the Third Annual Spring Symposium of the Homicide Research Working Group* (pp. 35–50). Washington, D.C.: National Institute of Justice.

LaFree, G. (1999). A summary and review of cross-national comparative studies of homicide. In M. D. Smith & M. A. Zahn (Eds.), *Homicide: A sourcebook of social research* (pp. 125–145). Newbury Park, CA: Sage.

Land, K. C., McCall, P. L., & Cohen, L. E. (1990). Structural covariates of homicide rates: Are there any invariances across time and social space? *American Journal of Sociology, 95*, 922–963.

Logan, J. R., & Messner, S. F. (1987). Racial segregation and suburban violent crime. *Social Science Quarterly, 68*, 510–527.

Mann, C. R. (1995). The contribution of institutionalized racism to minority crime. In D. F. Hawkins (Ed.), *Ethnicity, race, and crime: Perspectives across time and place* (pp. 259–280). Albany, NY: State University of New York Press.

Mansbridge, J. (1999). "You're too independent!": How gender, race, and class make many feminisms. In M. Lamont, (Ed). *The cultural territories of race: black and white boundaries.* Chicago, IL: University of Chicago Press.

Martin, D. (1983). *Battered wives.* New York: Pocket Books.

Messner, S. F., & Golden, R. M. (1992). Racial inequality and racially disaggregated homicide rates: An assessment of alternative theoretical explanations. *Criminology, 30*(3), 421–429.

Messner, S. F., & Rosenfeld, R. (1999). Social structure and homicide. In M. D. Smith & M. A. Zahn (Eds.), *Homicide: A sourcebook of social research* (pp. 27–41). Newbury Park, CA: Sage.

Messner, S. F., & Tardiff, K. (1986). Economic inequality and levels of homicide: An analysis of urban neighborhoods. *Criminology, 24*(2), 297–315.

Moracco, K. E., Runyan, C. W., & Butts, J. D. (1998). Femicide in North Carolina, 1991–1993: A statewide study of patterns and precursors. *Homicide Studies, 2*(4), 422–446.

Oliver, W. (2000). Preventing domestic violence in the African American community: A rationale for popular culture interventions. *Violence Against Women, 6*(5), 533–549.

Parker, R. N. (1989). Deterrence, poverty, and type of homicide. *Social Forces, 67*, 983–1007.

Parker, K. F. (2001). A move toward specificity: Examining urban disadvantage race- and relationship-specific homicide rates. *Journal of Quantitative Criminology, 17*(1), 89–110.

Parker, K. F., & Johns, T. (2002). Urban disadvantage and types of race-specific homicide: Assessing the diversity in family structures in the urban context. *Journal of Research in Crime and Delinquency, 39*(3), 277–303.

Parker, K. F., & McCall, P. L. (1997). Adding another piece to the inequality-homicide puzzle. *Homicide Studies, 1*(1), 35–60.

Peterson, R. D., & Krivo, L. J. (1993). Racial segregation and black urban homicide. *Social Forces, 71*(4), 1001–1026.

Rennison, C. M. (2001). Violent victimization and race, 1993–1998. *Bureau of Justice Statistics Special Report.* NCJ 176354. Washington, D.C.: U.S. Department of Justice.

Rennison, C. M (2003). Intimate partner violence, 1993–2001. *Bureau of Justice Statistics Crime Data Brief.* NCJ 197838. Washington, D.C.: Department of Justice.

Richie, B. (2000). A black feminist reflection on the antiviolence movement. *Signs: A Journal of Women in Culture and Society, 25*(4), 1133–1137.

Russell, D. E. H. (1974). *The politics of rape.* New York: Stein and Day Publishers.

Salfati, C. G. (2001). A European perspective on the study of homicide. *Homicide Studies, 5*(4), 286–291.

Sampson, R. (1985). Structural sources of variation. *Criminology, 23*(4), 647–673.

Smith, M. D., & Kuchta, E. S. (1995). Female homicide victimization in the United States: Trends in relative risk, 1946–1990. *Social Science Quarterly, 76*(3), 665–672.

Sokoloff, N. J. (1992). *Black women and white women in the professions.* New York: Routledge.

Sokoloff, N. J. (Ed.). (2005). *Domestic violence at the margins: Readings on race, class, gender, and culture.* Piscataway, NJ: Rutgers University Press.

St. Pierre Ruffin, J. (1895). Address to the first national conference of colored women.

Retrieved June 1, 2008 from http://www.
blackpast.org/?q=1895-josephine-st-pierre-
ruffin-address-first-national-conference-
colored-women

Sykes, A. O. (n.d.) *An introduction to regression
analysis.* Inaugural Course Lecture Chicago
Working Paper on Law & Economics.
Chicago: University of Chicago.

Truth, S. (1972). Ain't I a woman? In M. Schneir
(Ed.), *Feminism: The essential historical writ-
ings* (pp. 93–95). New York: Random House.
Original publication in 1851.

Vieraitis, L. M., & Williams, M. R. (2002).
Assessing the impact of gender inequality on
female homicide victimization across U.S.
cities: A racially disaggregated analysis.
Violence Against Women, 8(1), 35–62.

Wells, W., & DeLeon-Granados, W. (2004). The
intimate partner homicide decline:
Disaggregated trends, theoretical explanations,
and policy implications. *Criminal Justice Policy
Review, 15*(2), 229–246.

Whaley, R. B. (2001). The paradoxical relationship between gender inequality and rape:
Toward a refined theory. *Gender & Society,
15*(4), 531–555.

Whaley, R. B., & Messner, S. F. (2002). Gender
equality and gendered homicides. *Homicide
Studies, 6*(3), 188–210.

White, D. G. (1985). *Ar'n't I a woman? Female
slaves in the plantation south.* New York and
London: W.W. Norton & Co.

Wing, A. K. (2003). Introduction. In A. K. Wing
(Ed.), *Critical race feminism: A reader.* (2nd
ed.). New York: New York University Press.

Yllö, K. (1983). Sexual equality and violence
against wives in American states. *Journal of
Comparative Family Studies, 14*(1), 67–87.

Zahn, M. A., & McCall, P. L. (1999). Trends and
patterns of homicide in the 20th century. In
M. D. Smith & M. A. Zahn (Eds.), *Homicide:
A sourcebook of social research* (pp. 9–25).
Newbury Park, CA: Sage.

Endnotes

1. Intimate partners include current or former husbands, (legal and common-law), boyfriends and former boyfriends, and same-sex partners.
2. Homicide includes murder and nonnegligent manslaughter. Nevertheless, I will use the terms homicide and murder interchangeably.
3. Intersectionality theory and path analysis will be discussed later in the chapter.
4. Cities without reported homicide data were excluded. In order to examine the intersection of race, those cities with less than a 2 percent Black population were excluded from this study.
5. While it would be optimal to investigate the killing of Latinas, those data are not readily available for many of the cities in the sample, including Philadelphia, Chicago, and New York. Asian women and women of other races are not included because there were so few reported femicides of these women that identifying any meaningful patterns would be difficult. For those reasons, this study disaggregates the femicide rates for only Black women and White women.
6. Every dependent variable has a disturbance (residual), which is the unexplained variance that is omitted from the model.
7. The division by four creates the per year rate because the data sets represent 1998–2001. Yearly fluctuations in the data are minimized by averaging the rates.
8. These multiple variables may be so related to each other that they measure the same effects, a phenomenon called multicollinearity (Sykes, n.d.). To eliminate any possible multicollinearity, a technique known as principal components methods is used. Based on the information from standard principal components methods, the variables are combined to create separate indices: gender, racial, and class inequalities, which measure the predictive effects of the structural variables on the femicide rates, including overall rates and race-specific rates.
9. The data for these measures are gathered from the U.S. Bureau of Census, the Small Business Administration, and Web sites of all the cities in the sample based on 2000 data. All the data are available online.

10. Professional and managerial occupations include management occupations, business and financial occupations, computer and mathematical occupations, surveyors, architects, cartographers, physical scientists, life scientists, engineers, lawyers, judges, magistrates, other judicial workers, physicians, and surgeons. Professional occupations not included are those generally not considered as high-prestige occupations, including nurses, paralegals, and teachers.

11. The same occupations used in the gender occupational variable are used in this racial occupational variable.

12. Statistical significance of path coefficients is measured using the Critical Ratio, which is interpreted as a z-score.

13. Standardized path coefficients show the amount of expected change in the dependent variable as a result of the change in the independent variable while controlling the remaining independent variables. The path model also shows the correlated, nonpredictive relationships between the independent variables, which are shown by curved arrows with double arrowheads.

14. The racial inequality index also includes a political inequality variable.

CHAPTER 7

RAPE MYTHS: IMPACTS ON VICTIMS OF RAPE

HEATHER C. MELTON

ABSTRACT

Rape myths, stereotypical views about rape, rape victims, and/or rapists, are embedded in the culture of U.S. society. These rape myths have great impacts, particularly for victims of rape. Studies have found that victims are less likely to disclose their rapes because of rape myths. They may be less likely to turn to the police because of rape myths. They may be less likely to identify what happened to them as rape because of rape myths. This chapter explores the concept of rape myths, theories surrounding their existence and acceptance, the impacts they have on victims, and the criminal justice response to rape and sexual assault. Because of the particularly negative impact rape myths have on the following as well as because of historical exclusion of these victims from studies, particular attention is paid to their effect on victims of color, poor victims, and nonheterosexual victims of rape and sexual assault.

INTRODUCTION

Rape and sexual assault continue to be serious problems facing the United States today. While it is suggested that rape may be one of the most underreported crimes, the following statistics on rape are staggering. The Uniform Crime Report states there were more than 93,934 rapes in 2005, indicating that the rate of rape is 31.4 per 100,000 in the population (Federal Bureau of Investigation, 2005). The most recent results from the National Crime Victimization Survey suggest even higher numbers—191,670 incidents of rape or sexual assault in 2005 (United States Department of Justice, 2006). Moreover, many argue that these numbers increase if you examine specific populations (e.g., college students). Clearly, rape is a major problem.

Society, criminal justice personnel, and the media all hold preconceived notions about victims of rape.[1] Certain types of victims continue to be seen as more "true" victims than many other victims of rape. We continue to define "true" victims as those that are walking alone late at night and have a stranger jump out of the bushes. However, in reality most sexual assault happens among people who are acquainted, with a high correlation between dating and marriage and sexual assault. Victims of rape and sexual assault report that in nearly three out of four incidents, the offender was not a stranger. Moreover, it is estimated that in 90 percent of sexual victimizations involving child victims, the child knows the offender (Greenfeld, 1997). This misconception about characteristics of rape victims has serious consequences for those true victims of rape and sexual assault.

This chapter will explore the realities and truths of victims of sexual assault. Attention will be paid to what are known as "rape myths" and "rape culture," theories regarding these concepts, and the effects these have on victims of sexual assault and rape. In addition, the effects these have on the criminal justice response to sexual assault will be examined. Finally, particular attention will be paid to the race, ethnicity, class, and sexual orientation of rape victims and how this effects how others view them as victims.

SEXUAL ASSAULT

Defining sexual assault and rape is difficult. Historically, the definitions were very limited and narrow in scope. For example, in English common law rape only included forced sexual intercourse between a man and a woman who is not his wife. Traditionally, rape has been defined as forced penile–vaginal intercourse committed by an adult male stranger against an adult female. Today, we know that sexual assault can occur among strangers, dating partners, marital partners, heterosexuals, people of the same sex, and young and old, and both men and women can be victims. Moreover, it may involve anal, oral, or vaginal–penile intercourse, or even assault using a foreign object. Lastly, many argue that rape does not necessarily have to involve force. While unfortunately, many legally continue to rely on force as evidence of rape, many researchers, practitioners, and laws against rape include coercive rapes in their definitions. Rape is defined as unlawful sexual intercourse by force or without legal or factual consent. Sexual assault is more broad and inclusive and can be defined as any forced or coerced sexual intimacy (unwanted touching with no consent) (Belknap, 2001).

Statistics on rape vary greatly. It is estimated that rape is one of the most underreported crimes. Studies have found that many victims are unwilling to report for many different reasons including the following: They do not want anyone to find out, they do not define what happened to them as rape (particularly in date or marital rape situations), they blame themselves, they do not want their friend, boyfriend, or husband to get into trouble, they fear how criminal justice personal will treat them, they think nothing can be done, and they just want to forget and get over it. Because of this, it is estimated that both official records (i.e., police reports, because many victims do not report for reasons discussed above) and victimization surveys (i.e., victims may still have many reasons for not disclosing) greatly underestimate rape. Moreover, the way rape is defined will change the numbers. For example, some studies only include completed rapes, while others include attempted as well. Finally, many have argued that certain types of rape are disproportionately reported (stranger rapes where victims are seen as "typical" victims), and thus, the numbers may be skewed. That being said, the following are some statistics on the prevalence of rape in the United States. As stated previously, the range for 2005 goes from 93,934 incidents of rape according to official records to 191,670 using victimization reports. Clearly, rape and sexual assault are serious problems.

While rape is typically seen as a crime occurring between strangers, it is now known that the majority of rapes occur among acquaintances. This could involve a family relationship, a martial relationship, a dating relationship, a working relationship, or an acquaintance relationship. Rape and sexual assault are considered problems of violence against women, meaning the majority of sexual assault and rapes involve a female victim and a male perpetrator.[2]

In addition to being a serious social and criminal problem, many argue that violence against women and sexual assault in particular may be viewed as health problems. Sexual assault and rape may have severe physical and psychological health impacts for the victims. Studies have found that rape victims report chronic pelvic pain, gastrointestinal disorders, back pain, and facial pain. In terms of psychological impacts, studies have found that victims report increased experiences of posttraumatic stress disorder, depression, and sleep disturbances. Because of the serious health impacts of sexual assault, it is particularly important that the appropriate criminal justice response be implemented, a response that takes into consideration the victim's wants and needs.

VICTIMS OF RAPE: WHO ARE THEY?

Numerous studies have been conducted to determine who is most likely to be a victim of sexual assault. First, it is clear that sexual assault is a crime of violence against women: Women are more likely to be victims of sexual assault than are men. The National Violence Against Women Survey indicates that 18 percent of women and 3 percent of men experienced a completed or attempted rape at some point in their lives, with rape defined as forced oral, anal, or vaginal intercourse. This translates into 1 in every 6 women and 1 in every 33 men experiencing an attempted or completed rape as a child or as an adult (Tjaden & Thoennes, 1998). Groth and Burgess (1980) estimate that only 1 percent of reported rape victims are men, excluding men who are raped in prison.

While it should be noted that everyone is a potential victim of rape, studies have attempted to identify risk factors for rape victims. Thus, the typical rape victim is a young (Greenfeld, 1997), female (Belknap, 2001; Brownmiller, 1975; Greenfeld, 1997), and is raped in or near her home or apartment (Belknap, 2001). Although more than half of all rape victims are White, Black females are overrepresented in rape rates (Greenfeld, 1997). Rapes occur mainly at night: Three-fourths take place between 6:00 P.M. and 6:00 A.M. Certainly, there are different types of rapists, and research shows that different rapists may rape at different times of the day. One in five rapists use no physical violence or weapons, but verbal threats or coercive behavior may be just as effective with many victims.

RAPE MYTHS AND RAPE CULTURE

Rape myths abound in our society. Burt (1980) defined rape myths as "prejudicial, stereotyped, or false beliefs about rape, rape victims, and rapists" (p. 217). Lonsway and Fitzgerald (1995) explain that rape myths exist surrounding victim precipitation, the definition of rape, male intention, the condition whether or not a victim deserves to be raped or enjoys being raped, a trivialization of rape, and an emphasis on the deviance of the act. Common cultural myths and stereotypes concerning rape and sexual assault include the following: Good girls don't get raped, women provoke rape by what they wear, rapist are strangers who jump out of bushes, rape is an act of sex, women cry rape when they have been rejected or engaged in consensual sex that they later regret, and any healthy woman should be able to resist rape, to name a few (Burt, 1980; Stewart, Dobbin, & Gatowski, 1996). Moreover, some rape myths include the stereotype of the Black rapist and the White rape victim (Mann & Selva, 1979). Finally, some argue that the "pedestal myth of women" also pertains to rape myths (Stewart et al., 1996). This myth holds women to a higher moral standard than men. Thus, if something bad happens to her, it must be because of something she did (Stewart et al., 1996), illustrating the victim-blaming nature of rape myths. These myths regarding rape do not occur in a vacuum. They have developed out of a more general context of myths and stereotypes regarding gender, gender roles, race, and class. These cultural myths regarding rape have huge implications for the victims of sexual assault, the criminal justice response to sexual assault, and societal views on sexual assault.

Moreover, rape myths have extremely negative implications for women of color, poor women, and nonheterosexual women. While White, affluent, and heterosexual women may be seen as "typical" victims if their rape fits certain criteria, women of color, poor women, and nonheterosexual women are never seen as "typical" victims. This, in turn, affects their experiences, their recovery, and the criminal justice intervention in their cases. Particular attention will be paid to this issue in this chapter.

Certain people may be more likely to rely on rape myths. For example, many studies have found that men have higher rape myth acceptance (RMA) than do females (Foley, Evancic, Karnik, King, & Parks, 1995; Lonsway & Fitzgerald, 1995; Whatley, 2005). Others have found that rape myths may function differently for men and women: While men may use rape myths to justify the behavior, women may use rape myths to deny personal vulnerability (Lonsway & Fitzgerald, 1995). Some have found that people who ascribe to more traditional values particularly about men and women are more likely to have higher RMA (Foley et al., 1995; Lonsway & Fitzgerald, 1994). Moreover, many studies have explored the impact of RMA by victims of rape (see discussion below) (Peterson & Muehlenhard, 2004).

Rape myths clearly serve certain functions. First, rape myths allow the denial and trivialization of the crime of rape (Lonsway & Fitzgerald, 1994). Many who rely on rape myths continue to maintain, incorrectly, that it is not that common (i.e., look at low official statistics) and that it is not that serious (i.e., look at the small number of victims who go to the hospital). This, unfortunately, continues the cycle of victims not reporting and the crime not being taken seriously. Second, rape myths function to support the just world hypothesis (see discussion in theory section). Finally, many maintain that rape myths function to continue the oppression and social control of women (Brownmiller, 1975; Burt, 1980; Lonsway & Fitzgerald, 1994).

Beyond rape myths, many argue that we live in a rape culture (Brownmiller, 1975; Buchwald, Fletcher, & Roth, 1993), and thus these rape myths are, in part, a result of our rape culture. A rape culture is one in which male sexual aggression and violence toward women is encouraged and supported. It is one in which violence is associated with sex and vice versa. It is one in which sexual violence against women is seen as the norm as opposed to the exception (Brownmiller, 1975; Buchald, et al., 1993; Crowell & Burgess, 1996; Price, 2005). Like rape myths, this rape culture has very important implications for victims of sexual assault and rape.

THEORY REGARDING RAPE MYTHS AND RAPE CULTURE

One of the biggest criticisms of studies exploring the impact on rape myths and rape victimization is the lack of theory. Lonsway and Fitzgerald (1994) state, "the ultimate value of rape myths construct depends upon the degree to which it contributes to our theoretical understanding of the existence and acceptance of sexual victimization" (p. 156). Further, they articulate that there needs to be an examination of the etiology and role of rape myths in a theory of culturally supported sexual aggression.

Several theories, though underdeveloped, have been explored in regard to rape myths. These include the just world hypothesis (Lerner, 1965), the defensive attribution hypothesis (Mason, Riger, & Foley, 2004), justifications/excuses (Scully & Marolla, 1985; Stewart et al., 1996; Sykes & Matza, 1957), and various feminist theories (Brownmiller, 1975; Burt, 1980; Lonsway & Fitzgerald, 1994; Price, 2005; Washington, 2001). Each of these will now be discussed.

The just world hypothesis, developed by Lerner in 1965, maintains that people have a need to think that the world they live in is just and that people get what they deserve (Furnham & Boston, 1996; Lerner, 1965; Lerner & Miller, 1978). Thus, good things happen to good people, and bad things happen only to those who deserve them (Lonsway & Fitzgerald, 1994). In terms of rape, evidence of "victims were asking for it" and "she got what she deserved" illustrates the just world hypothesis. For example, Furnham and Boston (1996) found that respondents commenting on rape scenarios attributed more blame to victims when they were dressed provocatively than when they were dressed conservatively. Their reasoning was that "she was asking for it" (Furnham & Boston, 1996, p. 224). Other recent studies have confirmed that respondents attribute more blame to victims if they are dressed a certain way (Whatley, 2005), if they are seen to have failed to maintain a certain moral standard (Stewart et al., 1996), or if they are seen as engaging in provoking behavior (Krahe, 1988).

Similarly, the defensive attribution hypothesis argues that people use personal relevance and situational relevance to decide how much blame to place on victims of negative events (Mason et al., 2004). Thus, if they perceive themselves to be like the victim (personal relevance) or are likely to ever be in a similar situation (situational relevance), they place less blame on the victim. Mason and colleagues (2004) tested this hypothesis by examining respondents' sexual history and made the prediction that victims who were previously sexually assaulted would be less likely to place blame on victims of rape for their victimization. They did not find any support for their hypothesis and thus dismissed the defensive attribution hypothesis (Mason et al., 2004). However, more empirical testing of this hypothesis should be conducted.

Numerous studies on various crimes have explored the impact of using justifications and excuses for offenders and techniques of neutralization by offenders in terms of committing their crimes (Scully & Marolla, 1985; Sykes & Matza, 1957). However, studies have also indicated that these justifications and excuses and acts of neutralization may play a role in the continuance of rape myths (Stewart et al., 1996). Justifications and excuses and techniques of neutralization are used in order to make a behavior acceptable to the offender. For example, if an offender commits a murder, the offender may justify it to himself by saying, "It wasn't really my fault because I was drunk" or "the victim had it coming," and so on. Stewart and colleagues (1996) argue that rape myths may function in the same way: They allow people to justify and excuse rape and construct and reconstruct the reality of rape based on these cultural myths.

Many argue that the most powerful theoretical tool to examine rape myths and the rape culture in the United States lies in feminist theory (Brownmiller, 1975; Burt, 1980; Price, 2005). In applying feminist theory to sexual assault, rape myths, and rape culture, the following is argued. Feminist theories focus on male domination as of central importance in an effort to explain violence perpetrated by men against women. Many argue that rape is not a crime of sex, but rather one of domination and control (Brownmiller, 1975; Crowell & Burgess, 1996; Price, 2005). The starting point for many is that men's use of threatening, intimidating, and violent behaviors are not the exception, but rather the rule and as such has its origins in our culture and structures (Brownmiller, 1975; Crowell & Burgess, 1996; Price, 2005). If the behavior is normal, its origins are shared rather than distinctive (Price, 2005). Feminists argue that men's use of violence arises from men's power over women in the family and in society (Belknap, 2001; Dobash & Dobash, 1979; Dobash & Dobash, 1998; Price, 2005; Yllo, 1993). In patriarchal societies, historically men have been socialized to be aggressive and even encouraged to use violence to keep women in line (Dobash & Dobash, 1979), and evidence suggests that violence against women is more prevalent in patriarchally organized societies. A central component of patriarchy is the predominance of violence by both men and male-dominated organizations. Physical and sexual violence by men, then, is a manifestation of patriarchy. Dobash and colleagues (2000) state that "pro-feminist perspectives consider violence as intentional behavior chosen by men as a tactic or resource associated with attempts to dominate, control, and punish women." In writing specifically concerning gang rape, Brownmiller (1975, p. 187) states,

> No simple conquest of man over woman, group rape is the conquest of men over women. It is within the phenomenon of group rape, stripped of the possibility of equal combat, that the male ideology of rape is most strikingly evident. Numerical odds are proof of brutal intention. They are proof of male bonding, and proof of a desire to humiliate the victim beyond the act of rape through the process of anonymous mass assault.

Rape myths and the rape culture developed in a patriarchal context and have become embedded in our culture to such a degree that many who may not want to identify as upholding patriarchal beliefs still believe in and perpetuate rape myths.

This chapter is grounded in feminist and sociological theories which hold that our "environment conditions not only what our experience is, but also how we think about it" (Andersen, 1988, p. 6). Moreover, in the tradition of recent feminist theory, this chapter focuses on how inequalities not only among men and women affect us, but also on the impacts of the social construction of race, class, gender, and sexuality.

STUDIES ON RAPE MYTH ACCEPTANCE

Studies on rape myths have focused on the link between rape myths and various variables. First, some studies have focused on RMA and demographic or background variables. Predicted by feminist theory, the variable that is consistently linked to higher RMA is gender: Men are more accepting of rape myths than women (Foley et al., 1995; Furnham & Boston, 1996; Lonsway & Fitzgerald, 1994, 1995; Nagel, Matsuo, McIntyre, & Morrison, 2005; Whatley, 2005). Feminists might argue that men should be expected to score higher on RMA because it goes along with masculine ideology (patriarchy).

Studies conflict on the link between race/ethnicity and rape myths, with some finding people of color are more accepting of rape myths than Whites (Nagel et al., 2005), while others finding no consistent differences (Lonsway & Fitzgerald, 1994). Other studies have examined age (Nagel et al., 2005), education, occupation, knowledge of a rape survivor, and awareness/knowledge of rape (Lonsways & Fitzgerald, 1994), all with mixed results. One reason put forth for the mixed results is because of the numerous interaction effects that may be occurring (Lonsway & Fitzgerald, 1994). For example, it may not be younger age that explains lower RMA, but rather changes in education regarding rape and sexual assault. However, clearly demographic variables play a part in explaining RMA, particularly gender.

Other studies have focused on various beliefs that people hold and how these beliefs impact RMA. In terms of definitions of rape, most studies find that people with greater RMA are less likely to label a scenario rape even when it meets the legal criteria for rape (Kahn, Mathie, & Torgler, 1994; Lonsway & Fitzgerald, 1994; Peterson & Muehlenhard, 2004). Moreover, Peterson and Muehlenhard (2004) found that female victims of rape were more likely to describe their experience as rape if it corresponded to rape myths. In other words, victims themselves may use rape myth to determine if what happened to them was rape (Peterson & Muehlenhard, 2004). Kahn and colleagues (1994) also found that unacknowledged rape victims (e.g., those who fit the legal criteria for experiencing rape, but do not self-identify as rape victims) were more likely to describe typical rape scenarios as those involving strangers, occurring in public places, and where force is used. Clearly, this illustrates how many victims of rape continue to subscribe to rape myths regarding "real" rape (Kahn et al., 1994). This has important implications for treatment and intervention in rape cases that will be discussed later.

Numerous studies have explored the link between RMA and attribution of blame in rape situations. Most studies find that the higher RMA one has, the more likely they will blame the victim in a rape situation (Frese, Moya, & Megias, 2004; Krahe, 1988; Lonsway & Fitzgerald, 1994; Mason et al., 2004; Peterson & Muehlenhard, 2004; Stewart et al., 1996). Some have explored how this varies by type of rape. For example, Frese and colleagues (2004) found that RMA was most related to victim blame in acquaintance rape situations.

Some studies have focused on the relationship between adversarial sexual beliefs and RMA. Burt (1980) defined adversarial sexual beliefs as "the expectation that sexual relationships are fundamentally exploitative, that each party to them is manipulative, sly, cheating, opaque to the other's understanding, and not to be trusted" (p. 218). Many studies have found that the endorsement of the above is related to higher levels of RMA (Foley et al., 1995; Lonsway & Fitzgerald, 1994). However, some have argued that the scales used to measure the above may be a better measure of hostility toward women (Lonsway & Fitzgerald, 1994) and that may be more highly correlated with RMA than adversarial sexual beliefs per se.

Important to a discussion of rape myths is the impact of attitudes on RMA. Numerous studies have examined this and they have focused on the relationship between attitudes toward women and sex roles and acceptance of interpersonal violence and RMA. Not surprisingly, studies have found that higher levels of RMA are associated with negative and stereotypical attitudes toward women and more traditional views on sex roles (Burt, 1980; Foley et al., 1995; Lonsway & Fitzgerald, 1994; Whatley, 2005). Moreover, studies have found that people who are more accepting of interpersonal violence score higher in RMA (Burt, 1980; Lonsway & Fitzgerald, 1994). Once again, this would be predicted from feminist theory. These attitudes and beliefs are associated with patriarchy and belief in them further perpetuates patriarchal ideals.

Finally, many studies have focused on the link between RMA and actual behaviors. Specifically, studies have found that people who behave in sexually aggressive ways score higher in RMA than those who do not (Lonsway & Fitzgerald, 1994). Regarding experiencing sexual assault and RMA, most studies have not found a link (Lonsway & Fitzgerald, 1994; Mason et al., 2004). Surprisingly, two studies have (Peterson & Muehlenhard, 2004; Stewart et al., 1996). These studies conclude that many victims themselves adhere to rape myths and that this may have profound effects on their lives (e.g., on their reporting practices, see discussion below).

CRIMINAL JUSTICE SYSTEM

A major area of research regarding rape myths has been exploring the impacts rape myths have on the criminal justice system. This has included studies examining rape myth effects on reporting practices of the victims, on recommendations from others for reporting to the police, on police practices, on prosecutorial decisions, and on conviction and sentencing decisions.

VICTIMS

Much research has focused on reasons why victims of sexual assault do not report their victimizations to the police. This research finds that victims do not report because of guilt, embarrassment, shame, not wanting others to find out, denial, fear, and views of the criminal justice system (specifically that criminal justice personnel will engage in victim blaming and not take it seriously) (Bachman, 1993). Konradi (1996) focused on steps that victims take to prepare for dealing with the criminal justice process, arguing that victims are very aware of the hostility and negative reactions they face in the criminal justice process. Much research has focused on the role rape myths play in reporting practices of victims of sexual assault and rape. Du Mont, Miller, and Myhr (2003) found that there is a positive association between reporting rape and two overtly violent components of the "real" rape myths—the use of physical force and the occurrence of injury. In other words, they found that women who experienced physical force and sustained injuries during their sexual assault were much more likely to report than women who did not. However, they also found that for rape myths in general, a victim's acceptance or rejection of them did not impact their reporting: Women who had high RMA were just as likely to report as those who did not (Du Mont et al., 2003). Stewart and her colleagues (1996) also examined this issue. They found that victim's definitions of what they saw as "real" rape (rape myths) affected whether or not they reported. Victims who did not think they fit the criteria of a "real" victim were less likely to report their rape (Stewart et al., 1996).

RMA may also affect others around the victims, specifically the recommendations they give to victims, which, in turn, could affect what the victims choose to do. For example, if those around the victim are telling her not to report, she may be less likely to report the incident to the police. Because of the importance that others' advice may play in reporting practices of victims of rape, Frese and colleagues (2004) examined the impact of RMA on recommendation to report the incident to the police. Not surprisingly, they found that people with high RMA are less likely to recommend that victims report the incident to police than people with low RMA (Frese et al., 2004). This may have important implications for victim reporting practices. Moreover, they found that it varied by type of rape. For example, they reported that people were much more likely to recommend reporting to the police if the rapist was a stranger (illustrating one of the rape myths). This may further perpetuate rape myths by the continuance of only "real" rapes (i.e., those involving strangers) being reported to the police. Clearly, RMA may affect victims even if they do not support them, but if they have others around them who do.

POLICE

Police are the gatekeepers to the criminal justice system. As such, victims depend on the police to make their case (i.e., whether or not the case will go forward in the criminal justice system). Studies have found that police routinely base their arrest decisions on variables independent of the facts of the particular case (Du Mont et al., 2003; Kerstetter, 1990). For example, some studies have found that police rely heavily on "rape myths" in their arrest decisions (Du Mont et al., 2003; Stewart et al., 1996). Specifically, Stewart and colleagues (1996) found that police were more likely to question a case if the victim did not report right away. Moreover, for both police and district attorneys, the following were reported as the major reasons for case rejection: 1) prior relationship between the victim and the offender, 2) delay in reporting, 3) being a prostitute, 4) being a Black woman, 5) being a welfare recipient, 6) being a hitchhiker, 7) being obese, 8) being on drugs, and 9) engaging in risky behavior (Stewart et al., 1996). Clearly, police and other criminal justice personnel are relying on extra-legal variables, and more specifically, rape myths, to guide their decision making in rape cases. Similarly, others have found that police base much of their decision making on the victim–offender relationship (i.e., they are more likely to better investigate and go forward with cases involving strangers than cases involving acquaintances (Kerstetter, 1990) and personal attributes of the victim (Kerstetter, 1990)).

The above may have particularly important implications for victims of color. For example, studies have concluded that women of color may be particularly reluctant to disclose rape to the police (Foley et al., 1995; Washington, 2001). Foley and colleagues argue that one of the reasons for this is the difficulties a Black woman faces in disclosing rape because it goes against many of our rape myths (Foley et al., 1995). In part, this has to do with the historical acceptance of forceful sex between White men and Black women (Foley et al., 1995; Washington, 2001; Wyatt, 1992). Historically, rape was not treated as a crime in the above situations and the rape of Black women has not been treated seriously by the criminal justice system (Foley et al., 1995; Wyatt, 1992). Washington (2001) found that many Black women report not disclosing to others because of the "lived memory of racism in the criminal justice system." These women discuss that Black women are more likely to face violence from criminal justice person-nel, not have their cases taken seriously if either the assailant or the victim is Black, and prior negative experiences with the criminal justice system (Washington, 2001). In addi-tion, she found that women did not disclose in an effort to protect Blacks as a group from negative publicity (Washington, 2001). Moreover, Wyatt (1992) argues that "there is reason to believe some African American women may be convinced that rape is not treated any differently today than in the past" (p. 79). Foley and colleagues (1995) found that respondents perceived a comparable forceful encounter as less serious when the victim was a Black woman compared to a White woman. Thus, the researchers conclude that Black women may be right to feel more vulnerable because they are less likely to be seen as victims and less likely to receive protection from the criminal justice system (Foley et al., 1995).

CRIMINAL JUSTICE PROCESSING

It is often said that sexual assault victims are re-victimized by the criminal justice system. Some studies find that one reason victims do not report their victimization to the police is because of fear of how they will be treated by the police and other criminal justice personnel (Bachman, 1993, 1998). Konradi (1996) found that victims are very aware of the stereotypes and victim blaming that they will face as the prosecution of their rapists progresses. She argues that victims engage in specific activities to prepare for the court process: appearance work, rehearsal, emotion work, team building, role research, and case enhancement. All these activities are geared toward helping the victim through the criminal justice process (Konradi, 1996). Research has found that the processing of sexual assault cases is influenced by victim behavior that is seen as risk-taking, by evidence of victim "misconduct," by the victim's reputation, by victim charac-teristics (age, race, education, and occupation), by the victim–offender relationship, and by the timeliness of the reporting of the victimization (Kerstetter, 1990; LaFree, 1981; Myers & LaFree, 1982; Reskin & Visher, 1986); many mirror common rape myths.

Others have examined how the criminal justice system processes sexual assault cases. For example, it is argued that sexual assault cases are more likely than other cases to be unfounded (i.e., a process in which police or prosecutors decide that a sexual assault has not taken place) (Brownmiller, 1975; LaFree, Reskin, & Visher, 1985; Russell, 1984; Temkin, 1995). Studies have examined the conviction rates for sexual assault cases. For example, Estrich (1987) found that less than 35 percent of arrests for rapes end up in convictions. Russell (1984) found that of the 670 reported attempted and completed rapes, only 1 percent ended up in convictions. LaFree (1989) found that 37 percent of sexual assault cases reported to the police ended up in arrest and 12 percent ended up in convictions. Finally, a more recent study, conducted after many reforms have been made in rape laws, still found that less than half of all rape arrests end up in convictions (Greenfeld, 1997).

Like police, prior research on prosecutorial decision making in rape cases indicates that prosecutors use nonlegal variables to determine whether to go forward with a case or not. For example, Frohmann (1991) found that prosecutors tried to find discrepancies in victims' statements, determine if victims had ulterior motives for alleging rape, and see if victims fit criteria as "typical" victims in deciding whether to charge a rape case. Others have also found that whether or not a case moves forward is more dependent on victim characteristics than on circumstances surrounding the case (Spohn & Holleran, 2001). Once again, these studies illustrate a heavy reliance on rape myths by criminal justice personnel in the processing of rape cases.

Little research analyzes judges' perceptions of rape victims and cases. One study that examined judges found that, like police and prosecutors, many decisions in rape cases are based on who the judges viewed as "real" rape victims (Spohn & Spears, 1996). It is expected that their perceptions can have just as much impact on sexual assault cases as those of police and prosecutors.

DISCUSSION

RAPE MYTHS AND RAPE CULTURE: EFFECTS ON VICTIMS

Clearly, rape myths and rape culture are important for perceptions and understanding of rape and its consequences. Of particular importance is the impact rape myths and living in a rape culture have on victims of rape. The majority of women who get raped do not fit our culturally accepted rape myths. This leads them to engage in self-blame for their victimization; for them not to report their rapes to the police; when they do report, for their cases to not be taken seriously; and for their recovery process to be greatly delayed. Moreover, the acceptance and use of these rape myths allow for the further marginalization of many women of color, poor women, and nonheterosexual women. While their White counterparts at least may fit in the criteria for a "real" rape, women of color will never fit in our rape myths. This means that they are even less likely to disclose their victimization, less likely to report, less likely to ever have any action taken against their rapists, and less likely to seek help from the resources that are available to help women recover from rape. Clearly, rape myths have profound effects on victims of rape and need to be dealt with before we can ever hope to help victims of rape.

THE CRIMINAL JUSTICE SYSTEM

Rape myths and their continued use by criminal justice personnel in the processing of rape cases illustrate, in many ways, the continued biased and sexist nature of jurisprudence in this country. While criminal justice personnel may not necessarily act any differently than most (see discussion of how rape victims themselves adhere to rape myths), the consequences of their use is dramatic. Victims do not report. Cases do not get processed, and ultimately, justice is never done in a large number of rape cases. This is a detrimental effect of rape myths that must be dealt with before we will ever have any sort of resolution for intervention in cases of rape in the United States.

IMPLICATIONS

The question becomes what we can do about these rape myths and the rape culture that we live in. Some have argued for educational interventions. In their review of the rape myth literature, Lonsway and Fitzgerald (1994) found some evidence that some of these programs work. For example, they report that RMA has been reduced through 1) an educational debriefing program, 2) a sex-educational or rape-educational film, 3) a human sexuality course with a lecture devoted to sexual violence legislation, 4) a live or videotaped rape education workshop, and 5) a psycho-educational intervention (Lonsway & Fitzgerald, 1994). However, numerous studies have also reported that many education interventions are not successful (see Lonsway & Fitzgerald, 1994).

Others have argued for change through legislation. For example, rape shield laws may be an example of specific laws written to block rape myths from becoming part of the criminal justice processing of rape cases. Rape shield laws protect victims of rape and sexual assault to be questioned about their sexual history unless it bears directly on the case. This deals with the rape myth that "only promiscuous girls get raped." Most states and the federal government have some form of rape shield law. Some are quite restrictive, whereas others grant the judge considerable discretion in their enforcement. These laws have been upheld as constitutional by the U.S. Supreme Court in the 1991 case *Michigan v. Lucas*. However, while it is an important step forward that these laws are on the books, many have argued that they do not change the realities of processing rape cases (Stewart et al., 1996). Judges, who many claim share the same reality of rape myths as the rest of society, continue to use their discretion and allow the defense in cases of rape to get around rape shield laws (Stewart et al., 1996). Thus, many have questioned the utility of changing rape myths through the legislative process.

In order to eradicate rape myths, the solution must come from the theory that explains their existence. Feminists and others have suggested that until we remove male privilege and patriarchy from society, rape myths and a rape culture will persist. This may be done by the above methods (education, legislation, and so on), but it must be a multi-faceted effort directed at all levels and institutions of society.

In conclusion, rape myths are a great obstacle for victims of sexual assault. They determine how they view themselves, the criminal justice response to rape, and their own recovery. This may be particularly important for marginalized victims as they almost never fit into our culturally embedded rape myths. This leads to their further marginalization, which will, in turn, only have negative effects on our society. As long as rape myths persist, they will continue to have negative impacts on victims of sexual assault.

Discussion Questions

1. Identify what some of the existing rape myths convey and the sources of origin.
2. What are the factors contributing to rape myths being accepted as truth in our society?
3. How do the different theories discussed in this chapter explain the existence of rape myths?
4. Discuss how rape myths are stated to impact victim interaction with the police and court personnel and also criminal justice system processing of sexual violence cases at various stages.
5. What are some of the effects of the existence of rape myths on the victims of sexual violence?

References

Andersen, M. L. (1988). *Thinking about women: Sociological perspectives on sex and gender*. New York: Macmillan.

Bachman, R. (1993). Predicting the reporting of rape victimizations: Have rape reforms made a difference? *Criminal Justice and Behavior, 20*, 254–270.

Bachman, R. (1998). The factors related to rape reporting behavior and arrest: New evidence from the National Crime Victimization Survey. *Criminal Justice and Behavior, 25*, 8–29.

Belknap, J. (2001). *The invisible woman: Gender, crime, and justice*. Belmont, CA: Wadsworth.

Brownmiller, S. (1975). *Against our will: Men, women, and rape*. New York: Simon and Schuster.

Buchwald, E., Fletcher, P. R., & Roth, M. (1993). *Transforming rape culture*. Minneapolis, MN: Milkweed Editions.

Burt, M. R. (1980). Cultural myths and supports for rape. *Journal of Personality and Social Psychology, 38*, 217–230.

Crowell, N. A., & Burgess, A. W. (1996). *Understanding violence against women*. Washington, D.C.: National Academy Press.

Dobash, R. E., & Dobash, R. (1979). *Violence against wives: A case for patriarchy*. New York: The Free Press.

Dobash, R. E., & Dobash, R. (1998). *Rethinking violence against women*. Thousand Oaks, CA: Sage Publications.

Dobash, R. P., Dobash, R. E., Cavanagh, K., & Lewis, R. (2000). Confronting violent men. In J. Hanmer, C. Itzin, S. Quaid, & P. Wigglesworth (Eds.), *Home Truths about Domestic Violence: Feminist Influences on Policy and Practice, A Reader* (pp. 289–309). London: Routledge.

Du Mont, J., Miller, K. L., & Myhr, T. L. (2003). The role of "real rape" and "real victim" stereotypes in the police reporting practices of sexually assaulted women. *Violence Against Women, 9*(4), 466–486.

Estrich, S. (1987). *Real rape*. Cambridge, MA: Harvard University.

Federal Bureau of Investigation. (2005). *Uniform Crime Report 2005*. Washington, D.C.: Federal Bureau of Investigation.

Foley, L. A., Evancic, C., Karnik, K., King, J., & Parks, A. (1995). Date rape: Effects of race of assailant and victim and gender of subjects on perceptions. *Journal of Black Psychology, 21*(1), 6–18.

Frese, B., Moya, M., & Megias, J. L. (2004). Social perception of rape: How rape myth acceptance modulates the influence of situational factors. *Journal of Interpersonal Violence, 19*(2), 143–161.

Frohmann, L. (1991). Discrediting victims' allegations of sexual assault: Prosecutorial accounts of case rejection. *Social Problems, 38*(2), 213–226.

Furnham, A., & Boston, N. (1996). Theories of rape and the just world. *Psychology, Crime, and the Law, 2*, 211–229.

Greenfeld, L. A. (1997). *Sex offenses and offenders: An analysis of data on rape and sexual assault*. Washington, D.C.: U.S. Department of Justice.

Groth, N., & Burgess, A. (1980). Male rape: Offenders and victims. *American Journal of Psychiatry, 137*(7), 806–809.

Kahn, A. S., Mathie, V. A., & Torgler, C. (1994). Rape scripts and rape acknowledgment. *Psychology of Women Quarterly, 18*, 53–66.

Kerstetter, W. A. (1990). Gateway to justice: Police and prosecutorial response to sexual assaults against women. *The Journal of Criminal Law and Criminology, 81*, 267–313.

Konradi, A. (1996). Preparing the testify: Rape survivors negotiating the criminal justice process. *Gender and Society, 10*(4), 404–432.

Krahe, B. (1988). Victims and observer characteristics as determinants of responsibility attributions to victims of rape. *Journal of Applied Social Psychology, 18*(1), 50–58.

LaFree, G. D. (1981). Official reactions to social problems: Police decisions in sexual assault cases. *Social Problems, 28*, 582.

LaFree, G. (1989). *Rape and criminal justice: The social construction of sexual assault*. CA: Wadsworth.

LaFree, G. D., Reskin, B. F., & Visher, C. A. (1985). Jurors' responses to victims' behavior and legal issues in sexual assault trials. *Social Problems, 32*, 389–407.

Lerner, M. J. (1965). Observer's evaluation of preformation as a function of performer's reward and attractiveness. *Journal of Personality and Social Psychology, 1*, 355–360.

Lerner, M. J., & Miller, T. D. (1978). Just world research and the attribution process: Looking back and ahead. *Psychological Bulletin, 85*, 1030–1051.

Lonsway, K. A., & Fitzgerald, L. F. (1994). Rape myths: In review. *Psychology of Women Quarterly, 18*, 133–164.

Lonsway, K. A., & Fitzgerald, L. F. (1995). Attitudinal antecedents of rape myth acceptance: A theoretical and empirical reexamination. *Journal of Personality and Social Psychology, 68*(4), 704–711.

Mann, O. R., & Selva, L. H. (1979). The sexualization of racism: The Black as rapist and White justice. *Western Journal of Black Studies, 3*(3), 168–177.

Mason, G. E., Riger, S., & Foley, L. A. (2004). The impact of past sexual experiences on attributions of responsibility for rape. *Journal of Interpersonal Violence, 19* (10), 1157–1171.

Myers, M. A., & LaFree, G. D. (1982). Sexual assault and its prosecution: A comparison with other crimes. *The Journal of Criminal Law and Criminology, 73*, 1282–1305.

Nagel, B., Matsuo, H., McIntyre, K. P., & Morrison, N. (2005). Attitudes toward victims of rape: Effects of gender, race, religion, and social class. *Journal of Interpersonal Violence, 20*(6), 725–737.

Peterson, Z. D., & Muehlenhard, C. L. (2004). Was it rape? The function of women's rape myth acceptance and definitions of sex in labeling their own experiences. *Sex Roles, 51*(3/4), 129–144.

Price, L. S. (2005). *Feminist frameworks: Building theory on violence against women.* Halifax: Fernwood Publishing.

Reskin, B. F., & Visher, C. A. (1986). The impacts of evidence an extralegal factors in jurors' decisions. *Law and Society Review, 20*, 423–438.

Russell, D. E. H. (1984). *Sexual exploitation: Rape, child sexual abuse, and workplace harassment.* Beverly Hills, CA: Sage.

Scully, D., & Marolla, J. (1985). Rape and vocabularies of motive: Alternative perspectives. In A. Burgess (Ed.), *Rape and sexual assault* (pp. 294–312). New York: Garland.

Spohn, C., & Holleran, D. (2001). Prosecuting sexual assault: A comparison of charging decisions in sexual assault cases involving strangers, acquaintances, and intimate partners. *Justice Quarterly, 18*, 651–688.

Spohn, C., & Spears, J. (1996). The effect of offender and victim characteristics on sexual assault case processing decisions. *Justice Quarterly, 13*(4), 649–676.

Stewart, M. W., Dobbin, S. A., & Gatowski, S. I. (1996). "Real rapes" and "real victims": The shared reliance on common cultural definitions of rape. *Feminist Legal Studies, 4*(2), 159–177.

Sykes, G., & Matza, D. (1957). Techniques of neutralization: A theory of delinquency. *American Sociological Review, 11*, 335–354.

Temkin, J. (1995). *Rape and the criminal justice system.* Aldershot: Darthmouth Publishing Company Limited.

Tjaden, P., & Thoennes, N. (1998). *Prevalence, Incidence, and Consequences of Violence against Women.* U.S. Department of Justice. Research in Brief.

United States Department of Justice. (2006). *Criminal Victimization in the United States: 2005 Statistical Tables from the National Criminal Victimization Survey.* Office of Justice Programs, Bureau of Justice Statistics. Retrieved January 16, 2008, from www.ojp.usdoj/bjs/pub/pdf/cvus05.pdf

Washington, P. (2001). Disclosure patterns of black female sexual assault survivors. *Violence Against Women, 7*(11), 1254–1283.

Whatley, M. A. (2005). The effect of participant sex, victim dress, and traditional attitudes on causal judgments for marital rape victims. *Journal of Family Violence, 20*(3), 191–200.

Wyatt, G. (1992). The sociocultural context of African American and white American women's rape. *Journal of Social Issues, 48*, 77–92.

Yllo, K. (1993). Through a feminist lens: Gender, power, and violence. In R. Gelles & D. Loeske (Eds.), *Current controversies on family violence* (pp. 47–62). Newbury Park: Sage.

Endnotes

1. The term *victim* is used instead of *survivor* because of the importance of the term *victim* to rape myths, the focus of this chapter.

2. Thus, the focus of this chapter is on sexual violence perpetrated by males against females.

CHAPTER 8

DOMESTIC VIOLENCE: OVERVIEW OF THEORETICAL ETIOLOGY, PSYCHOLOGICAL IMPACT, AND INTERVENTIONS

SHARON BOYD-JACKSON

ABSTRACT

This chapter examines the nature, extent, and etiology of domestic violence. As a gendered victimization, domestic violence affects females at an alarming rate. As a result, the various forms of domestic violence must be understood. This chapter focuses on describing the nature and frequency of physical, sexual, and stalking abuse. After a discussion on what is domestic violence, the chapter moves to address some of the more general causal factors in three different schools of thought, specifically sociological, psychological, and feminist views. Although these are distinct social scientific fields of study, one can see overlap. Focus will be placed on the uniqueness of each viewpoint as well as identifying where they converge in theoretical analysis of domestic violence.

WHAT IS DOMESTIC VIOLENCE?

Imagine you are coming home after working a full day and looking forward to a night of relaxation. You open the door to your home to find glass smashed on the floor, the sofa turned upside down, and a hole punched in the living room wall. You immediately stiffen all over, overwhelmed by familiar fear you realize that your roommate has once again become violent. What do you think of when you hear the term *domestic violence*? Most people imagine a female being battered by a male. However, violence can take place in a variety of ways in any one household and can happen to anyone at anytime. While adult males battering adult females is probably the most common type of domestic violence, abuse directed toward adult males, female and male children, same-sex couples, and the elderly is also considered domestic violence (Klein, 2004; Walker, 2000). Domestic violence is often referred to as intimate partner violence because of the frequency of reported instances of violence between couples. Violence inside of the home undoubtedly has an impact on each and every family member. However, that violence can extend to incidents that occur outside of the home between couples and family members.

Domestic violence has a broad definition. While physical abuse is probably the most common type of domestic violence, sexual abuse, neglect, and emotional abuse can all be part of the domestic violence paradigm inside or outside of the household. In addition, it is not uncommon for domestic violence to occur among individuals who are noncohabitant couples, friends, or formal couples (Klein, 2004). The term *domestic* typically connotes to the intimacy and/or closeness of individuals. However, research has found that "the strongest risk factor for being a victim of domestic violence is being a woman" (Wilson, 2006, p. 8). Several studies highlight statistics that reveal women and girls as more likely to experience violence in their lifetime than men and boys (Abbey, 2005; Bachman & Saltzman, 1995; Harned, 2004; Monore et al., 2005; Tjaden & Thoennes, 1998; Wasco, 2005; Wilt & Olson, 1996). This chapter will further explore the broad definition of domestic violence and abuse (see Box 8.1), as well as various theoretical explanations with a primary emphasis on the domestic violence of females.

The prevalence of domestic violence is convoluted and impacted by the broad definition, which is inclusive of many types of violence and the range of victims of violence. Kilpatrick and Ruggiero (2004) point out that the results from major national studies conducted to assess violence cannot be used as comparable data. While most national governmental studies should be commended for their assessment of a long neglected issue of violence against women, the studies are not without their flaws. Kilpatrick actually compared the National Women's Study (NWS) conducted in 1989–1991 with the National Violence Against Women Survey (NVAWS) conducted in 1995–1996. Both studies were able to obtain incidents of violence and abuse that were not reported to the authorities; however, they queried different populations and types of victimizations. As pointed out by Tjaden and Thoennes (1998), while the NVAWS focuses on those 18 years of age and older, the National Crime Victim Survey (NCVS) questions individuals 12 years and older. Furthermore, "the NVAW Survey estimate for forcible rape is being compared to a NCVS estimate that includes rape and other forms of sexual assault, such as grabbing, fondling, and verbal threats of a sexual nature" (p. 4). It is difficult to compare these studies given the major differences. It is important to specify the population studied and the definitions of abuse when interpreting statistical data in this area. Nevertheless, there is consistency in reporting that women tend to be at greater risk of intimate partner violence (Tjaden & Thoennes, 1998).

The risk of intimate partner violence is not just prevalent in the United States, it is worldwide. The United Nations is presently grappling with the legal issues of eligibility for immigrant women who seek asylum for reasons of domestic violence. It is estimated that in some Third World countries one in every six women is exposed to domestic violence (Kotlowitz, 2007). The estimate of women in the general population of the

BOX 8.1

Domestic violence has a broad definition. While physical abuse is probably the most common type of domestic violence, sexual abuse, financial abuse, neglect, and emotional abuse can all be part of the domestic violence paradigm in any one household.

United States being subjected to some type of severe domestic violence in their lifetime ranges anywhere from 9 to 30 percent (Wilt & Olson, 1996). These estimates are too high for anyone of us to be comfortable with the potential violence women face. While all women can be potential victims of violence, young women and minority women tend to be reported at a greater risk, especially Native American women (Centers for Disease Control and Prevention, 2006; Tjaden & Thoennes, 1998; Wilt & Olson, 1996). What do you think of when you hear these statistics and the word "victim"? Do you view them as weak and feel sorry for these women? Should they feel sorry for themselves? Do you blame these women for being at a greater risk of domestic violence?

Women are too often blamed for their "victim" status when faced with the threat of harm or actual abuse. The term *victim* connotes a passive as well as negative viewpoint as you have learned in the first section of this book. Therefore, for our purposes this chapter will also focus on women as survivors of domestic violence, and the term *survivor* will be used when describing this population.

PHYSICAL ABUSE

Many social scientists describe the *physical abuse* that occurs in domestic violence as any behavior that inflicts bodily harm on another person such as punching, kicking, slapping, pinching, spitting, pushing, or any type of hitting (Tjaden & Thoennes, 1998; Wilson, 2006; Wilt & Olson, 1996). Some literature actually extends this destructive behavior to the actual threat of bodily harm and/or the destruction of property such as punching holes in walls, breaking furniture, or starting fires (Klein, 2004). Furthermore, laws generally define domestic violence to include "violence," "abuse," assault, and/or battery. Additionally, these laws recognize attempted, threatened, and completed violence. In fact, the legal definition of the many types of relationships that constitute domestic violence can vary from state to state. For example, the state of California defines the domestic violence relationship between spouse and/or cohabitant and violent behavior as intentionally causing corporeal injury to another person. The state of Hawaii distinguishes less serious assaults between household or family members as misdemeanors and matters for family court, while more severe assaults are tried in state criminal courts. And New York defines domestic violence as assaults that occur not only between current household members but between individuals who may have previously lived together (Klein, 2004). The relationships that constitute domestic violence can expand to common law, to adopted and step children, and to significant other relationships depending on the state of jurisprudence.

According to the NCVS (Bureau of Justice Statistics (BJS), 2006), in 2005 the prevalence of assaults involving nonstrangers was toward 51 percent of the population surveyed. That is, half of the assaults in this national study are related to acquaintance violence or domestic violence. This might be generalized to assuming a large portion of the U.S. population has been exposed to violence. This certainly does not sound so far-fetched when we think about the daily media stories of violence. There are several reports of domestic violence among famous athletes or former athletes. For example, Jim Lampley, a veteran sportswriter mostly known for his work as a boxing commentator for HBO, was arrested for domestic violence. He allegedly attacked Candice Sanders, a former Miss California USA. She "wrote in her request for a restraining order that she received injuries to her 'head, neck and back from his throwing me against the walls and door' " (Associated Press, 2007, p. 1). Lampey lost in court, he was sentenced to a 52-week domestic violence program. Pro NBA basketball player Jason Kidd was also arrested for suspicion of domestic violence in 2001. He was accused of hitting his wife during one of their disagreements. He was fined and ordered to attend anger management (Robbins, Eligon, & Schweber, 2007).

Violence in relationships can range in the severity of physical harm and frequency, but violence is always damaging in one way or another. Often the first time it occurs, it may be unexpected. In addition to the amount of times violence has been reported in the media, it is often exclaimed by a neighbor or friend of a person attacked that "I never would have imagined any violence like that to happen in this neighborhood." How many of you can say that about your own neighborhoods? What about sexual assaults? The NCVS (BJS, 2006) also reveals that rape and sexual assault involving nonstrangers was found in 65 percent of the population surveyed.

SEXUAL ABUSE

Probably the second most prevalent type of domestic violence is *sexual abuse*, which has an even broader definition than physical abuse. Sexual abuse can range from the inappropriate exposure of sexual materials or acts and unacceptable sexual touching to brutal rape (Kilpatrick & Ruggiero, 2004; Walker, 2000; Wasco, 2005). The latter two instances may even be considered a more harmful form of physical abuse. However, each form of sexual abuse listed above can be more devastating depending on the age of the victim. For example, inappropriate exposure of sexual materials may be more damaging for a young child than for an adult. And of course, rape as the more severe form of sexual abuse can be extremely damaging psychologically as well as physically. There are horrible accounts of rape and sexual assaults being reported among teenagers in the schools almost daily. According to the Centers for Disease Control and Prevention (CDC) (2007), 54 percent of all rapes of females occur before their 18th birthday while 22 percent occur before they are 12 years old.

The National Crime Victimization Survey (BJS, 2006) defines rape as forced penetration but emphasizes that force can be of physical means or inflicting a psychological fear of physical abuse. Therefore, a woman who did not scream or fight off her attacker after being threatened that he would kill her if she did so has been inflicted with psychological fear. The survey also expands penetration beyond vaginal and anal to oral and possible incidents of foreign object intercourse. The federal definition of sexual abuse is even more expansive. "The Federal Criminal Code of 1986 (Title 18, chapter 109A, section 2241-2233) does not use the term rape, but uses the term, *aggravated sexual abuse* to define what is typically described as rape" (Kilpatrick & Ruggiero, 2004, p. 3). Kilpatrick further describes the federal definition of two types of *aggravated sexual abuse*: 1) *aggravated sexual abuse by force or threat of force*—this includes any type of forced sexual act and all types of forced penetration; and 2) *aggravated sexual abuse by other means*—this refers to other means such as use of drugs, alcohol, and statutory rape. This definition is inclusive of all types of sexual abuse whether it is unwanted, forced, and illicit and/or inflicted by devious means. The Federal Criminal Code is clearly inclusive of some common types of sexual abuse that we as a society may have difficulty distinguishing between such as sexual harassment and date rape.

Sexual abuse includes *sexual harassment*, which is any unwanted sexual advances, exposure, or touching (Walker, 2000). When a person directs a request to the perpetrator (especially one who has power over another) of unwanted sexual advance to discontinue his behavior and the behavior continues, it is clearly sexual harassment. Have you ever been exposed to sexual harassment? Walker (2000) states that there is a thin line between actual harassment and the usual flirting or banter between two people who may be attracted to one another. Usually the line is drawn when the person on the receiving end begins to feel uncomfortable. The following is a hypothetical case designed to help you examine your ideas and to think critically about various aspects of domestic violence (see Box 8.2). This case will be developed and discussed throughout the chapter.

As the complexities of sexual harassment are contemplated, you might wonder what if a person decides to date another out of obligation. How far does the obligation go? Can you change your mind? This brings the focus to another aspect of sexual abuse, which is *date rape*. There is no accounting for how many young women have been affected by date rape. This is probably one area of sexual abuse and violence that is the most underreported. Do you know any females who have been a victim of date rape? Is it possible to rape a female if you are on a date with her and she gives clear signals that she is not interested in engaging in sex? What if the signals are mixed? Let's return to the case of Marsha and Derrick in Box 8.3.

The prevalence of rape is astounding for women and girls in this country, as indicated in the above statistics. Most women do not report incidences of date rape for fear of embarrassment and self-blame for the incident. It is questioned if some men actually

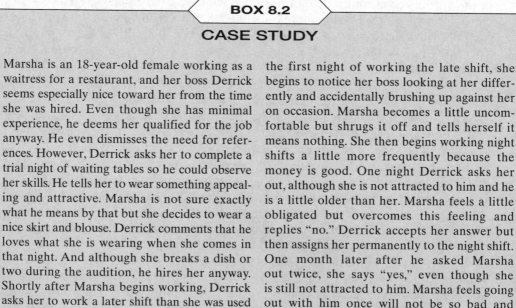

BOX 8.2

CASE STUDY

Marsha is an 18-year-old female working as a waitress for a restaurant, and her boss Derrick seems especially nice toward her from the time she was hired. Even though she has minimal experience, he deems her qualified for the job anyway. He even dismisses the need for references. However, Derrick asks her to complete a trial night of waiting tables so he could observe her skills. He tells her to wear something appealing and attractive. Marsha is not sure exactly what he means by that but she decides to wear a nice skirt and blouse. Derrick comments that he loves what she is wearing when she comes in that night. And although she breaks a dish or two during the audition, he hires her anyway. Shortly after Marsha begins working, Derrick asks her to work a later shift than she was used to working.

Although she does not want to, she agrees because Derrick has been so nice to her. On the first night of working the late shift, she begins to notice her boss looking at her differently and accidentally brushing up against her on occasion. Marsha becomes a little uncomfortable but shrugs it off and tells herself it means nothing. She then begins working night shifts a little more frequently because the money is good. One night Derrick asks her out, although she is not attracted to him and he is a little older than her. Marsha feels a little obligated but overcomes this feeling and replies "no." Derrick accepts her answer but then assigns her permanently to the night shift. One month later after he asked Marsha out twice, she says "yes," even though she is still not attracted to him. Marsha feels going out with him once will not be so bad and that maybe he will stop asking after that. In this scenario, is Marsha being sexually harassed?

BOX 8.3

CASE STUDY—CONTINUED

Marsha decides to go out with her boss Derrick who is 12 years older than her. He picks her up and they go out dancing to a club. The date is not bad, Marsha actually has fun, and she feels a slight attraction toward Derrick. At the end of the night after they both probably had a little too much to drink, Derrick convinces Marsha to stop by his place. Once they get there, after a few more drinks and dancing, Derrick and Marsha kiss. Immediately, Marsha realizes that she has had too much to drink to have allowed that to happen. She asks Derrick to take her home. He replies "in a minute" and tries to kiss her again. Although she allows him to kiss her again, she stops him from going any further. She again asks to be taken home. This repeats one more time before Derrick becomes very aggressive and forces himself on Marsha. He rapes Marsha then takes her home. Marsha is devastated, confused, angry, and afraid. She does not go back to work and quits her job. She never tells anyone about this incident. Why is Marsha confused? Did Derrick follow Marsha's lead? Did he go too far?

know this and attempt to use it to their advantage when dating. Certainly, there are some men who actually plan without the knowledge of his date to end the night with sexual relations when out on a date. However, without the benefit of communicating this to their date, this can cause serious miscommunication and expectations about the evening events. Is miscommunication an acceptable reason for a male raping a female? Proponents of the miscommunication myth (see Belknap, 2007) say "no." Then there are others who state that men may simply get "carried away" in the heat of the moment. Is getting "carried away" a rational reason or excuse for rape? Whatever the reason, forcefully following through with a sexual act when a woman says "no" is tantamount to rape. Dating can be confusing, difficult, and stressful at anytime but especially when you are young adults at the beginning stages of developing more serious intimate relationships. Furthermore, because of societal stigmatization of homosexuality, this can cause added stress for individuals in same-sex relationships. Can a woman be raped by another woman? If you utilize our definition, the answer is "yes." It is important to note here that there are also reported incidences of rape in lesbian relationships (Wasserman, 2004).

Date rape and dating violence is most prevalent among the college student population. One survey found that "21 percent of students reported that they had experienced violence in a relationship with a current partner and 32 percent with a previous partner" (Wasserman, 2004, p. 17). The current estimated prevalence rate for dating violence in relationships for college women over their entire college year is approximately 20 percent (Berkel, Furlong, Hickman, & Blue, 2005; Wasserman, 2004).

The Federal Crime Code of *aggravated sexual assault by other means* often applies when identifying date rape. This allows the justice system to aptly prosecute when substances such as "date rape" drugs are used in rape cases. Generally, these drugs are slipped unknowingly into a person's drink at a party or social gathering. GHB (gamma hydroxybutyric acid), Rohypnol (flunitrazepam), and Ketamine (ketamine hydrochloride) are three drugs that are most commonly used in date rape

(National Women's Health Information Center, 2005). Although different, they each have similar physiological effects such as relaxing the body, drowsiness, nausea, and causing problems with eyesight and memory. Rohypnol and Ketamine may also affect motor function and coordination difficulties, while Rohypnol also lowers blood pressure and can cause confusion and stomach problems. Yet GHB probably the most dangerous of the three can cause a person to slip into a coma and may even cause death. A number of young adults manage to get a hold of these drugs even though they are not available over the counter in your local drug store. According to the National Women's Health Information Center (2005), Rhypnol is legal in some European countries and in Mexico but not in the United States; whereas GHB and Ketamine are legal, they are only used for medicinal purposes. GHB was only recently made legal to treat issues related to narcolepsy, and Ketamine is used as an anesthetic (National Women's Health Information Center, 2005). Alcohol, cocaine, crack, and heroine are some other drugs that are associated with violence against women. The violence women experience can be more severe when the perpetrator is under the influence (Walker, 2000). Do you know anyone who has used these drugs or who has been a survivor of abuse from a person who was under the influence? How can you make certain that you are not a victim of these drugs? Box 8.4 provides some helpful hints.

STALKING ABUSE

There are often signs that may indicate whether or not a person has the potential to be abusive or not in domestic violence cases. Stalking may be one of those signs. Stalking can almost be considered an extreme form of sexual harassment. Interestingly, stalking is considered a fairly new form of abuse and violence, and only since 1990 have laws been legislated to protect the public (Dennison & Thomson, 2005). The NVAWS comprehensively defines *stalking abuse* as "a course of conduct directed at a specific person that involves repeated visual or physical proximity, non consensual communication; verbal, written, or

---

BOX 8.4

Helpful hints for young adults and others to protect themselves from these "date rape" drugs:

1. Do not share drinks or accept drinks from others.

2. Do not leave drinks unprotected; take them with you to the dance floor or if you decide to go speak with someone at another table or go to the bathroom.

3. Even though these drugs may not have an odor, do not drink anything that may smell or look strange, or if you are suspicious of it in any way (GHB often has a salty taste).

4. Drinks such as punch or premixed drinks may already have the drug blended in so be careful of these types of drinks.

Finally, if you have been or think you have been drugged or raped, you should go to the hospital and call the police right away. Try not to urinate because the drugs do not remain in your system for too long. You may need to use this for evidence in order to prosecute the perpetrator (National Women's Health Information Center, 2005).

implied threats, or a combination thereof that would cause fear in a reasonable person (with repeated meaning on two or more occasions)" (Tjaden & Thoennes, 1998, p. 13). Stalking behavior can include being followed, receiving an unreasonable number of telephone calls or telephone or e-mail messages, and/or having someone show up at your job, your favorite hang out, or home unannounced. Ultimately, it elicits fear in the person who is being stalked. Have you ever been stalked?

If you have ever been a target of the paparazzi, collection agencies, telemarketers, or a persistent salesperson, you may have felt the pressure of being stalked. The impetus to develop stalking laws was due partially to protect celebrities from the paparazzi and partially to protect the general public from unwanted harassment and intimidation by others. Legislation in the United States identifies stalking as repeated harassment with the intention or threat of harm (Dennison & Thomson, 2005). This leaves lots of room for debate. How do you prove the intention of harm if there is no direct threat? One might ask, can the harassment itself cause psychological harm? The person who is the object of stalking behavior can certainly describe her own reactions, emotions, and likely fear she may experience. But again, what if her reaction is an overreaction to innocent behavior? For example, what if the roles had been reversed between our hypothetical case study with Marsha and Derrick? Would Marsha be more or less likely to be labeled as a harassing boss and maybe even a stalker?

Stalking is a common form of dating violence on college campuses (Wasserman, 2004) and a growing form of violence. Tjaden and Thoennes (1998) argue that since 1.4 million people in the United States are being stalked, there should be serious concern and legislation directed toward this abuse. Additionally, they cite that 8 percent of women in the United States report being stalked at one time in their lives. Case studies show that stalking can lead to serious dangerous behavior especially due to the obsessive and/or vindictive nature of the individual and the seemingly lack of behavior control. One case in point highlights the female astronaut Captain Lisa Nowak who was accused of attempted murder after allegedly stalking a female colleague she believed to be a competitor for the affections of another male astronaut. It was reported that she actually drove 900 miles wearing an adult diaper to confront her perceived competitor, Colleen Shipman. The diaper was to help expedite her trip from Texas to Florida and cut down on potential stops to the bathroom. When she arrived she was reported to have confronted Ms. Shipman and sprayed her with pepper spray. She also had in her possession a "disguise, a compressed air pistol, a steel mallet, a knife, latex gloves and garbage bags" (Schwartz & Blumenthal, 2007, p. 1). Although she did not specify how, Ms. Shipman later reported that Ms. Nowak had been stalking her for two months prior to this unfortunate meeting. Although there were no signs of unstable behavior of Ms. Nowak in the past, her present behavior seems to warrant at least some type of psychological assessment and investigation and possible treatment. This is an example of when stalking can become deadly especially if Ms. Nowak had not been stopped by authorities.

Another popular case points to the seriousness and possible harm of *cyber stalking*, which is the elicit use of the computer and Internet to harass and harm others. In 2006, a New York police officer, "Michael Valentine was indicted on 197 counts of stalking, unauthorized use of a computer and other charges after hacking into the Yahoo e-mail account of a woman he had briefly dated and posing as her in online communications" (Zeller, 2006, p. 2). He had a possible intent to harm this woman as he set up dates in her name and gave out her address resulting in at least two men showing up at her door for a date. An even more extreme case is of a former security guard, Gary S. Dellapenta, of Los Angeles, who posed as his ex-girlfriend and entered chat rooms and personal sites expounding rape fantasies and giving her address. Although federal anti-cyber stalking was just instituted in January 2006, state laws became effective in 1991 with California leading the way (Zeller, 2006).

THEORETICAL EXPLANATIONS OF DOMESTIC VIOLENCE

Given the wide range of abuse within domestic violence, it would be impossible in this chapter to cover every possible reason or cause of such violence. However, this section will address some of the more general causal factors in three different schools of thought that relate to domestic violence. The sociological, psychological, and feminist views will be explored in this section. Although these are distinct social scientific fields of study, you will find some overlap in ideology of each area. Focus will be on the uniqueness of the each viewpoint as well as identifying where they converge in theoretical analysis of domestic violence.

SOCIOLOGICAL PERSPECTIVE

The sociological perspective views male-perpetrated domestic violence as a result of numerous structural factors that may or may not converge to impact relationships. In many ways, violence itself is interwoven into the structure and fabric of our way of life. Furthermore, "violence has been institutionalized as an acceptable means of solving conflicts" (Kaufman, 2006, p. 535). Much of the sociological analysis of violence in our society implies that violence is learned by witnessing and experiencing social violence. There are many forms and levels of social violence from parental corporal punishment, rage responses due to jealousy and competition in relationships to wars between countries to resolve turf conflicts, acceptable cultures, and ways of life such as religion and/or leadership ideology. "The racism, sexism and heterosexism that have been institutionalized in our societies are *considered* socially regulated acts of violence" (Kaufman, 2006, p. 535). Kaufman describes the violence men perpetuate against women as a definite expression of relative power. He further describes men's violence against women as related to a need to express and confirm a strong sense of masculinity. However, he also denotes that this type of violence usually confirms the precariousness of an individual's masculinity.

Anderson (1997) points out that sociologists "find strong relationships between domestic violence and age, co-habiting status, unemployment and *poor* socioeconomic status" (p. 655). This information directs our attention to a tendency for violence among the younger generation. Based on this information, it may be plausible to assume that maturity level, living status, educational level, and finances may all play a role in the level of tension and frustration that may lead to violence in any one household. There may even be cultural support for violence within households in the United States. We reside in a society with many cultural roots and influences. Culture highly influences the roles taken on in families.

In traditional relationships and family structures, there is a tendency for males to take the dominant role. *Resource theory* explains that violence in relationships is used as a means for individuals to gain power (Anderson, 1997). The individual in the relationship with the least amount of power, such as the least amount of income, education, etc., may use violence to obtain power. Utilizing resource theory to explain male-perpetrated domestic violence would help to clarify why some men may resort to violently attacking their female partners. In the case of Derrick and Marsha, however, this theory cannot suitably explain the violence. Derrick is already in a position of power; in fact he uses his power to manipulate his relationship with Marsha. In this case power is relative, and one must question not only what defines power but what influence power can have on any one individual. So we may have to be careful in using this explanation to identify types of power, the extent of power, and even aspects of perceived power. Does Derrick have perceived power in all aspects of his life? The feminist approach also focuses on the need for power in relationships as well as the tendency to control. The next section will look at power from a gender role perspective.

FEMINIST PERSPECTIVE

The feminist perspective emphasizes how the social construction of gender role development can impact the acceptance of violence in relationships. The masculinity assigned to the male gender role clearly supports more traits of aggression, assertion, and confrontation than the feminine role. Males are more aptly rewarded for their heroism, ability to be competitive, and their strong control over emotions. Male bonding occurs within aggressive sports, the work environment, and the exercise gym and entertainment arenas such as bars and clubs. While male bonding is an appropriate way to develop male friendships, for some men there is a thin line between an evolving friendship and an intimate attraction (Pharr, 2006). The pressure of some men to offset any feelings of intimate attraction is often compensated by homophobia, a coping mechanism to defend against attraction to other men.

> The failure to find safe avenues of emotional expression and discharge means that a whole range of emotions are transformed into anger and hostility. Part of the anger is directed at oneself in the form of guilt, self-hate, and various physiological and psychological symptoms . . . part is directed at other men . . . part of it is directed at women. (Pharr, 2006, p. 544)

This perspective recognizes patriarchy and sexism as systems of disadvantage that subordinates women and helps men maintain power and control. The lack of equal pay, unequal status, and accessibility to resources resonate with the lack of power women have in this society. Traditionally, women have been socialized to be passive, subordinate, and nurturing when interacting with others. Societal messages inform women that they are vulnerable and devalued. Media images reveal women as conniving, untrustworthy, back stabbers, inferior, and sexual objects. These messages can be viewed in the numerous movies that show women being raped, abused, or even killed (Pharr, 2006). However, Pharr (2006) aptly states that it is not the violence but the threat of violence that may control the lives of women (negative reinforcement) (also see Belknap, 2007). Women often restrict their movements and activities in order to protect themselves from violence and physical and psychological harm. Women are told not to travel or go out alone. They have to be careful, for example, not to jog in the park too late or too early and not to tarry in the mall parking lots or even in their own driveways. However, in domestic partner violence the threat is with the person you trust. How does an individual develop a gender role that can lead to violence? Let's return to our case and review the backgrounds of Derrick and Marsha in Box 8.5:

This description of Derrick's background supports the feminist perspective of at least the aggressiveness associated with the traditional male gender role within which he was socialized. Yet, Marsha's upbringing was very different, as shown in Box 8.6.

As you can see, Marsha had more freedom in choosing characteristics and activities that define her gender role identity. This demonstrates the idea of the social construction of gender role development and the cultural influences. The values and beliefs of Marsha's family assisted in her freedom of choice. But why did Marsha tend to be attracted to men who were controlling and protective? Maybe the psychological perspective can help to further explain the abusive relationship of Marsha and Derrick.

BOX 8.5

CASE STUDY—CONTINUED

Upon further discovery, we learn that Derrick is the youngest child of six children. He has four sisters and one brother. Derrick who is 10 years younger than his older brother and 3 years younger than the sister closest to his age was always considered the baby in the family. He admired his older brother who always considered Derrick too young to hang out with him. Although he did on occasion take him to baseball games and go to an occasional game when Derrick played on the local soccer and baseball teams from the age of 7 to 10. Derrick's brother received a degree from a nearby community college. He graduated with honors and was offered a scholarship to an Ivy league university. Derrick's sisters treated him with ambivalence. There were times when they were extra nice to him because he was the baby, but at other times they berated, rejected, and isolated him because they resented having to care for him.

Derrick's parents were hardworking each with two jobs to try to make ends meet, feed, and clothe six children. Because Derrick's parents were never home, he was often supervised by his older sister. Derrick's parents believed in strict gender role adherence. They taught the girls to follow traditional feminine roles throughout the household and expected the boys to adhere to traditional masculine roles. When Derrick's older brother was not around, his sisters would often tease and taunt him by sometimes dividing up snacks and not giving him any, making him do housework that was not required of him, and sometimes even hitting and punishing him unjustly. Derrick often found himself frustrated, angry, and alone at the hands of his sisters. He received frequent reports from school about his aggressive behavior, sometimes fighting and at other times disobeying especially his female teachers. Derrick would also often get beatings at the hands of his father for not standing up for himself when relating to his sisters. His father operated under the idea that to be male meant to be in control, independent, assertive, and even aggressive.

> **BOX 8.6**
>
> ## CASE STUDY—CONTINUED
>
> Marsha comes from a family of four. She has an older brother with whom she is very close. He often described her as a princess and took pride in protecting her. Marsha's parents are also hardworking, and although Marsha and her brother had some traditional gender roles growing up, their parents were not strict in maintaining these roles. For example, when Marsha wanted to join the boys' soccer team in grade school, her parents allowed it without much resistance. Marsha was always eager to explore new and different activities. She was friends with a diverse male and female group of average popularity in high school. Marsha began dating boys in her junior year of high school. She describes most of her boyfriends as somewhat controlling and protective of her. Marsha has always struggled to maintain her own independence in relationships. She feels she has clear goals and expectations regarding relationships, but she just often ends up choosing the wrong guy.

PSYCHOLOGICAL PERSPECTIVE

The psychological literature attempts to understand abuse by assessing individual characteristics and the individual relationship among an abusive couple as well as social stressors, interactions, and pressures. Although there is no identified personality for an abuser or a survivor of abuse, many studies have attempted to distinguish traits that are at least associated with abuse.

The battered women's syndrome (BWS) was introduced in psychological literature in the 1970s based on the research of Walker (1979). As a clinical researcher, Walker based her theory on qualitative accounts of clients she interviewed and treated for domestic partner abuse. Although BWS is not recognized as a clinical diagnosis, it has been widely used in the social science literature and in judicial matters. In addition, because of the lack of rigorous empirical evidence, the term BWS remains a controversial one to date (Dixon, 2002). BWS is considered a subcategory of posttraumatic stress disorder. The symptoms include memory impairment, confusion and uncertainty of perceptions, difficulty with decision making, anxiety, avoidance behavior, and depression (Walker, 1979). A woman who is being abused may experience all of the above symptoms and more depending on the intensity of the abuse. The confusion of awareness in a domestic violence situation can be seen as a useful defense to help reduce the painful reality of the abuse. Often a person who is being abused may minimize or in some way justify what is happening to her, especially if she is feeling trapped in the relationship. The paralyzing fear that one can feel in an abusive domestic partnership can induce feelings of high arousal and hyper vigilance. The survivor of abuse may often feel fragile that she is "walking on egg shells" around her abuser and careful not to do anything that she thinks may provoke the perpetrator. With this type of avoidance behavior, it takes a great deal of energy to withhold spontaneous thoughts and emotions. It can also lead to a sense of depression as the individual withdraws inward and loses her sense of assertiveness and only becomes responsive to others in their interactions. The theory behind such a depressive reaction is called learned helplessness. Seligman (1975) identified learned helplessness as behavior that occurs after experiencing the loss of external control. The inability to predict and/or control negative assaults can lead to a sense of helplessness and depression.

BWS has also been used as a defense for woman who attack and even kill their abusers. There have been a number of cases that have utilized BWS as a reason for any retaliation on the part of the survivor of abuse. It may seem logical that if a woman is distraught at the hands of the abuser she may lash out eventually. Seligman's theory of learned helplessness may help to further explain BWS. A woman who may be experiencing physical and/or sexual abuse at the hands of her domestic partner may begin to feel hopeless and helpless if all attempts made to end the abuse are rendered ineffective. The theory of learned helplessness dictates that a person may give up in despair after so many attempts to change an abusive situation. Can a dejected person who has been consistently and persistently abused turn around and attack her perpetrator? The BWS and learned helplessness have been utilized to explain such behavior. The BWS has been utilized in the courts as an explanation to defend the survivor. Part of the controversy of the BWS is that it also pathologizes the survivor (Dixon, 2002). A judge may discount the survivor's testimony if she is considered mentally ill. The BWS syndrome for some may also be recognized as the cause of the abuse. So the use of the BWS in a courtroom situation can be useful or harmful to the survivor depending on the context it is placed in by either the prosecution or the defense. The utilization of the BWS is only one way of attempting to understand the psychological aspect of abuse. Still, other psychological literature has focused on relationship dynamics.

Bornstein (2006) distinguished between three different types of dependency that may be found in a domestic violence relationship such as objective dependency, subjective dependency, and dependent personality. Objective dependency is defined as the disparity of economic resources between a couple engaged in domestic violence. This can relate to the amount of income, availability of alternative financial support or housing, and whether or not children are involved. This also relates to lack of control over external needs and practical concerns of survival for the survivor of abuse. On the other hand, subjective dependency has a lot to do the perceptions of the individuals involved in a domestic partner abuse relationship. Individuals may be perfectly capable of taking care of themselves independently, yet become uncharacteristically dependent on their spouse for nurturance, financial support, and security. Often there is a tendency to relinquish the control established when embracing independence after uniting with someone in a relationship. The pattern of past relationships may impact how dependency may influence any one relationship. Intimacy may conjure up a desire to acquiesce to the needs of another.

Finally, an individual who may have a dependent personality presents another aspect of dependence within a couple experiencing domestic violence. This type of dependency leads to a strong sense of vulnerability, a need for nurturance, and insecurity. A person experiencing dependent personality disorder may show clinging behavior, submission to others, and fear of separation. Emotional dependency is often equated with dependent personality disorder. Bornstein describes a "dependence model" as a theoretical framework with which to view domestic partner abuse that relates to the strength of commitment. This model focuses on the perception of fulfilling certain emotional needs. Although the relationship overall may have a lot to be desired, a high emotional dependency may preclude an abused partner from leaving the relationship. However, most researchers agree that economic dependency usually plays a stronger role in maintaining abusive relationships. Realistic and/or unrealistic perceptions of financial dependency may prevent a woman from leaving an abusive relationship more often than an emotional need. However, while some believe that if one has a personality disorder there appears to be a severity of abuse, there needs to be further research to corroborate this idea. It is important to understand that an individual who may be diagnosed with a dependent personality will not necessarily become engaged in an abusive relationship.

Returning to the case of Derrick and Marsha can help integrate some thoughts about the psychological perspective. Although it is not specified, Marsha was probably battered during the rape she experienced at the hands of Derrick. However, the limited information can at this point only lead to speculation about the plight of this relationship. Based on the psychological perspective, consider the following questions. Can Marsha be described as a battered woman or someone experiencing the BWS? Was she was somewhat dependent on her relationship? Derrick was her boss and as was stated, she needed the job. Did she have a dependent personality? Or would her dependency be considered objective or subjective according to Bornstein?

CONCLUSION

In summary, the three perspectives seem to be similar in that they focus on attempting to understand the etiology of intimate partner violence by assessing external factors, especially the economic connection. However, the sociological, feminist, and psychological perspectives also differ in theoretical emphasis of some internal and external factors. The sociological perspective focuses on external social structures that impact intimate partner violence such as violence in parenting, religious conflicts, and societal wars. Social violence is also related to social constructs of racism, sexism, and heterosexism (Kaufman, 2006) and seems to be correlated with socioeconomic status, unemployment, and cohabiting status (Anderson, 1997). This perspective is concerned with how external structures impact male perpetrators who are concerned with power and/or resources to obtain power.

The feminist perspective focuses on the socialization of roles and gender issues. There is a certain acceptability of aggression and violence assigned to the male gender than female. The sexism and homophobia that are abundant in society provide fertile ground for violence against women in intimate relationships (Pharr, 2006). This perspective also emphasizes the role the media play in possibly influencing intimate partner violence against woman.

Finally, the psychological perspective assesses individual personality characteristics that may either be a result of or influence intimate partner violence. There are various types of dependencies found in violent relationships that relate to economic resources, perceived dependency that may not be realistic, and a dependent disposition (Bornstein, 2006). The combination of violence and dependency in a relationship could result in symptoms related to the BWS. The BWS while not an official diagnosis is a controversial concept that has been used in judicial cases of intimate partner violence (Dixon, 2002).

Although the etiology and impact of intimate partner violence can be seen from a different theoretical lens, the result of this violence can be devastating to any individual. The difficulty of getting assistance especially when children are involved and there are extreme financial concerns can be perceived as almost insurmountable to some. There are many different steps to intervention depending on the individual's situation. It is recommended that any individual experiencing intimate partner violence seek the professional assistance of a counselor. However, the following list of resources can also be helpful as a starting point to self-empowerment.

RESOURCES

- National Crime Victims Survey (www.icpsr.umich.edu/NACJD/NCVS/)
- Cyber Abuse Help (www.WiredSafety.org)
- Working to Halt Online Abuse (www.haltabuse.org)
- National Sexual Assault Hotline at 1-800-656-HOPE (www.rainn.org)
- Men Can Stop Rape at 202-265-6530
- National Violence Against Women Survey (www.ncjrs.gov/pdffiles/172837.pdf)
- National Center for Victims of Crime, 800-394-2255
- National Institute on Drug Abuse, 800-662-4357 (www.drugabuse.gov)
- National Women's Health Resource Center (www.healthywomen.org/)
- United Nations (www.unsystem.org/)
- Centers for Disease Control and Preventions (www.cdc.gov/)

Discussion Questions

1. Define what is meant by the term *domestic violence*.
2. Discuss the different types of victimization occurring within contexts of physical abuse, sexual abuse, and stalking.
3. Reflecting on the research, discuss what is known about the nature and extent of domestic violence. What are some challenges to comprehending the full scope of domestic violence in society?
4. Compare and contrast the different sociological, feminist, and psychological perspectives discussed to explain the perpetration of domestic violence.
5. What are some of the effects on victims from experiencing domestic violence? How can some of these serve as barriers for victims to ending the abusive relationship?

References

Abbey, A. (2005). Lessons learned and unanswered questions about sexual assault perpetration. *Journal of Interpersonal Violence, 20*(1), 39–42.

Anderson, K. L., (1997). Gender, status, and domestic violence: An integration of feminist and family violence approaches. *Journal of Marriage and the Family, 59*(3), 655–669.

Associated Press. (2007, February 22). Sports briefing. *The New York Times*. Retrieved February 27, 2007, from http://www.nytimes.com/2007/02/22/sports/22sportsbriefs.html?pagew

Bachman, R., & Saltzman, L. E. (1995). *Violence against women: Estimates from the redesigned survey*. Bureau of Justice Statistics, Special

Report: National Crime Victimization Survey: U.S. Department of Justice.

Belknap, J. (2007). *The invisible women: Gender, crime, and justice* (3rd ed.). Belmont, CA: Wadsworth/Thomson Learning.

Berkel, L. A., Furlong, A. N., Hickman, A. A., & Blue, E. L. (2005). A qualitative examination of black college women's beliefs about abuse in relationships. *Professional Psychology Research and Practice, 36*(3), 283–290.

Bornstein, R. F. (2006). The complex relationship between dependency and domestic violence. *American Psychologist, 61*(6), 595–606.

Bureau of Justice Statistics. (2006). *Criminal victimization in the United States, 2005 Statistical tables.* Bureau of Justice Statistics, Special Report: National Crime Victimization Survey: U.S. Department of Justice.

Centers for Disease Control and Prevention. (2006). *Intimate partner violence: Fact sheet.* Atlanta, Georgia: National Centers for Injury Prevention and Control. Retrieved March 3, 2007, from http://www.cdc.gov/ncipc/factsheets/ipvfacts.htm

Centers for Disease Control and Prevention. (2007). *Sexual violence: Fact sheet.* National Center for Injury Prevention and Control, Atlanta Georgia. Retrieved March 3, 2007 from, http://www.cdc.gov/ncipc/factsheets/svfacts.htm

Dennison, S. M., & Thomson, D. M. (2005). Criticisms or plaudits for stalking laws? What psycho-legal research tells us about proscribing stalking [Electronic Version]. *Psychology, Public Policy, and Law, 11*(3), 384–406.

Dixon, J. (2002). Battered Woman Syndrome. *Expert Law.* Retrieved August 6, 2007, from http://www.expertlaw.com/library/domestic_violence/battered_women

Harned, M. S. (2004). Does it matter what you call it? The relationship between labeling unwanted sexual experiences and distress. *Journal of Counseling and Clinical Psychology, 72*(6), 1090–1099.

Kaufman, M. (2006). The construction of masculinity and the triad of men's violence. In T. Ore, (Ed.), *The social construction of difference and inequality* (3rd ed., pp. 533–549). New York: McGraw-Hill.

Kilpatrick, D. G., & Ruggiero, K. J. (2004). Making sense of rape in America: Where do the numbers come from and what do they mean? National Crime Victims Research and Treatment Center. Retrieved March 12, 2007, from http://new.vawnet.org/Assoc_Files_VAWnet/MakingSenseofRape.pdf.

Klein, A. R. (2004). *The criminal justice response to domestic violence.* Belmont, CA: Wadsworth/Thompson Learning.

Kotlowitz, A. (2007, February 11). The way we live now: 2-11-07: IDEA lab; asylum for the worlds battered women. *The New York Times.* Retrieved February 27, 2007, from http://www.nytimes.com

Monore, L. M., Kinney, L. M., Weis, M. D., Dafeamekpor, D. S., Dantzler, J., & Reynolds, M. (2005). The experience of sexual assault: findings from a statewide victim needs assessment. *Journal of Interpersonal Violence, 20*(7), 767–776.

National Women's Health Information Center. (2005). *Date rape drugs.* U.S. Department of Health and Human Services, Office on Women's Health. (March), Retrieved February 27, 2007, from http://www.womenshealth.gov/faq/rohypnol.htm#1

Pharr, S. (2006). Homophobia as weapon of sexism. In T. Ore (Ed.), *The social construction of difference and inequality* (3rd ed., pp. 550–559). New York: McGraw-Hill.

Robbins, L. Eligon, J., & Schweber, N. (2007, January 10). Pro Basketball: Kidd files for divorce, adding to a trying season for the nets. *The New York Times.* Retrieved February 27, 2007, from http://www.nytimes.com

Schwartz, J., & Blumenthal, R. (2007, February 8). Astronaut's arrest spurs review of NASA testing. *The New York Times.* Retrieved February 27, 2007, from http://select.nytimes.com/search/restricted/articl

Seligman, M. (1975). *Helplessness: On depression, development and death.* New York: Wiley.

Tjaden, P. & Thoennes, N. (1998). *Prevalence, incidence, and consequences of violence against women: Findings from the National Violence Against Women Survey.*

Walker, L. E. (1979). *The battered woman.* New York, NY: Harper and Row Publishers, Inc.

Walker, L. E. (2000). *A practical guide for the psychotherapist: Abused women and survivor therapy*. Washington, D.C.: American Psychological Association.

Wasco, S. M. (2005). Understanding rape and sexual assault. *Journal of Interpersonal Violence, 20*(1), 127–131.

Wasserman, C. (2004). *Dating violence on campus*. (Fall 2003/Winter 2004). Networks: National Center for Victims of Crime. Retrieved March 12, 2007, from http://www.ncvc.org/ncvc/AGP. Net/Components/documentViewer/Download. aspxnz?DocumentID=37929

Wilson, K. J. (2006). *When violence begins at home: A comprehensive guide to understanding and ending domestic abuse* (2nd ed). Berkeley, CA: Hunter House, Inc. Publishers.

Wilt, S., & Olson, S. (1996). Prevalence of domestic violence in the United States [Electronic Version]. *Journal of American Medical Women's Association, 51*(3), 77–82.

Zeller, T. (2006, April 17). Despite laws, stalkers roam on the internet. *The New York Times*. Retrieved February 27, 2007, from http://www. nytimes.com

CHAPTER 9

WORKPLACE VIOLENCE: IDENTIFYING GENDER DIFFERENCES AND SIMILARITIES

SHANNON A. SANTANA AND BONNIE S. FISHER

ABSTRACT

Research indicates that there are several gender differences in workplace violence. First, the types of victimizations suffered by males and females differ: Females are more likely than males to be victims of sexual assault, rape, and intimate partner violence in the workplace, while males are more likely than females to be victims of homicide, assault, and robbery in the workplace. Second, there are also differences in terms of the victim–offender relationship: Females who are victimized in the workplace are more likely than males to have been victimized by someone they know. Third, the occupations in which females are at high risk of being victimized differ from those of males. The implications of these findings for security and violence prevention as well as suggestions for future research will be discussed.

INTRODUCTION

On January 30, 2006, Jennifer Sanmarco shot and killed six of her former coworkers at the U.S. Postal Service's Santa Barbara Processing and Distribution Center in Goleta, California (Smith, 2006). On the rare occasion when a heinous workplace violent crime happens, the media are quickly on the scene to report it. The media's coverage of violent workplace incidents continues to fuel the public's perception that violence in the workplace is a recent epidemic that threatens the daily lives of the approximately 140 million employees in the United States (Bureau of Labor Statistics, 2004). Contrary to the media's depiction, violence has always been a part of the work setting. During some historical periods in the United States, workplace violence was commonplace. Despite continual efforts over time to address workplace violence, it is a labor force reality that no industry or occupation is immune.

Workplace violence has evolved into an occupational safety and health, and criminal justice issue. Since about the mid-1980s, workplace violence has received growing attention from a variety of parties concerned with employee safety and employer liability. Professional organizations and labor unions representing a large proportion of the labor force (e.g., transportation, law enforcement, education and nursing fields) continue to support workplace violence education and training and improved security for their respective constituency. Each branch of government— executive, legislative, and judicial—at every level has become involved in workplace violence issues. Their actions have included the passage of some state and local regulatory statutes and annual Congressional hearings (see Jenkins, 2006).

Their collective actions set the groundwork for a marked increase in scholarly work during the 1990s. Researchers from a range of different disciplines turned their attention to a variety of workplace violence issues. The issues they have addressed include estimating the extent of workplace violence, identifying individual, job, task, and work setting factors related to the likelihood of becoming a victim of workplace violence, and determining the physical and mental health-related consequences and financial costs of workplace violence (see Fisher, Jenkins, & Williams, 1998; Flannery, 1996; Hartley, Biddle, & Jenkins, 2005; Mullen, 1997). Researchers also continue to generate a growing body of research that addresses specific workplace violence-related issues such as domestic violence and coworker violence (Fisher & Peek-Asa, 2005; Tjaden & Thoennes, 2001).

Government agencies, such as the Bureau of Labor Statistics (BLS), the National Institute for Occupational Safety and Health (NIOSH), and the Bureau of Justice Statistics (BJS), also sustain separate national-level data collection efforts to estimate the extent, nature, and impacts of workplace violence and routinely publish reports to highlight their results (Bachman, 1994; Jenkins, 1996a; Toscano & Windau, 1994). During the early 2000s, workplace violence data from two new sources were produced by the federal government. First, NIOSH partnered with the BLS to administer to employers the Survey of Workplace Violence Prevention (SWVP). The SWVP data have been used to estimate the number of establishments and employees covered by a workplace violence prevention program or policy (Bureau of Labor Statistics, 2006). Second, NIOSH also partnered with the BJS and U.S. Census Bureau to administer the Workplace Risk Supplement (WRS) with the first six months of the 2002 National Crime Victimization Survey (NCVS). The purpose of the WRS is to provide data from employees about their perceptions of workplace safety, knowledge of in-place workplace violence prevention training and written materials and security measures, workplace victimization experiences, and self-protection behaviors (Jenkins, Fisher, & Hartley, 2007).

One issue that has not received much attention, even in these two new NIOSH data sources, is gender differences and similarities in workplace violence. While a few researchers have begun to examine gender issues (e.g., Duhart, 2001; Hartley et al., 2005; Richardson & Windau, 2003), there has been little systematic research designed to explicitly focus on gender differences and similarities in the extent and nature of workplace violence (for an exception, see Fisher & Gunnison, 2001). The purpose of this chapter is to provide an overview of what researchers know about gender differences and similarities in workplace violence in the United States.[1] The first section describes the extent and nature of workplace violence committed against male and female employees. The second section compares and contrasts workplace violence committed against female and male employees in terms of the perpetrators and their motives and impacts. The conclusion provides a discussion of the implications for security and violence prevention efforts that take gender into account.

WORKPLACE VIOLENCE AND GENDER

THE EXTENT OF WORKPLACE VIOLENCE COMMITTED AGAINST MALES AND FEMALES

Homicide

Numerous studies have examined the extent of homicide in the workplace among males and females. These studies reach several noteworthy conclusions. First, at least seven studies, using a variety of data sets and time periods, come to the same conclusion: Males are more likely to experience homicide in the workplace than females. For instance, Jenkins (1996a), using the death certificate-based National Traumatic Occupational Fatalities (NTOF)[2] surveillance system data, reported that 80 percent of the workplace homicides between 1980 and 1982 involved male victims. Similarly, Richardson and Windau (2003), using data from the BLS for 1996–2000, found that 81 percent of the homicides involved male workers while 19 percent involved female workers. Duhart's (2001) analysis of NCVS data for slightly different years (1993–1999) revealed the same average annual percentages: 81 percent of the workplace homicide victims were male while 19 percent were female. Kraus, Blander, and McArthur (1995), in their review of nine workplace violence articles published between 1980 and 1994, reported that work-related homicides rates were 3.0–5.6 times higher for males than for females. Likewise, Castillo and Jenkins (1994), using the NTOF data from 1980 to 1989, reported that the homicide rate for female workers was 0.33 per 100,000 workers compared with 1.02 per 100,000 workers for male workers—a rate three times higher than the rate of females. Similarly, Moracco et al. (2000), using data from North Carolina, found that the homicide rate for female workers was 0.32 compared with 1.19 for male workers. Finally, Kennedy (2004), using National Incident-Based Reporting System (NIBRS) data, found that males were approximately four times more likely than females to be murdered on the job. Thus, both national-level and some state-level data indicate that the homicide rate for male workers is higher than the homicide rate for female workers.

Despite the consensus among studies that males are more likely to experience homicide in the workplace than females, there are some noteworthy twists in the findings regarding homicide. First, although males have higher rates of workplace homicide, data from the 2004 Census of Fatal Occupational Injuries (CFOI) indicate that homicide is the second leading cause of death for females in the workplace but the fourth leading cause of death for males in the workplace (Bureau of Labor Statistics, 2004). In addition, the 2004 CFOI reveals that 24 percent of the fatal work injury incidents for females were the result of homicide compared with 9 percent of the fatal work injury incidents for males (Bureau of Labor Statistics, 2004). Other studies have found that homicides range from 10 to 30 percent of the work-related injury deaths for males compared with 31 to 57 percent of such deaths for women (Jenkins, 1996a, 1996b; Kraus et al., 1995; Richardson & Windau, 2003). Thus, while the rate of workplace homicide is higher for males than females, workplace homicide is a higher leading cause of death for females than for males (Bureau of Labor Statistics, 2004). Jenkins (1996b) attributed the differential risks of homicide victimization by gender to variations in employment patterns. Males suffer greater risks of accidental death than do women because they are more likely to work in hazardous industries such as agriculture/forestry/fishing and mining. These industries pose a greater threat to workers than the retail trade, services, and finance/insurance/real estate industries that have a greater gender balance of workers

(Jenkins, 1996b). Thus, even though a greater number of males are murdered in the workplace each year, homicide is a higher leading cause of death for females in the workplace compared with males (second vs. fourth, respectively) because male workers are more likely to suffer accidental deaths (e.g., falls, highway incidents, contact with objects and equipment) than homicides (Bureau of Labor Statistics, 2004).

The second noteworthy twist in the findings on homicide concerns the nature of work-related homicides. The research in this area is divided on whether there are gender differences in the types of homicides males and females experience in the workplace. For instance, Kraus (1987), in his study of work-related homicides in California from 1979 to 1981, found that while firearms accounted for 77 percent of all work-related homicides during this time period, females were more likely than males to be killed by cutting or stabbing instruments. Richardson and Windau (2003), on the other hand, found that shootings were the most common method of homicide for both males and females in the workplace (83% and 70%, respectively).

Rape and Sexual Assaults

Similar to patterns of sexual victimization more generally, data indicate that a much larger percentage of females experience sexual victimization in the workplace compared with males. Using data from the 1993–1999 NCVS, Duhart (2001) reported that the average annual percentage of rape and sexual assault victims who were female was 80 percent compared with 20 percent who were males.

Incident-level NCVS data reveal a similar pattern: Rapes and sexual assaults are committed far more frequently against females than males. Between 1992 and 1996, on average, 6.3 percent of the workplace incidents committed against females were rapes or sexual assaults compared with 0.6 percent of the incidents committed against males (Fisher & Gunnison, 2001).

Research ranking the frequency of different types of violence in the workplace has found sexual assaults to be the third most frequently occurring violent incident that females experienced in the workplace: 5 percent of the incidents, on average, were sexual assaults. A little over 2 percent of the incidents against females were rapes. For males, on average, both sexual assault and rape incidents were infrequent: Less than one-half of 1 percent of the total number of violent incidents committed against males in the workplace were rapes and sexual assaults (Fisher, 1997).

Robberies

Results from the 1993–1999 NCVS show that males were more likely than females to be victims of robbery while at work or on duty. Seventy percent of the workplace robbery victims were males compared with females who were approximately 30 percent of the workplace robbery victims (Duhart, 2001).

However, when examining the number of robbery incidents from the NCVS, Fisher and Gunnison (2001) found that the percentage of robberies committed against males and females was almost equal: 4.5 percent compared with 4.2 percent of their respective total number of incidents.

Aggravated and Simple Assaults

Using data from the 1993–1999 NCVS, Duhart (2001) reported that the percentage of males who had experienced an aggravated assault while working or on duty was almost 2.5 times greater than the percentage of females who did: 71.4 percent compared with 28.6 percent of the aggravated assault victims. He also reported a similar pattern for simple assaults: A larger percentage of males were simple assault victims compared with the percentage of female victims—64.1 percent compared with 35.9 percent of the simple assault victims. In contrast to Duhart's findings, data from the BLS's Survey of Occupational Injuries and Illness (SOII)[3] indicate that women were the victims in the majority (56%) of the nonfatal workplace assaults (Toscano & Weber, 1995). Toscano and Weber found that these acts usually took the form of "hitting, kicking, and beating." There is at least one methodological rationale for the difference between the BLS's SOII-based results and the BJS's NCVS-based results: The SOII is an injury and illness survey based on a sample of businesses (excluding the self-employed and government workers), whereas the NCVS is a victimization survey based on a sample of households. Also, the definition of assault differs across the two surveys.[4]

Other researchers, using NCVS data, have examined the number of assault incidents committed in the workplace and the ranking of the frequency of the different types of violence. As to the extent of assaults, Fisher and Gunnison (2001) reported that a similar percentage of the incidents committed against males and females in the workplace were simple assault incidents: 75.1 percent and 73 percent, respectively. A slightly different pattern emerges with respect to aggravated assault incidents in the workplace. A smaller percentage of aggravated assault incidents were committed against females compared with males: 15.1 percent versus 21.9 percent, respectively.

By far, simple assault was the most frequently occurring type of workplace violence among both males and females, followed by aggravated assaults (Duhart, 2001; Fisher, 1996; Fisher & Gunnison, 2001; Fisher et al., 1998). Although a larger percentage of males were simple assault victims while working or on duty, simple assault incidents were the most frequently occurring type of violence for both sexes.

Stalking

Stalking in the United States received relatively little attention until a short time ago. In fact, it was not until 1990 that California passed the nation's first state anti-stalking law (Doerner & Lab, 2005). While the prevalence of stalking in the United States was estimated through the National Violence Against Women Survey (NVAWS) in the 1990s,[5] there have yet to be any national-level studies focusing on the prevalence of stalking in the workplace.[6] However, given that females *in the general population* are more likely than males to be stalked (Tjaden & Thoennes, 1998), it is likely that females are also more likely than males to be stalked *in the workplace*. There is national-level evidence to support this speculation. Tjaden and Thoennes (2001), in their examination of coworker violence,[7] found that females were more likely to report being stalked by coworkers than were males. In addition, a larger proportion of the female victims reported being victims of stalking by coworkers compared with male victims: 39.5 percent of the female victims of coworker violence were stalked compared with 6.5 percent of the male victims of coworker violence. Research on stalking indicates that there are some differences between males and females in terms of the most common perpetrators. For example, the findings of the NVAWS indicate that females are more likely than males to be stalked by intimates (e.g., spouse, ex-spouse, boyfriend, ex-boyfriend) (Tjaden & Thoennes, 1998). Thus, it is likely that the perpetrators of stalking against females in the workplace are also intimates.

Given that women are frequently victimized by ex-intimates and given that the perpetrator of stalking is most likely to be an intimate, it is not surprising that Chenier (1998) reports that there is an increase in the number of women who are stalked in the workplace (see also Mullen, 1997). Chenier suggests that this increase may be due to the fact that increasing numbers of women are working and are thus able to leave abusive situations. However, although these women may be able to change their place of residence, they may not be able to change their work location, which is known to the perpetrator. In addition, Chenier argues that women are often reluctant to ask their employers for assistance in dealing with the problem. Even if the women do ask their employers for help, many companies do not have any procedures for protecting women from stalking and domestic violence.

Stalking in the workplace should be a serious concern for employers for a number of reasons. First, the average stalking situation persists for almost 2 years (1.8 years) and almost 20 percent of stalking victims move to avoid their stalkers (Tjaden & Thoennes, 1998). In addition to moving, it is likely that many of these stalking victims also quit or change jobs because their job may be one of the few places where the stalker knows where to find them. Second, 26 percent of the stalking victims in the NVAWS said they lost time from work due to being stalked. The average number of days missed from work for these stalking victims was 11 days; 7 percent of these victims said they never returned to work (Tjaden & Thoennes, 1998). Third, stalking should be a cause for concern because researchers have found a strong connection between stalking and other forms of violence in intimate relationships. For instance, results from the NVAWS indicated that a substantial percentage of females who were stalked by an intimate partner were also physically or sexually abused by that partner: 81 and 31 percent, respectively (Tjaden & Thoennes, 1998). Research indicates that intimate partner violence can have negative impacts on both employees and employers (see Fisher & Peek-Asa, 2005).

Domestic Violence

Data indicate that females are more likely to be the victims of domestic violence than males (Rennison & Welchans, 2000). There is some evidence indicating that this domestic violence may be carried over into the workplace. For instance, according to Lord (1998), the U.S. Department of Justice estimates that domestic partners were responsible for more than 13,000 nonfatal acts of workplace violence against women in 1993. However, in a study of full-time employees in state government agencies and universities in North Carolina, Lord found that few respondents reported that they had been victimized at work by domestic partners. Lord argues that it is likely that domestic problems do carry over into the workplace but that employees may be reluctant to report such incidents. Reasons that employees may be reluctant to tell their employers include fear of retaliation or fear of losing their jobs (Weiser & Widiss, 2004).

In contrast to Lord's (1998) study, a study of workers in North Carolina by Moracco et al. (2000) found that many females were victimized by current or intimate partners while in the workplace: 75 percent of the female victims of workplace homicide were victimized by current or former intimate partners.[8] The difference between the findings of this study and those of Lord may lie in the fact that Lord's study required victims of domestic violence in the workplace to self-report their victimization while Moracco et al.'s study analyzed homicide data from North Carolina's medical examiner system, thus not requiring victims to self-report their victimization.

As Fisher and Peek-Asa (2005) suggest, given the fact that approximately 1,200 women and 400 men are killed by an intimate partner each year, it is not surprising that some of these homicides will occur in the workplace. Lending further credence to this idea is Moracco et al.'s finding that not only did the victim–offender relationship differ for male and female employees (with male employees being more likely to be killed by coworkers followed by nonstrangers and customers and females being more likely to be killed by current or former intimates), but the nature of the homicide varied by gender. A larger percentage of the homicides of female workers were categorized as dispute-related compared with those of male workers who either tended to be killed while involved in law enforcement activities or tended to be robbery victims. In addition, not only were female workers more likely to be murdered in the context of disputes, when male workers were the victims of dispute-related homicides, the nature of the disputes tended to differ from the disputes of female workers: 75 percent of the dispute-related homicides of female workers occurred in the context of estranged intimate relationships while the majority of the dispute-related homicides of male workers were work-related (e.g., a fired or reprimanded employee). Moracco et al. note that all of the female victims who were murdered in the workplace by intimate partners had separated from these partners prior to the homicide. As suggested earlier, these women may be particularly likely to be victimized at work because the workplace may be the only location where the perpetrator knows he can find the victim (Moracco et al., 2000).

Besides Moracco et al.'s study, other research also indicates that domestic violence may be carried over into the workplace. However, some research suggests that certain *types* of workplace violence incidents may be more prone to domestic violence than others. For instance, Collins, Scarborough, and Southerland (2001) analyzed multi-site versus single-site incidents of workplace violence.[9] They found that females were more likely to be victims in multi-site incidents while males were more likely to be victims in single-site incidents. This finding is particularly startling given that they also found that multi-site workplace violence incidents were more likely to result in death. Based on their findings, Collins et al. conclude that there is a "family connection" between the victims of multi-site workplace violence and the offender. In other words, in multi-site incidents, females are often the victims of domestic violence in the workplace.

Understanding how and why domestic violence occurs is important as domestic violence can have negative impacts on employees and employers. Even acts of domestic violence that are not committed in the workplace can have negative impacts on the workplace (Fisher & Peek-Asa, 2005). For instance, victims of domestic violence may be late for work, miss work, quit, or function beneath their capability (American Institute on Domestic Violence, 2001; Farmer & Tiefenthaler, 2004; Weiser & Widiss, 2004). There is some data indicating that the *level* of domestic violence may be a factor in how negatively the domestic violence impacts the employee's productivity. For instance, Farmer and Tiefenthaler's (2004) analysis of Physical Violence in American Families (PVAF) data indicated that women who were more severely abused were more likely to report that their job performance suffered than women who were victims of less severe abuse. They also reported that battered women were *not* less likely to be employed; in fact, they argue that their results suggest that battered women are *more* likely to be currently employed than women with similar characteristics. It may be that battered women find it necessary to work outside the home in order to increase their economic independence should they decide to leave the relationship (Farmer & Tiefenthaler, 2004) or because they feel the workplace is safer than their home (Fisher & Peek-Asa, 2005). Given that females who are victims of domestic violence are thought to suffer from decreased productivity, the fact that there are a large number of battered females working outside the home may be detrimental to employers who are concerned with maximizing productivity.

Domestic violence may also negatively affect companies by increasing their health care costs. According to the American Institute on Domestic Violence (2001), the cost of providing medical and mental health services to victims of rape, physical assault, stalking, and homicide by intimate partners is almost $4.1 billion a year. In addition, companies are becoming increasingly concerned about domestic violence because they may be held liable if they fail to act when domestic violence crosses over into the workplace. For instance, one company was sued for $5 million when an employee's ex-partner killed the female employee and several of her coworkers. The female employee had said her partner had threatened to kill her at work. The company was found negligent for failing to act. Companies may also be held liable for negligent hiring and negligent retention (Braun Consulting News, 1998).

Workplace Aggression

One specific form of nonphysical workplace aggression is bullying.[10] Using a convenience sample, Namie (2000) reported that the majority of the victims of workplace bullying are females (77%). In addition, Namie (2003) found that bullies use different techniques depending on the gender of the victim. Female victims were more likely than male victims to 1) have their contributions to meetings discounted (74% vs. 61%, respectively); 2) be "mistreated when medically or psychologically vulnerable" (45% vs. 35%, respectively); 3) be "denied training or time to succeed in new job" (43% vs. 34%, respectively); 4) be "blocked access to equipment and resources for success" (30% vs. 21%, respectively), and 5) experience "uninvited invasion of office space and scrutiny of emails" (22% vs. 14%, respectively). Males, on the other hand, were more likely than females to be tormented because of a disability (26% vs. 18%, respectively). In addition, males were more likely than females to be threatened with physical harm (21% vs. 12%, respectively).

Namie (2003) also found a gender difference in the victims' perceptions of why they were chosen as a bullying target: 29 percent of the female victims indicated that they were chosen because the bully knew they could not afford to leave their job compared with 19 percent of the males.

One similarity between male and female victims of bullying is that they tend to be bullied by members of the same sex. In other words, females are more likely to be bullied by females and males are more likely to be bullied by males (Namie, 2003).

THE NATURE OF WORKPLACE VIOLENCE COMMITTED AGAINST MALES AND FEMALES

Sociodemographic Factors

Research also reveals some differences between males and females in terms of sociodemographic factors. For instance, Warren et al. (1999) cite a study by Klien and associates, using data from the NCVS, that reports that for males the risk of experiencing a work-related robbery and assault was higher for those under the age of 45 years with a family income of less than $40,000 but with more than a high school education. For females, the risk was higher for younger women (i.e., 18–34 years old) and for those who were not married. However, Tjaden and Thoennes (2001), in their analysis of coworker violence, found no significant differences between male and female victims in terms of race, age, or education. The difference between Klien et al.'s findings and those of Tjaden and Thoennes may partially be due to the different outcome variables and samples of the two studies: Tjaden and Thonnes focused on rape, physical assault, stalking, and threats by coworkers, while Klien et al. focused on robbery and assault in the workplace.

GENDER DIFFERENCES IN WORKPLACE VIOLENCE BY JOB CHARACTERISTICS AND OCCUPATION

Results from a number of studies, using a variety of data sources, suggest that certain job characteristics and occupations put females more at risk than males for experiencing workplace violence. Several job characteristics appear to be related to experiencing an incident of workplace violence. First, Mustaine and Tewksbury (1997), using data from the 1983 National Crime Survey's Victimization Risk Supplement, identify job characteristics that significantly increase the probability of women experiencing an incident of workplace violence. Their multivariate analysis suggests that males were more likely to be crime victims[11] if they did not have security at work, lived in a metropolitan area, worked in a place that is open to the public, and worked in a job that involved the protection of others or property. Females, on the other hand, were more likely to be victims if they were better educated and if their work involved late hours. Second, Hurrell, Worthington, and Driscoll (1996), in their study of public service employees, found some differences among males and females in the job stressors that were significantly related to whether an employee was assaulted on the job. Specifically, they found that while four stressor variables were associated with assaults among both males and females (low job decision control, high levels of responsibility for people, limited alternative job opportunities, and skill underutilization), two additional stressors were significantly related to assault for females: role conflict and low mental demands.

Other researchers have examined specific occupations and all report gender-related differences. First, Castillo and Jenkins (1994), examining data from the NTOF surveillance system, found that females had low rates of work-related homicide in three industries that were high risk for males: justice/public order/safety, hotels and motels, and eating and drinking establishments. Females had high rates of work-related homicide in liquor stores, gasoline stations, and grocery stores.

Second, Fisher and Gunnison (2001) found that a higher percentage of incidents of robbery occurred against women who worked at teaching institutions, in law enforcement, and in retail compared with males who worked in these occupations. Note, however, that Wooldredge, Cullen, and Latessa (1992), using a sample of faculty from one university, found no gender difference in the likelihood of personal victimization (i.e., robbery, aggravated assault, sexual assault, and assault with a deadly weapon). The reason for this discrepancy may be found in the composition of the two studies' respective samples: Fisher and Gunnison used a nationally representative sample from the population of U.S. residents, while Wooldredge et al. used a single sample of members of one type of occupation from one university.

In the next two studies, the researchers examined violence in a specific type of occupation. Keim (1999) cites results from a study conducted by Harlan in which four times more females than males in health care settings are injured by their patients. And finally, Hurrell et al. (1996) conducted a cross-sectional study on job stress among public service employees in a northeastern state in 1989. They found that 9 percent of the females and 17 percent of the males in their study reported that they had been physically assaulted while on the job during the past year. For females, the largest percentage of assaults occurred among mental health workers (29%), followed by clerks (8%), human services case workers (7%), and nursing personnel (4%). Within these job categories, 48 percent of the female mental health workers, 18 percent of the female human service case workers, 17 percent of the female nursing personnel, and 4 percent of the female clerks reported being assaulted within the past year. For males, the largest percentage of assaults occurred among state police personnel (21%), mental health workers (11%), guards (8%), and clerks (8%). Within these job categories, 65 percent of the male mental health workers, 51 percent of the male state police personnel, 35 percent of the male guards, and 11 percent of the male clerks reported being assaulted within the past year. Hurrell et al. (1996) also found that workers who had direct contact with clients had a higher likelihood of being assaulted while on the job, regardless of gender. According to Hurrell et al., this finding is consistent with other studies that have shown that the greatest risk of physical assault while on the job is from workers outside the organization (e.g., customers, clients, and patients), not from coworkers (see Tjaden & Thoennes, 1999, 2001).

Other evidence indicates that a greater proportion of female work-related homicides occur in the retail and service industries relative to other industries than do male work-related homicides (Jenkins, 1996a; Peek-Asa, Erickson, & Kraus, 1999; Richardson & Windau, 2003). One reason that females may be more likely to be victimized in retail and service industries than in other occupations is that the nature of retail and service positions puts women at greater risks of victimization. As discussed above, those at greatest risk of becoming a victim of workplace homicide are those who work alone or in small groups, those who work late at night, and those who work with cash (Jenkins, 1996a; Lord, 1998). These characteristics are typical of the retail positions in which women often work.

The last two studies focused on data from individual states. The first study, conducted by Islam, Edla, Mujuru, Doyle, and Ducatman (2003), used data from West Virginia's state-managed Workers' Compensation system for 1997–1999. They found that the incidence of physical assault was higher for females than for males: 136.2 versus 83.4 incident cases per 100,000 employee years, respectively. They also found an interaction effect between time of assault and gender with female health care workers experiencing a higher risk of assault injuries between 12:00 A.M. and 8:00 A.M. The second study, by Moracco et al. (2000), focused on workplace homicides in North Carolina. They reported that across different occupations, taxicab drivers had the highest homicide rate. All of the murdered taxicab drivers were men. The occupation with the second highest homicide rate[12] was law enforcement officer. Once again, all of the murdered law enforcement personnel were men.

GENDER DIFFERENCES IN THE RELATIONSHIP
BETWEEN THE VICTIM AND OFFENDER

The victim–offender relationship in workplace violence incidents can take various forms including coworker, ex-intimate, current intimate, relative, acquaintance, customer/client, and stranger. As noted above, the media often focus on incidents of coworker violence. Contrary to these media accounts, Tjaden and Thoennes (2001) present findings from the NVAWS that suggest that coworker violence is relatively rare: 1.7 percent of the respondents indicated that they had been victimized by a coworker sometime *during their life*, while 0.1 percent said they had been victimized by a coworker *during the past year*. When analyzing these statistics by gender, Tjaden and Thoennes (2001) found that females were significantly less likely than men to have been victimized by a coworker over their lifetimes while males and females were almost equally likely to have been victimized by a coworker in the past year.

Tjaden and Thoennes' (2001) findings also indicate that males and females experienced different types of coworker violence. The majority of victims of coworker rape (76.7%) and the majority of victims of coworker stalking (73.9%) were females, while the majority of victims of coworker assault (83.4%) and the majority of victims of threats by coworkers (80.6%) were males.

In addition to examining whether there was a working relationship between victims and perpetrators of workplace violence, several studies have also examined whether there was a personal relationship between victims and perpetrators. First, Bachman (1994), using data from the 1987–1992 National Crime Survey,[13] found that males who were victimized while working were more likely than females to be attacked by a stranger: 58 percent of the victimizations compared with 40 percent, respectively. Females, however, were more likely than males to be attacked by someone they knew while at work or on duty. For example, 35 percent of the workplace victimizations experienced by females were committed by an acquaintance whereas slightly less—30 percent—were against males. She found a larger difference with respect to victimizations committed by a person well known to the victim—a well-known person committed 19 percent of victimizations against females whereas such a person only committed 10 percent of victimizations against males. Additionally, Bachman found that husbands, ex-husbands, boyfriends, and ex-boyfriends were responsible for five percent of the attacks against females in the workplace compared with 1 percent for males. Intimate partner violence appears to be more of a problem for female employees than for male employees.

Second, Warchol (1998), using data from the NCVS, found that in 0.2 percent of the incidents committed against male workers, the victim and offender were intimates, compared with 2.2 percent of the incidents committed against female workers. In addition, he also found that a larger percentage of female victims reported that their attacker was an acquaintance compared with male victims: 46.2 percent and 29.9 percent, respectively. Males, on the other hand, were more likely to report that their attacker was a stranger compared with females: 65.0 percent versus 47.0 percent, respectively.

Third, Toscano and Windau (1998) also found that many female victims of workplace homicide knew their attacker. Specifically, they found that one-sixth of the female workplace homicides in 1996 were the result of domestic disputes. Fourth, Richardson and Windau (2003) found that of the workplace homicides that were committed by a relative (e.g., spouse or ex-spouse) or other personal acquaintance, 67 percent involved female victims.

In sum, there is a good deal of evidence indicating that females are more likely than males to be the victims of workplace violence that is committed by people they know. Part of this may be the result of domestic violence being carried over into the workplace.

GENDER DIFFERENCES IN MOTIVES BEHIND WORKPLACE VIOLENCE

In addition to the idea that some workplace violence is the result of domestic disputes carried over into the workplace, there is also some speculation suggesting that the advancement of women in the workplace may lead to feelings of resentment among men who feel they were unfairly passed over for jobs or promotions. For instance, an employee of the U.S. Postal Service shot three people and killed one other at work six weeks after his complaint to the Equal Opportunity Commission that he had been discriminated against in favor of female employees was dismissed (Mullen, 1997).

Other researchers suggest that females may face extreme risks of violence at work because they are viewed as vulnerable and as easy targets. For example, Kraus et al. (1995) suggest that criminals may perceive women as offering no resistance or being less likely to interfere during the course of a robbery.

Finally, some researchers suggest that males may use violence against females in the workplace as a means of maintaining power and control over them (Liddle & Widdowson, 1997). In sum, the research presented above suggests that women may be the victims of workplace violence for different reasons than are men.

GENDER DIFFERENCES IN THE IMPACTS OF WORKPLACE VIOLENCE

Researchers have consistently shown that experiencing an incident of workplace violence takes a negative toll on the victim (see Warren et al., 1999). When looking at the impacts of workplace violence on males and females, there is some research indicating that the toll may be different for males and females.

For example, Fisher and Gunnison (2001) examined the economic costs of workplace violence incidents committed against male and female employees. They found that in incidents where a person was injured, females were slightly more likely to miss time from work than were males. Similarly, Tjaden and Thoennes (2001), in their analysis of coworker violence, also found that females were more likely to miss time from work as a result of their victimization. In addition, there is some research suggesting that not only are females more likely to miss time from work, but they may also be absent from work for longer periods of time. For instance, Fisher and Gunnison (2001) found that, on average, female victims who were injured lost 22 days from work, while male victims who were injured lost 8 days.

There are other financial impacts to be considered. Fisher and Gunnison (2001) report that females were as equally likely as males to have lost pay due to injuries that were not covered by unemployment, insurance, sick leave, or other sources. However, female victims' household members were more likely to miss more than one day of work than were male victims' household members (49% compared with 35%).

Some research has focused specifically on the costs of workplace *homicides*. Using data from the 1992–2001 CFOI, Hartley et al. (2005) measured the societal costs of workplace homicides by summing medical expenses, future earnings from the year of death until the victim would have been 67, and household production losses such as child care and housework. They found the mean costs for males and females to be roughly equal: $800,000 and $799,000, respectively. The median costs for males and females were also almost equal: $784,000 and $783,000, respectively. However, because males are victims of homicide in the workplace much more frequently than females,[14] the total costs for males were estimated at $5.1 billion compared with just under $1.3 billion for females.

CONCLUSION

Gender differences do exist with respect to the extent, nature, motives, and impacts of workplace violence—male and female employees experience different types of violence for different reasons and they experience different impacts from their violent incidents. Research shows that there is variation among male and female workers in the frequency of the different types of workplace violence and the characteristics of the incidents. This variation will pose challenges for those developing and implementing workplace violence prevention and security policies and programs.

These differences need to be addressed as employers may be held liable for violence-related injuries suffered on the job (see Collins et al., 2001; Fisher & Peek-Asa, 2005; Hughes, 1999). Tailoring security and violence prevention strategies to fit the type of violence, type of work, the victim–offender relationship, and the motives of the perpetrator may be a valuable first step. For instance, because some research suggests that females are likely to be the victims of domestic violence in the workplace, employers need to incorporate measures to prevent and combat this type of workplace violence. In addition, because some research indicates that males are more likely to be the victims of disputes by coworkers, efforts should be made to address potentially hazardous work-related conflicts such as employee termination and unsatisfactory performance evaluations (Moracco et al., 2000).

Only by better assessing the gender and workplace violence relationship can our knowledge and understanding be put to good practice not only for preventing violence but also for securing a safer workplace for males and females. It is clear that efforts have to be made to educate the parties concerned—employers, employees, unions, professional organizations, government agencies—that gender differences exist in the extent, characteristics, victim–offender relationship, motives, and impacts of workplace violence. An education stage may be a first proactive step in the development of workplace violence prevention and security strategies and measures that address gender differences.

Discussion Questions

1. Describe the different types of victimization that occur in the workplace.
2. What is the utility of examining different data sources to inform about the nature and extent of workplace violence?
3. Discuss the risk of victimization in the workplace as it relates to job characteristics and occupation.
4. What factors assist in explaining the differential rates of victimization of men and women in the workplace?
5. What are some reasons for violence in the workplace?

References

American Institute on Domestic Violence. (2001). *Domestic violence statistics.* Retrieved January 4, 2007, from http://www.aidv-usa.com/Statistics.htm

Bachman, R. (1994). *Violence and theft in the workplace.* Washington, D.C.: U.S. Department of Justice.

Braun Consulting News. (1998). *Domestic abuse and workplace violence—a liability issue for employers.* Retrieved January 4, 2007, from http://www.braunconsulting.com/bcg/newsletters/spring2.html

Bureau of Labor Statistics. (2004). *Census of fatal occupational injuries.* Retrieved January 4, 2007, from http://stats.bls.gov/iif/oshwc/cfoi/cfch0003.pdf

Bureau of Labor Statistics. (2006). *Survey of Workplace Violence Prevention, 2005.* USDL 06-1860. U.S. Department of Labor. Washington, D.C.: U.S. Government Printing Office.

Castillo, D. N., & Jenkins, E. L. (1994). Industries and occupations at high risk for work-related homicide. *Journal of Medicine, 36*(2), 125–132.

Chenier, E. (1998). The workplace: A battleground for violence. *Public Personnel Management, 27*(4), 557–568.

Collins, P., Scarborough K., & Southerland, M. (2001). Workplace violence: "The family connection." *Crime Prevention and Community Safety: An International Journal,* 3(3), 7–18.

Doerner, W. G., & Lab, S. P. (2005). *Victimology.* Cincinnati, OH: Anderson Publishing.

Duhart, D. T. (2001). *Violence in the workplace, 1993–1999.* Bureau of Justice Statistics Special Report. NCJ 190076. Washington, D.C.: U.S. Department of Justice.

Farmer, A., & Tiefenthaler, J. (2004). The employment effects of domestic violence. *Research in Labor Economics, 23,* 301–334.

Fisher, B. S. (1996). *Analysis and report of the National Crime Victimization Survey: A summary report to DHHS, PHS, CDC, NIOSH, and ALOSH.* Cincinnati, OH: University of Cincinnati, Department of Political Science.

Fisher, B. S. (1997). *Analysis and report of the National Crime Victimization Survey: A summary report to DHHS, PHS, CDC, NIOSH,* *and ALOSH.* Cincinnati, OH: University of Cincinnati, Department of Political Science.

Fisher, B. S., & Gunnison, E. (2001). Violence in the workplace: Gender similarities and differences. *Journal of Criminal Justice, 29*(2), 145–155.

Fisher, B. S., Jenkins, E. L., & Williams, N. (1998). The extent and nature of homicide and non-fatal workplace violence in the United States: Implications for prevention and security. In M. Gill (Ed.), *Crime at work* (pp. 65–82). Leicester, UK: Perpetuity Press Ltd.

Fisher, B. S., & Peek-Asa, C. (2005). Domestic violence and the workplace: Do we know too much of nothing? In V. Bowie, B. S. Fisher, & C. L. Cooper (Eds.), *Workplace violence: Issues, trends, strategies* (pp. 97–120). Devon, UK: Willan Publishing.

Flannery, R. B. (1996). Violence in the workplace, 1970–1995: A review of the literature. *Aggression and Violent Behavior, 1*(1), 57–68.

Hartley, D., Biddle, E. A., & Jenkins, E. L. (2005). Societal cost of workplace homicides in the United States, 1992–2001. *American Journal of Industrial Medicine, 47,* 518–527.

Hughes, S. M. (1999). *Violence in the workplace: Identifying costs and preventive solutions.* Undergraduate Gold Medal paper awarded from the First Annual Student Paper Writing Competition, American Society of Industrial Security, February 2000.

Hurrell, J. J., Worthington, K. A., & Driscoll, R. J. (1996). Job stress, gender, and workplace violence: Analysis of assault experiences of state employees. In G. R. VandenBos & E. Q. Bulatao (Eds.), *Violence on the job: Identifying risks and developing solutions.* Washington, D.C.: American Psychological Association.

Islam, S. S., Edla, S. R., Mujuru, P., Doyle, E. J., & Ducatman, A. M. (2003). Risk factors for physical assault: State-managed workers' compensation experience. *American Journal of Preventive Medicine, 25*(1), 31–37.

Jenkins, E. L. (1996a). *Violence in the Workplace: Risk Factors and Prevention Strategies.* Washington, D.C.: National Institute for Occupational Safety and Health.

Jenkins, E. L. (1996b). Workplace homicide: Industries and occupations at high risk. *Occupational Medicine: State of the Art Reviews, 11*(2), 219–225.

Jenkins, E. L. W. (2006). *Active inaction symbolic politics, agenda denial or incubation period: Twenty years of U.S. workplace violence research and prevention activity.* Unpublished dissertation.

Jenkins, E. L., Fisher, B. S., & Hartley, D. (2007). *Safe and Secure at Work?: Findings from the 2002 Workplace Risk Supplement to the National Crime Victimization Survey.* Unpublished working paper, NIOSH, Morgantown, West Virginia.

Keim, J. (1999). Workplace violence and trauma: A 21st century rehabilitation issue. *Journal of Rehabilitation, 65*(1), 16–20.

Kennedy, J. F. (2004). *A comprehensive analysis of workplace violence: Utilizing NIBRS data in evaluating the typology of workplace violence.* Dissertation Abstracts International, A: The Humanities and Social Sciences, 64/11.

Kraus, J. F. (1987). Homicide while at work. *American Journal of Public Health, 77*(10), 1285–1289.

Kraus, J. F., Blander, B., & McArthur, D. L. (1995). Incidence, risk factors and prevention strategies for work-related assault injuries: A review of what is known, what needs to be known, and countermeasures for intervention. *Annual Review of Public Health, 16*, 355–379.

Licu, E., & Fisher, B. S. (2006). The extent, nature and responses to workplace violence globally: Issues and findings. In M. Gill (Ed.), *The handbook of security* (pp. 229–260). England: Palgrave Macmillan.

Liddle, J., & Widdowson, B. (1997). Women, violence, and the trade union. *Indian Journal of Gender Studies, 4*(1), 35–50.

Lord, V. B. (1998). Characteristics of violence in state government. *Journal of Interpersonal Violence, 13*(4), 489–503.

Moracco, K. E., Runyan, C. W., Loomis, D. P., Wolf, S. H., Napp, D., & Butts, J. D. (2000). Killed on the clock: A population-based study of workplace homicide, 1977–1991. *American Journal of Industrial Medicine, 37*, 629–636.

Mullen, E. A. (1997). Workplace violence: Cause for concern or the construction of a new category of fear? *Journal of Industrial Relations, 39*(1), 21–32.

Mustaine, E. E., & Tewksbury, R. (1997). The risk of victimization in the workplace for men and women: An analysis using routine activities/lifestyle theory. *Humanity and Society, 21*(1), 17–38.

Namie, G. (2000). *U.S. Hostile Workplace Survey 2000.* Retrieved January 4, 2007, from http://www.bullyinginstitute.org/res/2000wbti.pdf

Namie, G. (2003). *The Workplace Bullying Institute (WBI) 2003 report on abusive workplaces.* Retrieved January 4, 2007, from http://www.bullyinginstitute.org/res/2003results.pdf

Peek-Asa, C., Erickson, R., & Kraus, J. F. (1999). Traumatic occupational fatalities in the retail industry, United States 1992–1996. *American Journal of Industrial Medicine, 35*, 186–191.

Perrone, S. (1999). *Violence in the workplace.* Australian Institute of Criminology. Research and Public Policy Series, No. 22. Retrieved January 4, 2007, from http://www.aic.gov.au/publications/rpp/22/

Rennison, C. M., & Welchans, S. (2000). *Intimate partner violence.* Bureau of Justice Statistics Special Report. NCJ 178247. Washington, D.C.: U.S. Department of Justice.

Richardson, S., & Windau, J. (2003). Fatal and nonfatal assaults in the workplace, 1996 to 2000. In C. Wilkinson & C. Peek-Asa (Eds.), *Clinics in occupational and environmental medicine* (pp. 673–689). Philadelphia: Elsevier Inc.

Smith, S. (2006). *Occupational Hazards: The Authority on Occupational Safety, Health and Loss Prevention: The Rare Exception.* Retrieved January 4, 2007, from http://www.occupationalhazards.com/articles/14767

Tjaden, P., & Thoennes, N. (1998). *Stalking in America: Findings from the National Violence Against Women Survey.* Rockville, MD: U.S. Department of Justice, Bureau of Justice Statistics.

Tjaden, P., & Thoennes, N. (1999). *Violence by co-workers: Findings from the National Violence Against Women Survey.* Washington, D.C.: National Institute of Justice.

Tjaden, P. G., & Thoennes, N. (2001). Coworker violence and gender: Findings from the National Violence Against Women Survey. *American Journal of Preventive Medicine, 20*(2), 85–89.

Toscano, G., & Weber, W. (1995). *Violence in the Workplace.* Retrieved January 4, 2007, from http://www.bls.gov/iif/oshwc/cfar0005.pdf

Toscano, G., & Windau, J. (1994). The changing character of fatal work injuries. *Monthly Labor Review, 117*(10), 17–28.

Toscano, G. A., & Windau, J. A. (1998). Profile of fatal work injuries in 1996. *Compensation and Working Conditions*, 37–45. Retrieved January 12, 2007 from, http://www.bls.gov/opub/cwc/archive/spring1998art5.pdf

Upson, A. (2004). *Violence at work: Findings from the 2002/2003 British Crime Survey.*

Retrieved January 4, 2007, from http://www.homeoffice.gov.uk/rds/pdfs2/rdsolr0404.pdf

Warchol, G. (1998). *Workplace violence, 1992–96.* Washington, D.C.: Bureau of Justice Statistics: Special Report.

Warren, J., Brown, D., Hurt, S., Cook, S., Branson, W., & Jin, R. (1999). The organizational context of non-lethal workplace violence: Its interpersonal, temporal, and spatial correlates. *Journal of Occupational and Environmental Medicine, 41*(7), 567–581.

Weiser, W. R., & Widiss, D. A. (2004). Employment protection for domestic violence victims. *Clearinghouse Review, May–June*, 3–11.

Wooldredge, J., Cullen, F., & Latessa, E. (1992). Victimization in the workplace: A test of routine activities theory. *Justice Quarterly, 9*(2), 325–335.

Endnotes

1. This chapter will focus on workplace violence in the United States. For an excellent analysis of violence at work in England and Wales, see Upson (2004). For an analysis of violence at work in Australia, see Perrone (1999), and for an overview of workplace violence from an international perspective, see Licu and Fisher (2006).

2. The NIOSH maintains the NTOF system. The system is a death certificate-based census of occupational injury deaths to workers aged 16 years and older. Data are collected from all 50 states and the District of Columbia. This provides for complete coverage of all workers in the United States (see Jenkins, 1996b).

3. The SOII is an annual survey of approximately 250,000 business establishments in the private sector. Excluded from the sample are the self-employed, small farmers, and government workers (e.g., police and other law enforcement officers).

4. Nonfatal assaults in the SOII include hitting, kicking, beating, squeezing, pinching, scratching, twisting, biting, stabbing, shooting, all other specified acts (e.g., rape, threats), and unspecified acts. Assaults in the NCVS include an unlawful physical attack excluding rape or

sexual assault. This can include attack with a weapon, attack without a weapon when serious injury occurred, attack without a weapon resulting in either no injury or minor injury (e.g., cuts, scratches).

5. The NVAWS was administered from November 1995 to May 1996. It is a representative survey of 8,000 women and 8,000 men drawn from a national, random-digit-dialing sample of households in the United States.

6. In 2006, the NCVS administered a stalking supplement which will allow researchers to examine the incidence of stalking in the workplace. The results are scheduled to be available from the BJS sometime in 2009.

7. Tjaden and Thoennes (2001) used the NVAWS data in their analysis of coworker violence.

8. Male workers, on the other hand, were more likely to be killed by coworkers, followed by other nonstrangers and customers (Moracco et al., 2000).

9. Multi-site workplace violence was defined as a series of incidents of workplace violence that "occur over a short period of time at multiple sites, with at least one site being a workplace where at least one offender has some connection." By contrast, single-site

workplace violence was defined as incidents of workplace violence that occurred only at the workplace (Collins et al., 2001, p. 7).

10. Bullying can be defined as "repeated illegitimate mistreatment of a targeted employee by one or more persons characterized by acts of commission and omission which impair the target's psychological and physical health, and economic security" (Namie, 2000).

11. The authors do not distinguish type of crime. They only state that the victimization happened while the victim was working or on the way to or from work.

12. Law enforcement officer was actually tied with private security guard as the occupation with the second highest homicide rate in North Carolina.

13. The National Crime Survey was redesigned during the early 1990s. The redesigned version is titled the NCVS. Its administration was implemented in 1992.

14. The total number of male victims of workplace homicide in the United States from 1992 to 2001 was 6,314; the total number of female victims of workplace homicide was 1,611.

CHAPTER 10

CYBERBULLYING AND ONLINE HARASSMENT: RECONCEPTUALIZING THE VICTIMIZATION OF ADOLESCENT GIRLS

AMANDA BURGESS-PROCTOR, JUSTIN W. PATCHIN, AND SAMEER HINDUJA

ABSTRACT

Growing public awareness of electronic bullying and harassment among adolescents suggests the need to empirically investigate this increasingly common and problematic behavior. Although studies of cyberbullying and online harassment among young people are nascent, preliminary findings suggest that victimization can undermine the freedom of youth to use and explore valuable online resources, and may have negative emotional and physical consequences as well. This study presents both quantitative and qualitative data from an online survey of approximately 3,000 Internet-using adolescent girls to learn more about their experiences as victims of cyberbullying and online harassment. Though the results are exploratory and largely descriptive, this study helps broaden our understanding of the victimization experiences of adolescent girls in cyberspace.

My friend's cousin has lately been bullying me quite a bit. She calls me all sorts of bad things and curses me out . . . is sarcastic in everything she says to me and really is absolutely terrible to me. Through talking to me online while her cousin was watching her type she destroyed my friendship with my friend. The bullying and torment on [AOL Instant Messenger] and on my websites made me feel absolutely terrible . . . I was very upset even offline after it had happened, and it destroyed the friendship of what used to be my closest and most reliable friend. (9th grader from South Carolina)

My ex-boyfriend and his friends leave disgusting comments in my guest-book at [an online diary-hosting website]. Though I have locked my diary so that they no longer have access to it, they continue to leave hurtful comments in my guestbook. They have threatened bodily harm, and have even gone so far as to say that they would "kill me in my sleep." They have also OPENLY admitted to being "obsessed" with me while taking an online survey. I feel disgusted. (11th grader from New York)

INTRODUCTION

Research on the victimization of adolescent girls often focuses on crimes involving physical violence, such as sexual assault and child abuse (Finkelhor & Browne, 1986; Finkelhor, Hotaling, Lewis, & Smith, 2000; Kendall-Tackett, Williams, & Finkelhor, 1993; Lavoie, Robitataille, & Herbert, 2000; O'Keefe, 1997; Silverman, Raj, Mucci, & Hathaway, 2001). However, the above testimonials from adolescent girls who are victims of cyberbullying suggest the need to broaden our understanding of girls' victimization experiences to include bullying and harassment that occur through the use of electronic media. While academic inquiry into such behavior—alternately called *cyberbullying*, *online aggression*, *Internet-based harassment*, *cyberstalking*, and *cyberviolence*—is only just beginning to emerge, rapidly growing media attention suggests that Internet-using adolescents are all too familiar with cyberbullying (Chu, 2005; Meadows et al., 2005; Swartz, 2005). Still, the research on cyberbullying that does exist has not focused exclusively on the experiences of girls. This study represents one of the first known empirical investigations of the online victimization of adolescent girls. After first providing an overview of cyberbullying research literature to date, this chapter presents both quantitative and qualitative data from an online survey of approximately 3,000 Internet-using adolescent girls. The findings from this exploratory study reveal patterns in girls' online victimization experiences, as well as key themes that provide insight into how adolescent girls experience and respond to online victimization. More importantly, the results help facilitate the process of reconceptualizing victimization among adolescent girls to include bullying and harassment perpetrated using electronic media.

OVERVIEW OF CYBERBULLYING RESEARCH

Before we present an overview of the cyberbullying research literature, it is necessary to define "cyberbullying" and to differentiate it from "online harassment." Cyberbullying has been defined as "willful and repeated harm inflicted through the medium of electronic text" (Patchin & Hinduja, 2006, p.152). Cyberbullying behaviors can be carried out using cellular phone text messaging, electronic mail (e-mail), and Internet instant messaging and can take place in chat rooms, on personal websites, on social networking sites such as MySpace, on Internet bulletin boards, and in other web-based environments. Although in many cases cyberbullying involves traditional bullying behaviors (e.g., name-calling, spreading rumors or lies, and making threats) that are communicated electronically rather than in person, cyberbullying also can include behaviors unique to the Internet that have no corollary in traditional bullying. For example, "bombing" occurs when a bully uses an automated program to flood the victim's e-mail inbox with thousands of messages at once, potentially causing a failure of the e-mail software or of the entire computer system. The key to this definition of cyberbullying is "willful and repeated harm." Online victimization that is isolated or that is not intended to be malicious does not meet our definition of cyberbullying, and therefore falls into the broader category of "online harassment." Examples of online harassment include individual incidents of name-calling or threats, arguments between friends that occur over e-mail or instant messaging, and online comments that were not intended to be hurtful but which nonetheless were offensive to the victim.

In large part, the occurrence of cyberbullying and online harassment is reflective of how deeply Internet technology and electronic communications have permeated the lives of young people. According to the Pew Internet & American Life Project's "Teens and Technology" report, data collected in late 2004 from 1,100 teenagers and 1,100 parents nationwide indicate that 87 percent of those youth aged 12–17 use the Internet (Lenhart, Madden, & Hitlin, 2005). Almost three-fourths of respondents (73%) report having a desktop computer, 18 percent report having a laptop computer, 45 percent report having a cellular phone, and 33 percent report having sent a cellular phone text message. Nearly 90 percent of youth aged 12–17 communicate via e-mail and 75 percent communicate via instant messaging, and nearly half (48%) report using these methods of communication every day (Lenhart et al., 2005). Clearly, adolescents today are savvy and voracious consumers of electronic media; thus it should not be surprising that some who wish to tease, harass, or bully others use the electronic media with which they are so familiar. What may be surprising, though, is the extent to which cyberbullying occurs and the effect it has on its victims.

Results from the few cyberbullying studies that exist reveal some important information about this emerging form of adolescent aggression. First, it appears that a sizeable percentage of young people experience cyberbullying either as victims or as bullies.[1] In one study of Internet harassment (defined as "an overt, intentional act of aggression towards another person online"), Ybarra and Mitchell (2004) analyzed data from telephone interviews with 1,501 youth between the ages of 10 and 17. They found that 7 percent of young, regular Internet users were the victims of online harassment within the previous year, 3 percent were aggressors and victims, and 12 percent were aggressors. Similarly, Patchin and Hinduja (2006) conducted a pilot study of 384 adolescent Internet users to assess experience with various forms of cyberbullying, including bothering someone online, teasing in a mean way, calling someone hurtful names, intentionally leaving persons out of things, threatening someone, and saying unwanted sexually related things to someone. Approximately 29 percent of youth reported being the victim of such behavior, 11 percent reported engaging in such behavior, and almost half (47%) reported witnessing such behavior.

Second, although cyberbullying occurs in a virtual environment, the emotional and behavioral consequences of victimization are very real. For example, Patchin and Hinduja (2006) found that over 42 percent of victims were frustrated, almost 40 percent felt angry, and over one-fourth (27%) felt sad. The negative effects of online victimization extended beyond cyberspace, as 31.9 and 26.5 percent of respondents revealed that they were negatively affected at school and at home, respectively. Moreover, youth reported that being victimized often caused them to curtail their web usage, whether through avoidance of the venue where the victimization occurred (32%) or by staying offline altogether (20%) (Patchin & Hinduja, 2006). However, despite the negative effects of cyberbullying, adolescents appear reluctant to disclose their victimization to adults, preferring instead to seek support and understanding from friends (Patchin & Hinduja, 2006).

Third, it is unclear what factors place youth at risk of involvement in cyberbullying, either as a victim or as a bully. In a 2005 follow-up study of 1,388 youth (700 males and 688 females), Hinduja and Patchin (2008) found that neither sex nor race predicted likelihood of cyberbullying victimization or offending (but see the discussion of gender below), whereas older youth, youth who spent more time online, more computer proficient youth, and youth involved in offline bullying were all more likely to be involved with cyberbullying both as victims and as bullies. Additionally, both cyberbullying victimization and offending were significantly related to other adolescent problem behaviors such as scholastic difficulties, assaultive conduct, substance use, and traditional (offline) bullying.

However, there is some evidence to suggest that involvement in cyberbullying does vary by gender. After surveying 1,915 girls and 1,852 boys in 6th, 7th, and 8th grade from across the southwestern and southeastern United States, Kowalski et al. (2005) found that more girls than boys reported being bullied online (25% vs. 11%) and bullying someone else online (13% vs. 8.6%). When reporting on traditional bullying, however, this gender gap did not appear; similar numbers of boys and girls reported being bullied offline (12.3% vs. 14.1%), while more boys than girls reported bullying someone else offline (8% vs. 5%). Clearly, though, far more research is needed before conclusions can be drawn about girls' risk of involvement in cyberbullying offending or about their unique experiences with cyberbullying victimization. Indeed, it is with this latter question in mind that we framed the current study.

THE CURRENT STUDY

Despite preliminary support for the idea that girls have different experiences with cyberbullying than boys (Kowalski et al., 2005), the nature and extent of cyberbullying victimization among girls has not been fully parsed out, nor have the consequences of victimization for this population been adequately explored. In perhaps the first study of cyberviolence to use an exclusively female sample, Berson, Berson, and Ferron (2002, p. 63) studied online survey responses from 10,800 girls aged 12–18 and found that "a significant number of adolescent girls are engaging in very risky activities when online and continue potentially problematic offline practices as a result of these online interactions." Still, this study—while pioneering—examines girls' risky online behaviors rather than their experiences with cyberbullying per se. Thus, given the dearth of research on adolescent girls' online victimization, our understanding of this phenomenon is practically nonexistent. The current study is intended to help fill this void. In an attempt to learn more about the unique experiences of adolescent girls victimized by cyberbullying and online harassment, we identified the following research questions: (1) Who are adolescent girl victims of cyberbullying? (2) What cyberbullying behaviors do adolescent girls experience? (3) Who cyberbullies adolescent girls? (4) How do adolescent girls respond to being cyberbullied? (5) How does being cyberbullied affect adolescent girls?

METHODS

DATA COLLECTION

An online survey methodology was used to explore experiences with cyberbullying among 3,141 adolescent girls (a subset extracted from a data set of over 6,800 total respondents).[2] The cyberbullying questionnaire was linked to several adolescent-oriented websites; individuals who visited these websites were asked to participate in a survey of Internet behaviors.[3] Potential respondents who were under the age of 18 were instructed to obtain permission from a parent or guardian before completing the survey. It deserves comment, however, that it was not possible to verify whether minors actually obtained such permission.[4] Following an introduction and description of the research, the survey posed demographic questions as well as questions about the scope, extent, and frequency of cyberbullying victimization and offending that respondents may have experienced. Finally, the survey included several open-ended questions (e.g., "Tell us in as much detail as possible how cyberbullying makes you feel") that allowed respondents to describe their cyberbullying experiences in their own words. The primary benefit of an online survey methodology is the ability to reach a wide number of participants at an economical cost. Moreover, the subject matter itself was appropriate for this methodology because it involves a global phenomenon that occurs exclusively online.

ANALYTIC STRATEGY

This study uses a mixed-methods design, in which both quantitative and qualitative data are analyzed in order to gain the broadest possible understanding of adolescent girls' experiences with cyberbullying and online harassment. A mixed-methods design is particularly appropriate in this study for several reasons. First, qualitative methods are particularly useful when researching sensitive topics (Rosenblatt & Fischer, 1993). As cyberbullying victimization may be difficult for respondents to discuss, a mixed-methods design may elicit information more effectively than a quantitative design alone. Second, cyberbullying is a newly emerging form of adolescent aggression that is not fully understood. A universally accepted definition of cyberbullying does not exist, so the concept of cyberbullying may not be adequately captured by asking survey questions designed to measure the prevalence and frequency of specific cyberbullying behaviors. Indeed, the qualitative data allowed us to differentiate behavior that meets our definition of "cyberbullying" from behavior that is more appropriately labeled "online harassment." Third, in part due to the ambiguous definition of cyberbullying, as well as the vast spectrum of behaviors that adolescents are likely to label as cyberbullying, establishing the validity of a purely quantitative measure may prove difficult. Our quantitative measures were informed by traditional bullying research and from our own previous research on cyberbullying. Nevertheless, due to the embryonic nature of this line of research, it is in our best interest to keep an open mind in order to establish a comprehensive conceptual and operational definition of cyberbullying. In other words, without allowing respondents to discuss what online bullying means to them in the context of their individual experiences, researchers cannot be entirely confident that a survey instrument measures "cyberbullying" as it is perceived by the respondents. Therefore, including open-ended measures of cyberbullying helps ensure that respondents' victimization experiences are accurately measured.

We began by using the quantitative data to examine descriptive characteristics of our sample, from which we identified patterns in victimization experiences. Next, we used qualitative analysis to code the narrative responses to the open-ended survey question, "Please describe—in as much detail as possible—your most recent experience with being bullied online." In so doing, we looked to code around our five research questions. For this portion of the analysis, the first author read every narrative response and identified initial themes. Once initial themes were identified, the second and third authors each coded a subset of the responses in order to refine the initial themes. On the rare occasion when questions or disagreements about themes arose, all three authors discussed the findings until a consensus was reached. In general, however, the consensus level was very high, giving us confidence in our interpretation of the results.

RESULTS

WHO ARE ADOLESCENT GIRL VICTIMS OF CYBERBULLYING?

As noted above, data from 3,141 female respondents under age 18 were analyzed in the current study. As detailed in Table 10.1, respondents ranged in age from 8 to 17 years of age, with most girls falling in the 13–17 range (mean = 14.6 years). Similarly,

TABLE 10.1 Sample Characteristics (N = 3,141)		
	N	*%*
Age (years)		
8	1	<0.1
9	5	0.2
10	29	0.9
11	65	2.1
12	166	5.3
13	479	15.2
14	653	20.8
15	715	22.8
16	608	19.4
17	420	13.4
Mean age = 14.6		
Grade		
Do not go to school	24	0.8
1–5	51	1.6
6–8	821	26.1
9–12	2,171	69.1
College	55	1.7
Missing	19	0.6
Caucasian/White	2,460	78.3
Hispanic/Latino	199	6.3
Asian/Pacific Islander	189	6.0
Multiracial	104	3.3
African American	63	2.0
Indigenous/Aboriginal	9	0.3
Other	113	3.6
United States	2,352	74.9
Canada	301	9.6
United Kingdom	203	6.5
Australia	158	5.0
Other	127	4.1

most girls (69.1%) were high-school students in grades 9 through 12. Finally, girls in the sample were disproportionately Caucasian/White (78%) and from the United States (75%).

WHAT CYBERBULLYING BEHAVIORS DO ADOLESCENT GIRLS EXPERIENCE?

As seen in Table 10.2, 1,203 girls (38.3% of the sample) responded positively to the statement "I have been bullied online." Interestingly, when asked later in the survey whether they had experienced individual behaviors, including being disrespected and ignored by others online, a *greater* number of girls responded affirmatively. As we discuss below, this finding further supports the distinction between "cyberbullying" and the less insidious "online harassment" behaviors that appear to occur with some regularity among adolescent girls. Indeed, the two online victimization behaviors reported most frequently were being ignored (45.8%) and being disrespected (42.9%), both of which are relatively mild behaviors. Still, it is important to note that some girls did report serious behaviors like being threatened (11.2) that likely are more indicative of cyberbullying than online harassment. Finally, online victimization of any kind occurred most commonly in Internet chat rooms (26.4%), through computer text message (21.7%) and through e-mail (13.5%).

Online victimization behaviors identified in the narrative data overlap with those identified in the quantitative data. For example, *name-calling* was commonly reported by the girls in our study, who described being called "fat," "ugly," "slut," "bitch," and a host of other unpleasant names. Similarly, the spreading of *gossip*—including lies and

TABLE 10.2 Nature and Location of Online Victimization (N = 3,141)

	N	%
I have been bullied online	1,203	38.3
Nature of victimization		
Ignored by others	1,439	45.8
Disrespected by others	1,348	42.9
Called names by others	575	18.3
Rumors spread by others	452	14.4
Been threatened by others	352	11.2
Been e-mail bombed by others	334	10.6
Picked on by others	280	8.9
Been made fun of by others	264	8.4
Been scared for safety	195	6.2
Location of victimization		
In a chat room	829	26.4
By computer text message	683	21.7
By e-mail	425	13.5
On a bulletin board	229	7.3
By cell phone text message	146	4.6
In a newsgroup	40	1.3

rumors about the victim—was a very common occurrence. These themes make sense as examples of "being disrespected by others," a behavior reported by over 40 percent of the sample. Finally, the narrative responses lend support to the idea that adolescent girls do receive online *threats*, ranging from vague warnings ("she threatened to get me") to threats that are very specific ("she said she would knock me out and bash my head in") and very serious ("she [instant messaged] me saying that she would kill me"). However, it is interesting to note that the most common online behavior captured by the quantitative data, "being ignored by others," which was reported by over 45 percent of the sample, did not emerge as a particularly strong theme in the narrative data.

The qualitative data also revealed behaviors that were not captured by the quantitative data. First, many respondents indicated behaviors involving *duplicity*, or cyberbullies' use of *misrepresentation of self*. Such behavior occurred when the bully used another person's screen name or otherwise concealed her identity before contacting the victim, or when she passed off her own communications (e.g., inflammatory e-mail messages) as the work of the victim. Second, many girls described instances in which bullies used electronic communication devices (instant messages, chat rooms, e-mail) to *reveal confidential or sensitive information* about them to others. One victim described how "[the cyberbullies] brought up things [I] am not so proud of that happened last summer." A third very prominent example involves victims being *teased for sharing their opinions*. Again, though more indicative of online harassment than cyberbullying, many girls described being teased or ridiculed—usually in chat rooms, and often by several members at one time—based on their political beliefs, musical preferences, religious affiliations, and loyalty to particular bands or movie stars. While one might expect girls who are teased for sharing their beliefs to feel inhibited about expressing their opinion, this does not appear to be the case in our study. As we will discuss more fully below, many girls held firmly to their beliefs and dismissed affronts to their opinions as immature and nonthreatening. Finally, the narrative data revealed many examples of *sexual harassment* directed at adolescent girls, which appear to occur frequently in incidents involving strangers or anonymous sources. Behaviors mostly involved unsolicited sexual advances ("[I] was online playing a game and a guy asked me if [I] wanted to 'suck his cock'"), including requests for the victim to "cyber" (i.e., engage in cyber sex with) the aggressor.

WHO CYBERBULLIES ADOLESCENT GIRLS?

Respondents were asked how often they knew the person bullying them online (see Table 10.3). Of the 1,203 girls who reported being the victim of online bullying, only about 1 in 5 (20.5%) "never" knew who was bullying them. Thus, most victims appear to know the bully, and report that the bully was most often a friend from school (31.3%), someone else from school (36.4%), or someone from a chat room (28.2%). In general, the qualitative data taken from the narrative responses support the results of the quantitative analysis, indicating that girls most often were cyberbullied by *offline peers* such as friends, ex-friends, or other classmates and by *online peers* whose screen names they knew from online message boards or chat rooms. However, the qualitative analysis revealed two important sources of cyberbullying

TABLE 10.3   Relationship Between Bully and Victim (Victims Only, N = 1,203)

	N	%
How often do you know the bully?		
Once in a while	334	27.8
Never	247	20.5
Usually	224	18.6
Always	161	13.4
Missing	237	19.7
Bully was someone else from school	438	36.4
Bully was friend from school	376	31.3
Bully was someone in chat room	339	28.2
Bully was a relative	49	4.1
Bully was someone else	252	20.9

not identified in the quantitative data. First, there were several accounts of girls being cyberbullied by their *ex-boyfriends*, which typically involved name-calling and, in some cases, threats. Second, many girls reported victimization by *strangers*, usually someone with an unfamiliar screen name. Interestingly, stranger harassment was regarded as particularly frightening to some girls ("I didn't even know the person so I got really scared") and as relatively harmless to others ("I did not [feel] very scared since [the person] did not even know my name").

HOW DO ADOLESCENT GIRLS RESPOND TO BEING CYBERBULLIED?

Table 10.4 summarizes the responses to cyberbullying identified by those girls who reported being bullied online (N = 1,203). Many girls responded to online victimization by retaliating or "cyberbullying back" (27.3%). Notably, relatively few victims of cyberbullying informed a parent (13%) or another adult (7%) about their experiences with

TABLE 10.4   Responses to Bullying (Victims Only, N = 1,203)

	N	%
When bullied online		
I tell an online friend	559	46.5
I tell nobody	427	35.5
I bully the person back	332	27.6
I do nothing	295	24.5
I tell a friend	221	18.4
I stay offline	208	17.3
I tell my mom or my dad	161	13.4
I tell another adult	87	7.2

online victimization. Instead, victims were more far more likely to confide in an online buddy (46.5%) or another friend (18.4%). Some respondents felt forced to stay offline for a period of time (17.3%), while others did nothing different as a result of the victimization (24.5%). Finally, a significant number of girls did not respond to the victimization, reporting that they told nobody (35.5%) or that they did nothing at all (24.5%).

The narrative data confirmed that many girls responded through *retaliation*, or "cyberbullying back." There are several mentions in the narratives of girls responding to name-calling, harassment, or threats in kind. For example, one girl commented, "Some annoying kid in my school that I didn't really know [instant-messaged] me telling me that I had an eating disorder and [that] I was ugly. I was annoyed and told him to go f*** himself." This type of retaliatory response may be particularly common among victims of online bullying because there exists little threat of the situation escalating into physical violence, unlike in face-to-face bullying situations. Similarly, many girls reported that they received *protection from online peers*. Particularly in chat rooms and message boards, many girls reported being defended by online peers who, together with the victim, "fought back" against the bully on the victim's behalf. For example, one girl described this scenario, "A person I didn't know contacted me via computer text messaging and we . . . got into a verbal argument over the computer. We basically made fun of each other and my friend came in and supported me and made fun of the person I was in the argument with." Several girls also indicated that they had come to the defense of other cyberbullying victims.

The narrative responses also confirmed that a few girls responded by taking *official action*, such as contacting the Internet Service Provider (ISP), their parents, or friends, whereas others responded to their online victimization by *curtailing their web use*, such as avoiding particular websites, chat rooms, or message boards where they had been harassed. Interestingly, contacting law enforcement was never mentioned in the narrative responses, even though certain severe cyberbullying behaviors (such as death threats) are criminal acts.

On the other hand, many girls *did not respond* in any way to their victimization. Although it is possible that some girls did nothing or told nobody because they were scared of retaliation, as our discussion in the following section reveals, it seems far more likely that girls did not respond because they were not particularly bothered by this behavior. Additionally, it is noteworthy that cyberbullying victims can "walk away" from the situation in ways that victims of face-to-face bullying cannot. In fact, the *ease of removal* from the situation may be a characteristic that is unique to cyberbullying. With one simple motion, victims of cyberbullying and online harassment can block the user, log off the Internet, or shut off their cell phone, effectively ending the opportunity for continued victimization and eliminating the need to respond further.[5]

HOW DOES BEING CYBERBULLIED AFFECT ADOLESCENT GIRLS?

Finally, it is important to investigate how victims of cyberbullying were affected by the experience (see Table 10.5). Of the 1,203 girls who reported being bullied online, almost 35 percent reported feeling angry, over 30 percent felt sad, and 41 percent were frustrated by being cyberbullied. Victims also reported being affected at home (27.1%) and at school (22.7%). However, the majority of girls in our sample reported that they were not affected

	N	%
TABLE 10.5 Effects of Bullying (Victims Only, N = 1,203)		
When bullied online		
It did not affect me	667	55.4
I felt frustrated	494	41.1
I felt angry	419	34.8
I was not bothered	383	31.8
I felt sad	349	29.0
It affected me at home	326	27.1
It affected me at school	273	22.7

(55.4%) by being cyberbullied. This seemingly counterintuitive finding begins to make sense once the qualitative data are examined, as we discuss below.

First, adolescent girls who responded to our survey reported a wide variety of *emotional effects* of cyberbullying, including feeling "sad," "angry," "upset," "depressed," "violated," "hated," "annoyed," "helpless," "exploited," and "stupid and put down." While the quantitative data captured a few of these emotions, the narrative responses allowed us to understand the broader range of emotional impact of cyberbullying for victims. For example, some girls described how the victimization made them feel unsafe: "It makes me scared. I [sometimes don't] know the person so that makes me wonder if [I] have a stalker, and that gets me pretty scared." Other girls reported having extreme emotional responses to being victimized, including suicidal ideation. The dramatic words of one girl underscore this point:

> I was talking to two girls who used to be my friends . . . they went on a chat [that I] was also talking on and started saying horrible things about me . . . they used my [screen] name and everything . . . they even told one of my guy friends that [I] liked him since the day we met and he stopped talking to me . . . I was both depressed and angry . . . [I] wanted to die . . . [I] wanted to leave every thing behind. . . .

Another girl wrote of her online victimization, "[I]t made me feel so bad I started to cry. Nobody likes me." Clearly, although online victimization is easily dismissed for some girls, for others the experience is, in fact, quite painful.

However, the quantitative data also indicate that being cyberbullied had no negative effects for over half (55%) of the respondents. The narrative responses are particularly useful at explaining this seemingly perplexing finding, as they reveal that many girls exhibited attitudes of *dismissal*. Indeed, many girls share their belief that cyberbullies are merely "stupid," "pathetic," "bored," "just trying to amuse themselves," and "don't have anything better to do" with their lives. Further, it appears that attitudes of dismissal are particularly common in cases of online harassment rather than cyberbullying. From the narrative responses, it is clear that many girls who experience name-calling, gossiping, and other common forms of adolescent harassment perpetrated online exhibit healthy resilience to this behavior. What is less clear is the extent to which girls who are victims of more problematic cyberbullying behaviors are similarly able to ignore their victimization.

DISCUSSION

In this study we have identified some patterns in the victimization experiences of adolescent girls as well as some themes that help broaden our understanding of cyberbullying and online harassment in this population. This analysis has provided several important new insights into this behavior.

First, the narrative data in particular help clarify the range of behaviors that make up girls' online victimization experiences, and help distinguish "cyberbullying" from other, often less serious, forms of "online harassment." For example, the survey responses reveal that 31.3 percent of girls reported being "cyberbullied" by a friend from school and 36.4 percent reported being "cyberbullied" by someone else from school. However, upon closer inspection of the narrative responses, it is clear that most incidents of "cyberbullying" reported by the respondents are more accurately described as "online harassment" because they do not involve *willful and repeated harm*.[6] Repetition seemed to be the characteristic of the victimization experience that appeared to be missing most often. While one instance of harassment is often harmful, it fails to meet our definition of cyberbullying. Thus, much of the victimization adolescent girls experience by offline peers appears to be an extension of common adolescent behavior, including name-calling, arguing, and gossiping. Indeed, the narrative responses revealed that many of these conflicts with friends or ex-friends were resolved and ended with the parties going back to being friends, further distancing these examples from cases of true cyberbullying. Still, though informative, this finding raises many questions. How often does "true" cyberbullying occur? Do adolescents recognize or fully understand cyberbullying, or distinguish it from online harassment? Are instances of the former more or less memorable, and for what reasons? Can rationalizations and justifications be more readily employed because of the nontraditional context in which cyberbullying occurs?

Second, one particularly disturbing finding is how desensitized many girls seem to the threat of unwanted sexual advances that occur online. Based on the comments of several girls, unwanted sexual advances or sexually explicit communication is startlingly common online. In the words of one respondent, "I was on [MSN instant messenger] and somebody I've never met added me. I asked who it [was], and the person started saying inappropriate sexual things to me, so I blocked him and that was it. It didn't bother me because I know there are sick people out there." Still many questions remain. Is this awareness simply an extension of girls' awareness of unwanted sexual advancements in the offline world? Is exposure to unwanted sexual advances simply a fact of life for Internet-using adolescent girls? If so, what impact does this have for Internet-using girls?

Third, our data strongly suggest that many girls are simply not bothered by the online victimization they experience. The ease with which girls dismiss these incidents, coupled with the repeated assessments of cyberbullies as being "bored" or "pathetic," indicates that at least some portion of girls who experience online victimization do not suffer lasting negative consequences. Conversely, other girls reported having severe emotional responses to their victimization, up to and including prolonged crying, withdrawal, and thoughts of suicide. Though this information helps us better understand the range of effects that online victimization has on adolescent girls, it raises important questions. Are girls more inclined to be dismissive of these behaviors because the victimization does not occur in person? Do girls who experience more serious forms of cyberbullying suffer more serious consequences than girls who experience online harassment?

All of the questions raised by our analysis merit meaningful inquiry in future research endeavors. In addition, our study has several limitations that provide opportunities for future studies to improve upon our analysis. Most notably, our sample of adolescent girls is disproportionately Caucasian/White (78%) and from the United States (75%). Coupled with the potential problems associated with self-selection bias related to online survey methodology, generalization to a broader population of adolescent girls is very difficult. While the homogeneous nature of this sample is partially explained by the websites to which the survey instrument was linked (which likely attracted White female respondents from the United States), further research is necessary to better understand the relative lack of non-White and non-U.S. respondents completing our survey. In particular, the question of whether access to Internet technology is evenly distributed across social groups, and what implications this has for risk of online victimization, needs more exploration. Of course, research employing a random sample of a known population is necessary in order to avoid the complications inherent in our methodological approach.

One unexpected challenge involved in our analysis involved deciphering the shorthand language used by so many young people to communicate online.

> Sometimes referred to as *netspeak*, the language of the Internet entails both traditional linguistic forms and adapted ones including slang and non-standard forms that are sometimes used in offline life . . . The use of acronyms (e.g., "lol = laugh out loud," "brb = be right back,"), plays or variations on words (e.g., "cya = see you," "latah = later"), graphical icons that represent emotions called *emoticons* (e.g., :) or ;-{}) or graphical icons that represent a real person in a virtual context, called *avatars*, are all examples of language produced by online communicators. (Huffaker & Calvert, 2005, p. 2–3)

These factors, coupled with the disregard for conventions of standard English such as capitalization and punctuation that so often occur in online communication, can make reading and understanding online communications difficult for people who are unfamiliar with these customs. For example, the following passage is presented verbatim from one of the online survey responses: "i cant remember when i did get bullied. Its just been random names like bitch and things. If i do bully them and they get there friends who are shit hot at cussing. Im a bit arrr god what am i gonnna do? But i get over it." This example is representative of the syntax appearing in many of our survey responses, and it is clear that extracting meaning from passages like this can be a difficult task. Thus, one potential limitation of our study is that we may have misinterpreted the intended meaning of the respondents.[7] Certainly, future research should seek to more capably comprehend the complex character of cyberspace communication.

CONCLUSION

Data from this study of over 3,000 Internet-using adolescent girls have provided valuable information about their online victimization experiences. Both the quantitative and qualitative data identify patterns in girls' experiences with cyberbullying and online harassment and highlight themes that help us to broaden our understanding of this type of victimization as it ranges from trivial to serious in scope. Although our data indicate that much of the electronic victimization adolescent girls experience involves relatively minor forms of online harassment, the testimonials presented at the beginning of this chapter underscore the severe emotional and psychological consequences that can accompany cyberbullying victimization. Although many questions remain and much more research is needed, this exploratory study provides justification for reconceptualizing girls' victimization to include experiences with cyberbullying and online harassment.

Discussion Questions

1. What are some of the different types and contexts of online victimizations that adolescent girls have experienced?
2. What factors contribute to the existence of cyberbullying?
3. In what ways do adolescent girls respond to being victims of cyberbullying?
4. What are the consequences for adolescent girls of being cyberbullied?
5. What factors should be considered in the development of future efforts to prevent cyberbullying?

References

Berson, I. R., Berson, M. J., & Ferron, J. M. (2002). Emerging risks of violence in the digital age: Lessons for educators from an online study of adolescent girls in the United States. *Journal of School Violence, 1*(2), 51–71.

Chu, J. (2005). You wanna take this online? Retrieved August 1, 2005, from http://www.time.com/time/magazine/printout/0,8816,1088698,00.html

Finkelhor, D., & Browne, A. (1986). Impact of child sexual abuse: a review of the research. *Psychological Bulletin, 99*, 66–77.

Finkelhor, D., Hotaling, G., Lewis, I. A., & Smith, C. (2000). Sexual abuse in a national survey of adult men and women: Prevalence, characteristics, and risk factors. *Child Abuse & Neglect, 14*, 19–28.

Finn, J. (2004). A survey of online harassment at a university campus. *Journal of Interpersonal Violence, 19*(4), 468–483.

Hinduja, S. & Patchin, J.W. (2008). Cyberbullying: An exploratory analysis of factors related to offending and victimization. *Deviant Behavior, 29*(2), 1–29.

Huffaker, D. A., & Calvert, S. L. (2005). Gender, identity, and language use in teenage blogs. *Journal of Computer-Mediated Communication, 10*(2). Retrieved on May 23, 2008, from http://jcmc.indiana.edu/vol10/issue2/huffaker.html

Kendall-Tackett, K. A., Williams, L. M., & Finkelhor, D. (1993). Impact of sexual abuse on children: A review and synthesis of recent empirical studies. *Psychological Bulletin, 113*, 164–180.

Kowalski, R., Limber, S., Scheck, A., Redfearn, M., Allen, J., Calloway, A. M., et al. (2005). *Electronic bullying among school-aged children and youth.* Paper presented at the Annual Meeting of the American Psychological Association, Washington, D.C.

Lavoie, F., Robitataille, L., & Herbert, M. (2000). Teen dating relationships and aggression: An exploratory study. *Violence Against Women, 6*(1), 6–36.

Lenhart, A., Madden, M., & Hitlin, P. (2005). Teens and Technology. Retrieved August 2, 2005, from http://www.pewinternet.org/pdfs/PIP_Teens_Tech_July2005web.pdf

Meadows, B., Bergal, J., Helling, S., Odell, J., Piligian, E., Howard, C., Lopez, M., Atlas, D., & Hochberg, L. (2005, March 21). The web: The bully's new playground. *People*, 152–155.

O'Keefe, M. (1997). Predictors of dating violence among high school students. *Journal of Interpersonal Violence, 12*(4), 546–568.

Patchin, J. W., & Hinduja, S. (2006). Bullies move beyond the schoolyard: A preliminary look at cyberbullying. *Youth Violence and Juvenile Justice, 4*(2), 148–169.

Rosenblatt, P. C., & Fischer, L. R. (1993). Qualitative family research. In P. G. Boss, W. J. Doherty, R. LaRossa, W. R. Schumm, & S. K. Steinmetz (Eds.), *Sourcebook of family theories and methods: A contextual approach* (pp. 167–180). New York: Plenum.

Silverman, J. G., Raj, A., Mucci, L. A., & Hathaway, J. E. (2001). Dating violence against adolescent girls and associated substance use, unhealthy weight control, sexual risk behavior,

pregnancy, and suicidality. *Journal of the American Medical Association, 286*(5), 572–579.

Swartz, J. (2005). Schoolyard bullies get nastier online [Electronic Version]. *USA Today*. Retrieved March 6, 2005, from http://www.usatoday.com/tech/news/2005-03-06-cover-cyberbullies_x.htm

Ybarra, M. L., & Mitchell, J. K. (2004). Online aggressor/targets, aggressors and targets: A comparison of associated youth characteristics. *Journal of Child Psychology and Psychiatry, 45*, 1308–1316.

Endnotes

1. Research also suggests that online harassment occurs among young adults as well, including college students (Finn, 2004).
2. Survey was administered between December 22, 2004 and January 22, 2005.
3. Seven websites agreed to link to our survey, and included three online gaming sites, three musical artist homepages, and a Harry Potter site. More information on the specific data collection methods can be found in Hinduja & Patchin (2008).
4. Unfortunately, this is an unavoidable problem associated with web-based data collection from a spatially diffused sample, and is a limitation of which the authors are all too aware.
5. To be sure, in instances of more debasing forms of cyberbullying, such as when a web

page is created to make fun of the victim or when embarrassing information about the victim is posted in a public online environment, the victim cannot easily ignore or disregard the behavior.

6. Indeed, the fact that respondents indicated that their friends bullied them suggests a misinterpretation of the term "bullying." Although the online survey included a definition of cyberbullying, it appears that many respondents reported as cyberbullying behavior that did not meet that definition.
7. To overcome this possibility, the authors defined all acronyms and slang used in the narratives using an online dictionary, and when questions arose about responses, all three authors discussed the text in order to reach a consensus about its intended meaning.

PART III

SOCIETAL AND CRIMINAL JUSTICE RESPONSE TO FEMALE VICTIMIZATION

This book opened with a discussion of the gendered nature of victimization giving an explanation for this social fact. Part I of the book demonstrated how gendered victimization is defined by culture in general and criminal justice in particular. Part II provided examples of gendered victimization and the experiences of these victims. In Part III, the examination is completed with a look at responses to female-gendered victimization.

It is important to examine the social and justice responses to female victimization as these responses are derived from our social constructs of these events as well as work to reproduce them. Furthermore, these responses often label the female victim as deviant at some level. "Deviance is 'created by society . . . *social groups create deviance by making the rules whose infraction constitutes deviance,* and by applying those rules to particular people and labeling them as outsiders'" (italics present, Liazos, 1972, p. 170). Liazos, in an essay on the sociological study of deviance, emphasized that sociologists are so often fascinated by the "nuts, sluts, and perverts" that they ignore the destructive actions of the powerful individuals, groups, and institutions. These actions can affect people's lives in ways that can kill, maim, and destroy. Such destructive behaviors can include institutional racism and sexism, corporate pollution of the environment, and selective enforcement of the law. This labeling affects society in a way that the lives of female victims of crime are dissected in order to uncover the deviance that allows society to blame them. In this way, society tends to look at female crime victims as *nuts and sluts*. As many victims of female-gendered victimization are often labeled deviant and not awarded the victim status, this section provides a deeper examination of these problems. Questions that chapters in Part III examine include the following: Are social and justice institutions responding to myths of female-gendered victimization? What have been the changes in response in the last few decades? How can we improve social and justice responses to female crime victims?

Beginning a discussion on the response to female-gendered victimization, Chapter 11, "A Sheltered Life: Observations on a Domestic Violence Shelter" by Angela M. Moe, examines community response to female victims of domestic violence and examines the turmoil these women tend to experience when their power is further stripped. Moe examines the shelter as a total institution that works to further diminish female victims' power which sometimes results in a return to their abusers.

Gina Robertiello also focuses on shelter victims in Chapter 12, "In Their Own Words: Shelter Residents' Experiences with Police." In her examination, Robertiello focuses on those women who have escaped abuse, at least for now, and examines their stories. Robertiello finds that police response is experienced differently depending on geography, urban versus suburban. Furthermore, she finds that while many of the women are satisfied with the police response, there needs to be clearer and more concise and coordinated procedures in responding to domestic violence.

In Chapter 13, " 'I Don't Think a Cop Has Ever Asked Me if I Was OK': Battered Women's Experiences with Police Intervention," Hillary Potter takes our understanding of police response to domestic violence to a different level. In her research, Potter examines the fact that battered Black women perceive and experience police intervention differently than do battered White women. Particularly, Potter examines gender and racial identity and how these influence battered Black women's decisions to report this violence and outcomes of police intervention, such as arrest, victim satisfaction, and the effects of arrest. Among her many findings, Potter finds that while there is some inconsistency with the general research, battered Black women perceive that police are more likely to arrest battered Black women in the trend toward dual arrests and less likely to view them as victims due to their darker complexions.

Alesha Durfee moves the book's focus from police response to court response in Chapter 14, "The Gendered Paradox of Victimization and Agency in Protection Order Filings." Examining the cultural images of femininity and of battered women, Durfee argues that female victims face a paradoxical challenge. Particularly, women are required to be simultaneously helpless and agentic. Durfee examines this paradox by analyzing narratives within protection order petitions of domestic violence victims. She finds that the narratives submitted by female petitioners who received legal representation were more in line with gendered schemas enhancing their chances of obtaining protection orders.

In Chapter 15, "Misdemeanor Domestic Violence Cases in the Courts: A Description of the Cases," Joanne Belknap, Jennifer L. Hartman, and Victoria L. Lippen further examine domestic violence within the court system. They find that victims tend to more cooperative than social constructs have claimed. However, prosecutors do not give their cases much attention showing an unwillingness or inability to handle the magnitude of cases that go through the court.

Bringing our focus to the end of the criminal justice process, Susan F. Sharp (Chapter 16) examines the victimization histories of women incarcerated in Oklahoma, "The Victimization Histories of Women Prisoners in Oklahoma." Sharp found that many of the female inmates have experienced physical or sexual abuse as children or adults. Additionally, their victimization occurs at a higher rate than that of women in the general population. Sharp argues that correctional systems need to be educated on the impact of abuse on women and how to treat such traumas.

Closing this book, Patrick McManimon, in Chapter 17, examines the larger picture of the criminalization of female victimization, "The Criminalization of Victimization of Female Offenders and Emerging Correctional Responses." In his analysis, McManimon takes the reader through the juvenile justice system that punishes girls for escaping victimization within the home. McManimon describes how girls' survival strategies (i.e., running way and drug abuse) become the focus of most girls' experiences while victimization is ignored or denied. He then brings the reader to the adult female focusing on the battered women's syndrome and posttraumatic stress disorder resulting from sexual violence and domestic violence. McManimon closes his chapter with suggestions for halting these problems further exacerbated by the justice system.

Reference

Liazos, A. (1972). The poverty of the sociology of deviance: Nuts, sluts, and perverts. In H. N. Pontell (Ed.), *Social deviance: Readings in theory and research* (pp. 164–179). Upper Saddle River, NJ: Prentice Hall.

CHAPTER 11

A SHELTERED LIFE: OBSERVATIONS ON A DOMESTIC VIOLENCE SHELTER

ANGELA M. MOE

ABSTRACT

The focus of most research on woman battering[1] has centered on the effectiveness of various social and legal responses to the problem, particularly in terms of how well recidivism has been curbed and whether or not the victim returns to the relationship. While important, these conceptualizations of effectiveness remain short-sighted as there is also an experiential dimension to consider, which focuses on the lived experiences of women victims. This chapter elucidates such lived experiences within a shelter setting. Through semi-structured interviews and participant observation, the process of finding shelter, adjusting to shelter life, and planning for the future within a shelter setting is examined.[2] These findings are discussed within the conceptual framework of Goffman's (1961) "total institution," as adapted to account for the effects of shelter organizations.

INTRODUCTION

Over the last couple of decades, much has been written on the various social and legal responses to woman battering in terms of the law, justice system, social services, and victim services. Of particular concern has been the effectiveness of these responses with regard to ensuring victim safety and reducing recidivism. Comparatively, less attention has been given to the daily struggles of the women victims involved with these various institutions and agencies. What kinds of experiences do they have? What types of struggles do they face? How do they negotiate various avenues of assistance? This chapter considers these questions with regard to the shelter experience—finding shelter, living in a shelter, and exiting from a shelter. Data come from qualitative, life-history interviews with 20 women residing at a domestic violence shelter, as well as participant observation.

SHELTERS AS A SOCIAL RESPONSE TO BATTERING

The movement to develop institutional-based programs, including shelters, for battered women may be traced to a number of related social problems that gained notoriety during the late 1960s and 1970s. Among these were the identification of and response to child maltreatment (National Association of Counsel for Children [NACC], 2006; Wallace, 2005) and the increased reliance on shelters for the rising homeless population (Gounis, 1992; Stark, 1994). In fact, the link between various social problems and woman abuse was illustrated well in the first shelters for battered women, as they were intended for those who had been assaulted by alcoholic husbands (Schechter, 1982).

By and large, however, the strongest advocates for battered women were feminists who, because of their work against sexual assault during this same time period, were already cognizant of the ways in which battering connected to gendered social relations and patriarchy (Matthews, 1994; Schechter, 1982). The primary objectives of these early feminist activists were to end woman battering through broad social reforms targeted at acknowledging the social causes of male violence, while at the same time reforming the criminal justice system and social service programs that had previously ignored battered women's experiences (Bush, 1992; Dobash & Dobash, 1992; Loseke, 1992; Schechter, 1982; Tierney, 1982). In addition, an immediate objective of the movement was to provide emergency shelter and support for victims (Bush, 1992; Dobash & Dobash, 1992; Schechter, 1982; Tierney, 1982). Shelters seemed the most effective way of providing women with the time and safety they needed to begin healing and planning for the future, while also finding a sense of sisterhood and community among others in similar circumstances (Davis & Srinivasan, 1994; Dobash & Dobash, 1979, 1992; Gilman, 1988; Krane & Davies, 2002; Tierney, 1982).

Subsequently, small groups of activists across the country began advocating and providing services for battered women throughout the 1970s. In 1974 only a handful of shelters existed (Martin, 1976; Schechter, 1982); however, by 1982 the number had risen to 500 (Schechter, 1982). By 1989, as many as 1,200 shelters were operating (Dobash & Dobash, 1992) and by 1995 an estimated 1,250 existed (Roberts, 1995). Today, approximately 1,300 shelters are available to battered women (National Coalition Against Domestic Violence [NCADV], 2004). Early shelters were meager in structure, staffing, and residents, and often relied on egalitarian and participatory organizational models of management and development. However, as shelters grew in capacity and began making use of government sources of funding, structural and management questions arose. Bureaucratization occurred within many shelters, which facilitated a professionalization of staff and a hierarchal-based structure. With this came a relabeling of residents as "clients" and an overhauling of support services aimed at individual counseling, as opposed to group sharing, peer support, and empowerment (Ahrens, 1993; Davis & Srinivasan, 1994; Ferraro, 1981; Johnson, 1981; Mullender, 1997; Roche & Sadoski, 1996; Schechter, 1982; Srinivasan & Davis, 1991; Tierney, 1982).

SHELTERS AS "TOTAL INSTITUTIONS"

As Goffman (1961) originally defined it, a total institution is "a place of residence . . . where a large number of like-situated individuals, cut off from the wider society for an appreciable period of time, together lead an enclosed formally administered round of life" (p. xiii). While not originally included in this conceptualization, shelters, particularly those serving the homeless, have since been included in this framework (Bogard, 1998; Snow & Anderson 1993; Stark, 1994). As Stark (1994) attests, shelters become a type of total institution "when the role that the individual assumes as shelter resident blocks his or her ability to pursue the most basic human roles—those of friend, lover, husband, wife, parent, and so forth" (p. 557). It is my contention that most domestic violence shelters today also fit this conceptualization in many regards.

Within a shelter, there is little regard for autonomy or individuality. Residents are reduced to a dependent status, forced to rely on the institution for necessities (given either directly or through referral), inclusive of food, water, shelter, clothing, transportation, communication, education, therapy, and child care. Clear hierarchies exist between shelter residents and staff, with a strict bureaucracy supporting the creation, implementation, and enforcement of various rules and policies (Bogard, 1998; Snow & Anderson, 1993; Stark, 1994). While staff may retain discretionary decision-making power, there can often be no expectation by the residents that the utilization of such discretion will benefit them. In fact, it may be used in seemingly unjust or misunderstood ways, pitting residents against each other within a climate of scarce resources (Holden, 1997; Lipsky, 1980). A peculiar contradiction is thus created, wherein the goals of providing a nurturing and empowering environment for victims are couched against a structure that relies on obedience, conformity, and personal strife (Ferraro, 1981). Interesting parallels may be drawn in this regard to the environment the shelter residents are trying to escape—that of a coercive, imbalanced power structure, minus the more obvious forms of physical, sexual, and emotional abuse (Panzer, Philip, & Hayward, 2000).

Despite this obvious contradiction, widespread co-optation and professionalization within the shelter movement have left little room for more egalitarian practices (Johnson, 1981; Schechter, 1982; Tierney, 1982). Indeed, bureaucratically based organization and supervision over residents are often seen as a necessity not only for maintaining order but for creating a structure that is, of all things, facilitative of self-sufficiency (Williams, 2003). The rationale here is that structure is necessary for emotional healing, personal growth, and future planning, with the presumption that women in shelters are incapable of creating their own sense of structure and self-discipline. Such logic is disturbingly similar to prominent child-raising philosophies geared toward correcting misbehavior, wherein structure and boundary-setting are considered central to development (Borba, 2003; Christopherson, 1998; MacKenzie, 2001). Many women resent the fact that they were forced to leave their homes in the first place, as opposed to their abusers being forced to leave due to their behavior— being treated as if they cannot or are not able to think and act for themselves only contributes to a form of revictimization. Moreover, having to rely on a shelter, regardless of the type, carries with it a perceived and often realized social stigma—that of a person who is incapable of regulating her own affairs. Indeed, such a stigma is closely related to the original conceptualization of the total institution, in that such facilities have traditionally been associated with persons who are seen as threats to the larger community (e.g., mentally ill, criminal offenders, people with contagious diseases) (Stark, 1994).

METHODOLOGY

Following the common suggestion within qualitative field work of "starting where you are" (Lofland, Snow, Anderson, & Lofland, 2006, p. 9), I realized the potential for this study in the early 2000s when I became a volunteer at a domestic violence shelter in a suburb of Phoenix, Arizona. As I became more active in the shelter, eventually being hired as a fill-in "client care worker," I became more cognizant of the ways in which the agency's bureaucratic structure affected the daily functioning of the women residing there. I increasingly recognized the contradictions inherent in this structure, which was supposed to be empowering for women, yet operated as a type of total institution, relying on dependency-producing rules and policies. Upon being granted permission to conduct interviews with the residents for a related study, I remained open to hearing the women's experiences of living in the shelter.

Because the interviews were semi-structured, the questions varied and were left intentionally open ended, so as to provide the women with opportunities to shape the flow and content of their responses (Reinharz, 1992). I asked general questions about their childhoods and experiences with school, friends, and family, moving eventually to their adult experiences and what circumstances had preceded their shelter stay. Along these lines, efforts at various means of help-seeking and survival were addressed. It was within this context that experiences with and opinions about Tami's Place,[3] or other shelters and victim-based agencies, were shared. Certainly, all interviews were conducted under the strictest of confidences such that despite my role as staff member, the women were also made aware of my role as a researcher and were guaranteed full privacy through a university-approved informed consent process. With this protection and an open-ended, semi-structured format, the interviewing strategy yielded richly detailed and nuanced information about the women's lives that would not have been gleaned from other means of data collection (Kvale, 1996), while simultaneously allowing the women to remain within their personal boundaries of comfort and safety.

Relying on standpoint feminist theory (Harding, 1987; Smith, 1989), I approached the interviews with the goal of understanding the participants' lives from their own perspectives, acknowledging that their voices are often silenced amongst other available "master narratives" (Romero & Stewart, 1999, p. xiii), such as police, social workers, attorneys, court personnel, and even advocates themselves. Indeed, these women's voices were socially positioned, and may not be seen as representative of all victims of interpersonal violence. They may also only represent partial truths, as our social realities are indeed multifaceted. However, in this particular context, I viewed the epistemic privilege of this marginalized group to be appropriate for describing at least some of the ways in which our society responds to woman battering (Collins, 1989; Hartsock, 1987; Smith, 1987).

During a five-month period in the early 2000s, I conducted 20 interviews with shelter residents. All of the women expressed a great deal of trust in and seemed comfortable with me during the interviews, sharing their experiences with what seemed to be a great deal of honesty and candor. In this way, the interviews seemed to be facilitated through my position as a staff member in the shelter. They were conducted at the discretion of the women within private rooms of the facility and lasted an average of 55 minutes. Each woman was given the opportunity to provide her own pseudonym and $10 remuneration. All of the interviews were later transcribed and coded for emergent and recurring themes.

Overall the sample was fairly diverse in terms of race/ethnicity, age, and education. Ten women (50%) identified as White, four (21%) as Black, two (11%) as Native American, two (11%) as Latina, and two (11%) as biracial. Their ages ranged from 20 to 44 with an average of 29. Eight (42%) reported less than a high-school education, five (26%) had graduated from high school or received a GED, and seven (35%) had attended at least some college. Most (17% or 85%) were mothers, with an average of 2.4 kids each. All but one of these kids were minors and most resided at the shelter with their mothers. Four women were also pregnant at the time of the interviews. All of the women had experienced multiple forms of abuse; from their descriptions, it was found that 18 (95%) had been abused physically (e.g., pushes, shoves, punches, slaps, restraints, burnings, stabbings), 17 (85%) psychologically or emotionally (e.g., threats, degradations, insults, name-calling, belittling), 14 (70%) financially (e.g., having property destroyed, stolen, or misused), and 6 (40%) sexually (e.g., harassment, rape, unwanted fondling, forced pornography or prostitution). All but one (who was being abused by her parents) had been abused by male partners. It was most often the case that the women had actually been abused by more than one partner (average of two) over the course of their lifetimes. Only one woman reported being abused by a female partner; however, she had been abused by a male partner as well. All of the women had sustained injuries that merited medical attention.

FINDINGS

SEEKING SHELTER AS A LAST RESORT

Tami's Place was one of eight shelters for victims of family violence in the Phoenix area. It was one of the only shelters in the area to accept both women and men, as well as adolescent boys. While it regularly served victims from throughout the metropolitan area, it also took in those from other towns, cities, counties, and states, because many had been forced to flee long distances. The shelter was able to house 24 adults and children over two years of age (12 sets of bunk-beds), as well as four infants (4 cribs) within four cottage-style apartments. Each cottage housed between four and eight people, usually within only two bedrooms, and each was equipped with a kitchen, small living area, and single bathroom. A small courtyard was situated in the center of three of the four cottages and contained two picnic tables and a small swing-set. There was also a main house of approximately 1,400 square feet, which contained a community kitchen; large meeting room; library/sitting area with a single client phone and computer; main office/reception area with a couch and two staff workstations; four bedroom-sized offices, one of which was dedicated to children's therapy and play groups; bathroom; and basement.

The shelter's location was not publicly known, a common tactic in shelters across the country (Roberts, 1998). Because the facility was located within a residential neighborhood and appeared to be some sort of small housing or apartment complex, it was not distinguishable to passers-by. In fact, women who drove themselves to the shelter often telephoned several times for clarification on the location, as it was very easy to unsuspectedly pass by the complex. Residents, staff, and volunteers were required to sign confidentiality agreements, wherein they promised not to disclose the location of the shelter to anyone, even (especially) immediate family. Retaining the privacy of the location was very important, as no security or alarm system had as yet been installed on the grounds.

While by outward appearances, the shelter was a safe and comfortable setting, the women generally agreed that it was not a pleasant place. Melissa shared her thoughts:

The shelter life sucks. Everybody is in here for domestic violence and these women make more trouble and more drama in this place than is necessary. They're bitching about stuff . . . I hate that factor. Some of these women are dirty or they don't want to do anything. There are some really trashy women here who don't clean up after themselves or after their kids. And I understand they're depressed and they might not feel like it. There's sometimes I don't feel like doing anything either. But you still have to be considerate for everybody else. It's a good place, don't get me wrong. I thank God for the shelters. But these women make so much drama in this place. I try to stay out of their drama. It's really hard. They want to pair up and be friends with certain people because you didn't speak to them yesterday. That's how petty they are. . . . Shelter life is different . . . you have an added stress level. You don't have too much peace here. You always have somebody in the room with you.

Indeed, the shelter produced a particular kind of stress. Women entered the facility in a crisis state—upset, confused, angry, and scared. Their children were even more so and crying was the norm, rather than the exception. This was aggravated by the tight quarters throughout the facility, which was almost always at capacity. Any space that opened up was usually claimed within 12 hours. Moreover, because the buildings were dated (built in the 1950s) and dependent upon various governmental grants and private/philanthropic donations, necessary repairs and updates were subject to budgetary allowances and often neglected. Space constraints, coupled with the constant struggle to provide three meals a day for over two dozen residents, as well as varying standards of personal and environmental cleanliness, facilitated a mouse and cockroach problem, particularly throughout the main house.

Whether or not they knew what it was going to be like, seeking shelter was typically considered a final and desperate form of help-seeking, as has been documented elsewhere (Roberts, 1998). Indeed, even under conditions of abuse, who would hurry to leave their home, community, school, church, family, friends, and almost all of their possessions in order to hide in a secret place and live amongst complete strangers without any idea of what the future might hold? Indeed, stays in the shelter were a necessity, not a luxury, and according to the interviewees, they occurred after other means of help-seeking were exasperated. For instance, 13 (68%) of the women reported that they had told at least one friend or family member about their abuse and, in many cases, had asked for emotional or financial support from them. Six (32%) had moved on their own within the state to escape their abusive partners and four (21%) had moved out of state. Thirteen (68%) reported calling the police, requesting that their partner be arrested, and cooperating with investigators and district attorneys. Eleven (58%) had filed for restraining orders, sought divorce, and/or attempted to maintain full custody of their children. Fifteen (79%) had previously relied on victim-based services such as shelters, hotlines, support groups, and advocacy centers. Eleven (58%) had turned to social service agencies for assistance, including the welfare system, child protective services, the mental health care system, and child support enforcement. Six (32%) had sought medical attention. While details regarding their previous help-seeking efforts are discussed elsewhere (Moe, 2007), none of these efforts had worked to stop the abuse or otherwise helped the women feel safe, as they all had been forced to flee their homes. However, making the decision to seek shelter was just the first step—finding a place to go was a struggle in and of itself.

FINDING SPACE

In the year prior to this study, 16,600 women and children sought bed space in Maricopa County (the Phoenix metropolitan area) according to records kept by the eight area shelters. Of these, 14,164 were denied shelter, primarily due to a lack of availability (Arizona Department of Economic Security and Department of Health Services, 2001). Single women were the most successful at finding space, because they could be accommodated in any available bed. Women with many children had a much more difficult time finding space, particularly those with infants (who required cribs) and adolescent boys. As Nina, who had been forced to leave her sons with their father (her abuser), explained,

> My kids are nine, 11, 13, and 14. Most of the shelters don't take kids over 13 and most of the ones that do separate them overnight. I had to go all the way to New Mexico to get a shelter that would take me and my boys. Nobody here would take us. . . . they said they could find me a place . . . and then ended up with nothing unless I wanted to separate my kids and put them in different places . . . I wasn't going to leave them alone in someplace I didn't know. I told them, "Look, if you can't find someplace for all of us then we have no choice but to go back. You're pushing me to go back because now I've left and it's going to be twice as bad when I go back."

Nina went on to describe how her abuse had worsened when she left previously and was forced to return. Fearing for her life, she made the decision to come to Tami's Place just long enough to find alternative housing for her family.

In instances when space was available, fairly detailed telephone screenings took place in order to determine whether a woman was indeed in crisis, a victim of abuse, and appropriate for the services available at Tami's Place. Typically, the issue of crisis was not questioned—a potential resident would only need to express fear and the need for space. However, the issue of appropriateness was a much more stringent criterion. Women with current alcohol or drug addictions were not allowed at the shelter due to various regulations and policies, both internal (i.e., lack of substance abuse counseling on the premises) and external (i.e., funding stipulations) to the agency. For similar reasons, women with serious mental illnesses (SMI) were also typically weeded out of consideration and referred to other services, when available. While such policies exist elsewhere (Goodyear, 2001), explanations of them to potential residents were often not taken well. Staff had to regularly explain to disqualified women that the shelter simply did not have the services to accommodate their needs and that allowing them in the facility would only hinder their options, as well as cause a disturbance to other residents. If a woman was inappropriate for Tami's Place, or was accommodated but later seen to have an addiction or SMI, efforts were made to refer her to other area shelters or social-service-based programs.

Nina, whose struggles to find shelter for her entire family were discussed above, did not initially disclose the extent of her mental illness to staff. It was only because of her early meetings with counselors and observed behavior that it was discovered that she suffered from severe depression which facilitated regular attempts at self-mutilation and suicide. During the interview, she showed me some of the scars from these efforts, which ran up and down her arms, legs, chest, and abdomen. She also admitted to over-dosing twice and being hospitalized on numerous occasions. In recent months, her suicide attempts had increased because her abuser was hiding her medication. Though in dire need of a safe place to stay, regular access to medication, and psychiatric follow-up, the facilities and programming available through Tami's Place were not adequate for Nina's situation. In the days following her interview, she was removed from the shelter and referred to the county mental health authorities. As if predicting this, Nina commented during the interview, "I feel like I've fallen through the cracks of the system. There isn't any room for me . . . "

In fact, six (30%) of the women acknowledged mental illness (i.e., clinical depression, schizophrenia, and bipolar disorder) during their interviews, but most did not talk openly about it to other staff or residents, so as to avoid being referred from the shelter. The same was true for alcohol and drug addiction—six (30%) of the women were prior or current users; however, most did not openly disclose their history unless within the context of being in recovery, which was the only acceptable means of speaking about alcohol or drugs without risking dismissal.

ADJUSTING TO SHELTER LIFE

For those who did find space in Tami's Place, a period of second-guessing often occurred with regard to their decision to leave their homes and/or abusive partners. Part of this seemed related to the initial shock of the shelter, as already described, and the overwhelming feeling many experienced after realizing that other women were facing similar challenges. Lee reflected on her first few days at the shelter:

> First day here you're scared to death. Did I do the right thing? What am I going to do if he finds me? What am I going to do if I can't be here? What, what, what, what, what?!? You're stressed out and then you go to sleep. You realize you can go to sleep without somebody trying to kill you, nobody yelling and screaming. You sleep. Then you wake up and you're sort of like dazed, confused.

Compounding this shock was the recognition by several of the women that they still loved their partners, even if they were abusive. Terri's sentiments about her early attempts to leave her husband were typical of women who still loved their partners:

> I hated to see him suffer. I worried, "Who's getting his Diet Coke? Who's making sure it's not flat? Who's keeping his stuff separate? Doing his laundry? Making his bed?" I was just so concerned about him the whole time I was gone.

While there was a prominent feeling of concern about their partners for many of the residents, at least initially, there seemed to be little recognition among the shelter staff of this. Most of the conversations revolved around finding the resources that would allow the women to completely separate from their abusers, regardless of whether they were prepared to do so (Baker, 1997; Krane & Davies, 2002; Wharton, 1989).

An additional factor in these initial reactions to the shelter involved children, who often did not understand why they had left home. Many immediately showed resistance, resentment, and even hostility toward their mothers for leaving, as they missed their fathers or father-figures, friends, schools, extended family, and personal belongings (Krane & Davies, 2002). Some children were simply too young to understand why their surroundings were suddenly different. As Samantha explained with regard to her 14-month-old son, "The first week when I was here he had a really hard time. He would cry at night and he'd cling to me."

Women shared their children's frustration, as many were unable (due to safety concerns and shelter policy) to contact friends or family members. And as Renee described, there was the question of whether to return to an abuser:

> I've been depressed. I don't know if it's me or . . . I don't know . . . sometimes I think, "Should I go back or be in here?" And it's like, I know it's much different from being home and being here for him (her son). I think he gets depressed, too. He can't have his way . . .

Additionally, several were forced to leave their jobs, if they had them, or to travel longer distances in order to keep them (Moe & Bell, 2004). As Melissa described, after resigning from a management position at a food service company:

> So now I have to start all over. I got paid good. I was making $13 per hour plus I got paid overtime (OT) which is very rare for management to get paid OT so I was bringing, with the overtime I put in, about $700 to $800 a week alone . . . I couldn't have stayed because I don't have transportation back and forth, and being in management, I have to be accessible and I wouldn't have been accessible here.

For those who were able to get past the initial shock, a period of adjustment to the surroundings soon occurred. It was during this time that many residents began coming to terms with what they had been experiencing in their relationships, perhaps recognizing signs that the abuse had been occurring for a much longer time than they had initially believed. This was often a very emotional stage of adjustment as several women expressed regret, sadness, and disbelief about "putting up with it for so long." It was during this time that, despite the conditions, the

women were most likely to show appreciation for the shelter space. Cynthia's sentiments were illustrative:

> It's a place to stay. They give you food. They give you clothes. They give you the
> counseling you need. They try to make available to you services that you can
> get . . . assistance with housing and everything. This is a shelter. This is not
> home. You don't have to pay for anything here. The shelter has really helped
> me because I have self-worth. I have good qualities, I have talents, I have skills,
> I have the ability to be a healthy human being, and I just had to take time out
> and know that about myself.

Such sentiments served as powerful indicators as to the importance of shelters for
women with few options for assistance. However, they were not universally shared,
particularly for women who, often as time progressed, became disenchanted with the
shelter and their future prospects.

MANAGING BUREAUCRACY, EXPERIENCING DISCRETION

Much of the discontent about the shelter was driven by concerns about its rules and
policies, which dictated a fairly rigid schedule. Consistent with the notion that shelters
are a type of total institution because of their reliance on rules for control and order
maintenance (Goffman, 1961; Stark, 1994), residents were not allowed to sleep past
8:00 in the morning, unless they received prior permission to do so because of a work
schedule or other late-night necessity. Because the shelter's evening curfew was
between 5:00 P.M. and 8:00 P.M. (depending on the day of the week and season), in order
to stay out beyond curfew, residents needed to submit a "curfew extension" (a written
request made to the shelter supervisor). In language and policy comparable to that
used in a jail or prison setting (Dordick, 1996; Hammer, 2002), the shelter would go on
"lock down" later in the evening, typically by 10:00 P.M. At this time, all residents and
their children needed to be in their apartments, readying themselves for bed.
Moreover, all were required to maintain orderly and clean apartments and to complete
one communal house-keeping task per day, such as cleaning up the play-yard or wash-
ing house laundry (e.g., kitchen towels, linens, aprons, rugs). Both apartment cleanliness and daily chores were subject to inspection. All residents were also required to
sign up for dinner preparation once a week, as evening meals were served and eaten
communally at a similar time each day. Such practices are consistent with other shelters
(Davis & Srinivasan, 1994; Krane & Davies, 2002; Srinivasan & Davis, 1991).

   In terms of programming, all of the women were expected to keep an average of
two counseling appointments per week, as well as attend a weekly group therapy
session, group parenting class (if they had children), and house meeting. As was mentioned earlier, all of this programming was aimed explicitly at the assumption that the
women had decided to leave their abusers, when it was not clear that all had actually
decided to do so (Baker, 1997; Krane & Davies, 2002; Wharton, 1989). There was very
little by way of safety planning *during* a relationship, or strategizing on how to continue
therapy and/or involvement in the legal or social service system. Indeed, contact of any
kind with abusive partners during a woman's stay was strictly prohibited and grounds
for dismissal (Williams, 1998).

While the women acknowledged that many of the policies were necessary for order maintenance and security, they did compare the rules of the shelter with the control mechanisms used by their abusers (Panzer et al., 2000). According to Mandy,

> I don't know . . . as far as the curfews and stuff, I guess I kind of agree with them, but you know, they're like "Oh my God, you were controlled and that's just so horrible." And I don't know, they kind of control you here too. But I mean, I guess it's okay. I can't complain.

Some also commented on the isolation they felt because of the restrictions placed on their time, as well as the lack of meaningful activities:

> There's no interaction here. It's kind of like you're here and after 7:00 you're locked down. The only time we ever come together is during group. There's nothing to come together and be loose and be happy for. I don't know why they don't do some sort of ceremony for exiting. A ceremony so that you have the opportunity to say good-bye. Here, people leave and I'm like, "Oh, she left?" I just think they need more interaction with these women besides domestic violence. Women don't have transportation so the kids are stuck in these rooms. Being in these rooms is kind of a gloomy, depressed feeling. You can feel the negativity in these rooms, you really can. Have you ever seen a kid watch TV all day and you look at their face and they're zombied out? These women sit in the room doing nothing all day. . . . and they look like zombies, too. (Melissa)

There was also resentment about being treated like kids. Lee explained how she had been "grounded" by one of the counselors, a clear example of what Goffman (1961) called an "age grading system" (p. 43), meant to erode one's sense of self-determination and personal freedom:

> She grounded me to my apartment because I had a cold. She told me to go to my apartment and not to bring it out and not to bring it to the office. I was supposed to make calls yesterday and I couldn't come in to make them because I had a cold. . . . I couldn't go to group. I couldn't voice my opinion. I couldn't do nothin'. I had to go to my room.

Resident discontent was also aggravated by the ways in which resources and material goods were allotted. Because only one phone and computer were available for their use, residents were required to limit their time on both to 10-minute intervals and to sign up in advance during times of high demand. Sometimes they were not available when residents needed them, depending on when staff meetings occurred which necessitated privacy within the main house. During times that the main house was closed to residents, staff were supposed to take down phone messages and to post them on a community bulletin board. However, this did not seem to be a consistent practice. According to Lee,

> Well this is just another example. I went to the doctor yesterday and when I checked in they asked why I never went to take my mammogram and I said, "Because it's not until next week." "No, we got you in sooner and we called and left it with a (case-worker's name)." I never got it. (Q: It was never on the message board?) Nope. So that lost me that appointment so now it's two months away. Two months . . . just because somebody didn't bother to take the

message down. That makes five messages that I know of that I didn't get in the last week. What about all the other ones that I might have got, you know? I had called on housing. I called on vehicles. . . . They really need to work on getting their priorities and our priorities 'cause that's not cool. I've been working hard on my own . . .

In addition, residents needed to ask staff for almost everything, including medication (over the counter and prescription), monetary allowances, bus tokens, toiletries, personal hygiene products, diapers, clothing, and clean linens. Several concerns arose during the time of this study about the ways in which staff made use of their discretion in regard to enforcing rules and policies, as well as making resources and material goods available. A particularly severe example of this involved the padlocking of refrigerators. As a response to the perceived misuse of food, particularly milk, which some of the staff believed residents were stealing and hoarding within their respective apartments, the two refrigerators within the main house were padlocked. This then required residents to ask staff to unlock the refrigerators in order to get something as simple as a few eggs to fry. While the apartments also contained refrigerators, they were smaller in size and limited in supplies, so it was often the case that residents came to the main house's kitchen for perishable food. Padlocking the refrigerators seemed to incite much confusion and resentment by the residents who felt that the shelter administrators did not trust them with even the smallest amount of autonomy.

In general then, there appeared to be a love–hate relationship between residents and staff. On the one end, residents were thankful for the place to stay and the counseling and advocacy they obtained by virtue of being in a shelter. Most were cognizant of the fact that the shelter staff, particularly the staff member assigned to them as their primary "case-worker" could be a tremendous advocate, particularly with regard to negotiating the legal system, arranging future housing, and seeking employment. At the same time, the staff held enormous power over the women, in that they enforced the rules, penalized violators, and quelled disputes in ways that often made the residents resentful. Moreover, staff controlled access to various privileges, resources, and material goods. The women recognized this power and often felt that it could be misused and manipulated in ways that helped certain residents and hurt others. As Tazia explained,

> They're not consistent. I've noticed that you have to be on their good side for them to help you. You have to come into the office and ask them how they're doing. . . . 'cause women are women and they have their own issues at home too. There's probably three or four staff members who are really interested in helping women. . . . the other staff are not helpful. . . . there's been times when I've been devastated and crying and no staff would even ask if I wanted to talk.

Melissa also noted problems but generally had a more positive attitude toward the shelter staff:

> I haven't had any problems with staff except with the counselor. She really pissed me off the other day. But I went and I talked to her and I told her she really made me upset with the comments she had made. She said "Oh, I didn't realize. . . . " Most people don't realize when they say something to hurt your feelings. But, staff has been good. They've got a good team. You see a lot of

bonding between the staff which is really good. They'll help you. Some feel you have to do something extra for staff to make them like you, but they're pretty much friendly to everybody. And I know staff gossips 'cause everybody gossips. I haven't seen them turn down anybody or even heard of anybody saying that they were actually turned down by staff. They might say, "I didn't know," but they've been really helpful.

Interestingly, power hierarchies and misunderstandings thereof were recognized by staff as well, with frequent conversations about the "unpredictability" of residents. As I was told on one occasion by a more seasoned case-worker, "Some days they love you and some days they hate you." Of particular concern among staff was avoiding any accusations of favoritism in terms of making exceptions for certain residents over others. Even if an exception to a rule seemed appropriate due to the personal situation of a resident, staff questioned the fairness of making the exception and often consulted with each other on what the possible ramifications would be for making it. When exceptions were made and subsequently challenged by other residents, the standard response was, "There are individual circumstances with everybody and you don't necessarily know what they were in this case. You need to focus on yourself and not worry about what others are doing." This often did little to quell such concerns. In fact, it seemed to initiate greater resentment about not only the power hierarchies between staff and residents but also between residents themselves:

> The inconsistency is scary. That's what makes all the girls fight. You're put in situations that are bad enough . . . tempers are going to get crazy . . . (Lee)

Resentment was often worse against those staff who the residents knew were not themselves survivors of intimate partner violence and so, in their eyes, could not possibly understand what they were going through:

> There's a few people here that have never been in the situation of being without a home or being abused or being a victim. The last thing that somebody who's been on the street, been in the situation, needs is to be confronted or talked to by somebody who's just read it in a book. You don't respond well. (Lee)

In this way, it seemed that the shelter residents were more willing to deal with the authority of staff when they sensed that the staff somehow understood them on a deeper level by having been in a similar situation.

STRUGGLING AGAINST TIME

Regardless of the ways in which the women adjusted to the shelter or their feelings toward the staff, a concern shared by all was the struggle against time. Because the shelter was supported largely through government grants, strict regulations were placed upon it with regard to how long and in what capacities it served "clientele." Tami's Place was designated as a temporary crisis shelter, and its policies clearly stipulated a 30-day maximum stay, with formal extensions available for up to 90 days. The extensions were only given on a week-to-week basis, so women were required to constantly file requests, which was very anxiety-producing:

> You live week to week. If you get one write-up (documentation of a rule violation), you're out. You're terminated right there because you're on an extension. Your 30 days here just gets you comfortable. Everybody is constantly saying, "Relax, just get your head straight. Calm down. Know that you're safe. Don't dwell on anything. Don't worry about anything. Just make sure you make it to the meetings and calm yourself down. Get better." Then at the end of that 30 days, they're after you. "Well you know you gotta have housing or we're going to have to . . . " Tell me that's not a calming down just to shoot you over the collar. That's usually when people go back (to their abusers) . . . they're on you every week. (Lee)

Thus women were pressured to not only get over their initial shock and adjustment to the shelter, but to also quickly plan for the future in terms of housing, employment, child care, transportation, and the like. Little recognition was shown with regard to how emotional crisis, stress, anxiety, and depression can contribute to a person's inability to make quick and sound decisions (Lindsey, 1998; Williams, 1998). The "giving up" attitude/behavior that Lee speaks of has been documented elsewhere (Newman, 1993) in reference to the helplessness and fear women experience when being pushed to permanently leave their abusers without the appropriate emotional, financial, and legal supports to do so. Tazia made the point very well:

> They give you 30 days to do what you have to do, and then to get an extension and stay longer, you have to get documentation that you are working on getting a place to live. Not many women that have kids and don't have a car are able to hurry up and get a job within 30 days. Hurry up and get a place in 30 days. It's a lot of pressure and deadlines living here. I'm thinking that a shelter is a place for them to gain their self-esteem, to get out of that controlling situation, and give them the will power to be self-sufficient and independent and really there's more stress here with all the rules and extensions and groups and time limits. . . . it's not helpful to me at all. I've pretty much had to get out and get everything myself. I applied for DES (welfare subsidies through the Department of Economic Security) myself. I applied for school. I found daycare on my own. They helped me with bus tickets. They've given me thrift store vouchers. . . . This place is really stressful.

Tazia went on to say that some of the rules and constraints on availability of resources within the shelter impeded her ability to search for housing and employment:

> There's structure here at the shelter and that's understandable, but this particular shelter is not as resourceful. The phone is in the office to make your appointments to get business accomplished or whatever. . . . the office is closed the majority of the time. On Tuesdays, the office is totally closed from 11:00 to 5:00. . . . Curfew on Tuesdays and Wednesdays is 5:00 so you have very limited time to get things accomplished.

Moreover, these various logistical and pragmatic needs have to be addressed in a very short time frame, while living in a chaotic environment, without perhaps the necessary wherewithal or skills in self-advocacy. Indeed, it takes time to rebuild the self-esteem and personal efficacy which is so often destroyed within an abusive relationship.

Apart from her own situation, Tazia's frustration about the expectations and time limits within the shelter were offered with reference to her general observation:

> Women that come here are lost. They're so used to being in abusive relationships and controlling relationships and now they're on their own and they're like "Oh my God, what am I going to do?"

Cynthia recognized as much about herself: "I know I'm smart . . . I just don't have a lot of common sense and life skills, but all that comes from just being locked away for so long. I was basically locked in a prison . . . " Reorganizing one's life in 30–90 days was quite a challenge under these circumstances. For the majority of women, the most feasible options were to apply for public assistance that, if awarded, provided cash subsidies, food stamps, child care, and health insurance. For housing, the most feasible option involved applying for the local transitional housing program, which was supported through various grants and administered through one of the other shelters in the area.

The transitional housing program provided a semi-furnished apartment for up to two years, in which time women were given continued assistance with locating work so that they could gradually pay portions of the rent and save for the future. However, as is the case with short-term shelter, space within transitional housing was scarce and so competition for it was fierce. Women who applied for it had to meet strict criteria and, if accepted, continue to live under a form of administrative bureaucracy. Thus, staff at Tami's Place were fairly selective on who they allowed to apply for the program, knowing that only women who were seen as the most "appropriate" (e.g., those who had shown themselves to be able to manage personal affairs, meet deadlines, and obey agency polices) would have a chance at it (Donnelly, Cook, & Wilson, 2004; Ferraro, 1981; Lindsey, 1998; Marvasti, 2002). Samantha was one such resident:

> I can tell I'm doing the right thing because it seems like things are falling into place for me. I've got appointments with all of the different housing companies, I made all the deadlines on time, and it looks like I'm going to have my pick of housing. My job is holding my spot for me till I get my computer back. I've got day care if I go to work. Plus I have my vehicle. I applied for school and it's being fully paid for. And I've learned a lot in my counseling sessions. I'm becoming a completely different person in three weeks. I feel a lot better.

However, even she commented on the difficulty of lining up basic necessities within such a short time frame:

> I think they should lengthen the time. Thirty days is too short to be able to start your life over. After that you have to be able to have applied for housing or having an apartment getting ready for you, you have to have some sort of plan and know when you're going.

For women who did not qualify for transitional housing, particularly those who because of prior criminal records were excluded from many other related social services, time was even more of a concern. Five (26%) of the women had some sort of criminal record, although not all of them had disclosed such to their case-workers so as to hopefully still negotiate their way into transitional housing. Lee, who had a felony record for drug possession, expressed the following:

> There's supposed to be all this help out there. You get in here, you get safe and that's wonderful, and I've gotten better on a lot of things, but now I find out that they can't help me. Where do I go? I have all this ambition. I was going to be able to go to college. I was going to be able to go to a decent job. I was going to be away from all the drugs, all the drug users, all the dysfunctional . . . now to be just slapped in the face. "I'm sorry there's nowhere for you to go." What do you do? Nobody has an answer. It seems like the system is working more against me than for me.

In an even more damaging twist, Lee went on to share her concern about the way in which living in the shelter had broken down many of the "street smarts" she had relied upon in order to survive her abusive relationships and the drug-using milieu, one or the other of which she feared would become her most feasible option after using up her time at the shelter:

> You think going from a dysfunctional to a functional life would be so wonderful, and it is, until you realize that you're caught in the middle. You know dysfunction, you've lived it all your life, and you've been able to see functional but you can't quite get there. They keep closing a door or building another wall for you. You don't want to go back because you know you can't survive there now. I'm scared to death. I know I can't survive on the street now. I just don't see things now because I'm not up to date. So do I stick to my dream and hope and pray that something comes . . . or do I just revert back to my old training and just accept the fact that I'm not going to get anything and try to regroup on the dysfunctional so I can make it?

Indeed women like Lee, despite the best of intentions, seem to be falling through the cracks of the shelter system. The enforcement of prescribed goals and deadlines seemed to do little but facilitate anxiety, disenchantment, and hopelessness. It is no wonder that some of the women were not entirely truthful about their criminal history, just as they were not forthcoming about their mental health or addiction. As Faith admitted, "It's like you have to manipulate the system to get anything out of the system."

DISCUSSION AND CONCLUSION

This chapter examined the lived experiences of women within a domestic violence shelter. Through interviews with 20 women as well as personal observations, this chapter recounted struggles with seeking shelter, adjusting to shelter life, and planning for the future. Framed around the concept of Goffman's (1961) total institution, it is understandable that the women I interviewed opted for shelter as a last means of help-seeking. Prior to seeking shelter, many had disclosed their abuse to friends and family, called the police, worked within the legal system, used various social and victim-based services, and sought medical attention. Even if they had not experienced a shelter in the past, the women seemed to understand the possible ramifications of leaving one's home, neighborhood, children's schools, and perhaps job in order to stay in an institution that relies on the submission and dependency of its "clientele."

Upon recognizing that seeking shelter was a necessary step in trying to end their abuse, the women then recounted struggles in finding space, particularly when they had many children and/or older male children. In this way, before they even had the experience of residing in a shelter, these women learned of the bureaucratic nature of the shelter system, which restricted the size and age of eligible families. For those who found shelter, the next hurdle involved adapting to the shelter environment, which was often chaotic and emotionally challenging. Surviving the shelter experience was complicated by the many rules and policies that restricted their personal autonomy. In this way, the shelter worked as a total institution, relegating the women to a lowly status, contingent upon power differentials among themselves and staff as well as unquestioning submission to shelter policy and programming (Bogard, 1998; Snow & Anderson, 1993; Stark, 1994). Simultaneous and contradictory to the survival skills necessary within this total institution was the pragmatic need for planning independent and self-sufficient lives after the shelter stay (Ferraro, 1981). The women faced great pressure to work out the logistical details regarding housing, employment, education, transportation, and child care within a short time period.

While the intent here is not to lambaste the shelter in which this research was conducted, or the shelter system generally, it is important to recognize some of the shortcomings of this very important outlet for help. It was clear, from their descriptions of seeking shelter and by the myriad of other help-seeking efforts, that the women in this study viewed shelter as one of their last options for assistance. In this regard, shelter plays a pivotal role, beyond providing a temporary respite, in the ways battered women view their future in terms of options and safety. Unfortunately, what some of them learned about the shelter is that it became another form of social control, albeit a nonviolent one, in that in order to stay there they needed to submit to a barrage of rules, policies, deadlines, and bureaucracy. Such an experience may easily add insult to injury in the form of revictimization. Because many had already felt revictimized by various legal and social responses to their situations (Moe, 2007), they may be left with little hope when they face the same from a victim-based program.

Certainly, such negative experiences were not a universal finding—several women did indeed find the kind of support and assistance they needed within the shelter. These women were able to rebuild their lives in ways that allowed them to transition out of the shelter within specified time limits. What is important to recognize here is that these women also tended to fit the categories of "good," "deserving," or "appropriate" clientele (Donnelly et al., 2004; Ferraro, 1981; Lindsey, 1998; Marvasti, 2002), in that they obeyed the rules, did not question the authority of the staff, stayed out of others' business, and acted grateful for what they received. These women also stood good chances at finding employment and housing, particularly because they did not have criminal records, alcohol/drug addictions, or mental illness. They were, in this sense, the ideal client within a total institution—amiable, easy to please, and having a high probability of success (in terms of living safe, independent lives). We are left then to ponder the fate of women who do not fit this mold, who are not only victimized but revictimized and shunned by most if not all of the legal and social responses to battering. It is toward the needs and lived experiences of these women that the current shelter movement, and the violence against women movement in general, must turn with renewed focus and empathy.

Discussion Questions

1. Discuss Goffman's concept of the total institution. How does Moe apply it to the development and operation of domestic violence shelters?
2. What are some of the consequences for the victim of a shelter that resembles a total institution? Give some examples from the reading.
3. What does the author mean by egalitarian institutions? Describe how an egalitarian shelter would be organized. What are the benefits to such an organization?
4. How did residents respond to the problems of finding space and adjusting to shelter life?
5. What are obstacles residents face in struggling with time?

References

Ahrens, L. (1993). Battered women's refuges. In K. Winston & M. Bane (Eds.), *Gender and public policy: Cases and comments* (pp. 304–311). Boulder, CO: Westview.

Arizona Department of Economic Security and Department of Health Services. (2001). *Domestic violence shelter services in Maricopa County.* Phoenix, AZ: Author.

Baker, P. (1997). And I went back: Battered women's negotiation of choice. *Journal of Contemporary Ethnography, 26*(1), 55–74.

Bogard, C. J. (1998). The rhetoric of domination and its strategic use by homeless mothers. *Sociological Spectrum, 18*(3), 229–262.

Borba, M. (2003). *No more misbehavin': 38 difficult behaviors and how to stop them.* San Francisco, CA: Jossey-Bass.

Bush, D. M. (1992). Women's movements and state policy reform aimed at domestic violence against women: A comparison of the consequences of movement mobilization in the U.S. and India. *Gender and Society, 6*, 587–608.

Christopherson, E. R. (1998). *Little people: Guidelines for common sense child rearing* (4th ed.). Overland Press.

Collins, P. H. (1989). The social construction of black feminist thought. *Signs, 14*, 745–773.

Davis, L., & Srinivasan, M. (1994). Feminist research within a battered women's shelter. In E. Sherman & W. Reid (Eds.), *Qualitative research in social work* (pp. 347–357). New York: Columbia University Press.

Dobash, R. E., & Dobash, R. P. (1979). *Violence against wives.* New York: Free Press.

Dobash, R. E., & Dobash, R. P. (1992). *Women, violence, and social change.* London: Routledge.

Donnelly, D. A., Cook, K. J., & Wilson, L. A. (2004). Provision and exclusion: The dual face of services to battered women in three deep south states. *Violence Against Women, 10*, 1015–1035.

Dordick, G. A. (1996). More than refuge: The social world of a homeless shelter. *Journal of Contemporary Ethnography, 24*, 373–404.

Ferraro, K. J. (1981). Processing battered women. *Journal of Family Issues, 2*, 415–539.

Gilman, S. (1988). A history of the sheltering movement for battered women in Canada. *Canadian Journal of Community Mental Health, 7*, 9–21.

Goffman, E. (1961). *Asylums: Essays on the social situation of mental patients and other inmates.* New York: Anchor Books.

Goodyear, S. (2001). Give me shelter. *Ms. Magazine, 11*, 39–41.

Gounis, K. (1992). The manufacture of dependency: Shelterization revisited. *New England Journal of Public Policy, 8*, 685–693.

Hammer, R. (2002). *Antifeminism and family terrorism: A critical feminist perspective (culture and politics).* Lanham, MD: Rowman & Littlefield.

Harding, S. (1987). Is there a feminist method? In S. Harding (Ed.), *Feminism and methodology: Social science issues* (pp. 1–14). Bloomington, IN: Indiana University Press.

Hartsock, N. (1987). The feminist standpoint: Developing a ground for a specifically feminist historical materialism. In S. Harding (Ed.), *Feminism and methodology* (pp. 157–180). Milton Keynes, Great Britain: Open University Press.

Holden, D. (1997). "On equal ground": Sustaining virtue among volunteers in a homeless shelter. *Journal of Contemporary Ethnography, 26*, 117–145.

Johnson, J. M. (1981). Program enterprise and official cooptation in the battered women's shelter movement. *American Behavioral Scientist, 24*, 827–842.

Krane, J., & Davies, L. (2002). Sisterhood is not enough: The invisibility of mothering in shelter practice with battered women. *Affilia, 17*, 167–190.

Kvale, S. (1996). *InterViews: An introduction to qualitative research interviewing.* Thousand Oaks, CA: Sage.

Lindsey, E. W. (1998). The impact of homeless-ness and shelter life on family relationships. *Family Relations, 7*, 243–252.

Lipsky, M. (1980). *Street-level bureaucracy: Dilemmas of the individual in public service.* New York: Russell Sage Foundation.

Lofland, J., Snow, D., Anderson, L., & Lofland, L. H. (2006). *Analyzing social settings: A guide to qualitative observation and analysis* (4th ed.). Belmont, CA: Wadsworth.

Loseke, D. R. (1992). *The battered woman and shelters: The social construction of wife abuse.* Albany: State University of New York Press.

MacKenzie, R. J. (2001). *Setting limits with your strong-willed child: Eliminating conflict by establishing clear, firm, and respectful boundaries.* New York: Random House.

Martin, D. (1976). *Battered wives.* New York: Pocket Books.

Marvasti, A. B. (2002). Constructing the service-worthy homeless through narrative editing. *Journal of Contemporary Ethnography, 31*, 615–651.

Matthews, N. A. (1994). *Confronting rape: The feminist anti-rape movement and the state.* London: Routledge.

Moe, A. M. (2007). Silenced voices and struc-tured survival: Battered women's help-seeking. *Violence Against Women, 13*, 676–699.

Moe, A. M., & Bell, M. P. (2004). Abject economics: The effects of battering on women's work and employability. *Violence Against Women, 10*, 29–55.

Mullender, A. (1997). Domestic violence and social work: The challenge to change. *Critical Social Policy, 17*, 53–78.

National Association of Counsel for Children [NACC]. (2006). *Child maltreatment.* Denver, CO: NACC [On-line]. Retrieved April 13, 2006, from http://naccchildlaw.org/childrenlaw/childmaltreatment.html

National Coalition Against Domestic Violence [NCADV]. (2004). *National directory of domestic violence programs: A guide to com-munity shelter, safe home and service programs.* Denver, CO: NCADV.

Newman, K. D. (1993). Giving up: Shelter experi-ences of battered women. *Public Health Nursing, 10*, 108–113.

Panzer, P. G., Philip, M. B., & Hayward, R. A. (2000). Tends in domestic violence service and leadership: Implications for an integrated shel-ter model. *Administration and Policy in Mental Health, 27*, 339–352.

Reinharz, S. (1992). *Feminist methods in social research.* New York: Oxford University Press.

Roberts, A. R. (1995). *Crisis intervention and time-limited cognitive treatment.* Thousand Oaks, CA: Sage.

Roberts, A. R. (1998). The organization struc-ture and function of shelters for battered women and their children: A national survey. In A. R. Roberts (Ed.), *Battered women and their families: Intervention strategies and treatment programs* (pp. 58–75). New York: Springer.

Roche, S. E., & Sadoski, P. J. (1996). Social action for battered women. In A. R. Roberts (Ed.), *Helping battered women: New perspectives and remedies* (pp. 13–30). New York: Oxford University Press.

Romero, M., & Stewart, A. J. (1999). *Women's untold stories: Breaking silence, talking back, voicing complexity.* New York: Routledge.

Schechter, S. (1982). *Women and male violence: The visions and struggles of the battered women's movement.* Boston, MA: South End Press.

Smith, D. E. (1987). *The everyday world as problematic: A feminist sociology.* Toronto, Canada: University of Toronto Press.

Smith, D. E. (1989). Sociological theory: Methods of writing patriarchy. In R. A. Wallace (Ed.), *Feminism and sociological theory* (pp. 34–64). Newbury Park, CA: Sage.

Snow, D. A., & Anderson, L. (1993). *Down On Their Luck: A Study of Homeless Street People.* Berkeley, CA: University of California Press.

Srinivasan, M., & Davis, L. (1991). A shelter: An organization like any other? *Affilia, 6,* 38–57.

Stark, L. R. (1994). The shelter as "total institution." *American Behavioral Scientist, 37,* 553–562.

Tierney, K. J. (1982). The battered woman movement and the creation of the wife beating problem. *Social Problems, 29,* 207–220.

Wallace, H. (2005). *Family violence: Legal, medical and social perspectives* (4th ed.). Boston, MA: Allyn & Bacon.

Wharton, C. (1989). Splintered visions: Staff/client disjunctions and their consequences for human service organizations. *Journal of Contemporary Ethnography, 18,* 50–71.

Williams, J. C. (1998). Domestic violence and poverty: The narratives of homeless women. *Frontiers: A Journal of Women Studies, 19,* 143–165.

Williams, J. C. (2003). *"A roof over my head": Homeless women and the shelter Industry.* Boulder, CO: University Press of Colorado.

Endnotes

1. Several labels may be used to represent the victimization of women in intimate relationships—these terms often suggest a place, setting, or context for the victimization (e.g., domestic, interpersonal, intimate, relationship, dating/courting), the persons affected (e.g., partner, couple, family, woman, wife), and the actions involved (e.g., abuse, assault, battery, violence, victimization). They may be combined in various ways, according to the context, as well as individual and political preferences, such that terms like "family violence" subsequently refer to the various abuses that may occur within the family unit, whereas "wife abuse" refers explicitly to victimization against women within heterosexual marriage. Alternatively, terms like "woman battering" refer not only to the gendered nature of this victimization, but also recognize a multitude of relationship scenarios. In this chapter I use various terms, often interchangeably, that for the most part are intended to apply to the later context—abuse targeted at women by men or women, within or after marriage, cohabitation, or dating—unless the context of the word requires otherwise.

2. I broach this topic with reservations. My activism against woman battering has remained central to my professional and personal identity. I believe strongly in the utility of victim-centered agencies, and as a formally battered woman, I recognize the importance of having safe places to go and supportive people to talk to, both of which are central to the mission of crisis shelters. However, these facilities are not without problems. Just as unwavering support is vital to the existence of victim-centered agencies, so to is the ability to constructively critique their structure, philosophy, and daily operations. Such is an underlying goal of this chapter.

3. For confidentiality purposes, "Tami's Place" is a pseudonym for the shelter.

CHAPTER 12

IN THEIR OWN WORDS: SHELTER RESIDENTS' EXPERIENCES WITH POLICE

❧

GINA ROBERTIELLO

ABSTRACT

The following chapter summarizes the results of a study on shelter victims in New Jersey, and addresses the commonalities and differences between urban and suburban domestic violence victims who are shelter residents. In particular, police response to these victims was examined. Although the sample was small (30 victims), the findings reveal differences in victim–offender relationship dynamics, as well as the nature and extent of the abuse. Two major reasons for these findings include higher economic dependency and subsequent higher emotional dependency on the batterer by urban victims.

INTRODUCTION

Suzette is a 31-year-old White woman from a New Jersey suburb. The first time she was victimized was in 1995. Her boyfriend hit her when she found him using heroin. Her abuse escalated thereafter and continued for five years. She called the police 20–25 times during this relationship. It finally ended when

> he came home high and proceeded to beat me in the head after I questioned him about charges on my credit cards.

Suzette's interaction with the police was quite positive. They responded every time she called and her abuser was arrested on three occasions, including an arrest for the above-mentioned beating, which brought Suzette to a shelter.

Jessica obtained some assistance from the police. She is a 21-year-old Hispanic woman who was first beaten $2\frac{1}{2}$ years into her relationship. As with many battered women, her boyfriend began physically abusing her once he found out she was pregnant. According to Jessica,

> when he beat me while I was pregnant, I left him. I came back after I had the baby and left for good when he hit me in front of our child.

Jessica, a suburban victim, called the police three to four times, but the police only responded once. Her boyfriend was arrested on this occasion, but this did not deter him from abusing her upon his release.

Keiko was somewhat dissatisfied with the police response to her plight. She is a 22-year-old woman from suburban New Jersey. Her abuse began right after the birth of their child and lasted two years. The incident that brought Keiko to a shelter was when

> he came after me with a bat, tried to choke me, hit me with his fists on the back of my head, and threw me into our door.

The police were called three times during their relationship. Her husband was arrested twice, and she was arrested once when she grabbed him while being beaten and left nail marks on him. At that time, there were no visible signs of abuse on her (Robertiello, 2003).

These are just a few examples of different women with different stories. Their age, race, ethnicity, marital status, and socioeconomic status vary; the severity and type of victimization vary; and the number and type of contact with police also vary. Yet, these women are all survivors of domestic violence.

Their stories are not just sad but are also informative. By obtaining narratives from shelter residents, the differences and similarities in their experiences, particularly with the police response to their situations, can be examined. A set of interview questions were developed and administered to battered women currently living in two different shelters in New Jersey: one located in an urban city in New Jersey and the other located in a suburban neighborhood in New Jersey. Vast differences were expected between the two groups because most residents in the urban area (including domestic violence victims in this area) represent lower socioeconomic status groups than residents of the suburban area. The knowledge gained from these interviews assisted in determining victims' perceptions of the law and assisting police with combating domestic violence, as well as addressing the important critical issues facing police and victims today.

This chapter will review the scope of the domestic violence problem and some factors that influence rates of domestic violence. Mandatory arrest, temporary restraining orders (TROs), and satisfaction with police in general will also be discussed. The methodology used for this research project will be outlined. Detailed information from shelter victims was obtained, and their perceptions will be covered in depth regarding the above-mentioned topics, including their suggestions for improved justice. Finally, discussions of the findings will be summarized.

SCOPE OF THE PROBLEM

Estimates from the National Crime Victimization Survey (NCVS) indicate that about one million violent crimes are committed against persons by current or former spouses, boyfriends, or girlfriends (Catalano, 2006). In 2005, there were 75,651 domestic violence offenses in New Jersey. This represents a 1 percent decrease from 2004. Murders, harassment, false imprisonment, and stalking in New Jersey were also down. The percentage of arrests compared with 2004 decreased by 2 percent, and the number of domestic violence complaints decreased by 4 percent (New Jersey State Police [NJSP], 2005).

When examining New Jersey's domestic violence statistics by offense in 2005, there were 41 homicides, 33,674 assaults, 4,239 terroristic threats, 47 kidnappings, 190 criminal restraints, 35 false imprisonments, 217 sexual assaults, 30,602 harassment offenses, and 306 stalking offenses.

Even though each city/town in New Jersey experienced variations in the number of offenses, it is clear that domestic violence statistics vary greatly by geography. There were more domestic violence incidents and injuries in urban New Jersey than in suburban New Jersey. Furthermore, domestic violence offense data from the Uniform Crime Reports for the last 20 years (1990, 1995, 2000, and 2005) demonstrate a much higher rate of crimes related to domestic violence in urban New Jersey. In New Jersey overall, there were 3,461 domestic violence arrests involving restraining orders (NJSP, 2005).

FACTORS THAT INFLUENCE DOMESTIC VIOLENCE RATES

PROPER PROCEDURE

What factors influence rates of domestic violence? In the early 1990s, domestic violence victims could call police for help without committing themselves to the prosecution process. Today, there have been changes made in local and national response to these calls. Control is often taken away from victims due to pro-arrest policies, which encourage police officers to arrest under certain circumstances. In addition, some states *require* an arrest under certain conditions (mandatory arrest). New Jersey is one of the 22 states that require an arrest if probable cause exists.[1] According to the *New Jersey Police Manual* (2c:25-21), an arrest is required when law enforcement officers find probable cause to believe that domestic violence has occurred. Probable cause can be demonstrated by signs of injury on the victim, if a warrant or restraining order is in effect or if a weapon is believed to have been involved in the commission of the act of domestic violence.

In New Jersey, "warrantless" arrests are allowed for both felony and misdemeanor domestic violence as long as the woman has been beaten, even if no visible signs of injury exist (Buzawa & Buzawa, 1996). However, allowing "warrantless" arrests has not guaranteed that police officers will make that arrest. In fact, many arrest policies nationwide only *encourage* arrest (Hoctor, 1997). Officers can still decide to do nothing regardless of the law or policy in a particular state. However, according to Roberts (2002), it is a myth that police never arrest the batterer because they see domestic violence calls as a private matter. In fact, as of 2001, all 50 states had employed warrantless arrest policies, and there are specialized police domestic violence units, crisis response teams, as well as mandated domestic violence police training, and collaboration among groups (including victim advocates, police, and prosecutors). Thus, there has been an increase in offender accountability in the last few years (Roberts, 2002). Although it has taken years to implement some of the mandatory and pro-arrest policies on the books, recent research shows that 57 percent of domestic violence cases result in arrest (Jones & Belknap, 1999). NCVS research demonstrated that only 20 percent of these cases resulted in an arrest from 1992 to 1996.

In addition, police officers and criminal justice agencies, as well as victims and offenders, will each have various interpretations of the utility of such a law or policy.

There are also different definitions of "success" in a response to battering. For example, should we expect the high standard of deterrence from arresting a batterer when we do not expect this when arresting other criminals (Frisch, 1992)?

MANDATORY ARREST

Studies are mixed as to whether mandatory arrest of the batterer is *effective.* Maxwell, Garner, and Fagan (2001) studied the deterrent effects of arrest and found that arrest of batterers was consistently related to reduced subsequent aggression against female intimate partners. However, results were not statistically significant and the correlation between arrest and repeat offending was modest when compared with the correlation between recidivism and prior criminal record. They did not find an association between arresting the offender and increased risk of subsequent aggression against women (Maxwell et al., 2001).

Interestingly, studies do not find increased levels of satisfaction with higher levels of intervention by police. Some victims do not want their abusers arrested but would prefer a warning instead. Others just want advice, or to scare their partner, rather than have a punitive response (Hoyle, 1998). Yet, Smith (2000) found that 75 percent of women in a shelter supported the adoption of mandatory arrest. More White women supported the *no drop policies* than did Black women.[2] According to Lanza-Kaduce, Greenleaf, and Donahue (1995), victims view abuse as a criminal act, for which the appropriate penalty is arrest and jail. For the current research project, it is interesting to note that the victim responses indicated that mandatory arrest alone does not "work" because (1) not all police enforce the law as it is written, (2) not all women report domestic violence when they are victimized, (3) even when arrested, not all abusers discontinue their abusive behavior, and (4) it disregards the side effects associated with it, such as what to do with the children left in the home.

TEMPORARY RESTRAINING ORDERS

Another "option" to assist women, besides mandatory and pro-arrest policies, includes the use of TROs. Some studies show mixed results on the effectiveness of TROs. Roberts (2002), however, claims that it is a myth that TROs are rarely effective. He says that with the improved technological advances (such as advanced photographic techniques, DNA profiling, computers, and computer-aided investigation and dispatch) as well as automated case-study tracking, which offers a history of the battering offenders and the victim's reported victimization, TROs can be effective. In fact, evidence suggests a significant decline in the probability of abuse following the issuance of a protective order (Carlson, Harris, & Holden, 1999).

Balos and Trotzky (1988) examined the effectiveness of orders of protection in Minnesota. They found that 22 percent of those who obtained an order of protection were named in subsequent police reports of domestic violence. In every misdemeanor case where a not-guilty plea was entered, the case was dismissed. Yet, the authors concluded that for most individuals, an order of protection was an effective means of reducing domestic violence in felony cases. Holmes (1993) found that police officers were more apt to arrest if a TRO was violated, witnesses were present, the assault took place in public, and/or the offender was Black.

Chaudhuri and Daly (1992) found TROs increased police responsiveness. Yet, the chance of a victim being battered again depended upon numerous other characteristics such as the batterer's prior history, employment status, and substance abuse problems. They also found that the victims most likely to obtain restraining orders were younger, achieved a higher level of education and higher income status, and were in the relationship for a shorter period than the victims who did not obtain the restraining orders (Chaudhuri & Daly, 1992). Assessments from the interviewees who actually obtained these orders are discussed within this chapter.

SATISFACTION WITH THE POLICE

As mentioned above, different persons will have different interpretations of police response to a domestic violence call. Findings suggest the same holds true for other contact between the police and the public.[3] It may also lead citizens to decide not to contact the police because of a fear of what the police may do (Robertiello, 2004).

These findings may be interesting to take into account when examining domestic violence victims' perceptions of the police, and what police can do to assist them. Does she believe that the police will make an arrest? Is that her preference? Why would she not want her abuser arrested? These questions can be answered if police and victims are interviewed extensively on their expectations in a domestic violence encounter. The knowledge gained from research of that nature would be helpful at clarifying needs, preferences, and the confusion surrounding these volatile encounters. If police and victims know what is expected of them, they may be more satisfied when interacting with each other.

Interestingly, Coulter, Kuehnle, Byers, and Alfonso (1999) found that victims do describe officers in positive terms. In one study, 66 percent of victims expressed satisfaction with police when interviewed (Martin, 1997a). Others have found that 75 percent of victims thought police were helpful, but over half thought police should have removed the abuser and show more compassion (Yegidis & Renzy, 1994). On the contrary, in another study, many abused women revealed that police were the worst of all authorities they encountered (Erez & Belknap, 1998) (see Box 12.1).

BOX 12.1

FACTORS THAT INFLUENCE DOMESTIC VIOLENCE RATES

Proper criminal justice procedure. All 50 states have warrantless arrests and most states have pro-arrest policies. However, their utility is still being debated.

Mandatory arrest. Studies are mixed as to whether mandatory arrest of the batterer is effective. However, this study emphasizes that mandatory arrest alone does not work.

Temporary restraining orders. Twenty-two percent of those who obtained an order of protection were named in subsequent police reports of domestic violence.

METHODOLOGY

In this study, a set of survey questions was used to assess the experiences of 30 women who had recently been victims of domestic violence. Nineteen women who were residing in a domestic violence shelter in an urban community in New Jersey and 11 women who were residing in a shelter in suburban New Jersey were interviewed. Although the sample was small, the interviews were in-depth, adding to current knowledge on battering. The number of subjects was higher for the urban facility because there are more victims and more residents there. Turnover rates were higher at this shelter, allowing the researcher access to more victims. Further, the administration of the facility was open to allowing the researcher access to support group meetings where rapport was built with subjects through group and individual interaction. After these meetings, an interview schedule for each week was set up, and two victims per day, on average, were interviewed. Interviews lasted about 90 minutes. Occasionally, follow-up appointments were scheduled to clarify information after review of the narratives given by the subjects.

FINDINGS

DESCRIPTION OF FACILITIES

The physical appearance of both shelters varied. The urban shelter, which was located in an inner city, was cramped and furnished with older, worn materials. The suburban shelter, on the other hand, had relatively new furniture and was located in a residential area. The urban shelter offered the researcher a wonderful opportunity for interaction with the residents and the administration. The supervisors were much more open and cooperative than that of the suburban location. The suburban shelter did not allow the researcher to attend group meetings. Instead, an interview schedule was set up for each week through an administrator at the facility. Nevertheless, the volunteer residents at both locations were extremely helpful.

The character and intensity of the interview allowed the researcher to gain an excellent grasp of perceptions and problems experienced by the shelter victims. The questions concerned both the victimization itself and recollections of police response. Interviews were structured in a manner that encouraged in-depth responses and individual comments. Each woman had something unique and interesting to contribute. The results of this study should be useful in helping society and police understand victims and can assist in evaluating and revamping current policies and practices.

ENDING THE ABUSE

Victims were asked specific questions about their abuse including when and for how long the abuse occurred, as well as what particular incident brought them to a shelter. Evidently, the urban women experienced more severe abuse for a longer period of time. Eleven urban victims were abused immediately upon entering into the relationship, or shortly thereafter. Five were abused 18 months to $2\frac{1}{2}$ years into the relationship, and three were victimized between 5 and 9 years into the relationship. Four were beaten when pregnant. Most of the women reported coming to the shelter as a result of constant beatings or experiencing their worst beating at the hands of their abuser. One woman reported having her head cut open, and another reported that her abuser hit her in the head with a rock and threw soda at her. These victims experienced abuse with fists, weapons, and household objects, including workboots and a plaster lamp.

Abuse in the "facial area" seemed common, as the abuser may have wanted to make the victim feel ugly. Some victims reported being cut in the face, having their teeth knocked out, and being cut and/or choked in the neck area. One of the suburban victims, Terry, reported a similar story,

> He slammed the side of my face into the wall, then tried to bite me.

Some of their responses to the question of what incident brought them to this shelter demonstrated the escalation of the abuse. Many stated that the physical abuse began to occur daily, leading them to enter the shelter for protection. Carol stated,

> I was emotionally abused constantly by my husband for seven years-on and off until it increased to every day.

In addition to the frequency of the abuse was a concern about control. For example, Wanda, a 46-year-old Black woman with two sons stated that

> He became extremely controlling and would not let me go to church, threw my Bible and ripped all the phones out and threw the phone at me.

The abuse of the suburban victims ranged from very early on (one week into the relationship) to as late as 10 years into the relationship. The majority were victimized within the first three years of the relationship. Their reasons for leaving the abuser and entering the shelter were similar to the urban victims; the abuse became more frequent and more violent. Most victims were concerned about the safety of their young children, stating that they were fearful for them or that the abuser was beating all of them. Many had been threatened with knives and were mentally abused. However, two said their reason for leaving was *because* they were beaten while pregnant. Gail, a White woman from suburban New Jersey with a newborn daughter, stated,

> He came home breaking and throwing things, and frightened the baby. Jessica, who was pregnant at the time of her abuse, stated,

> I was having my second child and the abuse did not stop, and I was afraid of what would happen after I had the baby.

Janet was an exception to the rule; *he* actually left *her*. As a Black woman with no money or job, she had few options. She was abused for more than five years and had two children with her husband. She explained how her husband had no regard for her feelings and no respect for her. Instead,

> He decided he wanted to live with the woman he was having an affair with. Other than her situation, most of the victims fled in fear of their lives regardless of the geographic location. They also feared for the children or unborn children.

CALLS TO THE POLICE: RESPONSE TIME AND TREATMENT

Interestingly, negative perceptions about response time in general have led some of the victims to not even bother calling the police in the first place. Most of the urban victims claim to have never called the police during an abusive incident or to have only called once or twice. The majority also stated that "others" did not call the police for them. Over one-quarter of the victims called at least three times, and most of the urban victims claimed the police showed up every time they were called (14 of the 16 who called). Some victims did not call the police at all, and only a few victims claimed the police did *not* show up every time they were called. When asked why they did not contact the police, two victims reasoned that the abuse was minor, and one thought there was nothing police (or others) could do to help them.

Almost one-half of the urban victims thought the police responded quickly to their call, and almost one-half of the urban victims were satisfied with the outcome of the encounter. All but one suburban victim was satisfied with the police response time to their calls, as well as with the handling of the situation once they arrived at the scene. However, one-half of the urban victims thought the police took too long to respond (5–10 minutes or more), and were not satisfied with the response time of the officers.

However, most victims felt satisfied with the amount of time it took for police to arrive after the call for assistance. During one incident, the police actually returned to a home five times in one day. In this case, there were two occasions where the boyfriend was not arrested and three occasions in which he was arrested.

Denise, a young Black woman who was being abused for three years, claimed that her boyfriend sometimes knew the responding officer and that the officer would warn him of an impending arrest if the circumstances occurred again or just tell him to hurry up and leave the premises before he would be arrested. One unmarried urban victim, Bea, claimed that police just told her boyfriend to "take a walk." He would then get some alcohol and come back in 30 minutes. She also said,

> He was not scared by the threat of an arrest, and when my boyfriend was not arrested [and was instead just told to leave], he did not listen and returned immediately upon the police leaving the scene.

The abuse actually increased after the police left the scene. One time in particular, the officer said there was "nothing he could do." Even though the victim knew where the perpetrator had fled to, the police did not want to hear it. This was a standard response from the police for a few women. Some of these victims felt that the police could have acted and did not. These victims thought the police might have felt inconvenienced by their situations, or might have been ignorant of the law.

Asia was another victim who was not satisfied with the handling of the situation as it took three to four calls to the police just to get them to respond to her call. She claimed that there was an occasion where police responded to her call, witnessed signs of abuse, and did not make an arrest. Instead,

> They took over an hour to respond and did not even get out of the car or take a report. Police should investigate and get out of the car—make an arrest or at least take the abuser away.

This is a good example of how the law on the books differs from the law in action. Most of the victims interviewed, however, thought the police handled their situation professionally. They arrived in a timely manner (within minutes) and followed procedure: by seeing signs of abuse and making an arrest. According to Denise,

> The police did not take my situation serious enough—they saw him as a victim too.

For Tawanda, the situation police put her through was much more negative.

> They told me they would not come back again because I kept dropping charges against him. The police actually threatened to arrest me if I called them again. They took their time arriving and even told me I must like getting beat if I stay with him.

Kennedy and Homant (1983) found battered women were more satisfied with female officers who responded to the call for assistance than male officers. Studies also suggest that female officers are more likely to arrest the abuser. Interestingly, one of the urban interviewees from the current study commented that a victim should be allowed to choose the gender of the responding officer because she felt female police officers were more supportive of her. Monique was a 23-year-old Black victim from urban New Jersey. She was extremely open and vocal about her situation and made some interesting observations,

> Only the female police officer was helpful in dealing with my situation. She automatically arrested him when she saw visible signs of abuse and did not judge me. When a white, male police officer responds, I feel embarrassed for my race.

According to Lanza-Kaduce et al. (1995), most interviewed victims do not believe their problems with abuse will be solved effectively by the criminal justice system. Many of the urban and suburban victims in the current study felt similarly. According to Huda, "Arrest is not the best way to deter abuse because they just come back angrier."

Anna, a Hispanic 26-year-old victim who was abused for one year by her boyfriend stated the outcome as follows, "Arrest will not stop him in the long run, but it is the best response in the short run." Other victims felt similarly. Suzy said, "It is only a quick fix to the situation for that moment." Tara, a 21-year-old, Black single mother and college student agreed, "If they do it once, they will do it again." According to Sharon, who was a 36-year-old victim, abused for two years, and married since 1997,

> Arrest did not and has not prevented my dangerous situation from continuing. In my case, it further angered him and put more blame on me.

Yet, other assessments of arrest were more positive. According to Keiko, a Korean victim with two children,

> It is good that he was arrested because it is the law, but there is a huge backlash from the Korean culture. They do not believe in domestic violence or the shelter system.

Nancy concurred,

> They showed up quickly, made a radio call to try to locate him (the abuser) and went beyond their call of duty.

For most of the urban victims who called the police, the outcome of the police response was an arrest. In fact, most of these victims expected the police to make an arrest. Thus, most urban victims did not feel that there was a discrepancy between what they expected from the police and what the police did during their encounter. However, on seven occasions, the parties were separated, and on five occasions, the parties were only advised.

Just under one-half of the suburban victims expected the police to arrest their abuser. However, a few expected a warning or separation, and a few did not know what they expected. One only hoped to be taken out of the abusive situation. The majority of the suburban victims felt there was no discrepancy between what they expected the police to do and what the police actually did when they arrived at the scene.

When victims thought the police should have acted differently than they did, there were numerous explanations for the discrepancy. Some women accepted some of the blame, admitting to hitting their abusers back (and were subsequently arrested along with their partners). Others felt that the police did not care about them, that the police did not want to fill out the paperwork, or that the police sided with the abuser. Rochelle, a White suburban victim, thought the police did not make an arrest because "There were no visible signs of battering on either of us." Patricia thought they did not make an arrest because "I did not show them any signs of battering."

Clearly, some of these victims did not blame police for the discrepancy between what they expected the police to do and what they actually did. Some thought the police simply did not have the proper information and some took on part of the blame themselves for not revealing the entire story to the police. According to Sharon,

They were looking for every sign to try to make an arrest of him.

Interestingly, the majority of both urban and suburban victims thought the police were somewhat or even very helpful during their encounter. In fact, all but one suburban victim thought police were following the requirements of the law. However, only one-half of urban victims thought police were following the law.

Although some victims believed that mandatory arrest laws should be enforced, they still did not feel that their abusers would be deterred with arrest (at least not for long). Further, the majority of both sets of victims did *not* believe that *mandatory arrest* worked. In general, some victims believed abuse gets worse after an arrest (and eventual release from jail) because the abuser comes back for revenge. According to some victims, the abuse continues after the abuser is released from jail, and most abusers are not afraid of the law. Mandatory arrest only works if "bruises are on the face. I had them on my back, but it didn't matter." Nancy said it works only if

The man is arrested right away, because it gives the victim time to get away and get help.

UTILITY OF RESTRAINING ORDERS

When the urban and suburban victims were asked about the utility of retraining orders, there were some interesting (and some disheartening) responses. For example, one shelter claimed that after experiencing three years of beatings, she obtained a restraining order that works to stop the violence.

Sixteen of the 19 urban victims and all of the suburban victims obtained TROs. Yet, less than one-third of all victims actually found them effective. Six victims in total came directly to the shelter, so they were unable to determine whether the restraining orders worked for them in particular. According to Monique, obtaining the TRO was not effective. As a young Black woman, she felt the courts would not or could not help her. She was 23 years old at the time of the abuse and decided not to pursue the matter even though her abuser continued to accost her:

> He still came near me and I never went to court to finalize the restraining order.

Yolanda and Tawanda stated that their abusers were still harassing them or trying to get in touch with them. Tara said,

> The TRO was dismissed because the judge said I could not substantiate the domestic violence against me.

For Jessica, the TRO was "effective for a while, but then I dropped it." According to Wanda,

> He still comes near me and I see him from the shelter when I leave during the day.

These findings are very alarming, indicating that the abuser can locate these victims at the shelter and that the victims can never really feel safe. The idea of a shelter or safe house is to provide a safe and secure location for victims. Yet, many of the urban victims have stated that the location of the shelter is not a secret. This knowledge can only work to increase feelings of fear on the part of the victim and feelings of omnipotence on the part of the abuser. He can still control her even when she is supposed to be protected from him.

Thus, even after obtaining a TRO, some victims continued to be harassed. In fact, upon their abusers' release from jail, many victims claimed that they came directly back to them. Keiko said, "he violated the TRO right away—outside the courtroom." In Suzy's experience,

> He still came in the house, but I did not call the police because he cut off the phone.

Tonya put some of the onus on the police who respond to the call for assistance stating that

> They should explain the TRO and the choice of going to a shelter.

Of the urban victims who obtained the TRO, just under one-third claimed that the abuser did not subsequently violate it. Almost two-thirds claimed their abusers continued to contact them but that they did not tell the police.

Margie said he did not contact her, but *did* contact her friends and family. Terry stated,

> The TRO is just a piece of paper—he returned, I changed the locks, called the police, but he always left before the police arrived.

Nancy stated,

> He thought he was invincible. He would come over, get arrested, but [get] out the next day and harass me again.

The majority of urban and suburban victims said that the restraining order was easy to obtain. Jessica, however, got the runaround because

> Some of the abuse occurred in another town, and (town) did not want to issue the TRO due to this fact.

On the contrary, the suburban victims had little trouble with their abusers violating the TRO. It was the *urban* victims who claimed their abuser was not deterred by the restraining order. Further, because many did not tell police about the violations, the unrecorded frequency of violations is probably much higher making the effectiveness of restraining orders questionable for this group of victims.

In fact, of the 27 victims in this study who obtained TROs, only 5 urban and 3 suburban victims said it actually stopped the abuser from coming around. Patty claimed,

> The restraining order was effective because he knew all I had to do was call the police.

Lisa concurred,

> He has had no contact with me after I got the TRO.

It is interesting to note that Forell (1990) found that protective orders give women a false sense of hope. The orders have been ignored by batterers and by the police. Hoctor (1997) found that law enforcement officials often fail to arrest and prosecute batterers even when the victim has a TRO. Erez and Belknap (1998) found TROs to be largely unenforced and ineffective. On the basis of these results, they appear to be less effective than anticipated. Overall, most victims in this exploratory study did not believe TROs would deter their abuser.

DUAL ARREST AND PERCEPTIONS

Does fighting back in a life or death situation lead to dual arrest? Police officers sometimes feel obligated to arrest both parties if they cannot determine the identity of the "primary aggressor." Dual arrest is more common than most authorities realize, especially when police arrive at a scene and both parties show signs of injury. The state of Washington, for example, reported a dual arrest rate of 50 percent. Increased arrest of women becomes a deterrent to victims seeking police assistance. It may also reinforce their isolation and belief that no resources are available for them (Martin, 1997a).

For example, Bea, who was beaten for more than seven years of her relationship, admitted to picking up a knife when her boyfriend was about to beat her again. When the police arrived on the scene, they found her holding the knife and arrested both of them. Yolanda, who had an abusive boyfriend with drug problems and a criminal record, elaborated,

Him and some guys were on the porch—I mouthed off and he hit me and I hit him back. Then he hit me in the back of the head with his gun.

These are just two examples where the victim becomes the criminal when she fights back. Dual arrest may hurt the victim further by causing a loss of child custody and labeling to occur (Zorza, 1994).

Walker (1984) suggested that women, especially Black women, have often been misperceived as being angry and personally threatening. In addition, women are more inclined to use a weapon because of their weaker physical strength. Mandatory arrest has led to increased racial oppression, and increased incarceration of Blacks in general. It has also led to state controls over family relationships, which strengthens patriarchy from which feminists try to free themselves (Ruttenberg, 1994). It removes the power from the victim and may deter them from calling police because they do not want their spouse arrested (Gelles, 1993; Lyon, 1999; Ruttenberg, 1994). Further, arrest alone does not deter domestic violence from recurring (Binder & Meeker, 1992). This finding may be why Black victims are less satisfied with the police.

OFFENDER CHARACTERISTICS

According to the interviewed victims, the urban abuser was most likely to be a boyfriend, whereas the suburban abuser was more likely to be a husband. Comparatively, six urban abusers were husbands and four suburban abusers were boyfriends. Although one victim was beaten by an uncle (a one-time event) and one was beaten by a group of friends, for the majority of victims, the abuse was *not* a one-time event. Most urban victims said their abuse occurred for up to a year, and many said the abuse lasted for 2–5 years. For four victims, the abuse continued for 9–16 years, and for two victims, the abuse continued for over 18 years. One victim was abused for 30 of the 35 years of her marriage. Most of the suburban abuse lasted 3–5 years, and many said the abuse lasted for 1–2 years. However, one victim's abuse lasted for 7 years, and two victims experienced abuse for 13 years.

Thirteen of the 19 urban victims and 6 of the 11 suburban victims claimed their abusers were under the influence of alcohol at the time of the abuse. This finding supports the contention that many abusers are under the influence when they abuse, although this certainly does not cause, explain, or excuse their behavior (Zubretsky, 2002). For many, the mental abuse occurred on a daily basis and the physical abuse occurred whenever the abuser was drunk or high.

Almost one-quarter of the urban abusers, and almost one-third of suburban abusers, had a criminal history, and spent time in prison for their criminality. Two urban and two suburban batterers spent time in drug rehabilitation (for cocaine, marijuana, and heroin abuse). Fourteen urban abusers were Black, three were White, and two were Hispanic. Four suburban abusers were Black, five were White, and two were Asian.

Interestingly, the breakdown of abuser employment status was split quite evenly within the urban location: just over one-third were unemployed at the time of the battering incident, just under one-third were employed part-time, and just under one-third were employed full-time. Jobs ranged from manual laborers to computer programmers. One abuser was a pastor and one was a medical technician. On the contrary, in the suburban location, just over one-quarter were unemployed at the time of the battering incident, just under one-quarter were employed part-time, and just over one-half were employed full-time. Their jobs ranged from computer consultants and supervisors to manual laborers (construction and paving). One was a chef, one was a minister, and one was a State Trooper. Thus, it appears that the typical abuser (regardless of location) has a criminal history, but that race and employment status of the abuser vary by location.

As interesting as these findings are, it is most fascinating that one abuser was a State Trooper. Some statistics do show that domestic abuse is high in law enforcement due to the stress of the job and the "connections" officers have. They can probably get away with abuse more easily because they represent the law and usually have friends that will cover for them.

CHILDREN PRESENT: PERCEIVED INFLUENCE

All of the urban victims had at least one child and most had two. One victim actually had six children. Interestingly, most of them did not feel that their children influenced their decision to leave the abuser. All but one suburban victim had children. Most had one child, and one had four children. Interestingly, all but one of them thought their children influenced the decision to get out of the battering relationship. It appears children play an important role in the results of the encounter. Huda, a Hispanic mother of three young children, thought, "The police did not want to take us both in because we had children."

Many have been in battering relationships for most of their lives. Yet, almost one-half of the interviewed urban victims left for the first time. Almost one-third left either one or two times, and three victims left their abuses three or more times before. Three suburban victims never left their abusers until entering the shelter, and three left between one and two times. Two victims left three times and the other two suburban victims claimed to have left their abusers 20 and 30 times, respectively.

Although most women were victimized by their domestic partner, some claimed that their first batterer was their father. Some said their mothers were also beaten in the home. One victim was physically abused by her mother and sexually abused by her father. Many of these victims were abused in one relationship only to get out and into another abusive relationship. Much of the abuse also seemed to coincide with the pregnancy of the victim. This is a common finding because batterers often feel jealous of the growing baby or jealous of the attention the woman pays to her own belly.

One interesting comment that documents the severity of victimization and its effects on children came from Terry, who said,

Once is enough, get out as soon as possible and think about your kids.

CONCLUSIONS

After interviewing urban and suburban victims in New Jersey, what has been learned about a victim's experience? Most of the urban victims were Black women who were victimized by Black men. The abusers were often under the influence of drugs or alcohol while battering, and were most violent when the woman became pregnant.

Most abusers were not deterred by a TRO or an arrest. In general, the urban victims were battered for months to years before they were able to leave and many went back to their abuser after leaving the shelter. Police constantly received calls at the same locations numerous times per month and sometimes numerous times per day from these victims.

The urban victims were slightly less likely to call the police, obtain a TRO, or tell the police when their abusers violated it. They were slightly less likely to say police responded every time they were called and slightly less satisfied with the police response than were suburban victims. They were also more likely to say they never left their abusers before and more likely to believe mandatory arrest does not work (while a slight majority of suburban victims also did not believe mandatory arrest worked). Again, the definition of "success" needs more exploration when comparing views of the victims.

These victims were slightly different from the suburban victims. All suburban victims said they easily obtained TROs (not all of the urban victims did). Most of their injuries were less severe with abuse lasting for a shorter period of time, and beginning later into the relationship. Yet, individual victims from each area were more likely to have been beaten when pregnant, and all were likely to experience numerous incidents of abuse during their relationships.

The suburban abusers were more likely to be husbands than boyfriends, and their relationships were less likely to last long after the abuse began (up to 13 years vs. up to 30 years for the urban victims). The abusers were slightly less likely to be under the influence of alcohol during the battering incident, and the police showed up every time they were called. All suburban victims called the police at least once. Some urban victims never called the police at all.

Most urban and suburban victims were satisfied with the police handling of their situation and with the time it took police to respond. In addition, most said no "other" individual called the police if they did not call themselves. The outcome was most likely to be an arrest or separation for the suburban victims (as opposed to an arrest for the urban victims), and that was their preference. The urban victims were more likely to expect an arrest and to get one. This finding speaks volumes about victim preferences and a police officer's likelihood of listening to the victim. Both groups expected (and received) an arrest more often than any other response. However, suburban victims were almost as likely to expect a separation and to obtain that result.

If there was a discrepancy between what the women expected and what happened, the urban victims were more likely to express reasons that were extra-legal (i.e., their abuser was not arrested because he was a friend of the police officer, or the perception that the officer was being lazy). The suburban victims were more likely to believe legal factors precluded officers from making an arrest (i.e., not seeing visible signs of injury on either party).

The majority of both sets of women agreed that mandatory arrest in general did not deter the batterer. However, all but one of the suburban victims was likely to believe police were following this law. Only one of the suburban victims saw an occasion where police did not follow the law when witnessing signs of abuse, while three of the urban victims did. Only one-third of the urban victims thought mandatory arrest keeps the batterer away, whereas almost one-half of the suburban victims said mandatory arrest works.

Both groups experienced dual arrest and were victimized by abusers of various employment statuses. The jobs of the abusers ranged from working class positions to white-collar positions. However, the suburban abusers were more likely to be employed full-time, and the urban abusers were more likely to be unemployed. Thus, the assumption that there would be a difference between the abusers from urban and suburban areas regarding employment status was supported.

Interestingly, most victims (especially suburban victims) thought police followed the law. Most had mixed feelings on whether arrest was the best way to deter abuse, and most victims did not believe there was a discrepancy between what they expected from an encounter and the actual outcome. Alcohol abuse by the abuser was common for both sets of abused women, and rates of drug rehabilitation and criminal history of the abuser were also similar. Both sets of victims thought programs (in addition to arrest) were needed to deter and assist the abuser, and most had children. The urban victims tended to have more children and to be less likely to believe that having children affected their decision to leave. All but one suburban victim thought that having children did affect the decision to leave, and one did not have any children.

DISCUSSION AND LIMITATIONS

Although this was a pilot study with 30 subjects, several findings in the literature such as negative perceptions of police by poor inner-city residents and positive views of the police by suburban middle-class residents are supported by this research. Thus, perceptions of the police as well as treatment by them may be correlated with actual treatment during a domestic violence incident. Further, due to negative perceptions by minorities and members of poor inner-city areas, the victims, witnesses, and bystanders appear less likely to involve police, causing the victimization to occur for a longer period of time and causing it to escalate. Additionally, most of the urban residents (and domestic violence victims in this area) represented lower socioeconomic status groups than the suburban residents. This probably limits their opportunities to get out and affects their overall perceptions of the effectiveness of law enforcement. Some studies also pointed out that Black women are more likely to be perceived as angry due to racial oppression, which may cause the police to act differently toward them. Because more minorities have less money and fewer options, they may be less satisfied with police services. They are also less likely to seek TROs and more likely to cohabitate with their abuser, which may cause them to remain with a batterer for a longer period of time, be more financially and emotionally dependent, and be more at risk for severe abuse.

On the contrary, White women are less likely to cohabitate, more likely to support no drop policies, and more likely to be satisfied with police services in general. TROs are more likely to be obtained by higher educated and higher income victims, who are more likely to be nonminorities, and more likely to live in suburban areas.

However, many victims of domestic violence believed that the police who responded to them had followed the law, and most believed mandatory arrest and TROs were not panaceas. Further research is needed on a representative sample of the 2,000 shelters nationwide (at least 5 shelters from each of the 12 federal regions of the United States), and perceptions of shelter directors, residents, and police should be included.

CLEAR POLICY/CONNECT WITH VICTIM ADVOCATES

From the start, police need clear and concise information about the situation they are about to encounter. Dispatchers should notify an officer of the history behind each case (i.e., have the police been to this residence before, has a TRO been issued). This knowledge will probably cause officers to take the situation more serious and increase their likelihood of arresting or at least pursuing the alleged perpetrator.

Most research demonstrates the importance of measuring repeat victimization and statistical data. It has been suggested that an attempt be made to bridge police departments and crisis response teams so all victims can directly contribute to the body of knowledge on perceptions/expectations and how to better handle domestic violence situations. This information will allow statisticians to assess the impact of particular police response to the outcome of cases. This researcher is currently examining local crisis response teams and specialized domestic violence units to assist in bridging this gap.

Coordinated community response teams can also be utilized. These teams bring victims, advocates, and members of the community together to develop strategies, policies, and procedures that focus on the dynamics and prevalence of domestic violence and establish ways to end abuse (Roberts & Kurst-Swanger, 2002). However, the public needs to be educated on the realistic limits of police officer abilities and responsibilities. This is where Civilian Police Academy programs may fit in.

Most importantly, the voices of the victims must be heard. Many victims do not believe mandatory arrest works well enough. Victim input is needed to create policy, change police behavior, and improve the criminal justice system's response to their plight.

Discussion Questions

1. Describe the scope of domestic violence in the United States. Discuss the factors that influence domestic violence arrests. Discuss recent trends influencing arrest according to the research.
2. Examining research on satisfaction with the police, discuss what has been the overall response to police.
3. Reflecting on the overall research, discuss the predominant reasons why shelter victims end the abuse.
4. How did shelter victims feel about TROs? Were they likely to obtain them? Did they have problems having TROs enforced by the police?
5. What does the author mean by dual arrests? What are the consequences of dual arrests for domestic violence victims?

References

Balos, B., & Trotzky, K. (1988). Enforcement of the domestic abuse act in Minnesota: A preliminary study. *Law and Inequality, 6*, 83–125.

Binder, A., & Meeker, J. (1992). Arrest as a method to control spouse abuse. In E. S. Buzawa & C. G. Buzawa (Eds.), *Domestic violence: The changing criminal justice response* (pp. 129–140). Westport, CT: Greenwood Publishing Group.

Buzawa, E. S., & Austin, T. (1993). Determining police response to domestic violence victims: The role of victim preference. *American Behavioral Scientist, 36*, 610–623.

Buzawa, E. S., & Buzawa, C. G. (Eds.). (1996). *Do arrest and restraining orders work?* Thousand Oaks, CA: Sage.

Carlson, M. J., Harris, S. D., & Holden, G. W. (1999). Protective orders and domestic violence. *Journal of Family Violence, 4*, 205–226.

Catalano, S. (2006). *Criminal victimization, 2005.* Washington, D.C.: U.S. Department of Justice, Office of Justice Programs, Bureau of Justice Statistics. Retrieved May 26, 2008, from http://www.ojp.usdoj.gov/bjs/pub/pdf/cv05.pdf

Chaudhuri, M., & Daly, D. (1992). Do restraining orders help? In E. S. Buzawa & C. G. Buzawa (Eds.), *Domestic violence: The changing criminal justice response* (pp. 227–252). Westport, CT: Greenwood Publishing Group.

Coulter, M. L., Kuehnle, K., Byers, R., & Alfonso, M. (1999). Police-reporting behavior and victim-police interactions as described by women in a domestic violence shelter. *Journal of Interpersonal Violence, 14*, 1290–1298.

Erez, E., & Belknap, J. (1998). In their own words: Battered women's assessment of the criminal processing system's response. *Violence and Victims, 13*, 251–268.

Forell, C. (1990). Stopping the violence: Mandatory arrest and police tort liability for failure to assist battered women. *Berkeley Women's Law Journal, 6*, 215–262.

Frisch, L. A. (1992). Research that succeeds, policies that fail. *Northwestern University School of Law, 83*, 209–216.

Gelles, R. J. (1993). Constraints against family violence: How well do they work? *American Behavioral Scientist, 36*, 575–586.

Hoctor, M. (1997). Domestic violence as a crime against the state: The need for mandatory arrest in California. *California Law Review, 85*, 643–700.

Holmes, W. M. (1993). Police arrests for domestic violence. *American Journal of Police, 12*, 101–125.

Hoyle, C. (1998). *Negotiating domestic violence.* New York: Oxford University Press.

Jones, D. A., & Belknap, J. (1999). Police response to battering in a progressive pro-arrest jurisdiction. *Justice Quarterly, 16*, 249–273.

Kennedy, D. B., & Homant, R. J. (1983). Attitudes of abused women toward male and female police officers. *Criminal Justice and Behavior, 10*, 391–405.

Lanza-Kaduce, L., Greenleaf, R. G., & Donahue, M. (1995). Trickle-up report writing: The impact of a proarrest policy for domestic disturbances. *Justice Quarterly, 12*, 525–542.

Lyon, A. D. (1999). Be careful what you wish for: An examination of arrest and prosecution patterns of domestic violence cases in two Michigan cities. *Michigan Law Journal of Gender & Law, 5*, 253–298.

Martin, M. E. (1997a). Double your trouble: Dual arrest in family violence. *Journal of Family Violence, 12*, 139–157.

Martin, M. E. (1997b). Policy promise: community policing and domestic violence victim satisfaction. *Policing: An International Journal of Police Strategies & Management, 20*, 519–531.

Maxwell, C. D., Garner, J. H., & Fagan, J. A. (2001). *The effects of arrest on intimate partner violence: New evidence from the spouse assault replication program.* National Institute of Justice.

New Jersey State Police [NJSP]. (2005). *Crime in New Jersey: 2005 uniform crime report.* Retrieved May 20, 2008, from http://www.njsp.org/info/ucr2005/pdf/2005-ucr.pdf.

Robertiello, G. M. (2003). Victim perceptions of the utility of domestic violence arrests and temporary restraining orders. In A. R. Roberts (ed.) *Critical issues in crime and justice* (2nd ed., pp. 176–183). Thousand Oaks, CA: Sage Publications.

Robertiello, G. M. (2004). *Police and citizen perceptions of police power.* Lewiston, NY: The Edwin Mellen Press.

Roberts, A. R. (2002). *Handbook of domestic violence intervention strategies.* Oxford University Press.

Roberts, A. R., & Kurst-Swanger, K. (2002). Police response to battered women. In A. R. Roberts (Ed.), *Handbook of domestic violence intervention strategies* (pp. 101–126). New York: Oxford University Press.

Ruttenberg, M. H. (1994). A feminist critique of mandatory arrest: An analysis of race and gender in domestic violence policy. *Journal of Gender and the Law, 2*, 171–199.

Smith, A. (2000). It's my decision, isn't it? a research note on battered women's perceptions of mandatory intervention laws. *Violence Against Women, 6,* 1384–1402.

Walker, L. (1984). *The battered woman syndrome.* New York: Springer.

Yegidis, B. L., & Renzy, R. B. (1994). Battered women's experiences with a preferred arrest policy. *Affilia, 9,* 60–70.

Zorza, J. (1994). Women battering: High costs and the state of the law. *Clearinghouse Review, 28,* 382–395.

Zubretsky, T. M. (2002). Promising directions for helping chemically-involved battered women get safe and sober. In A. R. Roberts (Ed.), *Handbook of domestic violence intervention strategies* (pp. 321–342). New York: Oxford University Press.

Endnotes

1. AK, AZ, CO, CT, DC, IA, KS, LA, ME, MS, MO, NJ, NY, OH, OR, RI, SC, SD, UT, VA, WA, and WS.
2. New Jersey does not have a *no-drop policy*, so this is not an issue for the current study.
3. For example, Robertiello (2004) examined perceptions of the police in Newark, New Jersey, and determined that police and citizens do not have similar perceptions of what action police will take in a street encounter. Citizens thought police would be more intrusive than police thought they would be and expected particular demographic and situational characteristics (of police and suspects) to influence the outcome of an encounter. Yet, police officers did not believe those factors would be as influential in their own decision making. She concluded that citizens believed police would be tougher on citizens than the police really would be. This "attitude" may bias citizens' opinion of the police and lead to the expectation that police will abuse their powers in all encounters.

CHAPTER 13

"I DON'T THINK A COP HAS EVER ASKED ME IF I WAS OK": BATTERED WOMEN'S EXPERIENCES WITH POLICE INTERVENTION

Hillary Potter

ABSTRACT

This chapter examines battered Black women's perceptions of and experiences with police involvement in intimate partner violence (IPV) calls. This study analyzes the in-depth interviews of the participants' (1) perceptions of police and the criminal justice system, particularly as they concern race relations and relations with police in the United States and (2) use of police intervention for IPV occurrences. Factors such as Black culture, the Black community's relationship with police agents/agencies, and sociostructural impacts were found to affect the participants' views of police involvement and their reactions to this form of battering intervention, which were overwhelmingly negative. The implications of Black women's intersecting identities, stereotypical views of Black women, and police intervention used by battered Black women are discussed.

INTRODUCTION

Based on a variety of crime data sources, the overall rate of intimate partner violence (IPV) in the United States is presently lower than it was decades ago. Several explanations have been cited for this decrease, including improvement in police intervention methods for IPV incidents (Belknap, 2007; Dugan, Nagin, & Rosenfeld, 1999). Increased acknowledgment among police and lawmakers that IPV is a *crime* has resulted in greater oversight of the police in their responses to IPV; however, the ostensible advancement in the formal social control of IPV has not necessarily produced overwhelming satisfaction among battered Black[1] women. Several studies continue to demonstrate that, in general, African Americans are less satisfied with policing in their communities than their White counterparts (Hurst, McDermott, & Thomas, 2005; Smith, Steadman, Minton, & Townsend, 1999; Weitzer & Tuch, 2005a, 2005b). Although it has been established that the reporting rate of IPV to police is higher among Black women in comparison with White women (Bachman & Coker, 1995; Catalano, 2006; McFarlane, Willson, Malecha, & Lemmey, 2000; Rennison & Welchans, 2000),[2] Black women often remain suspect of those working in the criminal justice system and believe that what is in their best interest is not seriously considered. Many battered Black women frequently feel as though they are ignored by public agents who can assist them with their substandard relationships and other life dilemmas (Richie, 1996). Further, "[g]iven that white police officers are likely to be similar to the general white population in their racial views, it is likely that the majority hold negative stereotypes of African Americans" (Bolton & Feagin, 2004, p. 15). Consequently, assistance provided by police (and other system representatives) to victims of IPV has failed to result in parity, with African American women often not being afforded the same aid as that given to White women (Ammons, 1995; Robinson & Chandek, 2000).

Although there has been an increased amount of academic attention devoted to the experiences of battered Black women, particularly during the past decade, there remains a need to advance the field of IPV research by specifically seeking explanations for the disproportionate contact with the criminal justice system and the higher rates of IPV among African Americans. Accordingly, this chapter serves to supplement the extant research using a narrative approach that adds voice and nuance to aid in clarifying the inconsistency between high police reporting rates and low trust in police intervention among battered Black women. This investigation considers the perceptions and experiences of a group of African American women who were confronted with abuse from their male intimate partners and their dilemma of seeking ways to combat the abuse. The women's responses to IPV and the use—or lack thereof—of the police were vastly affected by the women's intersectional identities and life experiences as *African American* women as exacerbated by cultural and sociostructural dynamics.

RACE, GENDER, AND CLASS FACTORS IN POLICE INTERVENTION OF IPV

A substantial amount of research has resulted in specifying trends in the types of individuals who are most likely to utilize police to assist with controlling the violent behavior of their intimate partners and the responses by police personnel when they are called to intervene in these cases. Many of these investigations have determined variations by gender, race, or socioeconomic status, with some studies incorporating an *intersectional* analysis of these categories. A myriad of existing literature is available on reporting rates, circumstances surrounding arrests, effects of arrests, and the satisfaction experienced among women victims who consider these demographic factors (see Box 13.1).

REPORTING RATES

The many forms of advocacy around violence against women during the past 35 years have situated women to feel more comfortable and safer in speaking out against the abuse they face. Reports of IPV made to the police increased for women (and men) between 1993 and 2004, and women victims of IPV are more likely to contact the

---

BOX 13.1

INTERSECTIONALITY AND DOMESTIC VIOLENCE

Existing research reveals that issues of gender, race, and class, either separately or in an intersecting manner, do indeed affect how victims of IPV use police and how police react in these situations.

---

police than male victims (Catalano, 2006).[3] However, several factors still hinder women's ability to contact the police for assistance. Shame of being a "battered woman" often prevents women from calling the police after being abused by their intimate partners (Few, 2005). Catalano's (2006) examination of the National Crime Victimization Survey (NCVS) data determined that the most frequent rationale for not contacting the police is the belief that IPV is a private or personal matter, with more men (41.1%) than women (27.4%) citing this as a reason. Female victims also frequently indicated that fear of retaliation (15.2%) and wanting to protect the perpetrator (11.9%) prevented them from contacting the police. Though fear of retaliation by the batterers is a concern among battered women who call the police, in their analysis of NCVS data for 1992–2002, Felson, Ackerman, and Gallagher (2005) did not find evidence that batterers retaliate against their victims, even if police intervention resulted in an arrest. The three NCVS reasons for not contacting the police that were related specifically to *police* behavior garnered fewer positive affirmations by female respondents than other factors, (1) police will not do anything, 5.6 percent; (2) police ineffectiveness, 2.8 percent; and (3) police bias, 2.1 percent (Catalano, 2006; see also Fleury, Sullivan, Bybee, & Davidson, 1998; Tjaden & Thoennes, 2000).

Felson et al.'s (2005) 11-year review of NCVS data established that 56.5 percent of IPV victims (female and male) reported their victimization, with 22.2 percent of the reports resulting in arrest of the batterer (female and male). Another analysis of the NCVS data estimated that 53 percent of women IPV victims of all races from 1993 to 1998 notified police of their victimization, compared with 46 percent of male IPV victims (Rennison & Welchans, 2000). Concerning socioeconomic class, women victims who are at poverty level are significantly more likely to want their abusers arrested than those in higher classes (Hirschel & Hutchison, 2003; Jasinski, 2003). Additional research has found that women in higher socioeconomic classes prefer not to utilize the police (Erez & Belknap, 1998).

When distinguished by race, battered Black women have been found to be more likely to officially report their victimizations than White women (Bachman & Coker, 1995; McFarlane et al., 2000; Rennison & Welchans, 2000). The NCVS data reveal that from 1993 to 2004, 66.4 percent of Black women victims reported to police the violence perpetrated against them, compared with 53.6 percent of White women and 59.8 percent of Native American, Asian American, and Pacific Islander women combined (Catalano, 2006). Research in the area of policing intervention in IPV by race has also focused on the *desires* of women victims regarding the arrest of their batterers. Although many women may call the police to intervene, as demonstrated above, this does not necessarily mean that the women wish their batterers to be arrested once the police arrive. In concurrence with the police contact data from the NCVS, Black women victims were more likely than White female victims to want their batterers arrested (Hirschel & Hutchison, 2003; Jasinski, 2003). Hollenshead, Dai, Ragsdale, Massey, and Scott (2006) discovered that African Americans sought out police intervention more often than they sought social service interventions at a family violence center when both of these options were made available. The opposite was found among Whites in the study (i.e., a preference to use nonpolice services), with Black victims having sought assistance from the police four times more than Whites. Hollenshead et al. conclude that the difference in preference is likely due to African Americans being less aware of nonpolice services available to assist in combating IPV and the greater visibility of the police in many Black communities. In contrast to these findings, Richie (1996) found that battered Black women not only tended to avoid utilizing social services agencies but also had greater resistance to calling the police, while battered White women used all of these services with greater frequency.

Although much of the extant research has discovered that battered Black women contact the police at higher rates than other battered women, they may simultaneously be resistant to bringing in the police because they do not wish to call negative attention to the Black community and Black culture (Ammons, 1995; Kupenda, 1998; West, 1999). They may also worry about being considered an antagonist to the Black community by feeding the criminal justice system with even more African American men (Brice-Baker, 1994; Richie, 1996; Sorenson, 1996). Black women report being fearful of how their Black male partners will be treated by police officers based on perceived and real experiences of disparate arrests, excessive and unnecessary use of force, and other aggressive police behaviors (Brice-Baker, 1994; Fishman, 2002; Richie, 1996; Sorenson, 1996). These beliefs lead some battered Black women to feel the need to disregard their well-being in order to protect Black men. Bell and Mattis (2000, p. 528) stress that the "representations of African American men as victims who must be protected at all costs and the insistence that women must bear the responsibility for protecting men—even the men who harm them—contribute to the vulnerability of African American women." Regarding victims of IPV (as well as sexual violence from nonpartners), West (1999, p. 161) concludes, "Racism should be understood as thoroughly interwoven into all their life-choices, not as an isolated phenomenon that rears its head when the victim-survivor is trying to decide whether or not to call the police."

STIPULATIONS FOR ARREST

When police officers are called (or are already present) to attend to IPV, research has identified under which specific conditions officers are most likely to make arrests in these cases (see Belknap, 1995, and Jones & Belknap, 1999, for reviews of some of this research). Arrest policies, policing practices (regardless of official policy), and extralegal factors, such as race and class discrimination, affect the actions taken by police officers when they arrive on the scene of an IPV incident. Pro-arrest policies (also known as mandatory or presumptive arrest policies), which oblige officers to arrest IPV perpetrators when probable cause exists, were adopted in many U.S. cities subsequent to ineffective officer mediation (without arrest) efforts, feminist activism, successful lawsuits, and research support of the deterrent effect of arrest (Belknap, 2007). While there has been an increase in the rate of arrests of male (and women) batterers due to these factors,[4] IPV arrests in pro-arrest jurisdictions are reported to occur only 50 percent of the time when police respond to these incidents (Eitle, 2005). This is only 5 percentage points more than those jurisdictions without such a policy (see also Dugan, 2003).

Some investigations have indicated that police officers who respond to IPV calls tend to treat male batterers more leniently than other violent offenders (Buzawa, Austin, & Buzawa, 1995; Eigenberg, Scarborough, & Kappeler, 1996; Fyfe, Klinger, & Flavin, 1997).[5] Buzawa et al. (1995) found that in 75 percent of the IPV cases in their study the victims' preferences for arrests of their abusers were ignored, while in assault cases involving perpetrators who were strangers to the victims only 40 percent of the victims' preferences were ignored. These studies on arrest disparity were based on data collected from departments that did not adhere to pro-arrest policies at the time, even if pro-arrest statutes were in existence or policies were delineated in police procedure manuals. As follows, regardless of the existence of pro-arrest policies, the "leniency" finding remains important to consider in officers' decision to arrest a batterer. Clearly, police are frequently avoiding the arrest of batterers (see Belknap, 1995; Coulter, Kuehnle, Byers, & Alfonso, 1999; Jones & Belknap, 1999).

When police officers take action in IPV cases, they are more likely to take a report and make an arrest if the victim is female (Tjaden & Thoennes, 2000), but, again, gender differences are compounded by racial identity of the victim and/or offender. Regarding the presence of children, one study found the police were more than twice as likely to make arrests for battered White mothers as for battered Black mothers (Robinson & Chandek, 2000). Bachman and Coker (1995) found that Black men who were violent toward their Black female mates were more likely to be arrested than White men who victimized White women (see also Hutchinson, Hirschel, & Pesackis, 1994). This is an interesting finding considering that White women victims are often deemed more worthy of protection from personal, interpersonal, and social harms (Belknap, 2007; Madriz, 1997). This is evident in Avakame and Fyfe's (2001, p. 36) investigation, where they found that

> [P]olice are more likely to arrest if the victim is a wealthy, White, older, subur-
> ban female. . . . It may be the case that wealthy, White, middle-class, suburban
> females represent the 'quintessential woman' in U.S. society and that assaults
> on them symbolize an assault on the very fabric of U.S. society.

However, Avakame and Fyfe also found that an IPV arrest is more likely to occur if the attacker is African American. That Black men are arrested more frequently than White men for battering could be attributed to the typecasting of Black men as inherently criminal and in need of more formal social control. These findings and speculations are likely to play a critical role in interracial abusive relationships between a Black male abuser and a White female victim.

Even though officers have been found to still exert some discretion in departments with pro-arrest policies, there is indication that these policies may provide some relief from racial bias among police. Eitle (2005) discovered that pro-arrest policies reduce the significance of race in IPV arrests. He suggests, "Given the voluminous body of research devoted to exploring issues of race and the operations of criminal justice actors, these findings suggest that the implementation of formal policies restricting discretion may play a modest role in reducing bias in enforcement actions" (p. 592).

VICTIM SATISFACTION

Concerning satisfaction with the police, studies have found that most women victims of IPV are satisfied with their experiences with officers and would contact the police upon future IPV incidents (Apsler, Cummins, & Carl, 2003; Coulter et al., 1999). One investigation determined that women were more likely to report satisfaction with police when batterers were arrested upon the first police enforcement encounter (Stephens & Sinden, 2000). Nevertheless, there are still many cases where women victims of IPV believe police have not adequately protected and served victims. Stephens and Sinden (2000) identified four police attitudes that were recognized by a sample ($N = 25$) of mostly White female victims who had multiple encounters with officers responding to their battering situations. Respondents reported that officers minimized the situation, did not believe the victim, did not show care, and exhibited arrogance (see also Shoham, 2000). In a study of battered White and Black women in a rural setting, both groups of women reported feeling discriminated against by the police (Few, 2005). While the battered White women cited gendered discrimination, typically in the form of sexist attitudes, the battered Black women's negative experiences with police involved racial discrimination. This result demonstrates how the intersection of gender and race can have women of color facing added challenges in utilizing police assistance. Erez and Belknap (1998) asserted that these types of attitudes exhibited by police officers only enhance the despondency felt by IPV victims as a result of the abuse.

EFFECT OF ARREST

Studies have also centered on the deterrent effect of arresting male batterers. That is, what is the likelihood that a batterer will continue to abuse his intimate partner or be rearrested[6] after an initial arrest for IPV? Some of the research addressing this question, as mentioned above, resulted in the implementation of pro-arrest policies. However, the extant research has uncovered equivocal outcomes, where arrests have resulted in increases, no effect, and decreases in subsequent IPV and/or arrests in the various studies. In a study conducted by Bowker (1988), more than a third (39%) of the women victim participants reported that police intervention assisted in decreasing or ceasing the abuse by their intimate partners. Unfortunately, although a smaller proportion, 19 percent of respondents indicated that the violence perpetrated against them actually *increased* after police involvement.

A classic and well-documented study, which had astounding policy implications (Belknap, 2007), determined that the chance of rearrest for battering is dependent on marital and employment status of the batterer, Sherman, Smith, Schmidt, and Rogan (1992) found that the arrest of IPV perpetrators with a low "stake in conformity," namely, being unemployed and single, increased their rearrest or recidivism for IPV. By contrast, when married and employed individuals were arrested, it deterred further IPV. Hirschel and Hutchison (2003) found that women who did not want their batterers to be arrested were less likely to be revictimized than those who wanted their batterers arrested. This is in accordance with several studies that have ascertained that the violence perpetrated against women by their intimate partners did not significantly reduce after arrest at the scene of the incident (Berk, Campbell, Klap, & Western, 1992; Dunford, Huizinga, & Elliott, 1990; Hirschel, Hutchison, & Dean, 1992; McFarlane,

Willson, Lemmey, & Malecha, 2000; Sherman, Schmidt et al., 1992). Weisz (1996) argues that many of these studies failed to consider cultural background of the individuals, police conduct, and the couples' interactions prior to police contact, among other matters. However, a few studies did report contradictory evidence in regard to race and IPV recidivism. In the findings of the investigation conducted by Sherman, Smith et al. (1992), even though Black perpetrators had a higher rate of repeat violence than White perpetrators according to victim interviews, there was no significant relationship between race and the effect of arrest on recidivism. Maxwell, Garner, and Fagan (2002) determined that new IPV offenses were more likely reported for *White* offenders in victim interviews, but official criminal history records (arrest reports) showed that White offenders were less likely to recidivate. Finally, Mears, Carlson, Holden, and Harris (2001) found that Black women living in low-income neighborhoods had a greater risk of being revictimized after issuance of a protective order and/or an arrest than White women and women (including Black women) living in medium- and high-income settings.

This overview of the existing research represents that issues of gender, race, and class, either separately or in an intersecting manner, do indeed affect how victims of IPV use police and how police react in these situations. The findings of the study presented in this chapter will add to what is still a scant amount of inquiry into and understanding of battered Black women's experiences with the police and the criminal justice system. Regarding the implication of race in policing and the effect of academic research in this area on public policy, Harris (2007, p. 7) argues, "For everything that police, both individually and collectively, think they know about this topic, there is much more that they do not know. And what they do not know must begin with a discussion of how race may influence individual actions within the justice system."

METHOD AND DATA

The sole form of data collection for this study was narrative, which was based on an investigation into the way sociostructural factors, cultural factors, and African American women's identities affect how battered Black women respond to their abuse. Semistructured, in-depth interviews were used to gather the data. These exhaustive interviews provide a voice to members of a society who are traditionally ignored or "invisible" (Fontana & Frey, 1994). Specifically, having those who are disregarded because of their undervalued race and gender circumstances to be able to speak for themselves serves to better understand how race and gender are factors in studies of crime and the criminal justice system (Phillips & Bowling, 2003).

More than 90 potential informants responded to the recruitment efforts of this study between May 2003 and November 2003, and 40 women were ultimately interviewed. The majority of the participants were recruited through the posting of an advertisement in a monthly local newspaper based in Denver, Colorado, that is directed toward a primarily Black audience. The solicitation sought self-identified "African American" women over the age of 18 who had been or were previously in violent intimate relationships. This utilization of purposive sampling is appropriate when looking (a) at a small, select, and possibly hidden population, (b) for cases that are especially informative, and (c) to identify particular types of cases for in-depth investigation (Guest, Bunce, & Johnson, 2006). Twenty-nine of the women who responded to the advertisement were interviewed. An additional nine participants were referred to the study by the women who responded to the advertisement (i.e., snowball sampling), which resulted in four mother-daughter interviewee sets. The remaining two women who participated in the study were introduced to the study upon noticing a copy of the ad that was posted on a bulletin board at a Denver college campus.

Due to the highly sensitive subject matter of this study, the respondents were assured of their anonymity verbally and in writing using an informed consent form. Each woman was assigned a pseudonym to further protect her identity. The 40 audio-recorded interviews took place between May and September 2003, and were conducted in small meeting rooms in Denver-area public libraries, at an office on a downtown Denver college campus, or at the participants' homes. The interviews lasted anywhere between one and four hours.

The study yielded a diverse sampling of battered Black women. Although several of the women described multiracial and multinational ancestry, all of them identified that both birth parents were considered Black or African American and, except for two participants, all women were born and raised in the United States. Although the women lived in one state at the time of the interviews, there were varied residential histories among them. The women also varied by age, socioeconomic status, and level of education (see Table 13.1). The largest proportion of participants, 40 percent, was of the ages from 40 to 49 years, 15 percent of the participants were between the ages of 18 and 29 years, 27.5 percent between 30 and 39 years of age, and 17.5 percent between 50 and 59 years of age.

All of the participants reported that their abusive partners were male, and no women were identified as bisexual or lesbian or reported abuse by a current or former intimate female partner. In sum, none of the informants reported any female partners,

TABLE 13.1 Demographic Characteristics of the Sample at Time of Interview

	Total	Percent
Age		
18–19	1	2.5
20–29	5	12.5
30–39	11	27.5
40–49	16	40.0
50–59	7	17.5
Level of Education		
Middle school	1	2.5
Some high school	7	17.5
High school/GED	9	22.5
Some college	14	35.0
Associate's degree	5	12.5
Bachelor's degree	3	7.5
Master's degree	1	2.5

abusive or otherwise. Though the existing literature on Blacks and IPV usually focuses on abuse in African American couples, intimate interracial relationships were also considered for the current study. Four participants (10%) were abused by at least one non-Black batterer. Except for one batterer who was identified as a Black African (African continent nationality), the remainder of the batterers were described as African American or Black (U.S. nationality).

Socioeconomic status was categorized by the participants' statuses during their upbringings, during their abusive relationships, and at the time of the interviews (see Table 13.2). Fifteen (37.5%) of the participants were raised in low-income households and the same number was living in this status at the time of the interviews. These types of households were identified as being comprised of residents who are not regularly working and receive public assistance as a major means for survival. Fewer women ($n = 10, 25\%$) were in low-income abusive relationships. The working-class individuals were characterized by maintenance of regular employment, but in typically unskilled or lower skilled professions, or professions that do not draw adequate incomes. These individuals are often confronted with challenges of paying bills and affording necessities or material goods. Twelve (30%) of the participants were raised in working-class environments, including four participants whose fathers were in the military and lived on U.S. military bases during their childhoods. Twenty-five (62.5%) of the women were in working-class abusive couplings and 19 (47.5%) were in working class couplings at the time of the interviews. Members of the middle class were employed in professional, highly skilled, and/or college-level occupations. Their jobs often provided a stable environment and included benefits such as health insurance and retirement plans. Home ownership was also considered as a salient factor to classify the middle-class participants. Respondents reared in middle-class household of origin settings comprised 32.5 percent ($n = 13$) of the sample, while five (12.5%) were of this status during abusive relationships and six (15%) during study participation.

Although the interviews were conversational in nature, with the women free to tell their stories at their own pace and sequence, an interview schedule was developed to guide the interviews and assure consistency in data gathering. As this chapter is based on a segment of a larger study, the participants' responses to the inquiries about their experiences with and perceptions of police (particularly as related to battering incidents) are the sole focus of this chapter. Although trends in the women's experiences were being detected during the data collection process and in order to determine when data or theoretical saturation was reached, the transcribed interviews were read several times to further determine the themes and patterns in the women's lived experiences (see Guest et al., 2006). These themes and patterns were continuously recoded and refined throughout the data collection and data analysis processes.

TABLE 13.2 Socioeconomic Status of Sample

	Household of Origin	*During Abuse*	*Time of Interview*
Socioeconomic Status			
Low-income	15 (37.5%)	10 (25.0%)	15 (37.5%)
Working-class	12 (30.0%)	25 (62.5%)	19 (47.5%)
Middle-class	13 (32.5%)	5 (12.5%)	6 (15.0%)

RESULTS

RACIAL IDENTITY

As specified above, trends were identified during the assessment of the stories told by the assorted set of women. The participants openly discussed their beliefs and experiences in the context of how the criminal justice system deals with African Americans and other people of color regardless of the offending behavior, as well as in relation to IPV specifically. Essentially, the respondents felt they were not important enough to be heard, much of which was based on their identity as a Black woman. A significant aspect of this identity was their self-portrayal as strong women. Excerpts from interviews with four women hailing from various upbringings and socioeconomic statuses are just a sampling of the participants' perceptions of White women's *general* strength as distinguished from that of Black women:

- I know that Black women in general have to fight harder.
- I think Black women just have to put up with a lot more shit [than White women].
- Black women are strong. They go through everything. From the time I could remember.
- Black women have been going through hell. White women have been pampered.
- I think Black women are stronger. White women get more support, so they just *look* stronger. Their package looks better.

The women perceived that because White women are deemed more important in society, battered White women would be more willing to speak out and be heard. Even though some Black women *are* willing to expose the abuse to formal (official) sources, often they are not sincerely being paid attention to, as experienced by 32-year-old Aaliyah, who shared, "I have not once had anybody be sympathetic to anything that I've been through." Olivia, 48 years old, also summarized the sentiment felt by many of the participants concerning their position as African American women confronted with IPV:

> White America won't say anything [about abuse] unless it will be tragic. *We'll* say something but we're not being heard until something's really, really bad; then you want to lock us all up. We can't afford to get those Prozacs and Thorazines and twenty hours on the couch. We can't afford that. We have to pray to God and hope everything works out.

This outlook is depicted throughout the results that follow, where several trends were identified in the women's experiences with police support for controlling the violence perpetrated against them by their male intimate partners. To start, an overview of the respondents' general perceptions of the criminal justice system as a whole is provided, followed by an examination of (a) changes recognized in legal procedures and attitudes regarding IPV cases, (b) explanations for not calling the police, (c) effectiveness of police action when the police *were* called to the scenes of the IPV incidents, and (d) the few positive experiences with police intervention.

GENERAL PERCEPTIONS OF THE CRIMINAL JUSTICE SYSTEM

The respondents who were of middle-class status during their youth and/or at the time of the interviews, along with those women who had at least some college education, were, as a group, more vocal and forthright with their remarks about the effectiveness and fairness of the criminal justice system, particularly policing. These comments were typically disparaging and negative. This is consistent with previous research that has found that African Americans in the higher socioeconomic classes are more critical of the criminal justice system than African Americans in lower socioeconomic levels (Weitzer & Tuch, 1999). Even still, there was general sentiment among all the participants in the current study that the criminal justice system disfavors people of color. Forty-three-year-old Jacqueline, who was raised in the middle class, stated, "As far as dealing with Black people in general, it's a total imbalance." And Cicely, a 52-year-old high-school graduate raised in a low-income environment, advised that

> There's a lot of *in*justice when it comes to people of color, whether it's drugs, alcohol, or even assault. . . . I mean, no problem, "You do the crime, you do the time," but the system is unbalanced. You can have a Black man and a White man in there for the same crime, the same background history of their lives, where they went to school, degree, for the same crime. The Black man'll get 150 years while the White man will probably get five to 10 and out in two. Because the Black man is already stereotyped as, "You're never gonna be nothing. You're automatically a drug addict. You're automatically an alcoholic, and you're not working."

Forty-eight-year-old Olivia was raised in a middle-class household and has a high-school education. She also discussed the imbalance of treatment in the criminal justice system based on race:

> There's a law for them and there's a law for us. The criminal justice system is not equal like they say. The justice scale is unbalanced . . . and it's blindfolded because you don't know what you gonna get into. I've seen a lot of railroading us, a lot of bad things happening in the criminal justice system to good people.

The women also discussed the system's dealings with victims of crime. Michelle, like several of the respondents, is employed in a position where she works with victims of IPV. The 54-year-old, who was reared in the upper-class sector and holds a masters degree, spoke of how the system responds to IPV victims of color and victims with other disadvantages:

> I think the criminal justice system has a different response to women of color and immigrant women. I think the response is uneven. . . . The systems people I encounter, primarily White people, have absolutely no idea. . . . You know, they may take a one-hour class in cultural competency, which is meaningless. They have no empathy for women of color. To make it worse, battered immigrant women of color have almost no recourse in the criminal justice system. It is totally unresponsive. . . . We do have complaints about the system and about access, and not just from women of color and immigrant women, but also from deaf women and disabled women around access, and the fact that they'll have a TTY number and nobody will be there answering.

As illustrated by the narratives presented here, many of the women in this study ascertained that the distinctive life chances and experiences of African Americans and other people of color have been and continue to be a negatively significant factor in the criminal justice system's dealings with people of color.

RECOGNIZABLE CHANGES IN SYSTEM PROCEDURES AND ATTITUDES

The participants recognized the changes in the criminal justice system's response to IPV over time and after specific events. In particular, without prompting, some women mentioned the documented physical abuse inflicted on Nicole Brown Simpson by celebrated football player and entertainer O.J. Simpson that was revealed during his murder trial in 1994. In recalling her abusive relationships, 39-year-old Zora discovered the following:

> I've noticed a big difference in the way things were being treated before Nicole Simpson.[7] Right after that was when we broke up. I realized that when we had had issues before, even though he was the culprit, but after all of that happened, I think the law took a different turn on things. . . . Now, I feel like they're more on the victim's side. I felt like they were answering calls quicker and following up more on things that were happening. In some ways I feel like the criminal justice system is OK, but then in some ways I feel like it's not. . . . [U]ntil somebody gets killed, things don't happen. Somebody has to die to make a law change. I'm very happy that I don't have that in my life [anymore] where I need to have police coming to my rescue, and I hope that it remains that way. But until something very, very bad happens is when laws change or the criminal justice system is really on its toes. Until that point, I think I remain a little neutral about them.

This ambivalence in the usefulness of the implementation of pro-arrest policies for IPV was also found in the qualitative study conducted by Rajah, Frye, and Haviland (2006) where their participants were initially pleased to learn of the policies but ultimately dissatisfied because of their own arrests. Returning to the informants in the current study, Naomi is a 37-year-old with an associate's degree in criminal justice and pursuing further education in crime scene investigation. She has been on several ride-alongs with police officers as part of her school work. Naomi offered another viewpoint about the effect the Simpson case had on IPV when asked what she thinks about how police deal with IPV:

> I don't think it's good. They're overly doing it because of Nicole Brown Simpson. And it's almost like a game to the police because they're constantly going to the same houses. I do ride-alongs with the police department. You see the same people. Once they're out, the wife or the girlfriends take them back. It's the same cycle. You're knocking on the same doors telling the same woman, "This man is gonna kill you."

The women also discussed how they noticed the changes in the law caused more women victims of IPV (including some of the respondents) to be arrested for IPV-related offenses.[8] Other research has found that, indeed, there has been an increase in arrests of women, who were often victims of repeat abuse by their male mates (Miller, 2005). Much of these increased arrests of women victims are due to the implementation of pro-arrest policies. Forty-three-year-old Tammy discussed the outcome of such policies:

> Right now they're pretty strict 'cause somebody's going to get a case. . . . Sometimes they'll come out and talk, but either one of you are going or both of you are going to go. And once you get a domestic violence [case], that's just like a drug case on your record, 'cause people don't want you. Violent crimes or assaults, they don't want you in their apartments. Lot of places you have to get a criminal background history, and if you have domestic violence background a lot of times you can't even rent an apartment. It's almost like drugs on your record. It's not good. . . . I don't see no good habilitation in the criminal system.

Twenty-four-year-old Phoebe had a similar recollection and reported her experiences regarding this occurrence:

> I think now they're puttin' the women in jail more. . . . In most cases the women are still the ones being inflicted violence on, and they're puttin' the women in jail now. My sister went to jail. . . . It was a mutual thing. I guess she threw something at him, he hit her and strangled her. . . . She didn't want to press charges against him, so she didn't sign the paperwork. . . . He signed the paperwork. He prosecuted my sister when she was pregnant. She spent three or four days in jail. . . . But he would have been looking at more time than her, because he did choke her and kick her. . . . They put her in jail and she had to do a year of probation and a year of classes—domestic violence classes—behind this. So she really got the bad end of this. And now she has it on her record. She didn't have a record before. She was telling me about some of the women in the class. Like all of them were in there because their boyfriends had beat on them for years and years and then they finally hit 'em back and they end up going to jail because they hit back. I think that's a shame. I think the criminal justice system is really going down the wrong road. And then a lot of the cases, you know, [police] see so much domestic violence that I think they're getting the attitude that, "These women want this." So they're puttin' them in jail.

While many of the participants recognized that there have been policies and practices implemented to improve the official responses to IPV, they disapproved of the consequences of the practices, often referring to the way in which these policies have not been in the best interest of or positive for women, African Americans, and other people of color.

EXPLANATIONS FOR NOT CALLING THE POLICE

As indicated in the extant research outlined above, battered women have many reasons for not contacting the police after a violent threat or attack from their intimate partners. These reasons may be related to (a) a woman's fear of further abuse, (b) the economic status of a battered woman that would allow her to use her financial resources to leave the relationship instead of relying on the police, (c) the role battered women believe the police should play, and (d) the existence of other resources, such as familial and religious support. Regrettably, leaving an abusive relationship is rarely a one-time event. Ferraro (1997) reports that battered women typically make five to seven attempts at leaving abusive relationships before they do so permanently.

A major concern with police intervention is the effect arrests of batterers will have on future battering (recidivism rates). Often, the fear of further abuse will compel a battered woman to remain in the abusive relationship and not contact the police for assistance (Catalano, 2006). Interestingly, only a few women in the present study did not call the police due to *fear* of the batterers' greater abuse upon release. Naomi described her predicament:

> I went to the hospital. I was so out of it. I don't remember walking from the bathroom to the ambulance. I don't remember walking into the hospital or being taken to the hospital. I don't remember them taking pictures. I don't remember any of that. But when the MPs[9] came in and said, "Do you want to press charges?," I remember saying no, because I was so afraid to say yes.

Twenty-eight-year-old Isis described being fearful of her batterer, but was more fearful of the consequences of police intervention on her government-assisted living situation:

> I was afraid to [call the police]. He was an old gang member. I was staying in low-income housing. If I call the police on him and he's in my house—he could not have drugs on him [in the housing development]. That would jeopardize me and my kids' house. So I didn't call the police on him.

Erez and Belknap (1998) found that many of the victims in their investigation made attempts to *not* make use of the system's services. They argue that women with greater financial means may be less likely to utilize police for intervention. This is consistent with the respondents in the present study, as the five women in middle-class abusive relationships and many of the participants in the working-class couplings did not call the police themselves. (However, this does not mean there was never police intervention, since witnesses of the abuse may have been those who called in police agents to intervene.) In contemplating options for getting out of the abusive relationships, some participants felt it was necessary to find other ways to resolve the relationship instead of using the criminal justice system (Catalano, 2006). Forty-five-year-old Kim, who has lived in low-income settings throughout her life, concluded about the criminal justice system, "I don't care for it. I'd rather handle it in my own way." She elaborated by stating,

> We never called the police when we was growing up. It was just something you didn't do. You handle your own business. Handle your own business! What's the purpose of having a person in uniform there?

Laura, 42 years old and from a middle-class upbringing, also believed alternative methods should be used if at all possible:

> If you're lucky enough that the police and the courts will help you, sure, go try that, too. If you can do it a different way, go for the different way.

Both Kim's and Laura's assessment of police use were based on their familiarity of how detrimental the police can be for Black communities.

For many of the respondents, going a "different way" included relying on family or clergy members for assistance with stopping the abuse or getting out of the relationship. Religion and spirituality are significant elements in Black culture and the Black community and were especially strong factors in the lives of the women (see Potter, 2007).

Some of the women who were associated with a house of worship during their abusive relationships attempted to seek help from religious leaders instead of utilizing the police. The Muslim respondents ($n = 5$) reported greater general support than Christian participants. Sam, age 38, spoke of her mosque's stance on contacting the police for IPV incidents:

> They frown on it, I know that much. The Muslim men, they figure they take care of their own. Instead of calling the police, all you need to do is call your Wali. My Wali is like taking the place of my dad, while my dad is not here. If I need anything or have any kind of problems, this guy is the man I call. Call him and all the Muslim brothers will come and handle the individual. So that's the way they handle their's . . . If [my husband] has a problem with me, then he needs to call one of his Muslim brother's wives. They'll come and handle the situation; not fight or nothing like that, but come in, take you down and talk to you where you might not want to talk to your husband or wife. That's how they handle that, instead of calling the police. Right when we got married, after the ceremony, we were about to leave and my Wali came and said, "If you have any type of problems, you come and get us. Let the police be the last resort, because a Muslim man is more apt to listen to another Muslim man than the police." If it's a physical violence type thing, they'd probably understand. But if they can get to the situation before it becomes violent, then they prefer to do that.

EFFECTIVENESS OF POLICE ACTION

Although battered women may suspect that there will be harmful repercussions for contacting the police to arrest a batterer, many are willing to take this risk, as they deem it the best choice in certain situations. Regardless of the chance of continued battering after an arrest, some of the study respondents viewed the arrests of their batterers as a welcomed vacation from the abuse, allowing them to get rested for the next round of battles once abusers were released from police custody or jail. Forty-seven-year-old Vanessa said, "I called the police to put him out so I could go to sleep." Though some of the participants felt guilty for calling the police, none of the women felt guilty because they were providing the criminal justice system with yet another African American male. This varies from the extant research mentioned above, which found that one of the reasons battered Black women are reluctant to contact the police is because of feeling like or being viewed as a traitor to the Black community (Brice-Baker, 1994; Richie, 1996; Sorenson, 1996). If there were guilty feelings by the women, it was often for taking the children's fathers away by sending them off to jail or prison (see also Bennett, Goodman, & Dutton, 1999). When 45-year-old Deborah was asked if she felt guilty when she started calling the police on her batterer, she stated,

> Yeah, because the kids, they kind of wanted to know him, but they didn't. So I was feeling guilty about that. Other than that, about me, I didn't care. But the older they got and the more they saw it, I didn't feel guilty. It was mainly because of them.

Even with some satisfaction resulting from the arrests of their batterers, the women's thoughts about how the police dealt with the IPV situation were more in the form of disappointment than praise and appreciation. Research reviewed above found that many women victims of IPV did not want to call the police because they supposed the police could not do anything or would not believe them (Catalano, 2006; Fleury et al., 1998; Tjaden & Thoennes, 2000). Likewise, many of the women in the present investigation chose not to contact the police themselves or to admit that the batterer hit them when the police responded to the homes.

Some of the women were disappointed in police action when officers arrived to the scene. Jacqueline described her progression from not utilizing police protection to feeling the need to contact the police and the ensuing actions by the officers:

> I don't think I ever even thought about calling the police that first time. But, after going through it time after time after time, I did call the police, and they didn't do anything. . . . I was pregnant with our youngest son . . . like ready to deliver any day. He threw me into a refrigerator and broke my collarbone. That time I went to the hospital, and they called the police. No charges were pressed because he told them that I tripped, and they believed him.

Aaliyah described her impressions of the police when they were called to her home after one of her abuser's violent episodes:

> I don't have very much faith in—I don't want to say the criminal justice system—but in the police. First of all, as a Black woman on welfare, with a kid, you're dumb. That's what I think they think. I could have had a degree. They didn't ask me that. They even asked me, "Are you on welfare? Are you on Section 8?" . . . They don't look at you as if you have any sense . . . I just knew that there's no justice with the police officers. We're just basically scum of the earth.

On another occasion, after Aaliyah was brutally raped by her estranged husband who entered her home unlawfully, she was able to silently persuade her daughter to leave the house and contact the police. When the police arrived to the home, they informed Aaliyah that her husband's only infraction was violation of the restraining order Aaliyah had on her husband. Aaliyah stated,

> I feel like if it was a White lady up in [an upper-class neighborhood], I think the situation probably would have been handled differently. . . . I think she probably would have been treated better. . . . I've never been asked the question, "Are you OK? Do you need anything?" I don't think a cop has ever asked me if I was OK, ever.

In a few circumstances police officers would talk with the participants in the immediate presence of the batterer, as opposed to separating the couple to alleviate further victimization and to determine the nature of the situation. These participants expressed their dissatisfaction with this practice. Twenty-two-year-old Ebony described a situation when the officers responded to her home:

> I think they could have asked more questions. They're asking me questions, and he's standing right here. I think they should have separated us. Maybe

they could have got more out of me. . . . It should have been private. And then I don't like to talk in big groups, so if there's two or three police, I'm going to try to rush on. I know they're going to get in the car and laugh at the situation.

Further dissatisfaction among the respondents involved police officers' inability to detect evidence of abuse on the women because the color of their skin did not always easily show bruises. If there were no cuts, missing teeth, or other obvious lesions, the police typically failed to take action on behalf of the women. Naomi opined, "They're not trained to see what they need to see. . . . They're not looking at the signs, they're looking at physical symptoms." Deborah, a 45-year-old dark-skinned woman, spoke of the lack of physical evidence when the police arrived to her home after a battering incident that left indistinct bruising, "They didn't see nothing on me, no bruises or nothing. They would just make him leave the house." Though 45-year-old Renee is fair-skinned, she also encountered having a lack of evidence for official police action after her boyfriend hit her:

They didn't see any marks on me. It was my word against his. . . . Something has to be shown. Something has to be done. Somebody has to be found. And that didn't happen. They didn't see anything.

Naomi was one of the very few women in the study who typically did not fight back in any of her relationships, but she periodically attempted to make efforts to protect herself. In doing so on one occasion, Naomi, who has medium-brown skin, put marks on the batterer, who is a fair-skinned Latino. Naomi discussed the events that transpired when the police officers responded to the home:

I said, "This man hit me and you're looking at the scars on him because he's lighter than I am. Because of my complexion it's not gonna show up until later." [The officer said,] "No, no, it would show up right now. . . . " I could probably touch his cheek and it would turn red. . . . They put me down for third degree assault and put him down for harassment.

Some of the respondents offered insight on how they believed police and the remainder of the criminal justice system could better help battered women based on their interactions with system agents. Victoria, 33 years old, alluded to the need for improvement in system effectiveness when she explained her experience and within the context of being African American:

I wonder how come the system don't help me. That's what I don't understand. When we call the police and if the guy runs off, how come they don't give us a card, some agencies or something, instead of just leaving us to deal with it? Even though we are used to going through hard times, there should be some help for those that want some. I would have took the help a long time ago.

Other research also found what Victoria represents here; that is, that IPV victims were unsatisfied with police in their failure to provide counseling referrals (Apsler et al., 2003). In Few's (2005) analysis of her intensive interviews with 30 rural battered White ($n = 20$) and Black ($n = 10$) women, fewer of the Black women (20%) were provided with shelter information by the police than White women (60%).

POSITIVE EXPERIENCES WITH POLICE INTERVENTION

Although their experiences produced negative views of police interaction (both personal and those witnessed among family members and in the community), a small number of women in this study describe individual instances of positive police encounters. These instances are important to reveal because there are individual officers who uphold the expectations of their job and do not rely on racialized and gendered stereotypes in their interactions with those who require and request their assistance. Sam demonstrated this notion about police officers when she stated,

> The way they handled the situation as far as the domestic violence was cool, because basically they gave us the option, "OK, seem like both of you have bruises or whatever. So we have the option, we could take one to their mom's house . . . , one [has] the option to leave, or we'll take both of you to jail." They handled the situation all right . . . Not all police are bad police. There are some that take advantage of being a police officer. You know, just touch you any way they want to. Some of that is unnecessary. But all in all, police are good guys. As long as they're not taking me to jail, it's all good.

Gloria, 36 years old, had a great deal of gratitude for the additional protective measures taken and offered by an officer who responded to her call, even though the actions can be viewed as paternalistic and involving the misuse of police power:

> They took him to jail. The police officer asked me did I want him to beat him up. . . . [The officer] was a White guy. And I had on just my pajamas. He looked at me, he took off his coat and he put it around me. He said, "You know what? You did not deserve this and look how he's got you out here." He put me in the front seat [of the patrol cruiser] and then we sat down and he started talking. He said, "You know what? I can . . . kick his ass if you want me to." I was thinking, "I still love this man! No! No!" And after that, [the officer] would just ride around and just wave. He did that probably for about a month after that. And I thought that was really nice. . . . He was really sweet.

CONCLUSION AND IMPLICATIONS

The view of battered Black women as *strong* and *independent* women, which is often how these women view themselves, interferes with their propensity to reach out and use criminal justice system channels. Ultimately, many of the participants of the current study felt that as Black women, they were left to fend for themselves. Their views were based on the social position in which many African Americans are situated, one that is devalued and disregarded. The added circumstance of being a victim of IPV further exacerbated the study respondents' social status. The view of the Black woman as the *strong* Black woman also negatively affects how criminal justice officials respond to *battered* Black women. Although they may have intermittently sought out assistance from police to deal with abusive mates, the participants' preexisting views of deleterious policing of the Black community and any personal negative interactions with officers often compelled the women to be *self*-reliant. In addition to the cultural and structural factors that may formulate abused Black women's opinions about their victimization, and aside from relying on their own will to leave the relationships, battered Black women access police support and other criminal justice agencies at varying rates and varying levels of success.

The criminal justice system and its history of ineffectively dealing with African Americans were readily cited by the study participants, and, in general, the women believed the criminal justice system to be biased. However, the women occasionally used the system when they believed it would benefit them and they shared a small number of instances where the system worked in their favors and where individual police officers offered welcomed assistance. Many of the participants recognized the positive and negative changes in arrest policies of IPV perpetrators, such as those labeled as mandatory arrest. They were often pleased when batterers were arrested for their assaultive behaviors and none of the women felt guilty for their Black male mates being subjected to the criminal justice system, which is notably different from other research findings on African Americans and IPV. Nevertheless, the use of police as intervention in IPV was usually viewed as a temporary solution to the women's battering. It served as a form of respite or retreat from the batterers, providing time for the women to rest until the next battle. It also allowed the women the opportunity to reflect on the relationship and the next course of action.

Regrettably, the women were sometimes the subject of the criminal justice system's goal of formal social control, but as perpetrators or aggressors and not as defenders of their person, children, or property. This left these women bewildered about the role of police control of the violence perpetrated by intimate partners. As demonstrated above, previous investigations have acknowledged variations in experiences with police intervention in IPV incidents by race, gender, and class categories. Because evidence exists that Black women are more likely than White women to enter into the criminal justice system as offenders, much of which is based on discriminatory practices, it follows that police officers may not choose to speedily and effectively assist Black women with confronting their abusers (Joseph, 2006). Indeed, it has been shown here that police frequently possessed attitudes of misbelief and contention when dealing with complaints raised by battered Black women. These attitudes recurrently resulted in negative outcomes and satisfaction for many of the women in the study. Even basic policing methods for detecting evidence that a crime was committed were overlooked in some cases, as was apparent when officers looked for physical symptoms of trauma, such as bruising, but were unable to locate such evidence because of the darker pigmentation of some of the women.

An increasing array of research on policing considers the influence of a more racially diverse police force in efficiently managing the relationship between communities of color and the officers who patrol these areas (Bolton & Feagin, 2004), and such an increase in racial (and gender) diversity will improve the response to battered women of color (Huisman, Martinez, & Wilson, 2005). While African American representation (for both females and males) on police forces across the United States has considerably increased since the 1960s, Black officers in urban areas continue to be proportionately underrepresented in comparison to Black citizens (Taylor Greene, 2003). Although the addition of Black officers does not always translate into better relations between the Black community and the local police agency (Taylor Greene, 2003), a multitude of endeavors should be undertaken to mend this relationship and to underscore and address the tribulation experienced by battered Black women.

In addition to the need for more diversity among police officers in heterogeneous communities, adequate training must be implemented to equip officers with constructive skills to deal with IPV calls *and* issues of racism and sexism. Bolton and Feagin (2004, p. 270) argue that this is especially important for White officers, since "[i]t seems that only a minority of white officers and officials in law enforcement agencies have as yet entered the learning mode about how workplace racism harms not only officers of color and their agencies but also the larger society." Huisman et al. (2005) offer extensive direction on the best ways to train police officers in their approach to IPV issues, which, arguably, cannot be considered independent of the sociostructural problems of racism and sexism (Potter, 2006). Beyond assuring that this form of training is taking place in police departments, it is also important to consider those who are conducting the training. Whether the trainers are affiliated with academic or advocacy organizations or are officers specially assigned to carry out the training of their counterparts, trainers should be diversified by gender and race (Huisman et al., 2005). Moreover, the outcomes of the training must be regularly monitored, as the lessons communicated in classroom instruction are not always applied to police officers' work on the streets.

While this study resulted in a diverse group of African American women by socioeconomic status and education level, there were no major variations in their experiences and responses based on these characteristics. Instead, it was the women's interface with sociostructural and cultural factors as strongly affected by their intersecting gender and racial identity that amassed their experiences with police and which appeared to be more salient than class or educational attainment characteristics. Although it was a relatively small group of women whose experiences cannot necessarily be generalized to all battered Black women's experiences, their backgrounds were varied and their stories and experiences revealed some of the commonalities that are shared among Black women throughout the United States.

Overall, the respondents used police to intervene in stopping their partners' abuse, but maintained general mistrust in seeking police assistance based on their personal or vicarious experiences. This distrust and dissatisfaction can be traced to the practice of destructive and disadvantageous responses by criminal justice agencies (and their agents) to people of color (Bass, 2001; Brice-Baker, 1994; Fishman, 2002). Typecast and biased views about African American women may serve to form police officers' opinions about IPV among African Americans. This includes possessing stereotypes of inherent abuse among African Americans along with the impression of Black women as strong Black women, angry Black women, and uneducated women on welfare. These views by officers of battered Black women are essentially a form of racial profiling, but one that is moved from the streets and highways ("Driving While Black") and the airports ("Flying While Arab or Muslim"), where males are more likely to be targeted, to the homes of African Americans, where Black women may be placed on equal status with their male counterparts in the likelihood of arrest. Basing the level of intervention in these views may lead to the belief that Black women at IPV calls (a) need to be controlled (by way of arrest for their retaliatory behaviors), (b) can handle their abusive mates without further police assistance, (c) provoked or initiated the abuse perpetrated against them, or (d) are deserving of the abuse due to self-induced life circumstances and emasculating behaviors. Although the efforts of victims' advocates have improved awareness of IPV and have lead to the view of IPV as a *criminal* act, police officer attitudes regarding IPV, particularly as compounded by racialized and gendered viewpoints, clearly remain in continual need of positive adjustment.

Discussion Questions

1. Describe the racial disparities in domestic violence crime as well as in victim reporting of domestic violence.
2. Why do you think these racial disparities exist?
3. Describe the author's use of intersectionality. How does intersectionality describe arrest disparities?
4. According to the author, how does Black women's racial identity affect their experiences with police intervention?
5. Discuss the influences of Black culture and communities on Black women's decisions to seek police intervention.

References

Ammons, L. L. (1995). Mules, Madonnas, babies, bath water, racial imagery, and stereotypes: The African-American woman and the battered woman syndrome. *Wisconsin Law Review, 5*, 1003–1080.

Apsler, R., Cummins, M. R., & Carl, S. (2003). Perceptions of the police by female victims of domestic partner violence. *Violence Against Women, 9*, 1318–1335.

Avakame, E. F., & Fyfe, J. J. (2001). Differential police treatment of male-on-female spousal violence: Additional evidence on the leniency thesis. *Violence Against Women, 7*, 22–45.

Bachman, R., & Coker, A. L. (1995). Police involvement in domestic violence: The interactive effects of victim injury, offender's history of violence, and race. *Violence and Victims, 10*, 91–106.

Bass, S. (2001). Policing space, policing race: Social control imperatives and police discretionary decisions. *Social Justice, 28*, 156–176.

Belknap, J. (1995). Law enforcement officers' attitudes about the appropriate responses to woman battering. *International Review of Victimology, 4*, 47–62.

Belknap, J. (2007). *The invisible woman, gender, crime, and justice* (3rd ed.). Belmont, CA, Wadsworth.

Bell, C. C., & Mattis, J. (2000). The importance of cultural competence in ministering to African American victims of domestic violence. *Violence Against Women, 6*, 515–532.

Bennett, L., Goodman, L., & Dutton, M. A. (1999). Systemic obstacles to the criminal prosecution of a battering partner. *Journal of Interpersonal Violence, 14*, 761–772.

Berk, R. A., Campbell, A., Klap, R., & Western, B. (1992). A Bayesian analysis of the Colorado Springs spouse abuse experiment. *Journal of Criminal Law and Criminology, 83*, 170–200.

Bolton, K., Jr., & Feagin, J. R. (2004). *Black in blue, African-American police officers and racism.* New York: Routledge.

Bowker, L. (1988). The effect of methodology on subjective estimates of the differential effectiveness of personal strategies and help sources used by battered women. In G. Hotaling, D. Finkelhor, J. Kirkpatrick, & M. Straus (Eds.), *Coping with family violence, Research and policy perspectives* (pp. 80–92). Newbury Park, CA: Sage.

Brice-Baker, J. (1994). Domestic violence in African-American and African-Caribbean families. *Journal of Social Distress and Homeless, 3*, 23–38.

Buzawa, E., Austin, T. L, & Buzawa, C. G. (1995). Responding to crimes of violence against women: Gender differences versus organizational imperatives. *Crime and Delinquency, 41*, 443–466.

Catalano, S. (2006). *Intimate partner violence in the United States.* Washington, DC, Bureau of Justice Statistics, U.S. Department of Justice. Retrieved May 20, 2008, at http://www.ojp.usdoj.gov/bjs/intimate/ipv.htm

Coulter, M. L., Kuehnle, K., Byers, R., & Alfonso, M. (1999). Police-reporting behavior and victim-police interactions as described by women in a domestic violence shelter. *Journal of Interpersonal Violence, 14*, 1290–1298.

Dugan, L. (2003). Domestic violence legislation: Exploring its impact on the likelihood of domestic violence, police involvement, and arrest. *Criminology and Public Policy, 2*, 283–312.

Dugan, L., Nagin, D. S., & Rosenfeld, R. (1999). Explaining the decline in intimate partner homicide: The effects of changing domesticity, women's status, and domestic violence resources. *Homicide Studies, 3*, 187–214.

Dunford, F. W., Huizinga, D., & Elliott, D. S. (1990). The role of arrest in domestic assault: The Omaha Police Experiment. *Criminology, 28*, 183–206.

Eigenberg, H. M., Scarborough, K. E., & Kappeler, V. E. (1996). Contributory factors affecting arrest in domestic and non-domestic assaults. *American Journal of Police, 15*(4), 27–54.

Eitle, D. (2005). The influence of mandatory arrest policies, police organizational characteristics, and situational variables on the probability of arrest in domestic violence cases. *Crime and Delinquency, 51*, 573–597.

Erez, E., & Belknap, J. (1998). In their own words, battered women's assessment of the criminal processing system's responses. *Violence and Victims, 13*, 251–268.

Felson, R. B., Ackerman, J. M., & Gallagher, C. A. (2005). Police intervention and the repeat of domestic assault. *Criminology, 43*, 563–588.

Ferraro, K. J. (1997). Battered women: Strategies for survival. In A. P. Carderelli (Ed.), *Violence between intimate partners, Patterns, causes, and effects* (pp. 124–140). New York: Allyn and Bacon.

Few, A. L. (2005). The voices of Black and White rural battered women in domestic violence shelters. *Family Relations, 54*, 488–500.

Fishman, L. T. (2002). The Black bogeyman and White self-righteousness. In C. R. Mann & M. S. Zatz (Eds.), *Images of color, images of crime, Readings* (2nd ed., pp. 177–191). Los Angeles, CA: Roxbury.

Fleury, R. E., Sullivan, C. M., Bybee, D. I., & Davidson, W. S. (1998). "Why don't they just call the cops?" Reasons for differential police contact among women with abusive partners. *Violence and Victims, 13*, 333–346.

Fontana, A., & Frey, J. H. (1994). Interviewing: The art of science. In N. K. Denzin & Y. S. Lincoln (Eds.), *Handbook of qualitative research* (pp. 361–376). Thousand Oaks, CA: Sage.

Fyfe, J. J., Klinger, D. A., & Flavin, J. (1997). Differential police treatment of male-on-female spousal violence. *Criminology, 35*, 455–473.

Guest, G., Bunce, A., & Johnson, L. (2006). How many interviews are enough? An experiment with data saturation and variability. *Field Methods, 18*, 59–82.

Harris, D. A. (2007). The importance of research on race and policing: Making race salient to individuals and institutions within criminal justice. *Criminology and Public Policy, 6*, 5–24.

Hirschel, D., & Hutchison, I. W. (2003). The voices of domestic violence victims: Predictors of victim preference for arrest and the relationship between preference for arrest and revictimization. *Crime and Delinquency, 9*, 313–336.

Hirschel, D., Hutchison, I. W., & Dean, C. W. (1992). The failure of arrest to deter spouse abuse. *Journal of Research in Crime and Delinquency, 29*, 7–33.

Hollenshead, J. H., Dai, Y., Ragsdale, M. K., Massey, E., & Scott, R. (2006). Relationship between two types of help seeking behavior in domestic violence victims. *Journal of Family Violence, 21*, 271–279.

Huisman, K., Martinez, J., & Wilson, C. (2005). Training police officers on domestic violence and racism: Challenges and strategies. *Violence Against Women, 11*, 792–821.

Hurst, Y. G., McDermott, M. J., & Thomas, D. L. (2005). The attitudes of girls toward the police: Differences by race. *Policing, An International Journal of Police Strategies and Management, 28*, 578–593.

Hutchinson, I. W., Hirschel, J. D., & Pesackis, C. E. (1994). Family violence and police utilization. *Violence and Victims, 9*, 299–313.

Jasinski, J. L. (2003). Police involvement in incidents of physical assault: Analysis of the redesigned national crime victimization survey. *Journal of Family Violence, 18*, 143–150.

Jones, D. A., & Belknap, J. (1999). Police responses to battering in a progressive pro-arrest jurisdiction. *Justice Quarterly, 16*, 249–273.

Joseph, J. (1997). Woman battering: A comparative analysis of Black and White women. In G. K. Kantor & J. L. Jasinski (Eds.), *Out of darkness, contemporary perspectives on family violence* (pp. 161–169). Thousand Oaks, CA: Sage.

Joseph, J. (2006). Intersectionality of race/ethnicity, class, and justice: Women of color. In A. V. Merlo & J. M. Pollock (Eds.), *Women, law, and social control* (2nd ed., pp. 292–312). Boston, MA: Pearson Education/Allyn and Bacon.

Klinger, D. A. (1995). Policing spousal assault. *Journal of Research in Crime and Delinquency, 32*, 308–324.

Kupenda, A. M. (1998). Law, life, and literature: A critical reflection of life and literature to illuminate how laws of domestic violence, race, and class bind Black women. *Howard Law Journal, 42*, 1–26.

Madriz, E. (1997). *Nothing bad happens to good girls: Fear of crime in women's lives.* Berkeley, CA: University of California Press.

Maxwell, C. D., Garner, J. H., & Fagan, J. A. (2002). The preventive effects of arrest on intimate partner violence: Research, policy and theory. *Criminology and Public Policy, 2*, 51–80.

McFarlane, J., Willson, P., Lemmey, D., & Malecha, A. (2000). Women filing assault charges on an intimate partner: Criminal justice outcome and future violence experienced. *Violence Against Women, 6*, 396–408.

McFarlane, J., Willson, P., Malecha, A., & Lemmey, D. (2000). Intimate partner violence: A gender comparison. *Journal of Interpersonal Violence, 15*, 158–169.

Mears, D. P., Carlson, M. J., Holden, G. W., & Harris, S. D. (2001). Reducing domestic violence revictimization: The effects of individual and contextual factors and type of legal intervention. *Journal of Interpersonal Violence, 16*, 1260–1283.

Miller, S. L. (2005). *Victims as offenders: The paradox of women's violence in relationships.* New Brunswick, NJ: Rutgers University Press.

Phillips, C., & Bowling, B. (2003). Racism, ethnicity and criminology: Developing minority perspectives. *British Journal of Criminology, 43*, 269–290.

Potter, H. (2006). An argument for Black feminist criminology: Understanding African American women's experiences with intimate partner abuse using an integrated approach. *Feminist Criminology, 1*, 106–124.

Potter, H. (2007). Battered Black women's use of religion and spirituality for assistance in leaving abusive relationships. *Violence Against Women, 13*, 262–284.

Rajah, V., Frye, V., & Haviland, M. (2006). 'Aren't I a victim?' Notes on identity challenges relating to police action in a mandatory arrest jurisdiction. *Violence Against Women, 12*, 897–916.

Rennison, C. M., & Welchans, S. (2000). *Intimate partner violence.* Washington, D.C., Bureau of Justice Statistics, U.S. Department of Justice.

Richie, B. E. (1996). *Compelled to crime: The gender entrapment of battered Black women.* New York: Routledge.

Robinson, A. L., & Chandek, M. S. (2000). Differential police response to Black battered women. *Women and Criminal Justice, 12* (2/3), 29–61.

Sherman, L. W., Schmidt, J. D., Rogan, D. P., Smith, D. A., Gartin, P. R., Cohn, E. G., et al. (1992). The variable effects of arrest on criminal careers: The Milwaukee domestic violence experiment. *Journal of Criminal Law and Criminology, 83*(1), 137–169.

Sherman, L. W., Smith, D. A., Schmidt, J. D., & Rogan, D. P. (1992). Crime, punishment, and stake in conformity: Legal and informal control of domestic violence. *American Sociological Review, 57*, 680–690.

Shoham, E. (2000). The battered wife's perception of the characteristics of her encounter with the police. *International Journal of Offender Therapy and Comparative Criminology, 44*, 242–257.

Smith, S. K., Steadman, G. W., Minton, T. D., & Townsend, M. (1999). *Criminal victimization and perceptions of community safety in 12 cities, 1998.* Washington, D.C., Bureau of Justice Statistics, U.S. Department of Justice.

Sorenson, S. B. (1996). Violence against women: Examining ethnic differences and commonalities. *Evaluation Review, 20*, 123–145.

Stephens, B. J., & Sinden, P. G. (2000). Victims' voices: Domestic assault victims' perceptions of police demeanor. *Journal of Interpersonal Violence, 15*, 534–547.

Taylor Greene, H. (2003). Do African American police make a difference? In M. D. Free,

Jr. (Ed.), *Racial issues in criminal justice: The case of African Americans* (pp. 207–220). Westport, CT: Praeger Publishers.

Tjaden, P., & Thoennes, N. (2000). *Extent, nature, and consequences of intimate partner violence.* Washington, D.C.: U.S. Department of justice.

Weisz, A. N. (1996). *NIJ studies: Spouse assault replication program, studies of effects of arrest on domestic violence.* Retrieved July 13, 2004, at http://www.vaw.umn.edu/vawnet/arrest.pdf

Weitzer, R., & Tuch, S. A. (1999). Race, class, and perceptions of discrimination by the police. *Crime and Delinquency, 45,* 494–507.

Weitzer, R., & Tuch, S. A. (2005a). Racially based policing: Determinants of citizen perceptions. *Social Forces, 83,* 1009–1030.

Weitzer, R., & Tuch, S. A. (2005b). Determinants of public satisfaction with the police. *Police Quarterly, 8,* 279–297.

West, T. C. (1999). *Wounds of the spirit: Black women, violence, and resistance ethics.* New York: New York University Press.

Endnotes

1. Throughout this chapter, "African American" and "Black" are used interchangeably to describe U.S. citizens of Black African descent. Although there are instances where the term White will not be capitalized, it is only done so where direct quotes are included by others who do not capitalize the terms. There is no set standard for whether or not the term is to be capitalized when referring to race.

2. There have been a few studies that revealed Black women actually contacted the police at a lower rate than White women (see Joseph, 1997; Sorenson, 1996). However, it is plausible that investigations based on an especially large data set, the National Crime Victimization Survey, may be more generalizable (see Catalano, 2006; Rennison & Welchans, 2000). Also, in two analyses, Native American women are found to have reported the *highest* rates of IPV in comparison with all other races of women (see Catalano, 2006; Tjaden & Thoennes, 2000).

3. Because the NCVS underwent redesign in the early 1990s, the most accurate NCVS reports on IPV only date back to 1993, the year in which the first results from the redesign were first published. The redesign greatly improved the measurement of IPV (and sexual assaults) because of expanded questioning that includes explicit inquiries into criminal acts committed against survey respondents by intimate partners and familial relations.

4. An unintended consequence of these policies has been the significant increase in the arrest of women, many of whom were physically *retaliating* against their abusers (see Jones & Belknap, 1999; Miller, 2005).

5. An earlier study conducted by Klinger (1995) did not find variations in police responses to batterers and other violent offenders.

6. Though a batterer may continue to abuse her/his intimate partner, it does not necessarily lead to an arrest after each occurrence. Therefore, it is important that this is specified in the reporting of research findings.

7. When the participants make comments such as "before Nicole Simpson," as Zora does, they are referring to criminal justice system changes after O.J. Simpson's murder trial, not after the time when Nicole Brown Simpson was actually battered by O.J. Simpson during the 1980s, which was not readily reported in the national news media until the murder trial.

8. While a brief overview of the participants' perceptions of the criminal justice system in relation to arrests of women victims fighting back is presented here, it is outside the scope of this chapter to elaborate on what was a considerable aspect of the larger study.

CHAPTER 14

THE GENDERED PARADOX OF VICTIMIZATION AND AGENCY IN PROTECTION ORDER FILINGS

❧

ALESHA DURFEE

ABSTRACT

Female victims of domestic violence filing for civil protection orders face a paradox when asked by the courts to describe their abuse. Conventional images of "battered women" emphasize powerlessness and learned helplessness; "real" victims are pathologically weak, emotionally and financially dependent on their abusers, and are unable to leave or resist the abuser without external intervention. Women who do not fit these images are not considered "legitimate" victims, and their motivations for filing for a protection order are questioned. Thus, victims filing for protection orders face a paradoxical challenge: They must be simultaneously helpless and agentic. Neither of these expectations accurately reflects the lived experiences of domestic violence victims. This chapter compares these competing stereotypes of victimization and agency with the descriptions of abuse provided to the courts by women seeking protection orders. The analysis indicates that most petitions describe complex situations that offer conflicting images of both the victim and the abuser. Descriptions of violence found in the narratives of women who received legal assistance were more likely to be consistent with stereotypical expectations of abuse, and thus these victims had a higher likelihood of receiving a protection order. Implications of this disjuncture between lived experience, stereotypical expectations, and statutory requirements are discussed.

INTRODUCTION

Tonya was stunned. She had expected Steve to be angry about the realtor's commission. He had been angry since she had asked for a divorce six months ago, and his anger had significantly increased when they decided to sell their home. But she had never seen him like this. He yanked dollar bills from his wallet, throwing them in her face as he ranted about how much money they were wasting by using a realtor. Tonya repeatedly asked Steve to calm down. Instead, he pushed her up against the wall and told her that he would never agree to leave their home. As he spun around to leave, Tonya grabbed her cell phone and ran upstairs, where she called 911. When the police arrived, they told Tonya that since she and Steve had only a "verbal altercation," they could not arrest Steve unless Tonya had a domestic violence civil protection order against him. They recommended she file for an order immediately so "no one would get hurt."

Domestic violence civil protection orders protect victims of domestic violence by criminalizing contact between victims and their abusers. Because of their flexibility, protection orders have become important tools in combating domestic violence in the United States. Victims (called "petitioners," as they are petitioning the courts for an order) can request differing levels of protection depending on their specific needs. Between 1995 and 1996, an estimated 1.1 million petitioners, or 20 percent of all victims of reported intimate partner violence, filed for and received protection orders against their abusers (Tjaden & Thoennes, 2000, p. 54).

Many petitioners who may qualify for a protection order are unable to obtain one. It is estimated that only a little more than half of all women who file for an order receive one (Holt, Kernic, Lumley, Wolf, & Rivara, 2002). Information about the availability of protection orders is one problem. Only 34 percent of women who called the police after being physically assaulted by an intimate partner reported that the police referred them to the "prosecutor or court," and only 26 percent reported that they were given "advice on self-protective measures" (Tjaden & Thoennes, 2000, p. 49). Fear of the abuser's response to the order is another problem. Almost one-third of women who file drop their petitions due to pressure from abusers or because they fear retaliation (Harrell & Smith, 1996). Furthermore, it is estimated that between 50 and 70 percent of these orders are subsequently violated (Harrell & Smith, 1996; Tjaden & Thoennes, 2000).

One core set of problems that has received relatively little attention has to do with the protection order process itself. As many critical legal scholars have noted, the law *de jure*, or in theory, is quite different from the law *de facto*, or in practice. While the law *de jure* is a "set of rules and procedures," the law *de facto* is instead "a *process* that entails gendering, racializing, and classing practices" that reproduces social inequalities (Comack & Balfour, 2004, p. 10). Although *de jure* the protection order process appears to be relatively unbiased, there is a clear discrepancy between the law *de jure* and the law *de facto* in the protection order process. The petitioner in the case does not simply provide a "statement" to the courts that is then "objectively" interpreted. The assessment of a person's veracity, the legitimacy of an individual's claim to being a "victim," the altercasting of the respondent as a perpetrator, and the classification of a particular act as abusive are all factors that are contested in protection order filings, and each are influenced by—and assessed with—stereotypes about domestic violence, race, gender, class, ethnicity, immigration status, etc.

Female petitioners in particular face a core paradox about victimization and agency when filing for a protection order. When asked by the courts to describe their abuse, they must be simultaneously helpless and agentic. Conventional images of "battered women" emphasize powerlessness and learned helplessness; "real" victims are pathologically weak, emotionally and financially dependent on their abusers, and are unable to leave or resist the abuser without external intervention. To be considered legitimate victims of domestic violence, petitioners must be seen as powerless, fearful, unable to resist their abusers, and helpless enough to merit legal intervention. Women who are not passive, helpless, and/or fearful are not considered "legitimate" victims, and their motivations for filing for a protection order are questioned.

Yet, these same set of characteristics that legitimate a woman's claim to the status of victim also can be used to discredit her claims entirely. Victims must also been seen as agents of active (albeit unsuccessful) resistance. Victims who do not attempt to resist or leave their abusers are often portrayed as masochistic, pathological, and/or mentally ill. Furthermore, actors in the criminal justice system are often frustrated with victims who return to their abusers after intervention—and may assume that victims who do not have a history of resistance are not serious in their attempt to leave and are more likely to return. Victims with children who do not describe attempts to protect their children from violence may also be portrayed as unfit mothers and risk having their children removed from their custody.

Thus, paradoxically female petitioners must be powerful and powerless; they must be actively resisting their abusers but be ineffective in their efforts. Petitioners, often in crisis and without any form of legal assistance, must carefully craft their narratives of abuse to meet not only statutory requirements but also competing expectations based on stereotypes about domestic violence, gender, race, ethnicity, class, and immigration status. These negotiations about identity, agency, and culpability do not occur in a neutral setting, but in an institutional context where structural inequalities already exist— where individuals with broader social advantages "come out ahead" in contested cases (Galanter, 1974, p. 103).

This chapter explores how women employ stereotypes of victimization and agency when filing for protection orders, and how these stereotypes in turn influence the ways in which commissioners adjudicating the case interpret these narratives. In these documents, petitioners and respondents use gendered cultural images and stereotypes about domestic violence victims and abusers in an attempt to obtain or block the entry of a protection order. The legitimacy of these attempts, and thus the outcome of protection order hearings, is based on the efficacy of each party's attempts to use these stereotypes, which is, in turn, based on the social location of these parties. The outcome of each of these cases, taken as a whole, then reifies the very stereotypes that they draw upon.

EVIDENDCE, BUREAUCRATIZATION, AND STRATIFICATION IN THE PROTECTION ORDER PROCESS

Domestic violence is a difficult crime to prove (Cahn, 1991). Abuse most often occurs in private, with few witnesses outside of the immediate family. Abusers often isolate their victims from their social networks, preventing the disclosure of abuse to others who can later corroborate the victim's claims of abuse. Many victims are hesitant to phone police, go to the hospital for medical treatment after a violent incident, or may not have access to routine medical care where a provider can note signs of abuse, so they do not have external documentation of the history of abuse to substantiate their statements when they file for a protection order.

Because of these evidentiary concerns, many cases of domestic violence never reach the criminal courts. The civil protection order process is designed to allow victims of domestic violence to access legal protections without the necessity of criminal charges or the additional burden of proof associated with criminal proceedings. To obtain a protection order, the victim must show that a "preponderance of the evidence" indicates that acts of domestic violence have occurred (not "proof beyond a reasonable doubt"). While other definitions of domestic violence include sexual, economic, or psychological abuse, Washington State law limits domestic violence to those acts that cause

(a) Physical harm, bodily injury, assault, or the infliction of fear of imminent physical harm, bodily injury or assault, between family or household members; (b) sexual assault of one family or household member by another; or (c) stalking as defined in RCW 9A.46.110 of one family or household member by another family or household member. (RCW 26.50.010(1)).

Although the specific procedures for filing vary, most jurisidictions allow petitioners to enter as evidence a written description of the abuse they have experienced. These narratives of abuse often serve as the only evidence that judges have to make their determination as to whether a protection order is warranted. Of the cases analyzed in this chapter, only 12 percent of petitioners offered other materials in addition to their petitions to support their claims of abuse. Thus, these narratives of abuse are critically important to the case.

To facilitate access to protection orders for those with limited financial resources, petitioners in Washington State (as in most jurisdictions) are allowed to file *pro se* (without legal assistance), and most choose to do so. Many petitioners are unfamiliar with the legal system and the statutory requirements for the entry of a protection order; consequently, there is a wide variation in content, structure, and form of these narratives. Furthermore, few petitions filed *pro se* share the same content, structure, and form of other documents generated in the legal system. Petitioners not only focus on but also describe in extensive detail events, dates, and acts that are of importance to them, but that may not be legally relevant to the case.

In an attempt to standardize petitioner narratives, the form used to file for protection orders in Washington State, the form DV-1.020 (6/96), includes explicit instructions as to how it should be completed. Box 14.1 provides an example.

BOX 14.1

INSTRUCTIONS FOR PETITION FOR ORDER FOR PROTECTION

Domestic violence includes physical harm, bodily injury, assault, stalking, OR inflicting fear of imminent physical harm, bodily injury or assault, between family or household members.

STATEMENT: The respondent has committed acts of domestic violence as follows.

(Describe specific acts of domestic violence and their approximate dates, beginning with the most recent act. You may want to include police responses.

Most recent incident or threat of violence and date: _____. (Underscore in original document)

SOURCE: Washington Courts Website (2008). Courts Form, Domestic Violence. Retrieved May 7, 2008 from http://www.courts.wa.gov/forms/index.cfm?fa=forms.contribute&formID=16.

Additional sections of the form ask for the "history of threats and violence" in the relationship, "violence or threats towards children," "injuries treated by doctor," and "use of weapons or objects."

By providing the legal definition of violence in Washington State, asking for the dates and descriptions of "specific acts," and indicating the court's preferences for external documentation of abuse such as police calls, reports, and medical records, the court system is attempting to solicit a particular type of information from the petitioner in a standardized form. The rules and procedures here—the law *de jure*—provide "equal protection" to all victims of domestic violence. If specified elements exist in the case, and are presented in court, a certain result occurs: Either an order is entered because there is a history of domestic violence, or the petition is denied because the events described do not meet the legal standards. Other variations between cases such as the use of legal assistance to complete the petition, race, ethnicity, class, gender, education level, etc., should not affect the outcome of the protection order hearing.

However, rather than producing standardized, concise descriptions of acts committed by the respondent that are legally "domestic violence," the protection order petition instead elicits narratives that vary greatly in content, structure, and form. The problem is that these variations in petitioner narratives are not simply due to differences in individual case histories. The ability to present claims about domestic violence in a form consistent with both other legal discourses and broader social conceptions of domestic violence is both differentially distributed by other, non legally relevant characteristics of individuals, including gender, race, class, and nativity, and results in the entry of a protection order in contested cases (Durfee, 2004). In this way, narratives not only draw on but, more importantly, reproduce "existing ideologies and hegemonic relations of power and inequality" (Ewick & Silbey, 1995, p. 212) through the denial or entry of a protection order. On a macro level, the aggregation of these individual case outcomes then reinforces the very "master narratives" of domestic violence on which they are based.

THE SOCIAL PRODUCTION OF VICTIMIZATION

Social cognition is a theoretical perspective that analyzes how people use knowledge—the ways in which people selectively process, store, and retrieve information (Howard & Hollander, 1997). Cognitive schemas about domestic violence, gender, and victimization influence the narratives of abuse filed by petitioners. Cognitive schemas are expectations or theories about people, social groups, and events; they include elements such as what people are like, how they are likely to behave in or react to certain situations, and what their motivations are for their behavior. People use cognitive schemas to manage the constant barrage of information they are presented with in everyday life. Not only do they employ schemas to determine their behavior, but they also selectively attend to and remember details about events, people, etc. depending on their cognitive schemas.

According to this perspective, when petitioners write their own stories of abuse, they selectively choose to include and exclude certain types of information based on their cognitive schemas about domestic violence, gender, and victimization. They will include those acts or persons that they believe are abusive and/or that caused them to seek the protection order, drawing on schemas about both gender and victimization. The gender of the petitioner in this way shapes the narrative. When writing their stories, petitioners "perform" gender by focusing on certain types of information that are consistent with gender schemas.

One could argue that men and women experience quantitatively and qualitatively different abuse and that is why the stories they submit are so disparate. The first part of this statement is obviously true. With the exception of the National Family Violence Survey (Straus, Gelles, & Steinmetz, 1980), most quantitative data measuring the prevalence of domestic violence in the United States indicate that men are more likely than are women to physically or sexually abuse an intimate partner (Bachman & Saltzman, 1995; Tjaden & Thoennes, 2000). Women are more likely than men to be injured during an assault by an intimate partner[1] (Felson & Cares, 2005; Tjaden & Thoennes, 2000) and to be victimized multiple times by the same partner,[2] and those victimizations occur over a longer period of time[3] (Tjaden & Thoennes, 2000).

However, it does not necessarily follow that the reason that their protection order petitions are different is because the events they have experienced are different. The petitioner does not and cannot provide the commissioner with detailed information about every event that has occurred. For example, petitioners will often talk about actions that, while significant, cannot legally be classified as acts of domestic violence before they talk about more serious (as measured by the Conflict Tactics Scale), legally relevant acts of violence. Furthermore, they often talk about these "less serious" events in more detail than the "more serious" events (Durfee, 2004). They selectively choose certain events and persons in order to portray themselves as victims of domestic violence—whether that means offering details about events that are consistent with cognitive schemas of victimization or providing excuses and justifications meant to deflect negative associations with victimization.

When composing their narratives, female petitioners perform both gender and victimization by providing relatively few details about sexual violence and instead focusing on physical abuse. Female petitioners describe this physical abuse in detail, highlighting their powerlessness, helplessness, fear, and the dangerousness of the respondent and potential for future violence. At the same time, these women also include excuses and justifications as to why they were in the situation, why they did not leave their abuser, why they did not contact police, etc., that are intended to minimize any potential culpability for their abuse.

This "performance" of both gender and victimization is most critical when the respondent contests the petitioner's request for a protection order. When the narratives of abuse presented to the courts do not reflect societal schemas about domestic violence victims, male respondents are often able to block the entry of an order. They do this by reframing the events as nonabusive, the narrative as not credible, and/or describing the petitioner as someone who is mentally ill, is unstable, or has ulterior motives and is herself abusing the respondent through her manipulation of the court system. Thus, women who do not carefully navigate the gendered paradox of victimization and agency are less likely to have their petitions granted than are those women who successfully perform gender, victimization, and agency.

DATA AND METHODS

The data for this analysis come from 101 of the 2,361 petitions for a permanent protection order filed in King County, Washington Superior Court in 2000. Each of these cases is the first filing for a protection order between the two parties; cases with previous rulings were excluded from the analyses. As the dynamics of domestic violence, as well as judicial decision making, may be different for same-sex couples, only those cases where a female petitioner was filing against a male respondent, or a male petitioner was filing against a female respondent, were retained. Of the petitions included in the sample, 63 percent were granted, 14 percent were denied, 20 percent were dismissed, and 4 percent were reissued. Eighty-five percent of the petitions were filed by women against men; 15 percent were filed by men against women. Women filing for orders were more likely than men to have their requests granted; 66 percent of cases with female petitioners compared with only 40 percent of cases with male petitioners resulted in the entry of a protection order.

Narrative analysis is a qualitative, sociolinguistic approach used to analyze oral or written "narratives" that are solicited in a variety of settings (Crang, 1997; Ewick & Silbey, 1995; Lieblich, Tuval-Mashiach, & Zilber, 1998; Ochberg, 1994; Riessman, 1993; Toolan, 1988). One of the strengths of narrative analysis is the explicit emphasis on the linkages between macro-level power structures and micro-level everyday, lived experience. Using this approach, researchers focus on the ways in which the narratives individuals construct both draw on and reinforce "master narratives," thereby reproducing "existing ideologies and hegemonic relations of power and inequality" (Ewick & Silbey, 1995, p. 212).

This qualitative approach has been used by others to study protection orders (Trinch & Berk-Seligson, 2002), women's experiences of abuse in a broader context (Cobb, 1997; Lempert, 1994; Riessman, 1992), and other types of cases in the civil court system (Conley & O'Barr, 1990). The focus of this analysis is not on ascertaining the veracity of the claims made by the petitioner or the respondent, making some sort of "objective" assessment as to whether a request for an order should be granted, or whether the respondent has in fact committed acts of violence that can be legally classified as domestic violence. The narratives submitted by petitioners are, like all stories, "constructions, partial stories, inventions" (Katz, 1992, p. 503). In these stories, certain events are "picked upon" and defined as "turning points," while others are omitted or disregarded as irrelevant (Crang, 1997). The core focus of this analysis is the ways in which cognitive schemas about gender, domestic violence, and victimization shape both the construction of narratives by victims and the subsequent interpretations of these narratives by judges and commissioners. The complexity of these often competing cognitive schemas makes it difficult for many victims to obtain protection orders.

VICTIMIZATION AND GENDER IN THE NARRATIVES OF ABUSE

DISCLOSURE OF SEXUAL ABUSE

Relatively few petitioners described acts of sexual violence in their petitions. Only 13 percent of female petitioners indicated on the protection order petition that they had been sexually abused by the respondent; 8 percent said that the respondent had sexually abused their child(ren). Not one of the 15 male petitioners claimed that they or their children had been sexually abused by the respondent. This is consistent with other national studies on domestic violence, including the National Violence Against Women Survey (NVAWS; Tjaden & Thoennes, 2000), the National Crime Victimization Survey (NCVS; Bureau of Justice Statistics, 2006), and the National Incident Based Reporting System (NIBRS; Bureau of Justice Statistics, 2006), which indicate that women are sexually victimized by intimate partners at a much higher rate than men. According to the NVAWS, an estimated 0.3 percent of American men and 7.7 percent of American women will be sexually abused by an intimate partner at some point during their lifetime.

It is notable that not one male petitioner reported any form of sexual abuse against either themselves or their children. While existing survey data indicate that comparatively few men report sexual victimization, much of this reticence to identify certain events as sexual abuse or disclose those events in the protection order petition may also be attributable to cognitive schemas about masculinity.

While there are multiple forms of masculinities in society, some forms are marginalized or subordinated and others are "culturally exalted." Hegemonic masculinity is an idealized form of masculinity that "embodies . . . .the dominant position of men and the subordination of women" (Connell, 1995, p. 77). One of the core components of hegemonic masculinity in American society is "compulsory heterosexuality," with an emphasis on men having sexual power and domination over women to the point of sexual aggressiveness (Rich, 1980; Connell, 1995; Messner, 1997). This conception of male sexuality is so pervasive in our society that even boys who are sexually abused by adults "are less likely to report abuse and less likely to label an abusive experience as such" because of the stigmatization associated with male sexual victimization (Hines & Malley-Morrison, 2005, p. 113). To claim that a female intimate partner has sexually abused them disempowers and emasculates male petitioners in a way that claims of physical or psychological abuse do not. However, due to hegemonic masculinity, we cannot know if the sexual assault was omitted from the narrative or if it did not occur.

The reticence of many female petitioners to disclose or describe sexual abuse may be due to cognitive schemas about female sexual victimization. These include the belief that women routinely lie about rape for ulterior motives and that only certain women—those who are promiscuous or deviant in some way—are sexually assaulted (Lonsway & Fitzgerald, 1994). Even if the judge believes the victim, she may hold the victim partially culpable for the sexual abuse because of these cognitive schemas regarding allegations of sexual abuse.

Although some female petitioners do claim that they have been sexually abused by the respondent, most mention it only briefly, especially in comparison with the lengthy descriptions provided about physical abuse, psychological abuse, and the dynamics of the relationship in general. For example, one petitioner who filing for a protection order for both herself and her 17-year-old daughter first states,[4]

- My daughter and I have experienced ongoing abuse, mainly threats, for example last week he threatened to disable the car so I could not take her to work. He disables the phone so my daughter cannot contact me when she needs to. These have occurred in the past and over a long period of time.
- In Aug 1999 he threatened to harm me kill me & the children & was arrested.
- Approximately 4 yrs ago (her daughter) was given a black eye & bloody nose during a confrontation with (the respondent).
- He has sexually abused her.

Note that the petitioner gives approximate dates for the events described, provides contextual information about the events (he is disabling the car so she cannot go to work; disabling the phones so that her daughter cannot contact her; physically abusing her daughter during a "confrontation," most likely to assert his authority over her), and mentions that he was arrested for the incident in August 1999.

The petitioner alleges that the respondent has sexually abused her daughter, but in comparison with the description of the events above, she provides very little information about it to the courts. She simply states, "He has also sexually abused her" and does not reference it again in the document. From her narrative, we do not know the nature, duration, or frequency of the sexual abuse, when it occurred, whether it was reported to any governmental or law enforcement agency, whether the sexual abuse is ongoing, and whether the petitioner believes that it will happen again in the future. This petition was granted.

This lack of detail about sexual victimization is representative of most of the petitions that included allegations of sexual abuse against either the petitioner and/or her children. Only four petitioners describe the sexual abuse of their children or themselves in detail. Petitioners may be hesitant to write about this type of abuse due to the stigma associated with sexual victimization or because of cognitive schemas about victims of sexual abuse. Furthermore, mothers may not include allegations of sexual abuse against children because they are afraid of being portrayed as "unwilling to act to protect or properly care for their children" and eventually losing custody of them (Dunlap, 2004).

Finally, issues of consent, resistance, and culpability may also impact a petitioner's decision as to whether and how to describe sexual abuse. Susan Estrich, in her book *Real Rape*, notes that "rape is unique . . . in the definition that has been given to non-consent—one that has required victims of rape, unlike victims of any other crime, to demonstrate their 'wishes' through physical resistance" (1987, p. 29). Petitioners may feel that unless they can prove that they physically resisted their sexual abuse and/or that their victimization included physical abuse, they will be seen as somehow culpable for their abuse and thus they will not be considered "real" victims.

> [M] raped me forced me on him I repeatedly said <u>no</u> I did not want this he just kept doing it holding me down to the floor almost ripping my clothes off of me as I was telling him to please stop and get off of me. . . . . After a while of being on me holding me down to the floor doing what <u>I did not want</u> he hit me 2–3 times on my left cheek so hard I could not sleep on that side that night.

This narrative focuses more on the verbal and physical resistance of the petitioner, and the physical injuries she received because of her resistance, than on the attack itself. The physical injuries from her resistance are what disrupts her sleep "that night," not the violent rape itself. This emphasis on the impacts of the physical assault is notable given that "victims of wife rape suffer worse psychologically than victims of stranger rape" (Hines & Malley-Morrison, 2005, p. 183).

FOCUS ON PHYSICAL ABUSE

Female petitioners were more likely to describe acts of physical and sexual abuse than were male petitioners. While 81 percent of female petitioners said they had been physically abused by the respondent or described acts of physical violence that could be legally classified as abusive, only 66 percent of male petitioners made these same assertions.

As with physical abuse, these distributions are consistent with findings from other studies on intimate partner violence, including the NVAWS, the NCVS, and the NIBRS.

Female petitioners are not only more likely to disclose physical abuse, but they also discuss it in very specific ways. When describing their physical victimization, female petitioners emphasize their powerlessness, helplessness, the ineffectual nature of their resistance, their visceral fear of the respondent, and the dangerousness of the respondent.

POWER, HELPLESSNESS, AND RESISTANCE

The narratives filed by female petitioners often reflect conventional images of domestic violence and "battered women," emphasizing the utter fear they have experienced, as well as their powerlessness and learned helplessness. Cognitive schemas about domestic violence victims emphasize that victims are pathologically weak, emotionally and financially dependent on their abusers, unable to protect themselves or their children, and unable to resist the will of their abusers. The performance of victimization is also a performance of gender, as the traits we associate with victimization—passivity, helplessness, dependence, and vulnerability—are consistent with societal schemas about femininity (Hollander, 2001).

When female petitioners include descriptions of resistance in their narratives, those actions are often portrayed as inherently ineffective and nonthreatening. For example, one petitioner, who worked for the same company as the respondent, was in the respondent's office showing him some personal photos when he "instigated an argument" after seeing "one picture in particular." Afraid for her safety, she attempted to leave,

> I gave [D] pictures of [J] and other pictures of my daughter etc. . . . [D] exploded when he saw one picture in particular. [D] instigated an argument. I started grabbing my things. I was afraid and tried to leave as fast as I could. He was screaming and ran out into the hallway and persisted in yelling. [D] yelled during this time for me to get out. I was collecting my pictures and trying to get around him. I had a large tote bag, book, pictures. [D's] behavior was so erratic I grabbed my pop can. I told myself that if he did anything my defense (only defense) would be to hit him with the can. [D] then stopped screaming and pushed me against the whiteboard. I dropped my can of pop, I think that alarmed him because I dropped it on his desk. While he was looking down I ran around him and left.

Both the incident itself and the decision to include it in the narrative are significant. Of all the objects that were likely in the respondent's office (scissors, letter opener, etc.) and that the petitioner was carrying (large tote bag, pictures, and other heavy objects), her "weapon" was the lightest and most innocuous item. Similarly, while the respondent "exploded," "pushed," "yelled," and "screamed"—all very physical and threatening actions—her resistance was to drop the can of pop on his desk. While irritating and distracting, her act is difficult to interpret as physical, threatening, or aggressive; in fact, dropping the can is also an expression of fear. Her act of "resistance" also underscores her need for external intervention; if the only option available to her was to drop a can of pop, how can she resist future acts of violence, especially if they do not occur in a public area where she can easily escape while he is distracted? The petitioner's story reflects schemas about gender, victimization, and agency, and in this case, a protection order was granted.

While the petitioner above was able to leave when she resisted, the narratives of other women reflected their utter powerlessness. Another petitioner who had gotten into an argument with the respondent over their car stated that she "got away" from him when he tried to hit her, but then found that despite her repeated requests,

> He would not leave. He kept pounding on my windows and my door for about two hours. Finally, my landlord came out and told him to leave and he would not leave. . . . He continued to bang on my doors and windows. After another couple of hours of him banging my landlord and I called the police. . . . My landlord told Mr. [M] and the officer that we did not want [M] back on the property.

In this filing, like the previous one, the petitioner provides little information about the instigating event: We know that there was some sort of argument, but the details are vague. Attention is thus diverted from the initial argument to the subsequent actions of the respondent, and, as there is little information about the argument, it is difficult to attribute responsibility to the petitioner. Similarly, there are few details as to how the petitioner "got away"; the petitioner attempts to portray herself as agentic but not aggressive.

However, unlike the office worker, this petitioner is unable to end the incident by her act of resistance. She describes (in far greater detail) the continued aggression of the respondent, which is only stopped through the actions of others in positions of power and authority—her landlord and the police officer. Thus, her narrative successfully portrays her as simultaneously agentic and helpless, and the courts granted her request for a protection order.

FEAR AND DANGEROUSNESS OF THE RESPONDENT

Throughout their narratives, many female petitioners emphasize both the dangerousness of the respondents and their fear of future violence in order to persuade the commissioner to grant their request for a protection order. Although the events that the petitioner chooses to include in the narrative clearly affect assessments of the respondent's dangerousness and the likelihood of future violence, the way in which the petitioner describes those events, and the amount and type of detail given about them, often has greater impact on the case. The following two narratives illustrate how differences in the "perceived dangerousness" and "perceived vulnerability" (Hollander, 2001) of the respondent and the petitioner are often influenced more by the ways in which the events are described than the seriousness of the events themselves.

> I was sitting in a club on (date) and [C] came in. He sat at the table next to me and watched me. I think he is following me because he comes to places where I am. I am afraid of him. He calls me at home all the time. Today (date) he called me 10 times. The first 3 times I answered the phone and he called me bad names and said I was going to die in a car accident. I did not answer the phone the other times because I have caller I-D and it was his number. He has friends call me and speak Chinese and I don't understand Chinese. I don't feel good about this. I have changed my phone # many times because of him. I can't afford to keep changing. He said he will destroy everything of mine and destroy my life too.

The petitioner begins the narrative with an incident where the respondent "watched" her at a club. She does not indicate whether she had any other interactions with the respondent prior to this incident, nor does she state whether they had any kind of relationship (note she does <u>not</u> say that this was the first time they had met). Throughout the narrative, she focuses on his actions; he "watches," "calls," follows her, and threatens to "destroy" both her and her property. She does not provide any context or reasons for his actions, which render them less explicable and more frightening and erratic. Each sentence highlights his agency and power, while her agency is often excluded from the narrative. For example, she says that she was "watched" at the club, but does not explain when and how she left (or how she left other situations). She does not state how the respondent got her home phone number. These pieces of information, while they are not legally relevant to the case, often lead to discussions of culpability and provide the respondent with an opportunity to argue against her claim as a "victim" and to the relationship as "abusive."

In the narrative, the petitioner describes only one act of resistance/agency. She writes that she has changed her phone number "many times," but, as he and his friends are still calling her, the implication is that this is ineffective. Furthermore, she states that she cannot continue performing this resistance for financial reasons, and hence she needs a protection order. This petitioner's request for a protection order was granted.

In comparison, the narrative below attributes much more agency to the petitioner and much less agency to the respondent.

> [R] and I had an argument because he was supposed to pick up our son [C] for the weekend and he never showed up. When I called to see what was going on he got angry because I couldn't bring him to [R]'s house, there was an argument which he called me several inappropriate names and said my aunt and my grand-parents would be sorry the next time he was around us. . . . . . Thanksgiving of 1998 [R] locked himself in a closet with one of his rifles threatening to kill himself because I invited my mother and the rest of her kids over for Thanksgiving dinner because her power had gone out and she had no way of cooking for the kids. I don't know the date of this but he once threatened one of my friend's boyfriends with his rifle. . . . . . Not to mention all of the verbal harrassment because I want him to pay child support and spend quality time with our son [B] he says this is my fault because I chose to leave him.

While the first petitioner has one explicit goal—to obtain a protection order so that the respondent will leave her alone—the second petitioner describes a more complex situation that contains conflicting information that problematizes her claim to the status of "victim." The second petitioner has several explicit goals, none of which can be achieved by obtaining an order of protection. She wants the respondent to pick up her child from her when scheduled and as planned. She wants him to "spend quality time with our son." She wants him to pay child support. Not once does she explicitly state that she needs a protection order to protect her from actions that meet the legal definition of domestic violence in Washington State; verbal harassment other than "inflicting fear of imminent physical harm, bodily injury or assault" is not domestic violence, and thus is not grounds for the entry of an order. While the verbal harassment she and her family have experienced most likely meet this threshold, she does not provide specific evidence of this, and her request for a protection order was denied.

The first petitioner also explicitly states that she is "afraid" of the respondent, while the second petitioner does not—in fact, the opposite is conveyed when she states that she wants him to "spend quality time with our son" and attributes their argument to the fact that he never "showed up." The petitioner does mention that the respondent has previously made threats with a rifle against himself and against a friend's boyfriend—serious actions that indicate that the respondent is capable of escalating the situation from threats to actual violence against the petitioner. However, the focus of the narrative is not her fear of future violence or the dangerousness of the respondent, but instead the type of parent she wants him to be. This stands in stark contrast to societal stereotypes of domestic violence victims, who want to hide from and have no contact with their abusers, not co-parent with them.

VIOLATIONS OF FEMINIZED VICTIMIZATION

Those women whose narratives do not reflect the societal stereotypes above—who do not exclusively focus on their "victimization," who are agentic rather than helpless, and who actively and aggressively resist abuse—may not be considered "legitimate" victims. Judges and commissioners may then dismiss the seriousness of their claims and question their motivations for filing for an order (Cahn, 1991). For example, a petitioner filing for a protection order against a former boyfriend who was also a coworker wrote,

> 5/23/00 came into my personal workspace when asked not to, and left his personal belongings (given to him from me as gifts in the past). Followed me out to my car when I was leaving work. Left two threatening messages on my cell phone that he wanted everything he had ever given me back so he could smash them because I was viscious (sic) and filled with venum (sic).

While this narrative describes actions that meet the legal criteria for domestic violence, the petitioner does not describe them in ways that reflect cognitive schemas about victimization. Her petition provides more detail about the items in dispute (that they were gifts to him, that she considers them his personal belongings, and that he wants his gifts to her returned) than about acts committed by the respondent that might meet the legal criteria for the entry of a protection order (stalking, leaving threatening messages). When she describes his behaviors, she does not label them as "stalking." Unlike the previous petitioner who received threats on her cell phone, she does not describe any attempts to avoid contact with the respondent. Most importantly, at no time in her narrative does she explicitly express any fear of the respondent—in fact, she does not include any of her emotional reactions to the respondent's actions in her narrative. Each of these elements is inconsistent with schemas about victimization, and the denial order written by the commissioner reflects this assessment. The commissioner wrote,

> There is no evidence to support domestic violence as defined by the statute. This is a workplace romance that has had a bitter ending. Both parties conduct is less than appropriate, however. Supervisors apprised of this matter, addressing it if appropriate.

As in the case above, violations of feminized victimization (inconsistencies between the petitioner's narrative and cognitive schemas about gender, violence, and agency) also provide the respondent with opportunities to reshape the petitioner's narrative so that the courts do not enter a protection order. As the petitioner has not performed femininity and victimization in her narrative, she is not a legitimate victim and thus is not in need of a protection order. This is done in several ways: Respondents often portray petitioners as untruthful ("my wife has twisted the truth"), mentally ill ("she is bipolar and needs to be on meds"), manipulative ("You know, M., if you keep coming over here with this attitude, you'll never see your son again"), and as the "true" aggressor in the relationship ("she has hit me numerous times"). In the example of the workplace relationship above, the respondent could reframe the events as part of a normal "break-up" that the petitioner has misinterpreted or misconstrued in an attempt to block the entry of a protection order. If the petitioner's narrative is inconsistent with normative conceptions of domestic violence, the likelihood that the respondent's attempt will be successful greatly increases.

CONCLUSION

Cultural assumptions about domestic violence affect substantive law and methods of litigation in ways that in turn affect society's perception of women; both law and societal perceptions affect women's understandings of our own lives, relationships, and options; our lives are part of the culture that affects legal interpretation and within which further legal moves are made. Serious harm to women results from the ways in which law and culture distort our experience (Mahoney, 1991, p. 1).

Civil protection orders have a number of advantages over other legal and criminal justice interventions in combating domestic violence. Protection orders allow victims of domestic violence, who often do not have external documentation to substantiate their claims of abuse, to use their own stories as evidence. The burden of proof is also less than in criminal cases, and commissioners need only believe that a "preponderance of evidence" indicates that there has been domestic violence rather than "proof beyond a reasonable doubt." Unlike criminal no-contact orders, victims can request any of a number of provisions depending on their specific needs or, if they feel the respondent is no longer a threat, they can request that the order be dismissed altogether.

The protection order process also gives victims the opportunity to tell their stories in court, which is assumed to help empower them. Many domestic violence advocates, researchers, and survivors have argued that the retelling of abuse by the victim "enables her to transform her consciousness: to name the abuse, to interpret it as oppression, to re-experience her anger, and to make the transition from victim to survivor" (Riessman, 1992, p. 232). From this perspective, the act of writing the narrative for the protection order petition not only leads to empowerment (through the entry of a protection order) but is in itself empowering for the victim.

Like other areas of the legal system, however, the protection order process is situated in a broader social context. As noted by Mahoney (1991), "cultural assumptions"—cognitive schemas—about domestic violence, gender, and victimization shape both the construction of the petitions by victims and their subsequent interpretations by judges and commissioners. These schemas shape expectations as to what "true" victims are like, including expectations about the balance of power in the relationship, the agency and culpability of the victim, the victim's fear of the respondent, and the dangerousness of the respondent. To be seen as "legitimate" victims, women must present their clams so that they appear simultaneously (and paradoxically) helpless and agentic, powerless to stop the abuse, yet strong enough to engage in resistance. Female petitioners whose stories are not consistent with these schemas often do not receive protection orders.

For many petitioners, their ability to present their stories in a way that is consistent with schemas about gender and domestic violence is relatively unimportant because the respondent does not contest the allegations and/or the protection order petition. However, in contested cases, this ability becomes critically important. The respondent may be able to block the entry of a protection order in a contested case by (1) providing an alternative interpretation of events that is consistent with schemas about gender and domestic violence, or (2) by highlighting the ways in which the petitioner's narrative is inconsistent with these schemas, thereby casting doubt upon the petitioner's credibility or motives. In these cases, the opportunity to tell one's story in court may actually *disempower* the victim. Ironically, by allowing women to submit their own narratives as evidence for the entry of a protection order, the courts may have in fact made it more difficult for victims to obtain one.

Discussion Questions

1. What is the paradox described by Durfee? How is this paradox a problem for female protection orders petitioners?
2. What does the author mean by the law *de jure* and the law *de facto*? How are petitioners affected by this?
3. Discuss some of the gendered cultural images and stereotypes the petitioners and respondents use to obtain or block the entry of a protection order.
4. What is a cognitive schema? How does gender interact with cognitive schemas?
5. What does the author mean by empowerment? How does the protection order work to empower women? How does it work to disempower women?

References

Bachman, R., & Saltzman, L. E. (1995). *Violence against women: Estimates from the redesigned survey* (NCJ 154348). Washington D.C.: U.S. Department of Justice, Bureau of Justice Statistics.

Bureau of Justice Statistics. (2006). *Criminal victimization in the United States: 2005 Statistical tables from the National Criminal Victimization Survey.* NCJ 215244. Retrieved May 15, 2008, from http://www.ojp.usdoj.gov/bjs/pub/pdf/cvus05.pdf

Cahn, N. (1991). Civil images of battered women: The impact of domestic violence on child custody decisions. *Vanderbilt Law Review, 44,* 1041–1097.

Cobb, S. (1997). The domestication of violence in mediation. *Law & Society Review, 31,* 397–440.

Comack, E., & Balfour, G. (2004). *The power to criminalize.* Black Point, Nova Scotia: Fernwood Publishing.

Conley, J. M., & O'Barr, W. M. (1990). *Rules versus relationships: the ethnography of legal discourse.* Chicago, IL: University of Chicago Press.

Connell, R. W. (1995). *Masculinities.* Cambridge, UK: Polity Press.

Crang, M. (1997). Analyzing qualitative materials. In R. Flowerdew & D. Martin (Eds.), *Methods in human geography* (pp. 183–196). New York: Prentice Hall.

Dunlap, L. (2004). Sometimes I feel like a motherless child: The error of pursuing battered mothers for failure to protect. *Loyola Law Review, 50,* 565.

Durfee, A. (2004). *Domestic violence in the civil court system* (Doctoral dissertation, University of Washington).

Estrich, S. (1987). *Real rape.* Cambridge, MA: Harvard University Press.

Ewick, P., & Silbey, S. S. (1995). Subversive stories and hegemonic tales: Towards a sociology of narrative. *Law & Society Review, 29,* 197–226.

Felson, R. B., & Cares, A. C. (2005). Gender and the seriousness of assaults on intimate partners and other victims. *Journal of Marriage and the Family, 67,* 1182–1195.

Galanter, M. (1974). Why the 'haves' come out ahead: Speculations on the limits of legal change. *Law and Society, 9,* 95–160.

Harrell, A., & Smith, B. (1996). Effects of restraining orders on domestic violence victims. In E. S. Buzawa & C. G. Buzawa (Eds.), *Do arrests and restraining orders work?* (pp. 214–242). Thousand Oaks, CA: Sage.

Hines, D. A., & Malley-Morrison, K. (2005). *Family violence in the United States: Defining, understanding, and combating abuse.* Thousand Oaks, CA: Sage.

Hollander, J. A. (2001). Vulnerability and danger-ousness: The construction of gender through conversation about violence. *Gender & Society, 15*, 83–109.

Holt, V. L., Kernic, M. A., Lumley, T., Wolf, M. E., & Rivara, F. P. (2002). Civil protection orders and risk of subsequent police-reported violence. *Journal of the American Medical Association, 288*, 589–594.

Howard, J. A., & Hollander, J. A. (1997). *Gendered situations, gendered selves: a gender lens on social psychology.* Thousand Oaks, CA: Sage.

Katz, C. (1992). All the world is staged: Intellectuals and the projects of ethnography. *Environment and Planning. D: Society and Space, 10*, 495–510.

Lempert, L. B. (1994). A narrative analysis of abuse: Connecting the personal, the rhetorical, and the structural. *Journal of Contemporary Ethnography, 22*, 411–440.

Lieblich, A., Tuval-Mashiach, R., & Zilber, T. (1998). *Narrative research: Reading, analysis and interpretation.* Thousand Oaks, CA: Sage Publications.

Lonsway, K. A., & Fitzgerald, L. F. (1994). Rape myths. *Psychology of Women Quarterly, 21*, 35–51.

Mahoney, M. R. (1991). Legal images of battered women: Redefining the issue of separation. *Michigan Law Review*, 90, 1–94.

Messner, M. A. (1997). *Politics of masculinities: Men in movements.* Thousand Oaks, CA: Sage.

Ochberg, R. L. (1994). Life stories and storied lives. In A. Lieblich & R. Josselson (Eds.), *Exploring identity and gender: The narrative study of lives* (pp. 113–144). Thousand Oaks, CA: Sage.

Revised Code of Washington (RCW) § 26.50.010(1) (2008). Retrieved October 8, 2008, from http://apps.leg.wa.gov/RCW/default. aspx?cite=26.50.010.

Rich, A. (1980). Compulsory heterosexuality and lesbian existence. *Signs, 5*, 631–660.

Riessman, C. K. (1992). Making sense of marital violence: One woman's narrative. In G. C. Rosenwald & R. L. Ochberg (Eds.), *Storied lives: The cultural politics of self-understanding* (pp. 231–249). New Haven, CT: Yale University Press.

Riessman, C. K. (1993). *Narrative analysis.* Newbury Park, CA: Sage Publications.

Straus, M. A., Gelles, R. J., & Steinmetz, S. K. (1980). *Behind closed doors: Violence in the American family.* Garden City, NY: Anchor Press/Doubleday.

Tjaden, P., & Thoennes, N. (2000). *Full report of the prevalence, incidence, and consequences of violence against women.* Washington, D.C.: US Dept. of Justice, Office of Justice Programs.

Toolan, M. J. (1988). *Narrative: A critical linguistic introduction.* New York, NY: Routledge.

Trinch, S. L., & Berk-Seligson, S. (2002). Narrating in protective order interviews: A source of interactional trouble. *Language in Society, 31*, 383–418.

Washington Courts Website. (2008). Courts Form, Domestic Violence. Retrieved May 7, 2008, from http://www.courts.wa.gov/forms/index. cfm?fa=forms.contribute&formID=16

Endnotes

1. Felson and Cares report that of their sample, 38 percent of women and 26 percent of men reported that they were injured during an assault by an intimate partner.
2. On average, women who reported physical assault by an intimate partner had been victimized 6.9 times; for men, 4.4 times.
3. For women reporting physical assault by an intimate partner, the average number of years they were victimized is 4.5; for men, 3.6 years.
4. All excerpts from petitions included in this chapter reflect the spelling, grammar, and structure of the original documents.

CHAPTER 15

MISDEMEANOR DOMESTIC VIOLENCE CASES IN THE COURTS: A DETAILED DESCRIPTION OF THE CASES*

JOANNE BELKNAP, JENNIFER L. HARTMAN, AND VICTORIA L. LIPPEN

ABSTRACT

Most of the extant research on domestic violence and the criminal processing system focuses on the police response to the victims and batterers. Relatively little scholarly work attempts to understand the types of cases that reach the courts and how these cases are processed. This chapter draws on data from prosecutor reports, police reports, victim affidavits, and pretrial reports to provide a detailed description of misdemeanor domestic violence court cases in a large Midwestern urban area. The findings indicate that victims are more "cooperative" with authorities than is commonly assumed, but that prosecutors spend little time with them.

INTRODUCTION

A significant aspect of the second wave of the women's movement in the late 1960s and the 1970s was the identification of woman battering as a social problem (Dobash & Dobash, 1979; Schneider, 2000; Tierney, 1983). In addition to the women's movement, successful law suits brought by battered women against police departments for their failure to protect, and research indicating that arrest "works" to deter batterers, were influential in bringing about pro-arrest policies for intimate partner domestic violence cases (see Belknap, 1995; Sherman, 1992). The implementation of pro-arrest domestic violence policies across the United States and in many other countries not only marked a significant change in police practices but also resulted in an unprecedented amount of

*Prepared under Grant No. 96-WT-NX-0004, Research and Evaluation on Violence Against Women from the National Institute of Justice, Office of Justice Programs, U.S. Department of Justice. Points of view or opinions in this document are those of the authors and do not necessarily represent the official position of the U.S. Department of Justice. The authors would also like to thank Jeff Hayes of the University of Colorado for his statistical help and advice.

research on policing domestic violence, particularly on the effect of arrest on recidivism rates (for reviews and critiques of these studies, see Belknap, 1995; Bowman, 1992; Frisch, 1992; Lerman, 1992; Manning, 1993; Stark, 1993).[2]

While these pro-arrest policies indicate a strict departure from the wide latitude in police discretion, Davis and Smith (1995) contend that the pro-arrest policies have simply moved the point of discretion from the police to prosecutorial screening. In fact, a 1992 report indicated that despite a huge increase in domestic violence cases reaching the courts, prosecution is uncommon (Syers & Edleson, 1992, p. 491). Further, Roberts (1996) describes judicial intervention on behalf of battered women as a "recent phenomenon" (p. 97). To address this concern, a number of courts have implemented procedural changes such as no-drop policies to increase the convictions of intimate partner abusers (Ames & Dunham, 2002; Goodman, Dutton, & Bennett, 2000; Keilitz, 1997; Robbins, 1999). Notably, some feminists are concerned with the coercive and backfiring potential of no-drop court policies (e.g., Dasgupta, 2003; Ford, 2003; McDermott & Garofalo, 2004; Mills, 1999, 2003), while still other feminists are concerned that police pro-arrest and court no-drop policies are perhaps being dismissed too readily by feminists, without accounting for the women's lives they have positively impacted (e.g., Flanakin & Walsh, 2005; Stark, 2003, 2004). Given that through the pro-arrest policies, domestic abuse cases are reaching the courts in unprecedented numbers, and that the courts as well as the police have attempted to change policies and practices in domestic violence cases, studying the court processing of domestic violence cases is of a significant concern.

The purpose of the current chapter is to have a better understanding of misdemeanor domestic violence court cases. Specifically, the sample for this study is the total 1997 population misdemeanor intimate partner domestic violence cases that reached the courts in a large metropolitan area in the Midwest. The goal is to provide a detailed description of these cases, including such relevant but rarely collected data on victim "cooperation." Although the literature review uses the terms "domestic violence," "intimate partner violence," and "woman battering" interchangeably, we have chosen to include the entire intimate partner abuse cases in the research. Thus, while the written work on intimate partner violence indicates a strong gendered nature of this abuse (e.g., Dobash & Dobash, 1984; Dobash, Dobash, Wilson, & Daly, 1992; McLeod, 1983; Saunders, 1986; Tjaden & Thoennes, 2000; Vivian & Langhinrichsen-Rohling, 1994), there is a growing recognition of and concern about the number of women charged with this abuse (e.g., Jones & Belknap, 1999; Martin, 1994).

PRIOR RESEARCH

Similar to policing domestic violence, the limited research on the courts and domestic violence is fraught with assumptions about "reluctant" and "noncooperative" victims/witnesses. Indeed, to some extent the non-cooperative witness may be a self-fulfilling prophecy if prosecutors fail to take these cases seriously under the assumption that the battered women will not cooperate (see Cahn, 1992; Cannavale & Falcon, 1976; Cretney & Davis, 1997; Davis & Smith, 1981; Erez & Belknap, 1998; Ferraro & Boychuck, 1992; Hartman & Belknap 2003; Parnas, 1967; Pastoor, 1984; Schmidt & Steury, 1989; Sigler, Crowley, & Johnson, 1990; U.S. Commission for Civil Rights, 1982). Although one study reported that four-fifths of domestic violence cases were dismissed because the victim did not appear in court or appeared and requested the case be dropped (Quarm & Schwartz, 1985), it is crucial to understand the role prosecutors can play in this phenomenon. Ferraro and Boychuk (1992, p. 213) highlight how some prosecutors' assumptions and practices around their perceived images of battered women as reluctant or uncooperative likely *result* in this reluctance:

> Victim cooperation in cases of domestic violence is viewed as such a typical problem that prosecutors have established a 'cooling off' period for such cases. . . . . . . In our data, the majority of intimate victims were cooperative with prosecution (49 percent). However, a large proportion of intimate victims did request for charges to be dropped once filed (39 percent). . . . If it [a cooling off period] is a bureaucratic technique for eliminating the difficulty of working with victims who are emotionally and financially tied to their assailants, it would be helpful to provide assistance for the problems rather than discourage prosecution.

Assumptions about battered women's reluctance to "cooperate" with police and court officials overshadow six overlapping phenomena. First, many battered women who have sought help from the authorities have been denied this help (Abraham, 2000; Browne, 1987; Cahn, 1992; Erez & Belknap, 1998; Jones, 1994; Rosewater, 1988; Websdale, 1995; Websdale & Johnson, 1997). Second, some research suggests that the court and police officials often actively discredit and blame women abused by their intimate or former intimate partners (Belknap & Hartman, 2000; Eaton & Hyman, 1992; Erez & Belknap, 1998). Third, battered women in the stages of leaving an abuser are often in the riskiest and most lethal stage of the abusive relationship (Campbell, 1992; Ellis, 1987; Ellis & DeKeseredy, 1989; Erez & Belknap, 1998; Mahoney, 1991; Sev'er, 1997; Wilson & Daly, 1993). Fourth, many battered women fear reprisal from their abusers should they "cooperate" with police or court officials, and batterers often threaten them with abuse should they cooperate (Belknap, Fleury, Melton, Sullivan, & Leisenring, 2001; Buzawa & Austin, 1993; Ewing, 1987; Hardesty, 2002; Hart, 1993; Martin, 1994; McLeod, 1983; Ptacek, 1999; Quarm & Schwartz, 1985; Roberts, 1996; Singer, 1988). Fifth, some battered women want their cases dropped when they believe the serious abuse against them has been trivialized by court officials, such as charging them as misdemeanors or as crimes other than domestic violence (Corsilles, 1994; Hart, 1993; Langan & Innes, 1986; Martin, 1994; Ptacek, 1999). Sixth, the limited research on defense attorneys indicates that they often dissuade abused women from cooperating with the system, wear them down through continuances, and even inform them that they do not need to appear in court (Crenshaw, 1994; Ford & Regoli, 1993). Similarly, other studies report that some judges (Zorza, 1992) and police (Erez & Belknap, 1998) also try, often successfully, to talk victims out of pursuing charges. Given these phenomena, the police, prosecutors, and judges who fail to move these cases forward are deserving of the "reluctant" and "uncooperative" labels they issue the battered women (Gondolf & Fisher, 1988). Pro-arrest legislation and contemporary policies have limited effectiveness if prosecutors and judges do not treat these cases seriously.

Some research indicates that prosecution of domestic violence cases is still frequently handled leniently (e.g., Lerman, 1992; Martin, 1994; Mignon & Holmes, 1995; Syers & Edleson, 1992). For example, a study comparing simple assault prosecutions with the prosecution of misdemeanor domestic violence cases found that although the domestic assaults were often serious, the prosecution rates of these cases were significantly lower than those of the other assault cases (Martin, 1994). Other studies reported high rates of no prosecution in domestic violence cases: 66 percent in one study (Mignon & Holmes, 1995) and 79 percent in another (Martin, 1994). Other studies indicate that this may be because prosecutors have a higher standard of corroboration in domestic violence than in stranger assault cases (Kerstetter, 1990; Kingsnorth, MacIntosh, & Wentworth, 1999). Not surprisingly, then, one study of battered women whose cases were referred to court found that one-fifth of the victims who went to court did so despite the "barrier" of previous bad experiences with the court. Of those women who did not go to court, over a quarter reported previous bad experiences with the court as a reason for not going (Belknap, Fleury, Melton, Sullivan, & Leisenring, 2001).

The research findings are inconsistent regarding the role of victim injury on the decision to prosecute. Two studies report that victim injury increased the likelihood of prosecution (Hirschel & Hutchison, 2001; Schmidt & Steury 1989), and two did not (Martin, 1994; Rauma, 1984). Hirschel and Hutchison (2001) conducted a multivariate analysis to examine variables related to the decision to prosecute. They found that two legal factors were strongly associated (in the expected direction) with the decision to prosecute: victim injury and whether the victim wanted the case prosecuted (Hirschel & Hutchison, 2001). Another legal variable, the offender's record, however, had no impact on the prosecution decision. Another unique study of the effect of court disposition on recidivism (as measured by rearrest within six months) in domestic violence cases reported that the case disposition had no effect (Davis, Smith, & Nickles, 1998), but a more recent study found convicted batterers were less likely than nonconvicted batterers to recidivate within 12 months of the court verdict (Ventura & Davis, 2005).

METHOD

This study was part of a larger research project designed to examine misdemeanor intimate partner domestic violence in a large metropolitan area in the Midwest where the court processed cases for the large urban area and its surrounding county. The research design is a result of collaboration. The research–community partnership was between researchers and the Domestic Violence Committee (DVC), a community organization composed of judges, prosecutors, police officers and administrators, victim advocates, mental health and social workers, and others. Formed in 1995, the purpose of the DVC was to bring together key "players" in the criminal processing system's response to domestic violence (e.g., the police, prosecutors, and judges) in an attempt to improve the prosecution and conviction rate of batterers. A primary concern of the DVC leadership was to understand which factors were related to domestic violence case outcomes. To examine this problem and to identify solutions, the research team used a multi-pronged approach to collect data on misdemeanor domestic violence cases in the municipal court. In the larger research project, four data sets were collected to examine the court processing of misdemeanor court cases: pretrial data, court transcripts, court official (judge, prosecutor, and public defender) interviews and surveys, and victim interviews.

Misdemeanors constitute the vast majority of the domestic violence cases in this research site (approximately 80 percent). The misdemeanor cases are still believed by the DVC to include very serious cases of abuse; they are often batterers charged with a misdemeanor instead of felony simply because it was the first time he was arrested (not necessarily the first time he was abusive or that the police were called). This is not to deny the importance of studying court processing of felony domestic violence cases.

The current chapter reports on the pretrial data. To this end, 2,760 misdemeanor domestic violence cases were processed and collected by Pre-Trial Services in this jurisdiction in 1997. The head of the prosecutor's office in the jurisdiction of the study claims that there were 2,950 such cases for that year. Unfortunately, although the prosecutor's office had some means of tracking these cases, we were not made aware of it until the study was over and it was impossible to go backwards to get the missing (9.5%) cases. However, the method we used allowed us to collect data on over 90 percent of the cases, and we have no reason to think the cases we missed were different.

Pre-Trial Services conducted lengthy interviews with defendants and collected data on wide-ranging variables. In this study the "defendant" is a person who was arraigned in the research site between the period of January 1, 1997 and December 31, 1997 for one or more of these misdemeanor charges against a person living as a spouse: domestic violence, violating protection order or consent agreement or a related crime, menacing by stalking, and rape. The pretrial data were merged with two other data sets: police reports and prosecutor reports. The police were in the process of transferring to National Incident Based Reporting System (NIBRS) forms during the year of data collection. They had their unique form and then the NIBRS form. In this project we collected any police forms available for each of the cases (NIBRS and/or the one unique to this jurisdiction). Additionally, we believed it was important to obtain prosecutor data on these cases. Thus, we created a one-page form for prosecutors to complete for all of their intimate partner domestic violence cases in 1997. The prosecutors were asked about the status of the relationship between the defendant and the victim, the judges' and victims' demeanors, the case outcome, and so on.

The police in this jurisdiction operated under a "preferred arrest" policy, according to which they were not *obligated* to arrest, but were strongly encouraged to do so (at least in theory). There were no specialized dockets and no special services/policies regarding domestic violence cases in these courts. There were *no* victim advocates housed in the prosecutor's office or working with the prosecutors. Thus, victim services were quite distinct from the courts. There were approximately 250 cases heard daily in these courts (domestic violence combined with all other offenses). In sum, there were no innovative practices to address domestic violence operating in this jurisdiction in 1997, short of the DVC's efforts to gain funding and meet monthly.

It is useful to report the program structure of the victim advocacy program (VAP). The VAP oversees all cases in the county, but they are funded independently of the county (e.g., through the United Way, the city, and private donations). VAP advocates are in the courtrooms Monday through Friday. When the police service a domestic violence call, the police are to fax a copy of the report to the VAP. The VAP calls the victims before arraignment and educates them about the courtroom process and offers to stand up with the victim at the hearing. Moreover, they explain to the victim the meaning of the protection order, as well as to offer additional information on what services VAP offers. They also provide crisis intervention. VAP receives a copy of the daily docket and attempts to find the victim in the courtroom, if they have not already contacted the victim before. VAP tells the victims that, should their case go to trial, the victim can notify them and they will do their best to provide the above-noted assistance at that time. The prosecutors in this jurisdiction do not have any contact with the victims before arraignment; they rely on VAP workers and volunteers to notify the victims of the court time and date. After arraignment, the prosecutors are expected to contact the victims to ask and inform them the current case.

It is necessary to highlight some of the limitations of this study. First, this study is of one jurisdiction, and can hardly be said to be representative of all jurisdictions. The site is traditional in nature, and as Zimmerman and Owens (1989) have stated on their research comparing sites on family policy legislations, the local political culture "matters." Second, the police data are somewhat troubling. When examining the actual written reports, they each appear to be filled out very differently depending on the officer completing them. Third, the prosecutors also seemed to vary (though not nearly as much) in the detail they used to complete the forms. For example, many of the prosecutors did not complete the data assessing judicial demeanor. However, the data set is unusual in that it includes a large number of cases in a large jurisdiction with variables rarely or never collected in the existing studies on the court processing of domestic violence cases.

FINDINGS

SAMPLE DESCRIPTION

Table 15.1 describes the sample. Similar to national trends, over four-fifths of the defendants in the sample were male, and over four-fifths of the victims were female. About 86 percent of the cases were male defendants and female victims, and 14 percent were females charged with abusing their intimate male partners. These data certainly speak to the "double" or "dual" arrests as part of the backlash to pro-arrest policies (see Jones & Belknap, 1999; Martin, 1994). Less than 2 percent of the sample was same-sex partners.

TABLE 15.1 Domestic Violence Victim and Defendant Demographic Information (N = 2,670)

Variable	N^a	%	n
Defendant Sex	2,654		
Male		86.1	2,284
Female		13.9	370
Victim Sex	2,620		
Male		13.5	353
Female		86.5	2,267
Defendant Sex/Victim Sex	2,606		
Male/Female		85.7	2,234
Female/Male		13.0	338
Male/Male		0.5	14
Female/Female		0.8	20
Defendant Race	2,670		
African American		71.0	1,895

(continued)

TABLE 15.2 (continued)

Variable	N^a	%	n
White		28.3	756
Other[b]		0.7	19
Victim Race	1,726		
African American		65.9	1,137
White		33.8	583
Other[c]		0.3	6
Defendant Age ($0 = 31.4$)[d]	2,632		
18–24		25.6	674
25–29		22.4	590
30–34		18.2	478
35–39		16.0	422
40–45		11.4	301
46+		6.3	167
Victim Age ($0 = 29.5$)[e]	1,721		
14–19		10.7	185
20–24		23.9	411
25–29		21.2	364
30–34		17.5	301
35–39		13.9	239
40+		12.8	221
Victim–Offender Relationship	2,062		
Spouses		27.8	573
Ex-spouses		3.5	73
Boy/girlfriend		9.1	187
Ex-boy/girlfriend		5.4	113
Cohabitating/common law		37.0	762
Child-in-common		17.2	354
Residing Together at Time of Incident?	1,284		
Yes		73.2	940
No		26.8	344
Still Intimately Involved at Court Time?	957		
Yes		46.3	443
No		53.7	514

Sources: Prosecutor Form developed for this study, NIBRS data, and Pre-Trial data.

[a]Ns do not always total 2,670 due to missing data.

[b]Includes 3 Asians/Asian Americans, 2 Latinas, one Native American, and 19 coded as "other."

[c]Includes 4 Asians, 1 Latino, and 1 Southasia Indian.

[d]The median was 30 years and the mode was 25 years of age, and they ranged in age from 18 to 86 years.

[e]The median was 28 years and the mode was 20 years of age, and they ranged in age from 14 to 80 years.

There was some indication via casual courthouse conversation that same-sex partner domestic violence cases were more likely to be forwarded to mediation than heterosexual couple cases. Similar to many other studies and jurisdictions, this study explains that African Americans were grossly overrepresented in the court sample compared to the population. Over 70 percent of those charged with domestic violence were African Americans, and about slightly less than 70 percent of the victims were African Americans. Almost all of the remaining defendants and victims were White. The defendants' ages ranged from 17 to 86, with the average age in the early thirties. The victims ranged in age from 14 to just under 90. The average age for victims was almost 30.

The largest category of victim–offender relationship (VOR) was "cohabiting" or "common law." Almost two-fifths of the sample (37%) was in this category. The next most common VOR category, over one-quarter of the sample (28%), was "spouses," and the next most common VOR category, almost one-fifth (17%), was "child in common." Almost 10 percent of the couples were boyfriend/girlfriend, about 5 percent were ex-boyfriend/girlfriend, and fewer than 5 percent were former spouses (see Table 15.1). It is somewhat remarkable, from data on the prosecutor forms, how infrequently the prosecutors knew whether the victim and the offender (1) were residing together at the time of the incident, and (2) were still intimately involved at the time of the court case. For the 1,284 cases where prosecutors knew whether the victim and the offender were living together at the time of the incident, approximately three-fourths (73%) were living together. For the 957 cases where the prosecutors knew whether the victim and the offender were "still intimately involved at the time of the court case," they were fairly equally divided between those still involved and those no longer involved. Notably, however, and in contrast to the "Why don't women leave?" question, 54 percent were no longer intimately involved with their abusers according to the prosecutors; thus, over half had left.

PROSECUTORS' REPORTS OF THE CHARACTERISTICS OF THE COURT CASES

Table 15.2 presents information from the prosecutors' reports on the dynamics of the court case. The most common form of available evidence was the victim's testimony or statement (51% of the cases), followed by photographs of injuries or property damage (14%). Police testimony was available in about 7 percent of the cases. Notably, 911 tapes, medical records, and other eyewitness testimony each were available in fewer than 3 percent of the cases, respectively. Significantly, when we merged the data from the prosecutors' forms with the NIBRS data ($N = 2,486$), the availability of photographs of the injuries/damages increased from 14 to 19 percent, and the availability of medical records rose from less than 2 percent to over 3 percent. It suggests that the prosecutors were not aware of the evidence in all the cases, which could be troublesome.

According to the prosecutors, victims were not present in about one-third of the cases and were subpoenaed in almost half of the cases. Prosecutors reported that the victims changed their stories in 10 percent of the cases. Prosecutors infrequently seemed to know whether a victim advocate was present in court. In fact, they reported not knowing the status of the advocate almost 70 percent of the time. Of the 500 cases they reported knowing the status of the victim advocate, they reported advocates were present in about 3 percent of the cases.

Variable	*N*	%	*n*
TABLE 15.2 Prosecutors' Reports on Misdemeanor Domestic Violence Cases (*N* = 2,241)			
Available Evidence[a]	2,486		
911 tapes[b]		2.2	43
Photos of injuries/damages[b]		14.2	280
Medical records[b]		1.7	33
Victim's statement or testimony		51.2	1,007
Police testimony[c]		6.7	132
Other eyewitness testimony[c]		1.6	31
Victim Involvement[a]	1,968		
Not present		35.8	704
Changed story		9.9	195
Present for plea		70.2	1,381
Subpoenaed		46.7	920
Victim Advocate Present?	1,551		
Yes		3.3	51
No		28.3	439
Don't know		68.4	1,061
Victim Demeanor[a]	1,014		
Cooperative		57.7	585
Not cooperate		20.1	204
Withholding		19.2	195
Credible		40.0	406
Not credible		10.8	110
Reasonable		40.9	415
Unreasonable		6.7	68
Angry		7.6	77
Friendly		21.2	215
Belligerent		2.2	22
Mentally limited		4.4	45
Equally, or more at fault		8.7	88
Anxious, scared[c]		2.2	22
Intoxicated/drunk[c]		0.9	9
Judge's Conduct[a]	924		
Sensitive		37.4	346
Insensitive		0.3	7
Supportive		25.3	234
Nonsupportive		0.4	4
Appropriate		84.1	777
Inappropriate		1.2	11
Weapons Used?[d]	1,866		
Yes		23.1	431
No		76.9	1,435

(*continued*)

TABLE 15.2 (continued)			
Variable	*N*	*%*	*n*
Victim Injured?[e]	1,866		
Yes		47.9	893
No		52.1	1,286
No. Times Prosecutor Spoke with Victim on Phone (mean = 0.21)	1,934		
None		87.5	1,692
One		8.2	159
Two to three		3.5	67
Four to 10		0.8	16
Total Minutes Prosecutor Spoke with Victim on Phone (mean = 3.19)	1,169		
None		80.6	942
1–5 min		5.1	59
6–15 min		9.9	116
16–30 min		2.7	32
More than 30 min		1.7	20
No. Times Prosecutor Met in Person with Victim (mean = 0.53)	1,942		
None		51.6	1,003
One		44.4	863
Two to three		3.9	75
Four to seven		0.1	1
Total Minutes Prosecutor Spent Meeting with Victim (mean = 7.89)	1,501		
None		38.4	577
1–5 min		23.1	346
6–15 min		27.3	410
16–30 min		9.2	138
More than 30 min		2.0	30

[a]Cases could include more than one category.

[b]The 911 tape, photos of injuries, and medical records data reported here were strictly from the Prosecutor Form. However, when we combined data from NIBRS and the Prosecutor Form ($N = 2,486$), the 911 tapes rose to 2.4 percent ($n = 60$), photos of injuries/damages rose to 18.9 percent ($n = 469$), and medical records rose 3.1 percent ($n = 77$).

[c]These categories were listed by respondent under the "other" variable; thus they are likely to be a low representation of frequency in the respective category.

[d]Weapons include gun, knife, chair, rope, glass, bleach, and so on, but exclude body parts (e.g., hand, feet, head). This includes NIBRS data. A knife was present in 8.4 percent ($n = 145$) of the cases, a gun was present in 1.3 percent of the cases ($n = 24$), and a knife or gun was present in 6.2 percent ($n = 166$) of the cases.

[e]Police and/or prosecutors reported injuries including stabbed, shot, broken bones, black eye, scratched, bitten, or knocked out. This includes NIBRS data.

Table 15.2 also reports prosecutors' descriptions of victims' demeanor. In contrast to the media and research concentration on "uncooperative" victim/witnesses, the most commonly reported demeanor, used to describe almost three-fifths of the victims, was "cooperative." The next most common descriptions of victim demeanor, reported for two-fifths of the victims, were "credible" and "reasonable." About one-fifth was reported as "friendly." About one-fifth was also reported as "withholding" and "not cooperative." Roughly 10 percent were reported as "not credible." Fewer than 10 percent were reported as "equally or more at fault" (9%), "angry" (8%), "unreasonable" (7%), "mentally limited" (4%), and belligerent (2%). In the "other" category, about 2 percent of the prosecutors wrote in "anxious or scared" and almost 1 percent wrote "intoxicated/drunk." Thus, future research may want to include these categories in a checklist. The prosecutors reported that weapons were used in the incident in over one-fifth (23%) of the cases and that the victim was injured in almost half (48%) of the cases.

Table 15.2 also reports the prosecutors' perceptions of the judges' conduct, albeit for less than 1,000 of the cases. The most common description of the judge's behavior (84% of the cases) was "appropriate." Over one-third (37%) of the cases described the judge as "sensitive." One-quarter (25%) described the judge as "supportive." Thus, similar to descriptions of the victim, the descriptions most frequently provided regarding the judge were positive. About 1percent of the time prosecutors described the judges' behavior as "inappropriate," and in less than 1 percent of the cases the judges' conduct was reported as "non-supportive" or "insensitive." It is worth noting that the prosecutors all kept their completed forms in a common place in the prosecutors' office to be picked up, and it is likely that some of them may have been resistant to report "unkind" or "unprofessional" behaviors about the judges on these forms (thus a potential explanation to the somewhat low item response rate).

The remaining items reported in Table 15.2 concern the amount of time prosecutors spent with victims in person and on the phone. In almost nine-tenths of the cases, prosecutors reported that they never spoke with the victim on the phone, and in half of the cases they never met with the victims. In those cases where the prosecutors did meet and talk with the victims, it was typically in the courtroom five minutes before the court cases started. The average number of minutes prosecutors spent talking with victims on the phone was three minutes. In fewer than 2 percent of the cases did they talk more than 30 minutes with victims they represent.

OFFENDERS' CHARGES AND CASE DISPOSITIONS

Table 15.3 presents the information on the charges and dispositions (garnered from the prosecutor forms). Almost 90 percent of the charges were "M1," the most serious misdemeanor charge. Approximately half of the defendants' cases were "dismissed" and slightly over two-fifths were found guilty. About 5 percent were found "not guilty." The most common reason (70%) reported by prosecutors for the dismissal was victims' unavailability or "failure to appear." The next most common reason (9%) was that the defendant was given the option and took it to have the case dismissed if he (this was only available for male defendants) attended batterer treatment. In 7 percent of the dismissed cases, the prosecutor claimed the dismissal was due to the victim not cooperating with the prosecution. This is consistent with a study of sexual assault cases where Spohn, Beichner, and Davis-Frenzel (2001) found that victims' failure to appear and lack of cooperation with prosecutors were two of the major predictors of prosecutors deciding not to prosecute.

In the current study, when there was a guilty plea, over three-fifths (63%) were to an amended (lesser) charge. Ninety percent of the cases were "bench" cases (e.g., a judge not jury deliberates over the case), about 8 percent were settled in pretrial, and

TABLE 15.3 Present Charge and Disposition Information (*N* = 2,241)

Variable	N	%	n
Level of Charge[a]	2,104		
M1		88.4	1,860
M3		1.9	41
M4		9.7	203
Disposition	2,209[b]		
Dismissed		51.0	1,126
Guilty		43.9	969
Not guilty		5.1	114
Reason for Dismissal[c]	1,126		
Victim unavailable/fail to appear		68.9	776
Counseling (AMEND) attained		9.4	106
Victim uncooperative with prosecution		6.8	77
Plead to other charge		4.3	48
Private Mediation Services		3.0	34
Rule 29[d]		2.3	26
Cross-complaint warrant		2.1	24
Problem with Temporary Protection Order		1.3	15
No prior offenses		1.1	12
Request of prosecuting attorney		1.0	11
Defendant in jail or prison		0.8	9
Defendant did not show		0.2	6
Type of Guilty Plea	918		
To amended charge		63.4	582
As charged		36.6	336
Trial Type	1,055		
Bench		90.0	949
Jury		2.3	24
No trial/settled in Pretrial		7.8	82
Sentence: Days Incarcerated (mean = 62.1)[e]	895		
Zero		16.0	143
1–10 days		4.5	40
11–29 days		3.2	29
30–45 days		45.3	405
46–89 days		3.5	31
90–149 days		4.6	41
150–180 days		23.0	206
Sentence: Fines and Costs (0 = $119.74)[f]	895		
Zero		36.8	329
$1–100		35.6	319
$101–200		13.2	118
$201–999		10.8	97
$1,000–1,050		3.6	32

(*continued*)

TABLE 15.3 *(continued)*			
Variable	*N*	*%*	*n*
Sentence: Number of Days on Probation (mean = 209.1)^g	895		
None		31.4	281
1–29 days		10.5	94
30–179 days		1.5	13
180–359 days		14.0	125
360–499 days		34.2	306
500+		8.5	76

^{a}M1 is the most serious charge and M4 is the least serious charge.

^{b}Four cases were reported as being both not guilty and dismissed.

^{c}Cases could include more than one category.

^{d}The case went to trial AND testimony was taken; however, "reasonable minds" concluded that the state could not prove their case (e.g., victim plead 5th or victim recanted testimony).

^{e}The median and mode were 30 days.

^{f}The median was $100 and the mode was zero dollars.

^{g}The median was 180 days and the mode was zero days.

about 2 percent were jury trials. Although approximately 16 percent of the defendants were incarcerated zero days, the average number of sentenced days was 62 (the median and mode number of days sentenced to incarceration were 30 days). Note, some of the defendants who were later found "not guilty" or had their cases dismissed had spent time in jail waiting for their court date. In almost two-fifths of the cases, there was no probation sentence; the average number of days on probation was under seven months.

ABUSES REPORTED

Table 15.4 reports information on the abuses that were mentioned on one or more of the following documents: the prosecutor forms, NIBRS and other police reports, victim affidavits, or pretrial offender intake data. As stated previously, these variables, along with those reported in Table 15.5 (on weapons and injuries), may lack reliability. The police were inconsistent in how they completed the forms, which we suspect may hold true for the prosecutors, as well. It is our belief that, if anything, the rates reported in Tables 15.4 and 15.5 underestimate the occurrence of these abuses, injuries, and weapons. The police forms appeared to have a significant amount of missing information. Indeed, looking at these rates, one cannot help but wonder about what evidence the police used that resulted in many of the defendants' arrests. Clearly, there is a significant amount of missing data on the abuse, injury, and weapon variables. However, the prosecutors trying these cases were most likely relying on the same information we were able to find (except the significant difference of prosecutors who had access to the victims' input).

Perhaps one of the most notable findings from this study is that almost one-fifth of the victims reported a lethal threat from the defendant. Given that some research reports the psychological abuse as the worst type of abuse and that we know from everyday perusal of the news that some batterers *do* kill their victims, this rate is rather

TABLE 15.4 Information on Reported Abuses[a] (N = 1,867)		
Variable	**%**	*n*
Threats of Violence		
Nonlethal Threats of Physical Harm to Victim	11.5	215
Nonlethal Threats of Physical Harm to Others	1.2	22
Threaten Lethal Harm to Kill Victim	19.4	363
Threaten Lethal Harm to Kill Self	0.5	10
Threaten Lethal Harm to Kill Others	2.2	41
Threaten to Kidnap Victim's Children	0.9	16
Committed Violence/Abuse		
Slapped	13.1	244
Shoved/Pushed	31.3	585
Grabbed/Dragged	10.5	196
Punched/Hit	44.8	836
Hit with Held Object	7.5	140
Hit with Thrown Object	3.2	60
Kicked	7.3	137
Ripped Clothing	1.9	35
Pulled Hair	4.6	85
Bit	2.6	49
Spit on	0.9	16
Chased	0.7	14
Physically Restrained	4.1	76
Burned	0.4	7
Kidnapped	0.4	8
Choked/Strangled	17.5	327
Harmed a Pregnancy	0.4	8
Hit with a Vehicle	0.4	7
Knifed/Stabbed	6.8	127
Raped Victim	0.2	3
Physically Abused Victim's Child	0.2	4
Sexually Abused Victim's Child	0.2	4
Trespassed	3.2	59
Damaged Property	8.4	157
Harassed on Phone	1.9	35
Prevented from Calling 911	2.9	54
Stalking Behavior	2.3	43

[a]These data were collected from NIBRS, Police Reports, Pre-Trial, and Victims' Affidavits. More than one type of abuse and/or threat could be reported for any given case.

alarming. Indeed, it was the most common form of threat reported on any of the data sources (police reports, victim affidavits, etc.). The next most commonly reported threat was of nonlethal physical harm. Many of these on the police reports wrote quotes such as "I'm going to get you!" and "I'm going to f—you up!" Thus, perhaps they could be taken as lethal threats as well, but were not coded as such. For one-half

TABLE 15.5 Information on Weapons Used and Injuries Reported[a] (*N* = 1,867)

Variable	%	n
Weapons		
Any Weapon[b]	12.3	430
Knife/Sharp Instrument	9.1	169
Gun	1.8	33
Knife/Sharp Instrument or Gun	10.6	198
Telephone	1.3	25
Injuries		
Scratched	10.3	192
Bruised (includes black eyes, swelling, bite marks)	20.4	380
Cuts (includes bloody nose and split lip)	13.0	243
Broken Bones/Teeth	0.9	16

[a]These data were collected from NIBRS, Police Reports, Pre-Trial, and Victims' Affidavits. More than one type of weapon and/or injury could be reported for any given case.

[b]These weapons included a wide variety of objects, from guns, knives, belts, lamps, baseball bats, and telephones, to logs, walkers (for the disabled), and televisions thrown at the victim or used to beat the victim. Weapons do not include body parts such as hands/fists, feet, or heads used to slap, beat, or butt.

of 1 percent of the cases, there was a report that the defendant had threatened to kill himself. About 2 percent of the cases involved a lethal threat to someone other than the victim or the defendant (often the victim's child, mother, or sister), and 1 percent of the cases involved nonlethal threats of physical harm to others.

Table 15.4 also reports the types of violent or abusive behaviors that were reported in the various data sources. The most commonly reported abuse, reported in 45 percent of the cases, was being "punched or hit." The next most common, reported in almost one-third of the cases (31%), was being shoved. The third most frequently reported abusive or violent action was being "choked or strangled," reported in almost one-fifth (18%) of the cases. Thirteen percent of the cases involved some report of being "slapped," and about 11 percent had reports of being grabbed or dragged. Although slapping sounds more "minor" than many of the abuses listed, slaps frequently appeared to result in bloody noses and split lips. Similarly, while "shoved or pushed" sounds relatively tame, sometimes this involved being pushed/shoved out of a car, downstairs, or through a glass door or glass table. The cases of being "dragged" frequently involved being dragged by one's hair. Thus, consistent with some of the criticisms of the Conflict Tactic Scale measure (Cantos, Neidig, & O'Leary, 1994; Cascardi & Vivian, 1995; Dobash et al., 1992; Morse, 1995; Smith, 1994; Vivian & Langhinrichsen-Rohling, 1994), it is important to look at the *context* of the abuse incidents to understand their severity.

Property damage was reported in about 8 percent of the cases, and about 7 percent of the cases involved being knifed/stabbed with a sharp object, being kicked, or being hit with a held object (3% involved being hit with a thrown object). The range of objects used to hit or throw at victims was also varied. They were as "minor" as a stack of papers to objects as varied and serious as a television set, a vacuum cleaner, and a shovel.

The stabbing cases often resulted in a number of stitches, seemingly making a "misdemeanor" charge seem unsuitable. About 4 percent of the cases involved restraining the victims, often pushing them down and standing on their chests, or holding their hands behind their backs. While just fewer than 3 percent of the cases involved trespassing and preventing the victim from calling 911, a little over 2 percent of the cases had some report of stalking behavior and phone harassment (see Altizer, Turner, Hartman, and Kuhns (forthcoming) who report stalking and harassment behavior may be a precursor to more serious behavior). Although less than half of 1 percent of the cases reported "raping the victim" or "sexually abusing the victim's child," it is worrisome that any such police reports would be charged as "misdemeanors" (Table 15.4).

WEAPONS USED BY THE OFFENDER AND INJURIES REPORTED BY THE VICTIM

Table 15.5 provides information on any reports of weapons or injuries. Almost 10 percent of the cases involved a knife or sharp object (e.g., scissors or a screwdriver). Almost 2 percent involved a gun. Other types of weapons included lamps, belts, ropes, and flammable liquids. Although the weapons other than knives/sharp objects and guns were numerous and varied, there was not much reported in the way of patterns. We do, however, report the telephone as a weapon (1.3%). Even though this is rare, it was also a noted pattern in the court transcript data presented (not presented in this chapter but part of the same study). We argue that the telephone is symbolic: the victim's lifeline to safety. Telephones were often involved in the property damage reported in the last table, as well as the issue of being kept from calling 911.

Table 15.5 also reports information on the injuries. Similar to weapons, it was difficult to come up with patterns. For the most part, injuries were not reported regularly. The most commonly reported injury, in one-fifth of the cases, was bruises (including black eyes and bite marks). The next most common was cuts, at 13 percent (including bloody noses and split lips). Almost 1 percent of these misdemeanor domestic violence cases involved broken bones or broken teeth.

SUMMARY

The data reported in this study confirm the vast overrepresentation of people of color in the criminal processing system and the growing trend to arrest women as well as men for intimate partner violence. These data also indicate that victims participate in the prosecution of their abusers far more than is commonly assumed. In slightly over half the cases, the victims made some statement or testimony. Prosecutors reported that victims changed their stories in only one-tenth of the cases. The variables most commonly reported as describing the victims in each case by the prosecutors were "cooperative" (58%), "reasonable" (41%), and "credible" (40%). Only one-fifth were reported as "not cooperative" and "withholding." Slightly over one-tenth was reported as "not credible."

However, these data also indicate that *prosecutors* appear unwilling or unable to adequately prepare for many misdemeanor domestic violence cases. For example, the fact that the overwhelmingly majority of prosecutors reported never being in contact with the victims prior to the case being called (either on the phone or in person) is troublesome.

That is, in almost nine-tenths of the cases the prosecutors *never* spoke with the victims on the phone, and in half, they *never met with the victim in person*. To recall, the average number of minutes that prosecutors reported speaking with victims on the phone was 3.2, and the average number of minutes they met with the victims was 7.9. Of note, those times that the prosecutors did meet with the victim at least once, this was often immediately preceding the case being called into court. Seemingly, having the prosecutor meet with the victim and gain full understanding of the event would increase the likelihood that the case would come to some final decision and not be dismissed.

Another measure of prosecutor time/investment was the prosecutor caseload. Prosecutors with a higher than average caseload were less likely to have the defendants found guilty and were more likely to be involved in cases where the incarceration sentences represented fewer days (but the probation days were higher). These findings are particularly important given findings that battered women's intentions to reuse the criminal legal system are impacted by their experiences with the police and court personnel (Fleury-Steiner, Bybee, Sullivan, Belknap, & Melton, 2006).

These findings are in stark contrast to previous research that places the primary responsibility of case outcome on whether the victim cooperates or not. It is clear that this office is highly understaffed. In this jurisdiction, there were far more public defenders available ($n = 31$) than there were prosecutors available to the victims ($n = 18$). This indicates a serious structural problem in responding to intimate partner abuse victims. We fear that too much emphasis is placed on victims' testifying, particularly given the literature documenting many victims' fear of reprisal *and* the evidence in the prosecutor forms regarding the numerous victims who never knew when their cases were being tried. Finally, the evidence presented in this chapter suggests the very immediate need to focus on appropriate staffing for these cases and/or implement a victim advocacy office within or as a part of the prosecutor's office. It is likely that with more prosecutors, they could meet with victims more often, which would likely increase victims' participation and guilty verdicts and stricter sentences of intimate partner abusers.

References

Abraham, M. (2000). *Speaking the unspeakable: Marital violence among South Asian immigrants in the United States*. New Brunswick, NJ: Rutgers University Press.

Altizer, T., Turner, M. G., Hartman, J. L., & Kuhns, J. B. (forthcoming). Sexual harassment victimization during emerging adulthood: A test of routine activities theory and a general theory of crime. *Crime and Delinquency*.

Ames, L. J., & Dunham, K. T. (2002). Asymptotic justice: Probation as a criminal justice response to intimate partner violence. *Violence Against Women, 8*, 6–34.

Belknap, J. (1995). Law enforcement officers' attitudes about the appropriate responses to woman battering. *International Review of Victimology, 4*, 47–62.

Belknap, J., Fleury, R. E., Melton, H. C., Sullivan, C. M., & Leisenring, A. (2001). To go or not to go?: Preliminary findings on battered women's decisions regarding court cases. In H. M. Eigenberg (Ed.), *Woman battering in the United States* (pp. 318–326). Prospect Heights, IL: Waveland Press.

Belknap, J., & Hartman, J. L. (2000). Police responses to woman battering: Victim advocates' reports. *International Review of Victimology, 1*, 159–177.

Bowman, C. G. (1992). The arrest experiments: A feminist critique. *Journal of Criminal Law and Criminology, 8*, 201–209.

Browne, A. (1987). *When battered women kill.* New York: Free Press.

Buzawa, E. S., & Austin, T. (1993). Determining police response to domestic violence victims: The role of victim preference. *American Behavioral Scientist, 36*, 610–623.

Cahn, N. R. (1992). Innovative approaches to the prosecution of domestic violence crimes: An overview. In E. S. Buzawa & C. G. Buzawa (Eds.), *Domestic violence: The changing criminal justice response* (pp. 161–180). Westport, CT: Auburn House.

Campbell, J. (1992). If I can't have you, no one can. In J. Radford & D. E. H. Russell (Eds.), *Femicide: The politics of woman killing* (pp. 99–113). New York: Twayne Publishers.

Cannavale, F. J., Jr., & W. D. Falcon. (1976). *Improving witness cooperation: Summary report of the District of Columbia witness survey and a handbook for witness management.* National Institute of Law Enforcement and Criminal Justice Law Enforcement Assistance Administration, U.S. Department of Justice, D.C. Health and Company.

Cantos, A., Neidig, P. H., & O'Leary, K. D. (1994). Injuries of women and men in a treatment program for domestic violence. *Journal of Family Violence, 9*, 113–124.

Cascardi, M., & Vivian, D. (1995). Context for specific episodes of marital violence: Gender and severity of violence differences. *Journal of Family Violence, 10*, 265–293.

Corsilles, A. (1994). No-drop policies in the prosecution of domestic violence cases: Guarantee to action or dangerous solution? *Fordham Law Review, 63*, 853–881.

Crenshaw, K. (1994). Mapping the margins: Intersectionality, identity politics, and violence against women of color in the public nature of private violence. In M. A. Fineman & R. Mykitiuk (Eds.), *The public nature of private violence: The discovery of domestic abuse* (pp. 93–118). New York: Routledge.

Cretney, A., & Davis, G. (1997). The significance of compellability in the prosecution of domestic assault. *British Journal of Criminology, 37*, 75–89.

Dasgupta, S. D. (2003). *Safety and justice for all: examining the relationship between the women's anti-violence movement and the criminal legal system.* New York: Ms. Foundation.

www.ms.foundation.org/user-assets/PDF/program/safety_justice.pdf

Davis, R. C., & Smith, B. (1981). Crimes between acquaintances: The response of criminal courts. *Victimology: An International Journal, 8*, 175–187.

Davis, R. C. & Smith, B. (1995). Domestic violence reforms: empty promises or fulfilled expectations? *Crime and Delinquency, 41*, 541–552.

Davis, R. C., Smith, B. E., & Nickles, L. B. (1998). The deterrent effect of prosecuting domestic violence misdemeanors. *Crime and Delinquency, 44*, 434–442.

Dobash, R. E., & Dobash, R. P. (1979). *Violence against wives.* New York: Free Press.

Dobash, R. E., & Dobash, R. P. (1984). The nature and antecedents of violent events. *British Journal of Criminology, 24*, 269–288.

Dobash, R. P., Dobash, R. E., Wilson, M., & Daly, M. (1992). The myth of sexual symmetry in marital violence. *Social Problems, 39*, 71–91.

Eaton, S., & Hyman, A. (1992). The domestic violence component of the New York task force report on women in the courts: An evaluation and assessment of New York City courts. *Fordham Urban Law Journal, 19*, 391–497.

Ellis, J. W. (1984). Prosecutorial discretion to charge in cases of spousal assault: A dialogue. *Journal of Criminal Law and Criminology, 75*, 56.

Ellis, D., & DeKeseredy, W. (1989). Marital status and woman abuse. *International Journal of Law and Psychiatry, 10*, 401–410.

Erez, E., & Belknap, J. (1998). In their own words: Battered women's assessment of systemic responses. *Violence and Victims, 13*, 3–20.

Ewing, C. P. (1987). *Battered women who kill.* Lexington, MA: Lexington Books.

Ferraro, K. J., & Boychuck, T. (1992). The court's response to interpersonal violence. In E. S. Buzawa & C. G. Buzawa (Eds.), *Domestic violence: The changing criminal justice response* (pp. 209–225). Westport, CT: Auburn House.

Flanakin, N., & Walsh, C. (2005). Letter to the editor. *Violence Against Women, 11*, 822–827.

Fleury-Steiner, R. E., Bybee, D., Sullivan, C. M., Belknap, J., & Melton, H. C. (2006). Contextual factors impacting battered women's intentions to re-use the criminal legal system. *Journal of Community Psychology, 134*, 327–342.

Ford, D. A. (2003). Coercing victim participation in domestic violence prosecutions. *Journal of Interpersonal Violence, 18*, 669–684.

Ford, D. A., & Regoli, M. J. (1993). The preventive impacts of policies for prosecuting wife batterers. In E. S. Buzawa & C. G. Buzawa (Eds.), *Domestic violence: The changing criminal justice response* (pp. 181–208). Westport, CT: Auburn House.

Frisch, L. A. (1992). Research that succeeds, policies that fail. *Journal of Criminal Law & Criminology, 83*, 209–216.

Gondolf, E. W., & Fisher, E. R. (1988). *Battered women as survivors: An alternative to treating learned helplessness*. New York: Lexington Books.

Goodman, L. A., Dutton, M. A., & Bennett, L. (2000). Predicting repeat abuse among arrested batterers. *Journal of Interpersonal Violence, 15*(1), 63–74.

Hardesty, J. L. (2002). Separation assault in the context of post divorce parenting: An integrative review of the literature. *Violence Against Women, 8*, 597–625.

Hart, B. (1993). Battered woman and the criminal justice system. *American Behavioral Scientist, 36*, 624–638.

Hartman, J. L., & Belknap, J. (2003). Beyond the gatekeepers: Court professionals' self reported attitudes about and experiences with domestic violence cases. *Criminal Justice & Behavior, 30*(3), 349–373.

Hirschel, D., & Hutchison, I. W. (2001). The relative effects of offense, offender and victim variables on the decision to prosecute domestic violence cases. *Violence Against Women, 7*, 22–45.

Jones, A. (1994). *Next time, she'll be dead: battering and how to stop it*. Boston, MA: Beacon Press.

Jones, D., & Belknap, J. (1999). Police responses to battering in a progressive pro-arrest jurisdiction. *Justice Quarterly, 16*, 249–274.

Keilitz, S. L. (1997). *Domestic violence and child custody disputes: A resource handbook for judges and court managers*. Williamsburg, VA: National Center for State Courts.

Kerstetter, W. A. (1990). Gateway to justice: Police and prosecutorial response to sexual assaults to against women. *Journal of Criminal Law and Criminology, 81*, 267–313.

Kingsnorth, R. F., MacIntosh, R. C., & Wentworth, J. (1999). Sexual assault: The role of prior relationship and victim characteristics in case processing. *Justice Quarterly, 16*, 275–302.

Langan, P. A., & Innes, C. A. (1986). *Preventing domestic violence against women*. Bureau of Justice Statistics, Special Report, August, Washington, D.C.

Lerman, L. G. (1992). The decontextualization of domestic violence. *Journal of Criminal Law & Criminology, 83*, 217–240.

Mahoney, M. (1991). Legal images of battered women: Redefining the issue of separation. *Michigan Law Review, 90*, 2–94.

Manning, P. K. (1993). The preventive conceit: The black box in market context. *American Behavioral Scientist, 36*, 639–650.

Martin, M. E. (1994). Mandatory arrest for domestic violence: The court's response. *Criminal Justice Review, 19*, 212–227.

McDermott, M. J., & Garofalo, J. (2004). When advocacy for domestic violence victims backfires: Types and sources of victim disempowerment. *Violence Against Women, 10*, 1245–1266.

McLeod, M. (1983). Victim noncooperation in the prosecution of domestic assault. *Criminology, 21*, 395–416.

Mignon, S. I., & Holmes, W. M. (1995). Police response to mandatory arrest laws. *Crime and Delinquency, 41*, 430–442.

Mills, L. G. (1999). Killing her softly: Intimate abuse and the violence of state intervention. *Harvard Law Review, 113*, 550–613.

Mills, L. G. (2003). *Insult to injury: Rethinking our responses to intimate abuse*. Princeton, NJ: Princeton University Press.

Morse, B. J. (1995). Beyond the conflict tactics scale: Assessing gender differences in partner violence. *Violence and Victims, 10*, 251–272.

Parnas, R. J. (1967). The police response to the domestic disturbance. *Wisconsin Law Review, 2*, 914–960.

Pastoor, M. K. (1984). Police training and the effectiveness of Minnesota 'domestic abuse' laws. *Law and Inequality Journal, 2*, 557–607.

Ptacek, J. (1999). *Battered women in the court room*. Boston: Northeastern University Press.

Quarm, D., & Schwartz, M. D. (1985). Domestic violence in criminal court: An examination of new legislation in Ohio. In C. Schweber & C. Feinman (Eds.), *Criminal justice politics and women: The aftermath of legally mandated change* (pp. 29–47) . New York: The Haworth Press.

Rauma, D. (1984). Going for the gold: Prosecutorial decision making in cases of wife assault. *Social Science Research, 13*, 321–351.

Robbins, K. (1999). No-drop prosecution of domestic violence. *Stanford Law Review, 52*, 205–233.

Roberts, A. R. (1996). Court responses to battered women. In A. R. Roberts (Eds.), *Helping battered women* (pp. 96–101). New York: Oxford University Press.

Rosewater, L. B. (1988). Battered or schizophrenic? Psychological tests can't tell. In K. Yllo & M. Bograd (Eds.), *Feminist perspectives on wife abuse* (pp. 200–216). Newbury Park: Sage.

Saunders, D. G. (1986). When battered women use violence: Husband-abuse or self-defense? *Violence and Victims, 1*, 47–60.

Schmidt, J., & Steury, E. H. (1989). Prosecutorial discretion in filing charges in domestic violence cases. *Criminology, 27*, 487–510.

Schneider, E. M. (2000). *Battered women and feminist lawmaking.* New Haven, CT: Yale University Press.

Sev'er, A. (1997). Recent or imminent separation and intimate violence against women. *Violence Against Women, 3*, 566–589.

Sherman, L. W. (1992). *Policing domestic violence: experiments and dilemma.* New York: Free Press.

Sigler, R. T., Crowley, J. M., & Johnson, I. (1990). Judicial and prosecutorial endorsement of innovative techniques in the trial of domestic abuse cases. *Journal of Criminal Justice, 18*, 443–453.

Singer, S. I. (1988). The fear of reprisal and the failure of victims to report a personal crime. *Journal of Quantitative Criminology, 4*, 289–302.

Smith, M. D. (1994). Enhancing the quality of survey data on violence against women. *Gender and Society, 8*, 109–127.

Spohn, C., Beichner, D. B., & Davis-Frenzel, E. (2001). Prosecutorial justifications for sexual assault case rejection. *Social Problems, 48*, 206–235.

Stark, E. (1993). Mandatory arrest of batterers: A reply to its critics. *American Behavioral Scientist, 36*, 651–680.

Stark, E. (2003). Race, gender and woman battering. In D. Hawkins (Ed.), *Violent crime: Assessing race and ethnic differences* (pp. 171–197). New York: Cambridge University Press.

Stark, E. (2004). Insults, injury, and injustice: Rethinking state intervention in domestic violence cases. *Violence Against Women, 10*, 1302–1330.

Syers, M., & Edleson, J. L. (1992). The combined effects of coordinated criminal justice intervention in woman abuse. *Journal of Interpersonal Violence, 7*, 490–502.

Tierney, K. J. (1983). The battered women movement and the creation of the wife beating problem. *Social Problems, 29*, 207–220.

Tjaden, P., & Thoennes, N. (2000). Prevalence and consequences of male-to-female and female-to-male intimate partner violence as measured by the national violence against women survey. *Violence Against Women, 6*, 142–161.

U.S. Commission on Civil Rights. (1982). Under the rule of thumb: Battered women and the administration of justice. Washington, DC: National Institute of Justice.

Ventura, L. A., & Davis, G. (2005). Domestic violence: Court case conviction and recidivism. *Violence Against Women, 11*, 255–277.

Vivian, D., & Langhinrichsen-Rohling, J. (1994). Are bi-directionally violent couples mutually victimized? A gender-sensitive comparison. *Violence and Victims, 9*, 107–124.

Websdale, N. (1995). Rural woman abuse: The voices of Kentucky women. *Violence Against Women, 1*, 309–388.

Websdale, N., & Johnson, B. (1997). The policing of domestic violence in rural and urban areas: The voices of battered women. *Policing and Society, 6*, 297–317.

Wilson, M., & Daly, M. (1993). Spousal homicide risk and estrangement. *Violence and Victims, 8*, 3–15.

Zimmerman, S. L., & Owens, P. (1989). Comparing the family policies of three states. *Family Relations, 38*, 190–195.

Zorza, J. (1992). The criminal law of misdemeanor violence, 1970–1990. *The Journal of Criminal Law & Criminology, 83*, 46–72.

CHAPTER 16

THE VICTIMIZATION HISTORIES OF WOMEN PRISONERS IN OKLAHOMA

❧

Susan F. Sharp

ABSTRACT

This chapter addresses the victimization histories of women incarcerated in Oklahoma prisons. The study focuses on both sexual and physical victimizations that the women experienced both as minors and as adults. The study is based on data collected as part of a larger study on incarcerated women and their children. Treatment services received by the women both prior to incarceration and while incarcerated are examined.

INTRODUCTION

There is a strong link between victimization and offending among females. Our knowledge of this, however, is still developing. It has only been in relatively recent years that much attention has been paid to incarcerated women. Until the mid-1980s, women prisoners were largely an overlooked group (Belknap, 2001; Bloom & Owen, 1994; Chesney-Lind, 1986, 1997, 1998, 2003; Faith, 1993; Miller, 2005; Owen, 1998; Owen & Bloom, 1995; Pollock, 1986; Pollock-Byrne, 2001; Rafter, 1990). Beginning in the 1980s, the War on Drugs led to massive incarceration of women in the United States, and the female share of the total prison population more than doubled. By the beginning of the twenty-first century, women accounted for almost 7 percent of those in prison (Beck & Karberg, 2001). Thus, there is a growing need to make our prisons, if we are going to continue to use them at such high rates, more responsive to the needs of women (Hannah-Moffatt, 1995; Kruttschnitt, Gartner, & Miller, 2000; Sharp, 2003). This means we need to increase our understanding of women's pathways to crime. Having a history of abuse is perhaps one of the greatest predictors of female offending (Belknap & Holsinger, 2006). In this chapter, the victimization histories of female prisoners in Oklahoma are examined, as well as the services they have received.

THE RELATIONSHIP BETWEEN ABUSE AND OFFENDING

Certainly, most of those who are abused do not go on to become prisoners, despite the strong prevalence of abuse histories in incarcerated women. Overall, women are more likely than men to experience most types of abuse yet less likely to commit crimes. Females often respond to abuse with more self-directed types of deviance, such as self-harm (Belknap & Holsinger, 2006) and disordered eating (Sharp, Terling-Watt, Atkins, Gilliam, & Sanders, 2001). However, offending females report abuse histories at much higher levels than their nonoffending counterparts (Acoca, 1998; Rivera & Widom, 1990; Widom, 1989). Some have argued that victimization is in part a result of delinquent behavior, but these researchers acknowledge that it is more true for male adolescents, and they focus on types of victimization that result from lifestyles, such as the likelihood of being the victim of robbery (Lauritsen, Sampson, & Laub, 1991). Their research, however, ignores the types of victimization more often experienced by adolescent girls.

The gendered nature of abuse is most evident in the distribution of sexual abuse. According to the findings from the National Violence Against Women Survey (Tjaden & Thoennes, 1998), women are far more likely than men to experience sexual assault, both as children and as adults. This survey included 8,000 women and 8,005 men. Almost 18 percent of the women surveyed reported an attempted or completed rape in their lifetimes, with over half of these occurring before the age of 18. In comparison, 3 percent of men reported experiencing rape (Tjaden & Thoennes, 1998). These findings are similar to those from other research (see, for example, Michael, Gagnon, Lauman, & Kolata, 1994). Additionally, more than half of American women and two-thirds of American men reported experiencing physical assault as a child or adult. There are also some gender differences in terms of the perpetrator of abuse with women being far more likely to report a current or former spouse raped or assaulted them (Tjaden & Thoennes, 1998).

There is considerable evidence that abuse is even higher among prisoners than in the general population, but with the same type of gendering of victimization. Histories of both physical and sexual abuse are particularly prevalent among women prisoners and may be linked to their criminal involvement (Marcus-Mendoza, Sargent, & Chong Ho, 1994; Sargent, Marcus-Mendoza, & Yu, 1993). Almost 60 percent of women prisoners have reported being sexually or physically abused. In more than one-third of the cases, the abuse started prior to age 18, with 12 percent of the women reporting childhood abuse only and 25 percent reporting abuse both as a child and as an adult. Additionally, 20 percent of women prisoners reported abuse that began after the age of 18 (Greenfeld & Snell, 1999).

The abuse suffered is arguably related to girls' and women's pathways into the juvenile and criminal justice systems. Widom (1989) found that victimization as a child increased the likelihood of both juvenile and adult offending. Additionally, adult female offenders frequently report that their first arrests occurred as juveniles. Unlike boys, girls' contacts with the juvenile justice system are often due to status offenses such as running away from home (Chesney-Lind & Shelden, 1998; Widom, 2000). It may well be that this "offending" is actually a survival strategy: Girls run away from abusive homes, then commit crimes for survival. When caught, they are punished for behavior that is actually self-protecting. Indeed, Belknap and Holsinger (2006) reported that nearly half of the delinquent girls in their study indicated that being abused was a contributing factor to their offenses. Similarly, in a recent study of female prisoners in Oklahoma, over

83 percent of the women who had multiple arrests as juveniles and who were placed in juvenile facilities reported experiencing childhood abuse (Sharp, 2005). Examining the relationship between juvenile confinement and adult offending from yet another angle, Widom (2000) reported that almost half of the girls with juvenile status offenses were subsequently arrested as adults.

Thus, it appears that a common path for females into prison begins with childhood abuse, followed by status offenses and survival crimes. Abused girls often engage in status offenses such as running away, as we have seen above. Once on the street, they may engage in prostitution or theft to survive. Once in the system, girls often find themselves labeled and their options limited. More disturbingly, the delinquent female is often revictimized by the system that is supposed to be intervening in her behalf. This can range from emotional abuse to sexual abuse (Acoca, 1998). Certainly, without treatment and intervention, the issues and mental health problems that led to their initial offenses are likely to continue and to get worse. Understanding the needs of incarcerated women, then, requires understanding their abuse histories. First, women are clearly incarcerated for different reasons than are males. Males are much more likely to be incarcerated for property offenses, while drug offenses and low-level property offenses are the most common among women (Greenfeld & Snell, 1999), and one study reported forgery and drug sales as the most common crimes committed by women prisoners (English, 1993). Second, a high proportion of female prisoners have abuse histories, and many have never received therapy of counseling for their past abuse. This is not surprising given the fact that recent research reports that two-thirds of female rape victims have not received counseling from mental health professionals (Tjaden & Thoennes, 2006). Third, having a history of abuse is linked to substance abuse (Acoca, 1998), and women prisoners have high rates of substance abuse and addiction. Clearly, dealing with the victimization of women prisoners is needed if they are to be able to reenter society successfully.

CONSEQUENCES OF ABUSE

The consequences of abuse include high levels of substance abuse and mental health problems (Acoca, 1998; Chesney-Lind & Shelden, 1998; Owen, 1998; Tjaden & Thoennes, 2006). Additionally, early pregnancy and failure to complete school are linked to childhood abuse (Acoca, 1998). Notably, in addition to being a common response to abuse, substance abuse is one of the major problems faced by women prisoners (Chesney-Lind, 1989). Not only does substance abuse create problems in other areas of the prisoners' lives, but drug charges are the most common offense type for which women are incarcerated.

SUBSTANCE ABUSE

Substance abuse is rampant among women offenders, but, unfortunately, drug treatment is not. In the United States, there is a serious problem with availability of drug treatment. According to a study conducted for the Governor and President Pro-Tempore of the Senate in Oklahoma, more than 530 women who needed substance abuse treatment were waiting for an open slot at the end of 2003 (Oklahoma Criminal Justice Resource Center, 2004b). In a conversation with the author, one warden pointed out a flaw in the corrections policy. The state has legislated that substance abuse treatment be made available only to minimum security women prisoners, excluding medium and maximum security prisoners. This means that some of those with the most serious problems do not receive help. Arguably, this policy is ineffective if not actually destructive. Many medium or maximum security level prisoners parole directly from that level of supervision. Thus, they will be returning home without much needed treatment.

MENTAL HEALTH ISSUES

Mental health problems are far more frequent and more serious in female prisoners than in male prisoners (Kaplan & Sasser, 1996; Warren, 2003), particularly depression and bipolar disorder (Belknap, 2003). Additionally, women prisoners may experience borderline or antisocial personality disorders or posttraumatic stress disorder (PTSD) (Jordan, Schlenger, Fairbanks, & Caddell, 1996; Morash & Schram, 2002; Warren, 2003). It is noteworthy that most women diagnosed with borderline personality disorder are victims of childhood sexual abuse. Furthermore, a diagnosis of borderline personality disorder often masks the presence of PTSD (Heney & Kristiansen, 1998).

The large number of drug offenders now incarcerated is at least in part the cause of the high number of women prisoners with mental health diagnoses. Psychiatric disorders may underlie substance abuse, with women self-medicating their symptoms with drugs and alcohol. When more women are incarcerated for drug offenses, higher numbers with psychiatric diagnoses will then end up in the system (Chesney-Lind, 1998; Warren, 2003). Co-existing mental and substance abuse disorders are quite common in women prisoners indicating special treatment needs (Anderson, 2003; Morash, Bynum, & Koons, 1995; Young & Reviere, 2006). These include treatment for PTSD. Stress, disempowerment, and low self-esteem are frequent results of abuse, particularly sexual abuse (Marcus-Mendoza & Wright, 2003; Widom, 2000; Young & Reviere, 2006; Zaplin, 1998). It is noteworthy that physical and sexual abuse have been reported in nearly 80 percent of women prisoners with mental health problems, and PTSD in women prisoners is thought to be most often the consequence of abuse (Ditton, 1999).

As noted above, many women prisoners are abuse survivors with subsequent mental health problems. Those problems may be exacerbated by treatment offered in correctional facilities, especially those based on a boot-camp or therapeutic community model. One study examined the negative impact of these types of treatment programs on women prisoners. They argued these programs could have serious negative effects on women due to the confrontational environments that are the foundations of therapeutic communities and boot camps (Marcus-Mendoza, Kleijn-Saffran, & Lutze, 1998). Similarly, Heney and Kristiansen (1998) point out that prison often mirrors the abuse experiences of women. They describe Finkelhor and Browne's Traumagenic Model of Child Sexual Abuse and how this may be replicated in the experiences of women prisoners. Body searches may be invasive and traumatic to the women, incarceration can lead to an increased sense of powerlessness, the women may feel an increased sense of betrayal by the society in which they live, and they may feel increasingly stigmatized (Heney & Kristiansen, 1998). Abused women frequently already experience disempowerment and low self-esteem (Heney & Kristiansen, 1998; Marcus-Mendoza et al., 1998). The confrontational measures employed in boot camps and similar programs can actually increase these problems (Marcus-Mendoza et al., 1998). Additionally, the feminist model of therapy emphasizes bonding with the counselors. Female prisoners can find themselves in conflicted relationships similar to those they experienced on the outside. Prisons are not conducive to the development of healthy therapeutic relationships. Instead, staff may serve as both therapists and "keepers" (Marcus-Mendoza et al., 1998; Marcus-Mendoza & Wright, 2003).

SPECIAL NEEDS OF WOMEN PRISONER

Having established that the pathways of women to prison are frequently different from those of men, it follows that women prisoners will also have different needs. One of the greatest needs faced by women prisoners is help in dealing with their mental health issues. Women prisoners are not "female versions" of male prisoners. Their life experiences and pathways to crime are different from those of men, and successful rehabilitation requires recognition of these differences. Women's life experiences result in different problems and needs, and treatment of women prisoners should address those. In particular, recognition of the role of victimization in subsequent offending is imperative to the development of programming for female prisoners. The presence of co-existing disorders (mental health and substance abuse) further complicates the needs of women prisoners. The most often adopted treatment of substance abuse is based on a medical model of addiction. The downside of utilizing this model for women prisoners is that it fails to address the complicated interrelatedness of abuse, psychiatric disorders, and addiction in incarcerated women (Covington, 1998).

Arguably, the current criminal justice system approach ends up punishing women who have been victimized. Many already feel that they have been doubly victimized, both by their abusers and by a system that fails to punish the abusers. For example, victims of rape rarely report the rape to authorities. However, even when the rape is reported, the likelihood of the abuser being punished is slim. According to a recent report, *Extent, Nature and Consequences of Rape Victimization: Findings from the National Violence Against Women Survey*, rapes were prosecuted less than one-third of the time (32.1%) if the perpetrator was an intimate of the victim and less than half the time (44.4%) if the perpetrator was a nonintimate. When the cases were prosecuted, convictions were still difficult to attain, particularly if the perpetrator was an intimate partner. In those prosecutions, only 36.4 percent of those charged were convicted. In nonintimate cases, only 61.9 percent were convicted. With only roughly 20 percent of the rapes being reported, it is easy to see how rape victims might feel that a system designed to protect them had in reality let them down, with only 2–5 percent of all rape perpetrators being convicted and 12–17 percent of the perpetrators in reported rapes being convicted (Tjaden & Thoennes, 2006).

In a just society, it would seem that we would work toward interventions other than incarceration as the response to victimized offenders. There is some limited progress being made in the diversion of female offenders. Drug courts are being used to divert some offenders from prison, but more than two-thirds of drug court participants in Oklahoma are male, despite the high rates of substance abuse problems among females (Oklahoma Criminal Justice Resource Center, 2004a). However, Oklahoma drug courts have greater impact on female offenders than on male offenders. In Oklahoma, the mean income at entry into drug court was $489.52 per month for women, compared with $1,071.58 for men. Upon successful completion, the women's mean income had increased 130 percent to $1,128.54, while the mean income for men had only increased 31 percent to $1,400.16 (Oklahoma Criminal Justice Resource

Center, 2004c). Similar results were seen for education. These programs, however, concentrate on substance abuse treatment, employment, and education. There is no recognition of the abuse histories of women prisoners, and no court mandated trauma programs. Instead, once again, the women are treated as if they were men.

Additionally, although women's success rates suggest that this kind of approach improves their life chances, there is a downside to the use of drug courts. Women offenders, due to their lower earning power, often have difficulty meeting the financial demands of drug courts. Inability to pay the court costs, administrative fees, and the costs of obtaining drug treatment often lead to revocation of their probation. The Oklahoma Criminal Justice Resource Center has recommended that the legislature explore this problem (Oklahoma Criminal Justice Resource Center, 2004b), but to date no action has been taken. Furthermore, without treatment of the underlying issues, it is quite likely that these women are being set up for failure in the long run. While they may successfully complete the requirements of the drug court in the short run, much female offending is a result of abuse histories. Failure to incorporate treatment for abuse into the requirements of drug court means that the women still have many of the same issues as they had before entering the system. Drug court is often viewed by authorities as a last chance. If the woman re-offends or uses drugs again, the assumption is often that she has had her chance. Clearly, a deeper understanding of women offenders is needed to improve the utility of drug courts in addressing the needs of female offenders.

Oklahoma's high female incarceration rate, an understanding of the relationship between abuse and offending, and the importance of examining both the needs of female offenders and the degree to which those needs were being met resulted in the state legislature requiring a study on incarcerated women in the state. The remainder of the chapter examines some of the findings of this study.

THE OKLAHOMA STUDY OF INCARCERATED WOMEN

The Oklahoma State Legislature passed a resolution in 2004, calling for a study on incarcerated women and their children. Two legislators became concerned about the incarceration of women prisoners upon realizing that Oklahoma had the highest per capita female incarceration rate in the United States (129/100,000 women), double the national rate of 64 women per 100,000 (Harrison & Beck, 2005). One of the legislators had visited a women's prison in her jurisdiction and spent time talking with the women incarcerated there. This led her to propose a study of the state's incarcerated women, resulting in the joint resolution between the two houses of the state legislature (Sharp, 2004). The study was conducted in three phases. For Phase I, the Oklahoma Department of Corrections drew a random sample of 250 women prisoners in the state, stratified by age, race, security level (maximum, medium, minimum, community corrections, halfway house), and length of time in the corrections system. The sample size was selected to include about 10 percent of the state's approximately 2,200 women prisoners. Participation in the study was voluntary, and no identifying information was included on the survey instrument in order to protect the subjects. The women were assembled in a large room, and the study was explained to them. Some chose not to participate, particularly at one prison where a staff member became ill and was removed by ambulance a few minutes before the survey was to be administered. This delay resulted in the survey administration overlapping with the lunch period, and several women decided not to participate due to time constraints. Additionally, the sample included women who were incarcerated for harm to a child, and these women did not participate. The final sample, collected in late 2004, was composed of 203 women prisoners from four facilities: a minimum security prison ($n = 92$), a mixed security level prison ($n = 56$), a community corrections center ($n = 41$), and a halfway house ($n = 14$). The survey included demographic information, information related to criminal records, questions related to abuse, and information about families such as contact with children, placement of children, and problems with children. Phase II participants were drawn from the initial sample through selective volunteering.

At the end of the survey, women were asked to volunteer to participate in the second phase of the study, which included a more in-depth examination of a number of issues.[1] One hundred forty women volunteered to participate in the second phase, and 119 women ended up completing the second phase instrument during two different data collection periods in 2005. The Phase II survey asked in greater detail about the women's personal histories as well as about their children, going into far greater detail on the women's childhoods, legal histories, mental health histories, substance abuse, physical and sexual abuse, placement of children, and problems with children. The final phase of the study focused on caregivers of the children. Little information gathered from this portion of the study is included in this chapter. Most of the data in the remainder of this chapter comes from the second phase of the study.

ABUSE HISTORIES OF WOMEN PRISONERS

In the recent Oklahoma study, almost 60 percent ($n = 71$) of the women prisoners reported sexual abuse before the age of 18, and about 53 percent ($n = 63$) reported experiencing childhood physical abuse. Of these, almost 40 percent reported both physical and sexual abuse as children ($n = 48$). Overall, nearly 74 percent reported experiencing at least one type of childhood abuse.

Even when the women were not the specific targets of physical abuse, they may have been traumatized by violent childhood homes. More than half ($n = 63, 52.9\%$) reported that one or both parents were violent around the family when they were growing up. Furthermore, the women were likely to report experiencing continued abuse as adults. Almost 80 percent ($n = 94$) of the women reported experiencing either sexual abuse or domestic violence since turning 18 years of age. There was also strong evidence of the continued victimization of these women. Victims of childhood sexual abuse were significantly more likely than other women in the sample to also experience sexual abuse as an adult ($n = 30, \chi^2 = 5.22, 1 \text{ df}, p \le .05$). Additionally, those who were victims of childhood physical abuse were significantly more likely to be victims of domestic violence as adults ($n = 58, \chi^2 = 11.87, 1 \text{ df}, p \le .001$).

More than one-third ($n = 42, 35.3\%$) of the women had received some type of mental health services prior to incarceration. Indeed, almost one in five had been hospitalized one or more times for mental health issues ($n = 21, 17.6\%$), and the same number had received psychotropic medication on an outpatient basis. However, it appears that the treatment received was less often geared to their abuse histories. Half of the women who experienced abuse as children had received no counseling specific to their abuse, and almost half of the 94 women who had been abused as an adult had received no abuse-specific counseling ($n = 42, 44.7\%$). Nor were those issues being addressed in prison. Less than half ($n = 55, 46.2\%$) of the women prisoners in the study were receiving some type of mental health service, with slightly more than one-fourth ($n = 33$, 27.7%) receiving counseling and about 18 percent receiving psychotropic medications ($n = 22$). Among those who had experienced childhood sexual abuse, about 38 percent ($n = 27$) were receiving counseling and 17.6 percent ($n = 13$) were receiving medication.

A variable was created to measure heavy substance abuse. Those who reported using any of the following drugs more than once per week in the month before being incarcerated (marijuana, crack, cocaine, methamphetamine, heroin, speedballs or cocaine and heroin together, nonprescription methadone, other narcotics, barbiturates, tranquilizers, PCP, LSD, or Ecstasy) were coded as heavy drug users, and all others were coded 0. Eighty-six (72.3%) of the sample reported heavy drug use in the month prior to incarceration. Forty subjects (33.6%) reported heavy alcohol use measured as more than once per week. These groups overlapped, resulting in a total of 93 (78.2%) subjects who reported heavy alcohol and/or drug abuse. Contrary to expectations, however, there was no significant difference in those with abuse histories of any sort and heavy substance abuse. Of course, with such a large percentage of the population reporting heavy substance use, this is not surprising.

The study also included some qualitative components that may help further illustrate the relationship between abuse and offending as well as the need for programs that take this into account. In the final stage of the study, a prisoner's grandmother gave a poignant account of the young woman's troubled childhood and her subsequent problems.[2] This young woman, a Native American, was the daughter of a man and woman with substance abuse problems of their own. By the time she was 10 years old, her mother was training her to be a professional thief as she "couldn't go to prison." The girl would be sent out with a list of things to steal for her mother. Not surprisingly, she developed an extensive juvenile history. She went to live with her grandmother, but by that time she had developed problems with anger and depression. Not only had she been introduced to crime by her parents, but she had also suffered severe physical and sexual abuse. She continued to get into trouble and began using drugs. She then met a young man who also had a drug problem. They had two children, and then the man was sent to prison for a drug offense. The young woman met another man and became pregnant again. While pregnant, she committed another offense. Her court-appointed attorney waived the right to keep her juvenile record sealed, and she was sentenced to 25 years on a blind plea, where the defendant enters a guilty plea not knowing what the sentence will be. Once in prison, she adjusted well, involving herself in any kind of class or activity that would help her better herself, including a number of college courses after completion of her GED. However, her abuse history eventually was linked to trouble inside the prison. She was celled with a woman who was in prison for abusing her children, and this triggered the young woman's past trauma. She got into a physical brawl with the other woman and ended up in lockdown as a result. To date, she has received no counseling or drug treatment.

Certainly, some women prisoners do receive substance abuse treatment. The most popular form of substance abuse treatment in the Oklahoma system is the modified therapeutic community format, but acceptance into the program is usually limited to younger White offenders. Those deemed more serious offenders and those with longer-standing drug problems are not considered to be "appropriate" for this type of program. As we have seen earlier in the chapter, the confrontational approach is not always the best approach with females who have been abused and are experiencing low self-esteem (Marcus-Mendoza et al., 1998; Marcus-Mendoza & Wright 2003). One woman talked about her inability to get any help with her substance abuse problems.

> I've been a meth addict for years. I know I need help, but I haven't been able to get into NADTC [a state public treatment program] because the wait is so long. Now, I can't get help here, either. I go to AA meetings, but they are not enough for me right now. We only have them twice a month for an hour, and we listen to speakers. How is that going to help me? I don't want to come back here. . . .

The multigenerational problem of abuse was brought up by yet another subject, who reported severe abuse in her own childhood. Her mother had been the primary perpetrator of her abuse, and now the woman's daughter was living with the prisoner's mother.

> My 14 year old daughter is being physically & verbally abused by my mother. . . . She is treated as a slave & a robot. She has been coached & trained on a daily basis what to say to child welfare if they are called. She has threatened to kill my daughter & repeatedly tells her she hates her. She also calls her very, very vulgar names. . . . She also bites her, pulls her hair and just so much more. Then after the abuse occurs she is made to feel sorry for my mother. If someone who just gets her out of there long enough, a professional can break her silence.

This subject had not received any counseling for her own abuse, and now she was dealing with reports of her daughter's abuse. She was in prison on a drug charge, and she believed that her daughter was in danger of following in her footsteps. Unfortunately, her status as a prisoner made reporting of the abuse difficult if not impossible. Prior research has pointed out the problem of placement of the children of female prisoners in households where the prisoners had experienced abuse as a child (Sharp & Marcus-Mendoza, 2001).

THEORETICAL CONSIDERATIONS

The findings of the Oklahoma study strongly suggest that Feminist Pathways Theory is a valid explanation of female crime, at least for these women. Because mainstream theories of offending may be more applicable to males, feminist scholars have developed theoretical approaches that focus on the paths into criminal behavior that are more typical of women (Belknap & Holsinger, 2006; Britton, 2000; Chesney-Lind, 1989; Daly & Chesney-Lind, 1988; Flavin, 2001). This body of work continues to advance the idea that men and women differ significantly in their pathways into crime. Mainstream theories are primarily drawn from research on male offenders, and therefore generalizability to women is problematic (Daly & Chesney-Lind, 1988). The study reported in this chapter did not address male offenders; therefore comparisons would not be appropriate. However, the histories of the women who participated in the study clearly indicate that abuse, both during childhood and adulthood, is almost ubiquitous in the lives of these women prisoners. Other research has indicated that the abuse histories of female prisoners are much higher than of females in the general population (Acoca, 1998; Rivera & Widom, 1990; Widom, 1989). Additionally, females are sexually abused at higher rates than males, although males are generally more likely to experience physical abuse (Tjaden & Thoennes, 1998). Finally, females tend to enter the justice system first as juveniles, frequently for status offenses such as running away (Widom, 1989). Furthermore, juvenile offending is strongly linked to adult offending, with about half of the girls arrested for juvenile status offenses ultimately being arrested as adults for criminal offenses (Widom, 2000). The study reported in this chapter adds to the body of knowledge about the high correlation between abuse and offending in female prisoners, thus adding support to pathways explanations of female crime.

CONCLUSIONS AND POLICY IMPLICATIONS

The Oklahoma study confirms much of the existing knowledge about women offenders. The vast majority of them have experienced physical or sexual abuse, either as a child or as an adult (Belknap & Holsinger, 2006; Marcus-Mendoza et al., 1994; Sargent et al., 1993). Furthermore, they have experienced abuse at higher rates than women in the general population (Acoca, 1998; Rivera & Widom, 1990; Widom, 1989).

Often, they have experienced multiple types of abuse, both as a child and as an adult. This clearly indicates the need for incorporating abuse-specific types of treatment into the prison programming for women. However, this is not occurring in Oklahoma's female prisons. Nor are these women receiving appropriate treatment prior to incarceration. Instead, prison is often just one more event in a long list of violent victimizations, and the women who end up there have in many ways been ignored by society until their behaviors were considered offensive in some way. Because much of the general public assumes that those who are incarcerated are "bad" people, little headway has been made in providing adequate services to the women. Furthermore, the services that do exist have been largely developed based on a male model of incarceration.[3] Despite more than three decades of scholarship on women offenders, very little has changed in our treatment of them. The field of criminology remains dominated by "malestream" approaches (Renzetti, 1993). Women who offend are seen as the female mirror images of men who offend. This leads to the conclusion that they should be treated exactly the same.

As I reached the end of this chapter, it occurred to me that I could find out how knowledgeable the Oklahoma Department of Corrections is about the women that are incarcerated. In this state, all prisoners go through an initial assessment when they are received into the system. This is accomplished in order to determine not only proper classification of the prisoner but also what types of programs should be completed. So, I asked a caseworker from the assessment center about the type of assessment done on women prisoners. I was somewhat encouraged to hear that a different instrument was used to assess female prisoners than the one used for males. However, when I asked whether the instrument included any questions about the abuse histories of prisoners, my optimism flagged. I was told that prisoners are asked whether or not they have abused others, but they are not asked whether or not they have been victimized. I pointed out that the majority of women prisoners are incarcerated for drug offenses and that drug use is linked to victimization, particularly in women. The caseworker told me that, as of now, this is simply not addressed in screening for program needs.

Obviously, if there is no assessment of abuse histories, it is highly unlikely that the prisoners will receive counseling or treatment specifically designed to help the women deal with past abuse. Instead, they are highly likely to complete their sentences and return to society with many of the same problems that led to their offending.

It is extremely important, therefore, that we educate correctional systems about the impact of abuse on women prisoners and the importance of providing counseling and programs specifically designed for the victims of abuse. While the victim offenders in prison do need other services, including education, training, and substance abuse treatment, the likelihood of successful rehabilitation is decreased by the lack of awareness of the pathways to offending that are common in incarcerated women. Perhaps, with repeated efforts to educate those in charge of developing and implementing programs in prisons, these women can at last step out of the cycle of victimization, substance abuse, and offending that has characterized their lives.

Discussion Questions

1. Why does the author argue that there is a growing need to make our prisons more responsive to the needs of women? Describe these needs.
2. Discuss the gendered victimization experiences by female and male inmates. Discuss the pathways of women and men to prison.
3. According to the author, what are the consequences of abuse? How can we work to change these consequences?
4. Discuss the histories of victimization among the women interviewed in this study.
5. What theory does the author propose is best suited to explain the criminalization of female victimization?

References

Acoca, L. (1998). Outside/inside: The violation of American girls at home, on the streets and in the juvenile justice system. *Crime & Delinquency, 44*, 561–589.

Anderson, T. L. (2003). Issues in the availability of health care for women prisoners. In S. F. Sharp (Ed.), *The incarcerated woman: Rehabilitative programming in women's prisons* (pp. 49–60). Upper Saddle River, NJ: Prentice-Hall.

Beck, A., & Karberg, J. C. (2001). *Prison and jail inmates at midyear 2000.* Washington, D.C.: U.S. Department of Justice/Bureau of Justice Statistics.

Belknap, J. (2001). *The invisible woman* (2nd ed.). Belmont, CA: Wadsworth.

Belknap, J. (2003). Responding to the needs of women prisoners. In S. F. Sharp (Ed.), *The incarcerated woman: Rehabilitative programming in women's prisons* (pp. 93–106). Upper Saddle River, NJ: Prentice-Hall.

Belknap, J., & Holsinger, K. (2006). The gendered nature of risk factors for delinquency. *Feminist Criminology, 1*, 48–71.

Bloom, B., & Owen, B. (1994). *Women in prison in California: Hidden victims of the war on drugs.* San Francisco, CA: Center on Juvenile and Criminal Justice.

Britton, D. (2000). Feminism in criminology: Engendering the outlaw. *Annals, 571*, 57–76.

Chesney-Lind, M. (1986). Women and crime: The Female offender. *Signs, 12*, 8–96.

Chesney-Lind, M. (1989). Girls' crime and woman's place: Toward a feminist model of female delinquency. *Crime & Delinquency, 35*, 5–29.

Chesney-Lind, M. (1997). *The female offender: Girls, women and crime.* Thousand Oaks, CA: Sage.

Chesney-Lind, M. (1998). The forgotten offender: Women in prison. *Corrections Today, 60*, 66–73.

Chesney-Lind, M. (2003). Reinventing women's corrections: Challenges for contemporary criminologists and practitioners. In S. F. Sharp (Ed.), *The incarcerated woman: Rehabilitative programming in women's prisons* (pp. 3–14). Upper Saddle River, NJ: Prentice-Hall.

Chesney-Lind, M., & Shelden, R. G. (1998). *Girls, delinquency and juvenile justice.* Belmont, CA: Wadsworth.

Covington, S. S. (1998). Women in prison: Approaches in the treatment of our most invisible population. In J. Harden & M. Hill (Eds.), *Breaking the rules: Women in prison and feminist therapy* (pp. 141–155). Binghamton, NY: Harrington Park Press.

Daly, K., & Chesney-Lind, M. (1988). Feminism and criminology. *Justice Quarterly, 5,* 497–538.

Ditton, P. M. (1999) *Mental health and treatment of inmates and probationers.* Washington, D.C.: Bureau of Justice Statistics (NCJ 174463).

English, K. (1993). Self-reported crime rates of women prisoners. *Journal of Quantitative Criminology, 9,* 357–382.

Faith, K. (1993). *Unruly women: The politics of confinement and resistance.* Vancouver, BC: Press Gang Publishers.

Flavin, J. (2001). Feminism for the mainstream criminologist: An invitation. *Journal of Criminal Justice, 29,* 271–285.

Greenfeld, L. A., & Snell, T. L. (1999). *Women offenders.* Washington, D.C.: U.S. Department of Justice/Bureau of Justice Statistics.

Hannah-Moffat, K. (1995). Feminine fortress: Women-centered prisons? *The Prison Journal, 75,* 135–64.

Harrison, P. M., & Beck, A. J. (2005). *Prisoners in 2004.* Washington, D.C.: U.S. Department of Justice/Bureau of Justice Statistics (NCJ 210677).

Heney, J., & Kristiansen, C. M. (1998). An analysis of the impact of prison on women survivors of childhood sexual abuse. In J. Harden & M. Hill (Eds.), *Breaking the rules: Women in prison and feminist therapy* (pp. 29–44). Binghamton, NY: Harrington Park Press.

Jordan, K., Schlenger, W., Fairbanks, J., & Caddell, J. (1996). Prevalence of psychiatric disorders among incarcerated women. *Archives of General Psychiatry, 53,* 512–519.

Kaplan, M. S., & Sasser, J. E. (1996). Women behind bars: Trends and policy issues. *Journal of Sociology and Social Welfare, 23*(4), 43–56.

Kruttschnitt, C., Gartner, R., & Miller, A. (2000). Doing her own time? Women's responses to prison in the context of the old and new penology. *Criminology, 38*(3), 681–717.

Lauritsen, J. L, Sampson, R. J., & Laub, J. H. (1991). The link between offending and victimization among adolescents. *Criminology, 29,* 265–291.

Marcus-Mendoza, S. T., Klein-Saffran, J., & Lutze, F. (1998). A feminist examination of boot camp prison programs for women. In J. Harden & M. Hill (Eds.), *Breaking the rules: Women in prison and feminist therapy* (pp.173–186) Binghamton, NY: Harrington Park Press.

Marcus-Mendoza, S. T., Sargent, E., & Ho, Y. C. (1994). Changing perceptions of the etiology of crime: The relationship between abuse and female criminality. *Journal of the Oklahoma Research Consortium, 1,* 13–23.

Marcus-Mendoza, S., & Wright, E. (2003). Treating the woman prisoner: The impact of a history of violence. In S. F. Sharp (Ed.), *The incarcerated woman: Rehabilitative programming in women's prisons* (pp. 107–117) Upper Saddle River, NJ: Prentice-Hall.

Michael, R. T., Gagnon, J. H., Lauman, E. O., & Kolata, G. (1994). *Sex in America: A definitive survey.* New York: Warner Books.

Miller, S. L. (2005) *Victims as offenders: The paradox of women's violence in relationships.* Piscataway, NJ: Rutgers University Press.

Morash, M., Bynum, T., & Koons, B. (1995). *Findings from the national study of innovative and promising programs for women offenders.* Washington, D.C.: National Institute of Justice.

Morash, M., & Schram, P. (2002). *The prison experience: Special issues of women in prison.* Prospect Heights, IL: Waveland Press.

Oklahoma Criminal Justice Resource Center. (2004a). *Analysis of Oklahoma drug courts: Fiscal years 2002–2003.* Oklahoma City, OK: Oklahoma Criminal Justice Resource Center.

Oklahoma Criminal Justice Resource Center. (2004b). *Special task force for women incarcerated in Oklahoma.* Oklahoma City, OK: Oklahoma Criminal Justice Resource Center.

Oklahoma Criminal Justice Resource Center. (2004c). *Gender, crime and incarceration in Oklahoma.* Oklahoma City, OK: Oklahoma Criminal Justice Resource Center.

Owen, B. (1998). *In the mix.* Albany, NY: State University of New York Press.

Owen, B., & Bloom, B. (1995). *Profiling the needs of California's female prisoners: A needs assessment.* Report to the National Institute of Justice.

Pollock, J. (1986). *Sex and supervision: Guarding male and female inmates.* New York: Greenwood.

Pollock-Byrne, J. M. (2001). *Women, prison and crime.* Pacific Grove, CA: Brooks/Cole.

Rafter, N. H. (1990). *Partial justice: Women, prisons and social control* (2nd ed.). New Brunswick, NJ: Transaction.

Renzetti, C. M. (1993). On the margins of the malestream (or, they *still* don't get it, do they?): Feminist analyses in criminal justice education. *Journal of Criminal Justice Education, 4,* 219–234.

Rivera, B., & Widom, C. S. (1990). Childhood victimization and violent offending. *Violence and Victims, 5,* 19–35.

Sargent, E., Marcus-Mendoza, S. T., & Yu. (1993). Abuse and the woman prisoner. In B. R. Fletcher, L. D. Shaver, & D. G. Moon (Eds.), *Women prisoners: A forgotten population.* Westport, CT: Praeger.

Sharp, S. F. (2003). Where do we go from here? In S. F. Sharp (Ed.), *The incarcerated woman: Rehabilitative programming in women's prisons* (pp. 185–189). New York: Prentice-Hall.

Sharp, S. F. (2004). *Oklahoma study of incarcerated mothers and their children—Phase I* (Report to the Oklahoma State Legislature). Oklahoma City, OK: Oklahoma Commission on Children and Youth.

Sharp, S. F. (2005). *Oklahoma study of incarcerated mothers and their children—Phase II* (Report to the Oklahoma State Legislature). Oklahoma City, OK: Oklahoma Commission on Children and Youth.

Sharp, S. F., & Marcus-Mendoza, S. (2001). It's a family affair: The effects of incarceration on women and their families. *Women and Criminal Justice, 12*(4), 21–49.

Sharp, S. F., Terling-Watt, T., Atkins, L. A., Gilliam, J. T., & Sanders, A. (2001). Purging behavior in a sample of college females: A research note on General Strain Theory and female deviance. *Deviant Behavior, 22,* 171–188.

Tjaden, P., & Thoennes, N. (1998) *Prevalence, incidence, and consequences of violence against women: Findings from the National Violence Against Women Survey.* Washington, D.C.: National Institute of Justice/Centers for Disease Control and Prevention, Research in Brief.

Tjaden, P., & Thoennes, N. (2006). *Extent, nature and consequences of rape victimization: Findings from the National Violence Against Women Survey.* Washington, D.C.: National Institute of Justice (NCJ 210346).

Warren, J. I. (2003). *Baseline psychopathology in a women's prison: Its impact on institutional adjustment and risk for violence.* Retrieved April 3, 2006, from the National Institute of Justice (http://www.ncjrs.gov/pdffiles1/nij/grants/198621.pdf).

Widom, C. S. (1989). The cycle of violence. *Science, 244,* 160–166.

Widom, C. S. (2000). Childhood victimization and the derailment of girls and women to the criminal justice system. In *Research on Women and Girls in the Justice System* (pp. 27–36). Washington, D.C.: National Institute of Justice.

Young, V. D., & Reviere, R. (2006). *Women behind Bars: Gender and race in U.S. Prisons.* Boulder, CO: Lynne Rienner Publishers.

Zaplin, R. (1998). Female offenders: A systems perspective. In R. Zaplin (Ed.), *Female offenders: Critical perspectives and effective interventions.* Gaithersburg, MD: Aspen.

Endnotes

1. A page at the end of the survey asked for volunteers, explaining the qualification of having children. This page asked for the volunteer's name, department of correction number, and the number of children and their ages. The pages were separated from the surveys and collected separately to maximize confidentiality by keeping the subjects' responses on the initial survey and their identifying information separated.

2. A detailed explanation of the interviews with caretakers can be obtained from the author.

3. Most of the programs in prisons were developed based on male prisoners because the vast majority of prisoners were male.

CHAPTER 17

THE CRIMINALIZATION OF VICTIMIZATION OF FEMALE OFFENDERS AND EMERGING CORRECTIONAL RESPONSES

Patrick McManimon

ABSTRACT

This chapter discusses the role the juvenile justice and criminal justice systems play in criminalizing female victimization. It examines the early and residual effects of the cycle of violence on future criminality that is often survival for female victims. Battered women's syndrome and the criminal justice system's failure to construct an effective response to its effects highlight the system's insensitivity toward females who experience various forms of domestic violence. Also examined are how this continued violence leads to the development of posttraumatic stress disorder and the consequences this disorder has on women's reaction to continued abuse. The physical and psychological effects are exemplified in a discussion of several well-publicized cases. Finally, this chapter discusses the emerging correctional systems' responses to female offenders. The reality that most female offenders are victims of violence at some point in the life cycle warrants this emerging programmatic emphasis on the part of correctional personnel.

INTRODUCTION

Female offenders are the progeny of androcentric laws often justified by a history of paternalism and chivalry, which are rationales for maintaining traditional female roles requiring obedience to male authority. Nowhere is this more evident than in the juvenile justice system. The majority of adult female offenders have a juvenile justice history. Thus a discussion of the legal system's victimization of female offenders should begin with the juvenile offender.

Similar to our counterparts in other countries, the United States has criminalized the behavior of girls in an effort to ensure their obedience to their fathers (and mothers) and to maintain their proper role and place in society. In the United States the criminal justice system, as the primary agent of social control, has the responsibility to punish behavior believed aberrant by the dominant class, who define which behaviors are punished and therefore what groups are most likely to be punished. Inadequate attention is paid to the fact that girls and women are more adversely affected by the juvenile and criminal justice systems that punish female victims.

THE CRIMINALIZATION OF JUVENILE VICTIMIZATION

Both male and female juvenile arrests are predominately for trivial offenses, whereas status offenses are particularly significant in the case of girls. In fact, in 1990 status offenses accounted for 24 percent of all girls' arrests (Chesney-Lind, 1995). Data collected by the Office of Juvenile Justice and Delinquency Prevention (OJJDP) for the year 2002 show that of the 125,700 arrests for "runaways" 60 percent were committed by girls. These statistics exemplify a consistent pattern over the last 20 years: Girls have been and continue to be overrepresented in arrests for running away and incorrigibility even though the National Youth Survey found no evidence of greater female involvement in any category of delinquency and that males were more likely to report status offense behavior than were females. Further data from the OJJDP show that girls are underrepresented in most offense categories demonstrating that official practices target female status offenses (Canter, 1982).

The importance of this relates to both the theories of delinquency (which are primarily rooted in male behavior and will not be discussed here) and the fact that girls are being victimized in their homes by relatives and acquaintances as well as by the juvenile justice system. Running away is, in many instances, the only way which girls can escape continued sexual and physical abuse perpetrated in their homes. Girls who have been abused are nearly twice as likely to be arrested. Often these arrests begin as status offense arrests and end in arrests for violent crimes as adults (Widom, 1998). As quoted from a 16-year-old girl who had been repeatedly sexually and physically abused and assaulted and started to run away from home, "I ran away so many times. I tried everything man and they wouldn't believe me . . . As far as they are concerned they think I am the problem. You know, runaway, bad label" (cited in Chesney-Lind, 1995, p. 73). She was arrested and charged as a runaway.

For many girls who face similar situations, running away is the only remedy they have to survive. Often this leads them to a life on the street, one filled with prostitution and drug use. These offenses begin a continued spiral of criminal activity that continues into adulthood (see Box 17.1).

These findings are supported by previous research into the phenomenon of criminalizing girl's survival. As many as 35 percent of women in the general public report being victimized before the age of 18, which many believe to be a low estimate (Hebert, Tremblay, Parent, Daignault, & Piche, 2006). Many end up in correctional settings, with those with histories of victimization as children to be twice as likely as their counterparts to have an adult criminal history. The issue here is that girls who are victims of sexual/physical abuse have their survival criminalized and this criminalization leads to further criminal conduct as adults. Researchers have found that the criminal persistence of abused and neglected girls can be quite significant and compelling. In fact, a significant portion of female offenders had offense patterns similar to "mid-rate chronic" male offenders (Widom, 1988; Widom, Nagin, & Lambert, 1998).

> ### BOX 17.1
>
> ## ARREST OF JUVENILE AND ADULT FEMALE CRIME VICTIMS OF SEXUAL AND PHYSICAL ABUSE
>
> - Juvenile and adult female victims are twice as likely to be arrested for criminal conduct.
> - Juvenile and adult female victims are 2.5 times more likely to be arrested for crimes of violence.
> - The majority of females who are arrested for sex crimes were abused or neglected (Maxfield & Widom, 1996).
>
> - Girls represent over 70 percent of those victimized sexually (Finkelhor & Baron, 1986).
> - Over 61 percent of females in juvenile correctional settings have experienced repeated physical and/or sexual abuse (American Correctional Association, 1990).

THE CRIMINALIZATION OF VICTIMS OF DOMESTIC VIOLENCE

As in the case of juvenile female offenders, women are victimized by the very system that is responsible for their protection. As a result, women are often left to "fight back" on their own in order to eliminate further victimization. This is never more evident than in cases of domestic violence where women are often left to feel entrapped due to isolation from family and friends, social services, and advocacy centers. Without the needed support, victims are often trapped at the hands of their abusers who are then supported by a patriarchal society. The institutions of that society, or rather the failures of these institutions, contribute to the feeling of entrapment and isolation.

Neglect by police to provide protection for battered women is well documented and aids in the feeling of powerlessness that many of these victims experience. Even when arrests are made, victims are often reluctant to pursue prosecution due to anticipated financial instability, if the bread winner is removed from the house for a long period of time, repeated past failures of the criminal justice system to provide protection from future assaults and victimization, and the prospect that future battering would increase in severity and often spill over to child abuse as a way to control the victim (Erez & Belknap, 1998).

Pro-arrest policies introduced in the late 1980s and early 1990s were followed up by new legislation that in many states required the victim to cooperate with prosecutors or face contempt charges, criminalizing their fears. Women were also prohibited from withdrawing complaints against their abuser, regardless of their personal needs and wishes, although research demonstrates that victims are better protected when the criminal justice system respects the abused women's wishes with regard to prosecution (Moe, 2007).

Orders of protection and restraining orders seek to provide the abused with legal protection without criminal prosecution. As a civil matter, there is a lower standard of proof required to obtain an order. This provides the victim a sense of empowerment over a process she has control over. However, restraining orders are often ineffective in preventing future abuse (Davis & Smith, 1995). Among other reasons are the inconsistent enforcement of these orders by police and the limited nature of the orders' scopes. Much of the police response to domestic violence is predicated on individual as well as organizational beliefs and biases, and the long held belief that domestic violence is a family matter.

Although there seems to be little dispute regarding women historically being the victims of domestic violence, the evidence is mounting that there is a change in the idea that males are the perpetrators of intimate partner violence (IPV). There is a large and growing body of evidence that women are using forms of physical aggression at roughly the same rate as men in interpersonal relationships (Archer, 2000). Many in the feminist community cite women as using aggression as a means of self-defense especially within the context of a continuing abusive relationship. Some estimate that as many as 25 percent of all domestic violence arrestees are women. The explanations range from dual-arrest practices by police to women actively defending themselves in the face of an abusive attacker with knives, guns, and other weapons. The latter certainly is contrary to images of the helpless, passive women who are in need of defending (Chesney-Lind, 2002a; Miller, 2001). One should keep in mind that it is the response to the situation (abuse) that is changing and not the fact that women remain the predominate victims of IPV. There is consistency in the research that women arrested for IPV are victims who are acting in self-defense, not initiators of the conflict in the vast majority of cases.

However, the criminal justice system routinely ignores the fact that women are the victims. As a result of years of physical and, in most cases, accompanying psychological abuse, women fight back, and they are treated as the perpetrators of violence. Their victimization history is ignored by the system. They are charged with a criminal offense and most likely will have to endure a trial which they cannot afford financially or personally.

VICTIM OR OFFENDER: THE CASE OF LORENA BOBBIT

Lorena Bobbitt's case is infamous both for the criminalization of years of victimization and the way in which the media and criminal justice system treat women who fight back against their abusers. The facts of the case are simple: On January 22, 1994, a jury in Manassas, Virginia, acquitted Lorena Bobbitt of malicious wounding. The previous summer, she cut off her husband's penis after he raped her, an act of violence to which she had regularly been subjected since they were married in 1989 (Weaning, 2000).

Unfortunately, the focus of the Bobbitt case has been carefully shifted away from the problem of violence against women to the fact that John Bobbitt's penis was cut off. The case also exemplifies the typical male response to such an act: "why didn't she leave?" The academic literature discusses the reasons for a woman's perceived inability to leave. Among the factors are that they are not financially able to do so, there have been threats against children—"if you leave I will kill the kids"—and there is no place to go.

In the case of Lorena Bobbitt, she was an immigrant from Venezuela who came to the United States at the age of 17. She was married three years later to John Bobbitt. She had no real frame of reference regarding the legal or social systems in the United

States. As is the case with many women, she was isolated from family and friends and had a marginal support system. Some reports find that women's shelters are fewer in number than animal shelters. Although acquitted of the crime of malicious wounding, for the next month, she was held at a mental hospital for tests. She has been painted as a dangerous, crazed, sexually frustrated woman and the butt of many jokes, but in reality, it is men like John Bobbitt, and public neglect of important issues like violence against women, that are dangerous. Media and public treatment of the Bobbitt case reveal a tragic case of domestic violence, a testament to the need for more education about violence against women, and a study in backlash (Weaning, 2000).

This case also opens the door to the examination of cultural differences within communities of the nondominant culture. During interviews with the victims' advocate in a large county in a northeastern state, this author discussed IPV in a Hispanic community. This county had a particularly large Guatemalan population. The advocate stated that she personally witnessed abuse so severe that the women were often not recognizable. However, the victims would often not seek medical care and would never call police to the scene, nor consent to file criminal charges. In that particular community, women would be ostracized if they called the police to report an assault by their partners. Not only would the community in this county ostracize the victim, but because they had no visible means of support, they would be returned to Guatemala, where they would face beatings from their families and possible death for bringing shame to them (Victim's Advocate Office, 2001).

Continuing the criminalization of victims' responses to severe and repeated IPV in the absence of formal measures of social control is hypocritical. Interpersonal violence is no longer America's dark secret. It is in the open and the criminal justice system has a responsibility to apply its resources to stem the tide. The long-term effects of IPV on juveniles are only now being explored. We do know that the cycle of violence continues from one generation to the next. The *status quo* is no longer an option. Women are taking matters into their own hands to protect themselves and their children. However, the results of that behavior have further deleterious effects, not the least of which is the arrests and sometimes prosecutions and convictions of women who are defending themselves. Their children are often lost to the social services systems. Male-dominated laws fail to protect women and children, and the laws need to change to require police intervention when orders of protections are issued. Criminal consequences for violation of orders of protection should be initiated where they do not exist and increased in places where the penalties are not significant enough to deter or incapacitate the perpetrators of IPV against children and women.

POSTTRAUMATIC STRESS DISORDER: THE CASE OF FRANCINE HUGHES

The case that began to change the legal and social reactions to the problem of violence against women was that of Francine Hughes. In 1977, a 29-year-old housewife, Francine Hughes, was charged with first-degree murder for killing her abusive husband. (Michigan Battered Women' Clemency Project, 2000). After enduring 13 years of vicious beatings, death threats, intimidation, and humiliation, Ms. Hughes set fire to the bed in which her husband was sleeping. For years before the murder, Ms. Hughes tried to escape from her husband without success. She actively sought help from lawyers, judges, social service agencies, and the police, all to no avail. Had she not killed her husband, it seems probable that she would have died at his hands (Michigan Battered Women' Clemency Project, 2000). Francine Hughes was found not guilty by reason of temporary insanity. This case gave rise to a movie "The Burning Bed" starring Farrah Fawcett. It also began to alter the collective conscience relative to domestic violence and the inevitable reactions of women abused for years.

BLURRING THE LINE: THE CASE OF SUSAN SMITH

The cases of Bobbitt and Hughes had a positive outcome for the defendants. There are other cases that ignore this abuse and women are confined, often for periods up to twice that of males who kill their female partners. One such case is that of Susan Smith. On October 25, 1994, Susan Smith released the emergency break on her Mazda and watched it role into the lake (Pergament, 2007). In the backseat of the automobile slept her two children Michael and Alex. The car slid into the lake as the children slept. Both boys drown and Susan made no attempt to save them. There seems to be little controversy about this case. She drowned her children because she was depressed over her failed marriage and the breakup with her new love interest. Neither were reasons sufficient to explain the taking of the lives of her children. In our society there is nothing more heinous or despicable. Susan Smith also blamed the "disappearance" of her children on a Black man who she alleged carjacked her automobile. Susan later confessed to the murder of her sons.

At the trial and sentencing phases, social workers and psychologists agreed that Susan had been sexually molested as a child by her step-father, been exposed to several suicides, including her father, with whom she was very close, and her marriage failed due to adultery of her husband. The defense argued successfully that she should be given consideration in sentencing because of her many years of abuse. Although the jury convicted her of murder, they spared her life. She was sentenced to life in prison for the murder of her children. She is eligible for parole in 2025.

This case raises issues that are much less clear cut and immediate than the above cited cases of Bobbitt and Hughes. In those cases the abuser was the object of the retaliatory assault. In the Susan Smith case, the social norms and expectations of the role of a mother predetermined the outcome of the case, in the face of an abusive history. Additionally, Smith did not fight back, she became caught in a system that provides little assistance for women suffering from depression. The offender's victimization is often lost as in this case. The effects of psychological abuse are not as well documented as are the issues of physical abuse and battering.

BATTERED WOMEN'S SYNDROME

The concerns raised in the Smith case are supported by research that finds psychological abuse affects a woman's psychological well-being to the same extent as physical abuse or battering and may actually be predictive of physical violence (Kelly, 2004). In 1977, Lenore Walker (1977) first labeled the battered women's syndrome. In her work she identified three stages of the syndrome beginning with tension, progressing to explosion of acute battering incidents, and ending in a calm, even a loving respite (see Box 17.2). Later, Walker found that there were consistent and unique psychological phenomena accompanying the physical abuse (Walker, 1983, 1984,

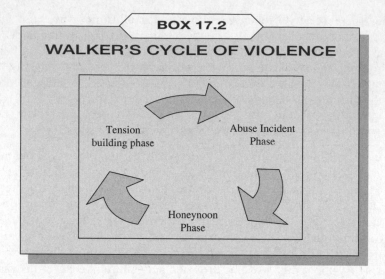

BOX 17.2

WALKER'S CYCLE OF VIOLENCE

Tension building phase

Abuse Incident Phase

Honeynoon Phase

1991). This study shifted the understanding and treatment of the syndrome. Walker's analysis revealed that victims were not staying in abusive relationships because of a psychological need to be a victim, but out of sheer terror at the thought of leaving the relationship solely on issues of safety; their safety and that of their children. (Kelly, 2004; Follingstad et al., 1990).

It is easy to identify physical abuse. Cuts, bruises, broken bones, and more severe physical injury are quantifiable and easily documented. The criminal justice system works best when evidence of a crime is clear and understandable to the common man. Photographs, X-rays, and even more sophisticated medical tests explained by physicians in court cases are easily understood by most people. However, psychological abuse and injury are difficult to quantify and therefore has been slow to be accepted in the courts.

In reality, the social construct of psychological abuse is not well established in the psychological community. As a result, there has been a slow acceptance of this defense within the criminal justice community. One of the major difficulties with the definition of psychological abuse and the battered women's syndrome is that the effects of the psychological abuse and the victim's responses are dependent upon a variety of individual factors. These factors include the intensity of the abuse, frequency of abuse, intent, and the level of the victim's fear (Tolman, 1992). Additionally, Tolman categorized psychological forms of abuse to include the creation of fear, economic abuse, and others. The point here is that although these categories seem very clear in a discussion such as this, they become less clear and difficult to quantify in a court. Further, the type and extent of the abuse can elicit different reactions from different victims.

As is often the case, law and research often experience a lag in knowledge and acceptance. The law often drags behind science and certainly drags behind social science due to the use of statistics to bolster scientific arguments of certainty. As an example, the use of DNA was not readily accepted in courts and law, but rather required a set of consistent results supporting previous findings raising the level of certainty to the level of certainty beyond a reasonable doubt. Social sciences lack the certainty required by law for several reasons, not the least of which is that there is little prestige for researchers to replicate research as is the case in the hard sciences. However, in the case of psychological abuse and the battered women's syndrome, the development of a broadly accepted definition has been slow. Much of the research was completed under the auspices of feminist criminology, which itself has not received the attention it deserves.

Although the social construct of psychological abuse continues to be a difficult task, the effects of this abuse and the evidence of its detrimental impact on victims are more agreed upon within the psychology community. Higher risks of depression and depth of depression are reported among groups of women who were abused than among women who were not. Lower self-esteem is also significantly correlated with abuse. Clearly, the psychological abuse suffered by women is a form of the battered women's syndrome obfuscated in use of the syndrome as a defense. However, the battered women's syndromc has been replaced in the last decade by a more well-known construct, posttraumatic stress disorder (PTSD) (Overa, McLeod, & Sharpe, 1996).

POSTTRAUMATIC STRESS DISORDER

Originally known as "shell shock" in veterans returning from war who had experienced psychological effects of war, PTSD is now used to explain the psychological deterioration of persons expericncing psychological trauma from a variety of sources including physical and psychological abuse at the hands of an intimate. Research into lethality by female victims of domestic abuse shows that women who kill their partners differ little from women who do not kill their abusers. A major factor is the frequency and severity of the abuse. A sense of helplessness overtakes the victim because of the lack of trust in the criminal justice system and a fear of the response of the perpetrator if the victim attempts to leave the situation. A varied and progressive set of escape strategies develop including increased alcohol and drug use, suicide attempts, and eventual murder. Walker's definition of battered women's syndrome is consistent with PTSD (Houskamp & Foy, 1991; Walker, 1991). There is a high level of PTSD symptoms present in women who kill their abusive partners when compared with women who do not use lethal force (Hattendorf, Ottens, & Lomax, 1999). For the purposes of the criminal justice system, the ability to quantify the effects, severity, and intensity of abuse allows the law to "catch up to science" making PTSD a viable defense for abused women.

Judicial acceptance of the battered women's syndrome has increased in recent years. The traditional defenses of duress, necessity, justification, self-defense, defense of others, and psychological impairment have evolved in contemporary legal circles as have the battered woman's/PTSD defenses. One of the key elements in the acknowledgment of the defense is the repetitive nature of abuse suffered by the "victim/perpetrator." This is a double-edged sword. On one hand, women are less likely to use deadly force, but women who do use deadly force are more likely to vicitimize their husbands or close relatives. However, women who kill their husbands have been more severely abused than those who do not kill their husbands (Ewing, 1987). Mann (1988) found that 59 percent of the women in her study who killed their husbands claimed self-defense and were severely beaten over a long period of time.

On the other hand, Mann also found that 58 percent of the women in her study indicated premeditation, a condition that removes the generally accepted self-defense argument. Mann concluded that the self-defense claim may be relevant in some domestic violence cases but not others, primarily due to the issue of premeditation.

The fact that woman react in a violent nature is contrary to the socially accepted roles of women. Gillespie (1989) posited that violence against women by intimates had been ignored until recent time, but violence by women violated traditional stereotypes of women. Women who were charged with murdering their spouses were expected to plead guilty. The battered women's syndrome defense has begun to gain acceptance, but tradition dictates that the battering by the husband or intimate is not an excuse for the women's actions of murder. The acceptance of the defense remains inconsistent across jurisdictions (Reid, 1994).

Judicial acceptance of the defense faced staunch resistance from a predominately male judiciary that found it difficult to accept a defense juxtaposed to traditional American roles. The defense was categorized as self-defense. Legal definitions of self-defense required the danger to self to be immediate or imminent. As in the above cases of Hughes and Bobbitt, the assaults were completed when the offenders were asleep, negating the claim of immediate or imminent danger. These cases are examples of the difficulty the legal system experienced in accepting the battered women's syndrome defense initially. The fact that the battering took place over a "long" period of time further complicated its sustainability.

However, the PTSD defense was seen as more acceptable. The fact that male soldiers experienced the symptoms and actions exhibited by female offenders as a result of battering may have made the judiciary more accepting of the defense. Also, the psychology community was able to agree on the symptoms of the disorder, and it appeared in the *Diagnostic and Statistical Manual of Mental Disorders (DSM-IV)* in 1994. The fact that psychologists were able to diagnose high levels of PTSD symptoms within populations of offenders who murdered their abusers gave the necessary credence to the use of the defense and made it more acceptable to the judicial community (Kemp, Rawlings, & Green, 1991). Research found that judges were more and more willing to admit expert testimony of battered women's syndrome and PTSD, "the older more experienced judges were less receptive to the defenses and the more cases judges heard, the less likely they were to consider trauma as a mitigating factor in sentencing" (Sigler & Shook, 1997, p. 1). As the judiciary changed and the psychology community became more expert in defining the role of abuse in criminal behavior of women, the more credence has been given to the battered women's syndrome defense. It is important to understand that self-defense, the category under which the battered women's syndrome and PTSD are classified, is an affirmative defense. It is a defense that needs to be proven—a task which is not always an easy undertaking. This burden victimizes women who believe they have no other alternative but to act decisively, taking matters into their own hands, because the system has failed to provide the necessary protection by increasing the burden of proof to beyond a reasonable doubt.

EMERGING CORRECTIONAL RESPONSES
TO FEMALE OFFENDERS

The relationship between women who have been abused and offending is important not only in and of itself, but because women are being arrested and convicted of violent offenses at a greater rate than ever before (Richie, 2002). While the actual numbers may be smaller than those for males, the rate of increase in arrest, conviction, and prison sentences are significantly higher. Much of the discussion has centered on victimization of women. It is important to understand the victimization of women both individually and systematically in order to enable one to examine the efficacy of the correctional system in addressing the needs of women offenders. A recent report by the Bureau of Justice Statistics indicated that over 50 percent of the women in prison and jail report physical, sexual, and psychological abuse before their imprisonment. Statistics seem clear that abused women comprise at least 50 percent of the population of women prisoners, and the exact number of jail inmates most likely exceeds that number.

A report commissioned by the Institute on Women and Criminal Justice finds that female imprisonment in the United States has skyrocketed 757 percent since 1977 (Frost, Greene, & Pranis, 2006). Women are the fastest-growing segment of the prison population, surpassing male prison population growth in all 50 states.

The gap between male and female prison population growth rates has widened recently, producing an annual rate of increase for women that roughly doubled the rate for men in six of the last seven years. The number of women added to the state prison populations each year remains high despite lower growth rates. In fact, the expansion that has taken place since 1999 (11,689 new female prisoners) exceeds the total female state prison population in 1980 (11,113 women) (Frost et al., 2006).

According to Frost, Greene, and Pranis, there are four themes which can explain female criminality:

1. "Most women in the criminal justice system come from neighborhoods that are entrenched in poverty and largely lacking in viable systems of social support.
2. Alarmingly large numbers of these women have experienced very serious physical and/or sexual abuse, often commencing when they were young children.
3. As adults, most of these women are plagued with high levels of physical and mental health problems as well as substance abuse issues. Often these problems are combined and compounded.
4. The great majority of the women who have suffered from these deprivations, histories of trauma and abuse, and health deficits are mothers—and they are far more likely than men in the criminal justice system to be the sole support and caregivers for their children" (Frost et al., 2006, p. 9).

The removal of female offenders from society has a more dramatic, direct effect on the social order, precisely because children are removed from the supervision of their parents and dumped into a child services system that is overwhelmed and often ineffective in maintaining safety.

Historically, women received lesser sentences than their male counterparts. As a result of mandatory prison sentences and sentencing guidelines, judges have less discretion and are treating women similarly to men. Chesney-Lind reports that 20 years ago, nearly two-thirds of the women convicted of federal felonies were granted probation, but in 1991, only 28 percent were given straight probation (2002b). The reality is that there are more women under correctional supervision than ever before. Much of the increase is attributed to the increased number of felony convictions in state courts between 1990 and 1996. The Bureau of Justice Statistics reported a 42 percent increase in felony convictions overall, and for violent crimes, there was a 27 percent increase over that period. Also, drug felonies increased 37 percent and property offenses increased 44 percent, while other felony convictions increased by 65 percent. These increases required many states to increase capacity in existing female correctional facilities (many states had only one facility for women), convert male facilities to female facilities, or build additional prisons for female offenders (Seiter, 2008).

Correctional agencies experienced a change in management as it relates to program disparity. In 1974, a federal court decision found that a disparity in programs between male and female inmates could not be justified simply because women were smaller in number and the costs would be prohibited (*Barefield v. Leach*, 1974). In *Butler v. Reno*, federal female inmates claimed gender discrimination due to denial of access to facilities, programs, and services available to similarly situated male inmates. The U.S. District Court for the District of Columbia agreed with the plaintiffs, and the Federal Bureau of Prisons agreed to provide parity in services and facilities including placing minimum-security females in camps with little physical security, reducing staff–inmate ratios, and providing work, parenting, recreational, and educational programs comparable with those provided to male inmates.

However, in 1995 the Eighth Circuit Court of Appeals in *Pargo v. Elliot* (1995) held that just the fact that there are differences in programs between males and females does not in and of itself violate the equal protection clause of the Constitution. In this decision, the Eighth Circuit recognized that women would look for different types of jobs after release and that there was a need for different types of vocational training and a need for parenting skills training and other child care issues that were not as important to male inmates. The Court basically paved the way for women to receive parity in programs without having to sacrifice specific gender needs as well as gender expectations.

Today the issue of parity has diminished as a result of the growth of the female inmate population. It is no longer a cost effectiveness issue with the growth in the female population. New prisons for females have increased program services for women. However, because women present a lower risk of repeat criminalization, prison administrators have made use of alternatives to incarceration more for female offenders. By far the most used alternative is the pre-release center. These facilities admit women who are three to six months from their release from prison. Female offenders learn life skills and are trained in job interviewing and preparation, and parenting skills. Offenders are also assisted in child care practices. In those cases where children are under the supervision of the child protection agency, women receive assistance in getting visitation rights and eventually their children back (Chesney-Lind, 2002b).

Female offenders seem to have higher substance abuse problems than their male counterparts, nearly 33 percent of female incarcerants have admitted committing a crime in order to obtain money for their drug habit, and nearly 80 percent of the women in state prison have a severe and long-standing history of drug abuse. Chesney-Lind suggests,

> Women's programs must, first and foremost, give participants strategies to deal with their profound substance abuse problems. They must also be gender sensitive in additional ways: they must understand that most women take drugs as a form of self-medication, and they must be sensitive to women's unique circumstances. (as cited in Seiter, 2008, p. 246)

As a result of this highly recognized need for substance abuse counseling, there are currently over 90 psychological programs nationally available within women's correctional centers. Their principal components include substance abuse counseling and domestic violence counseling. The interrelatedness of the two as we have seen cannot be overemphasized.

Gender-responsive programs include other important services for the female offender. Among them are such innovations as holiday parties for inmates and their children, often in partnership with a charity that will donate toys for the mothers to give their children. Girl Scouts Behind Bars assists inmate mothers with staying in contact with their children as female prisons permit the inmates and their daughters to participate in Girl Scouts within the prison (Moses, 1995).

Programs that involve children and offenders are predicated on the ability of children to be able to reach the prison. Many of the female prisons were located away from urban areas, where most of the offenders resided prior to commitment. Many Departments of Corrections are cognizant of this and provide transportation to children and family members who are their caretakers to ensure the success of these new programs (Clear, Cold, & Reisig, 2006).

One final area of discussion for prisons is the fact that for years female offenders have been classified using the same classification instruments and procedures that were developed for male offenders. This certainly had led to female inmates being overclassified. Overclassification is the placement of offenders in more secure prisons than is necessary. Many state Departments of Corrections and the Federal Bureau of Prisons have recognized the need to develop a gender-sensitive classification system and either have a different scoring system for females or use administrative overrides to reduce the security classification for women offenders (Seiter, 2008).

The tremendous growth in prison populations translates into more offenders than ever before in history being released to parole or other forms of community supervision. In 2001, 669,123 inmates, of which approximately 53,500 were female, were released from prisons across the country. This is a 66 percent increase from 1992. In some states and the federal system, inmates are returning to the community without any form of supervision due to the abolition of parole, particularly in the federal system. As a result there is a growing emphasis on prison reentry programs (Seiter, 2008).

REENTRY AND VICTIM–OFFENDER NEEDS

Female releasees face problems that compound the release difficulties. Among them are the continued issues surrounding domestic violence victimization. Gender-responsive strategies are now being integrated into services for female offenders.

One such strategy is a comprehensive approach to domestic violence victimization. This includes screening all women upon release to determine the scope of victimization. Several states including Oregon have hired domestic violence advocates to assist women releasees to develop safety plans. Recognizing the need to escape in a crisis is an important function that can assist women and prevent future criminalization. In some cases, an offender may be away from the residence for a period of time and probation officers need to be aware of the implications that domestic violence has on this problem. A pre-approved plan, kept confidential, can assist both the offender and the supervising agent in resolving a potential returnable offense without a revocation hearing (Neal, 2007).

Women offenders have a high rate of substance abuse and as a result need to address the issue in the community post release. State corrections departments are bridging services to offenders from prison into the community. Offenders begin treatment in the prison and the services are available to them in the community post release. In some states, such as Illinois, the bridge from prison goes to community correctional centers, to parole supervision, and to post supervision (Cervantes, 2007).

It is difficult for female offenders to find suitable means of financial support for themselves and their children. In the post–welfare era, this task has become more difficult because women must find employment. Given the fact that many females are not high-school graduates and are the sole means of support in their homes, this task can be overbearing, and criminality seems the most direct solution. As is the case with all post-release programs, parole agents and administrators need to ensure that programs for female offenders are gender-specific and employment is no different.

The probation trends in many ways mirror the trends of parole and vice versa. The movement toward case management and intensive probation supervision (ISP) has been recognized by practitioners and scholars as a positive approach to probation especially of female offenders. The case management model of ISP allows for lower caseloads, more frequent personal contact, and a readiness with the system to assist probationers with problems before they escalate to criminal behavior. This proved most effective for drug-involved women in San Francisco (Chan et al., 2005).

An important program being used in connection with probation and directly targeting substance abuse is drug courts. Current research demonstrates that female offenders are likely to be suffering from forms of mental illness, as discussed throughout this chapter. Therefore much of the research regarding success or failure ignores the fact that substance abuse is directly related to the mental health issues female offenders are encountering. Although bivariate correlations demonstrate gender differences at a statistically significant level, under multivariate analyses the relationship is no longer significant. Research shows that when mental health issues are added to the equation, they are more effective predictors of success, both for program completion and in relapse. Drug courts continue to be seen as a promising solution to substance abuse problems; however, it is important to ensure that the programs assess the mental health of the participants before determining the appropriate course of treatment. As women offenders demonstrate a higher incidence of both mental health issues (often directly related to abuse) and a profound dependence on drugs and alcohol, drug courts need to address both issues (Gray & Saum, 2005).

CONCLUSION

The trend in corrections relative to female offenders focuses on the recognition of the need for gender-specific programming and treatment. The break with tradition that one program fits all is an important step forward in the treatment of female criminality. Although the recognition has occurred within the criminal justice community, this realization has not fully translated over to the community at large. Getting the necessary information to the public is important for the success of future programming for female offenders.

Violence against women is established as a problem within society. Even in this new century, there is misunderstanding about the effects of physical and emotional abuse and their relation to crime. The literature discusses the cycle of violence and the effects of domestic violence on future generations. But too little emphasis is placed on the current generation of women who have engaged in retaliatory acts of violence to escape continued and repeated abuse. Further, and probably most significant, is the plight of young women who suffer the sexual abuse and physical abuse within the one place they should feel safest, their homes. The criminalization of survival in the forms of status offense convictions and incarceration should be abolished. In fact, the OJJDP continues to make this a priority.

The criminal justice system has begun the recognition that all offenders are not alike and male and females cannot be treated the same. Parity does mean identical. Different approaches and programs are needed and the courts have recognized this need. Corrections is not the best place in the system to begin to change the overall approach to female criminality. The continued walk down the path of mandatory sentencing and get tough on crime policies will only trap more female offenders in a system that does not or refuses to recognize gender differences in root causes of crime. For women it is a cycle, abuse, runaway, prostitution, drug addiction, and crime. Scholars and practitioners alike need to join forces to change the public perception of the female offender. The voices need to be loud and clear. They need to continue until the system changes. Too many women in our society are victims, and a growing number of these victims are being turned into offenders by the very system that is supposed to protect them.

Discussion Questions

1. How did the author make a case that female victimization is criminalized?
2. According to the author, what is the trend of the incarceration of female offenders who have been victimizes of violence?
3. Compare and contrast the cases of Lorena Bobbit, Francine Hughes, and Susan Smith with regard to the criminalization of female victimization.
4. How have the battered women's syndrome and posttraumatic stress disorder help women in excusing their violence? How have these worked to hurt women?
5. How does the author propose to correct the problem of the criminalization of female victims?

References

American Correctional Association. (1990). *The female offender: What does the future hold?* Washington, D.C.: St. Mary's.

Archer, J. (2000). Sex differences in aggression between heterosexual partners: A met-analytic review. *Psychological Bulletin, 126*(5), 651–680.

Barefield v. Leach, No. 10282 (D.N.M. 1974).

Canter, R. (1982). Sex differences in self- report delinquency. *Criminology, 20*, 373–393.

Cervantes, R. A. (2007). Interview with Casework Supervisor, R.A. Cervantes, Illinois Department of Corrections. August, 2007.

Chan, M., Gydish, J., Prem, R., Jessup, M., Cervantes, A., & Bostrom, A. (2005). Evaluation of probation case management (PCM) for drug-involved women offenders. *Crime and Delinquency, 51*(4), 447–469.

Chesney-Lind, M. (1995). Girls, delinquency, and juvenile justice: Toward a feminist theory of young women's crime. In B. R. Price & N. J. Sokoloff (Eds.), *The criminal justice system and women: Offenders, victims, and workers* (pp. 71–88). New York: Prentis Hall.

Chesney-Lind, M. (2002a). Criminalizing victimization: The unattended consequences of pro-arrest policies for girls and women. *Criminology and Public Policy, 2*(1), 81–90.

Chesney-Lind, M. (2002b). The forgotten offender, women in prison: From partial justice to vengeful equity. In T. Gray (Ed.), *Exploring corrections: A book of readings* (pp. 8–25). Boston: Allyn and Bacon.

Clear, T., Cold, G., & Reisig, M. (2006). *American corrections* (7th ed.). Belmont, CA: Wadsworth.

Davis, R., & Smith, B. (1995). Domestic violence reforms: Empty promises or fulfilled expectations? *Crime and Delinquency, 41*, 541–552.

Erez, E., & Belknap, J. (1998). In their own words: Battered women's assessment of systemic responses. *Violence and Victims, 13*, 3–20.

Ewing, C. P. (1987). *Battered women who kill: Psychological self defense as legal justification.* Lexington, MA: D.C. Health.

Finkelhor, D., & Browne, A. (1986). Initial and long term effects: A conceptual framework.

In D. Finkelhor (Ed.), *A source book of child sexual abuse* (pp. 180–198). Beverly Hills: Sage.

Follingstad, D., Rutledge, L., Berg, B., & Hause, E. (1990). The role of emotional abuse in physically abusive relationships. *Journal of Family Violence, 5*, 107–120.

Frost, N. A., Greene, J., & Pranis, K. (2006). *Hard Hit: The growth in the imprisonment of women 1997–2004.* Institute on Women and Criminal Justice. Retrieved August 5, 2007, from Women's Prison Association website: http://www.wpaonline.org/institute/hardhit/index.htm

Gillespie, C. K. (1989). *Justifiable homicide: Battered women, self-defense, and the law.* Columbus, OH: Ohio State University.

Gray, A., & Saum, C. (2005). Mental health, gender, and drug court completion. *American Journal of Criminal Justice, 30*(1), 55–69.

Hattendorf, J., Ottens, A., & Lomax, R. (1999, March). Type and severity of abuse and post-traumatic stress disorder symptoms reported by women who killed abusive partners. *Violence Against Women, 5*(3), 292–312.

Hebert, M., Tremblay, C., Parent, N., Daignault, I., & Piche, C. (2006). Correlates of behavioral outcomes in sexually abused children. *Journal of Family Violence, 21*, 287–299.

Houskamp, B., & Foy, D. (1991). The assessment of posttraumatic stress disorder in battered women. *Journal of Interpersonal Violence, 6*, 367–375.

Kelly, V. A. (2004). Psychological abuse of women: A review of the literature. *Family Journal: Counseling and Therapy for Couples and Families, 12*(1), 383–387.

Kemp, A., Rawlings, E. I., & Green, B. L. (1991). Post-traumatic stress disorder (PTSD) in battered women: A shelter sample. *Journal of Traumatic Stress, 4*, 137–148.

Mann, C. R. (1988). Getting even? Women who kill in domestic encounters. *Justice Quarterly, 5*, 33–51.

Maxfield, M., & Widom, C. (1996). The cycle of violence: Revisited six years later. *Archives of Pediatrics and Adolescent Medicine, 150*, 390–395.

Michigan Battered Women' Clemency Project. (2000). *Clemency for battered women in Michigan: A manual for attorneys, law students and social workers.* Retrieved on August 5, 2007 from http://www.umich.edu/~clemency/clemency_manual/manual_intro.html

Miller, S. (2001). The paradox of women arrested for domestic violence: Criminal justice professionals and service providers respond. *Violence Against Women, 7*(12), 1339–1376.

Moe, A. (2007). Silenced voices and structured survival: Battered women's helping seeking. *Violence Against Women, 13*(7), 676–699.

Moses, M. (1995). "Girl scouts behind bars": A synergistic solution for children of incarcerated parents. *Corrections Today, 57,* 124-126.

Neal, C. (2007). Women who are victims are domestic violence: Supervision strategies for community corrections professionals. *Corrections Today, 69*(4), 38–43.

Ovara, T., McLeod, P., & Sharpe, D. (1996). Perception of control, depressive symptomatology and self-esteem of women in transition from abusive relationships. *Journal of Family Violence, 11,* 167–186.

Pargo v. Elliot, 49 F.3d 1355 (8th Cir. 1995).

Pergament, P. (2007). *Susan Smith: Child murder or victim?* Retrieved Crime Library on August 10, 2007, from http://www.crimelibrary.com/notorious_murders/famous/smith/susan_3.html

Reid, S. (1994). *Crime and criminology* (7th ed.). New York: Holt Rinehart and Winston.

Richie, B. (2002). *Understanding the links between violence against women and women's participation in illegal activity.* Rockville, MD: National Criminal Justice Reference Service.

Seiter, R. (2008). *Corrections: An introduction* (2nd ed.). Upper Saddle River, NJ: Prentice Hall.

Sigler, R., & Shook, C. (1997). Judicial acceptance of the battered women syndrome. *Criminal Justice Policy Review, 8*(497), 365–382.

Tolman, R. M. (1992). Psychological abuse of women. In R. T. Ammerman & M. Hersen (Eds.), *Assessment of family violence: A clinical and legal sourcebook* (pp. 291–310). New York: John Wiley & Sons, Inc.

Victims' Advocate Office, Hudson County New Jersey (2001). Interview. (Name withheld by request).

Walker, L. E. (1977). Battered women and learned helplessness. *Victimology: An International Journal, 2,* 525–534.

Walker, L. E. (1983). Victimology and the psychological perspectives of battered women. *Victimology, 8,* 83–104.

Walker, L. E. (1984). *The battered women's syndrome.* New York: Springer.

Walker, L. E. (1991). Posttraumatic stress disorder in women: Diagnosis and treatment of battered women syndrome. *Psychotherapy, 28,* 21–29.

Weaning, M. (2000). Lorena Bobbitt story. In *The Trials of Lorena Bobbitt: A study in media backlash.* Retrieved August 5, 2007, from Harvard University Website: www.digitas.harvard.edu/~perspy/old/issues/2000/retro/lorena_bobbitt.html.

Widom, C. (1988). *Child abuse, neglect, and violent criminal behavior.* Unpublished manuscript.

Widom, C. (1998). Childhood victimization: Early adversity and subsequent pathology. In B. Dohrenwend (Ed.), *Adversity, stress, psychopathology* (pp. 81–95). New York: Oxford University Press.

Widom, C., Nagin, D., & Lambert, P. (1998, November). *The childhood victimization alters developmental trajectories of criminal careers?* Paper presented at the annual meeting of the American Society of Criminology, Washington, D.C.

INDEX

❧

Note: In this index figures are indicated by fig.; tables by tab.; notes by n. Published documents are presented in italics

A

Abuse, victimization and gender in the narratives of
  feminized victimization, violations of, 255–256
  physical abuse, focus on, 251–252
  power, helplessness, and resistance, 252–253
  respondent, fear and dangerousness of, 253–255
  sexual abuse, disclosure of, 249–251
Abuse, when and for how long, 205–206
"Accident-prone personality", 46
Acts of neutralization, 118
Adams, Abigail, 23
Adams, John, 22
Adolescent aggression, 164–166
African American Women, 73, 98, 122, 220, 222, 225–226, 238
"Age grading system", 190
Aggravated murder, 79, 94nn. 5, 6
Aggravated sexual abuse, 131
Aggression
  adolescent, 164–166
  feminist perspective, 137
  mandatory arrest, effect on, 203
  online, 163
  rape as, 31, 37
  sexual, 116, 117
  against women, 6
  womens' use of, 295
  workplace, 152
American Institute on Domestic Violence (2001), 152
American Law Institute, 27
Anthony, Susan B., 24
Arrest policies, 34–35
Arrest reports, 29, 225
Avatars, 174

B

Backlash, 105
Barefield v. Leach (1974), 302
Battered Black women, 178. *See also* Battered women, experiences with police intervention

Battered women, experiences with police intervention
  abstract, 219
  conclusion/implications, 236–238
  intimate partner violence (IPV), 219
  introduction, 219–220
  method and data
    demographic characteristics of the sample at time of interview, 226 tab. 13.1
    socioeconomic status of sample, 227 tab. 13.2
  race, gender, and class factors
    arrest, effect of, 224–225, 242n. 6
    arrest, stipulations for, 222–223
    intersectionality and domestic violence, 221 box 13.1
    introduction, 220
    reporting rates, 220–222, 242nn. 2, 3
    victim satisfaction, 224
  results
    criminal justice system, general perceptions of, 228–229
    not calling the police, explanations for, 221, 231–233
    police action, effectiveness of, 233–235
    positive experiences, 236
    racial identity, 228
    system procedures and attitudes, recognizable changes in, 230–231, 242n. 7
Battered Women's Movement, 51
Battered women's/PTSD defenses, 299–300
Battered women's syndrome (BWS), 139–140, 141, 297–299, 300
Battering. *See also* Domestic violence shelter, observations on; Intimate partner violence (IPV)
  arrest, effect of, 224, 232
  children present: perceived influence, 213

police action, effectiveness of, 233–235
post-traumatic stress disorder (PTSD), 299–300
shelters, as social response, 181
successful response to, definitions of, 203
victims, employment status, 212–213
Belknap, Joanne, 178, 259–278
Bench cases, 269
Black Civil Rights Movement, 25
Black feminists, 98
Black officers, 237
Blackwell, Henry, 24
Black women. *See also* African American Women; Femicide
  citizenship and, 24, 29
  criminal justice system, 121–122
  dual arrest and perceptions, 212
  homicide victims, 62
  no drop policies, 203
  police intervention, experiences with, 178, 219–242
Bobbit, John, 295, 296
Bobbit, Lorena, 295–296
"Bombing", 163
Bowman, Patricia, 4
Boyd-Jackson, Sharon, 70, 128–144
Bradley v. State of Mississippi (1824), 23 box 2.2
Bradwell, Myra, 23
Brewster, Dennis R., 2, 45–58
British common law, 33
Bryant, Kobe, 4
Brzonkala, Christy, 39–40
Brzonkala v. Morrison, 39–40
Bullying, 152, 161n. 10
Bureau of Justice Statistics (BJS), 64, 146
Bureau of Labor Statistics (BLS), 146
Burgess-Proctor, Amanda, 71, 162–176
"The Burning Bed", 297
Butler v. Reno, 302